Fractal Architecture

Fractal Architecture

**Organic Design Philosophy
in Theory and Practice**

James Harris, AIA

University of New Mexico Press
Albuquerque

Printed in China

17 16 15 14 13 12   1 2 3 4 5 6

Book design by David Fideler, Concord Editorial and Design

Library of Congress Cataloging-in-Publication Data

Harris, James, 1957–
    Fractal architecture : organic design philosophy in theory and
practice / James Harris.
        p. cm.
    Includes bibliographical references and index.
    ISBN 978-0-8263-5201-9 (pbk. : alk. paper)
    ISBN 978-0-8263-5202-6 (electronic)
  1. Geometry in architecture. 2. Fractals. I. Title. II. Title: Organic
design philosophy in theory and practice.
    NA2760.H37 2012
    704.9'49514742—dc23
                              2011041452

To my loving wife and my wonderful children,
who have brought me joy and happiness.

Contents

Introduction

Early in my architectural career, I developed an interest in the association between mathematics and architectural form. The marriage between architecture and mathematics is age-old, as exemplified by structures such as Stonehenge. This relationship continued and flourished from Greek civilization through the Renaissance. With the advent of computers, the relationship between architecture and mathematics has entered a new phase, in which previous areas of study are enhanced and new research possibilities are created.

In the course of my exploration, I was exposed to fractal geometry, in particular, through the work of Beniot Mandelbrot and Michael Barnsley. I was fascinated by the escape time fractals created by Mandelbrot, where, through a relatively simple mathematical formula, an ever-increasing self-similarity of extraordinary swirling structure is revealed with each level of detail. Although captivated by these beautiful mathematical compositions, I saw architectural possibilities in the work of Michael Barnsley and the iterated function system. The fractals created with this method had a direct correlation with a diverse array of structures found in nature. This connection appeared to hold the key to an innovative and intriguing source from which to create architectural form.

During the course of my exploration of the possible fusion of fractal geometry and architectural form, I became more aware and appreciative of nature's beauty and its forms. This transformation undoubtedly was a result of my exposure to nature's underlying fractal geometry. Michael Barnsley, in the introduction to his volume

Fractals Everywhere, stated, "Fractal geometry is a new language. Once you speak it, you can describe the shape of a cloud as precisely as an architect can describe a house."[1] Similar to learning a new language, which opens the door to understanding a new culture, it appears that comprehending the language of fractal geometry can reveal a deeper appreciation of nature. As this deeper appreciation of nature grew in me, so, too, did my confidence that the marriage of fractal geometry and architecture was inevitable.

As I experimented with fractals and architecture, I created forms, some of which were inconsequential or incomprehensible. The structures that were successful in producing an architectural statement resonated on an intuitive level regarding the suitability of the form. The configuration of visual forces produced by the relationships of the structure's elements struck an instinctive chord within me. I felt there must be a connection between my reaction to these forms and the emotions that are triggered by exposure to nature and its manifestation, through its vast array of natural forms. This reaction is unique, and if properly utilized, fractal geometry has the capacity to produce architectural expressions that are powerfully connected to the human infrastructure.

I wrote this book to expose the public to this possibility, offer insight into why these forms resonate with humans and to provide a more concrete methodology for achieving the marriage between fractal geometry and architecture than has been previously documented. This is a new, promising field of exploration; I hope I am only revealing the tip of its expanse of possibilities. I want to spur the reader to stand on my shoulders and reach up and attain greater success in producing architectural forms that resonate intuitively with the human perceptual, cognitive, and emotional infrastructure.

This book is organized into three parts, each composed of three descriptive chapters and concluding with a chapter on the generation of a building type utilizing fractal geometry. Part I explores man's relationship to nature; new concepts in the geometry of nature; and historically, how man has sought to integrate nature into his architecture. Chapter 1 is a recitation of the history of fractals and describes a particular class of fractals called iterated function systems. In chapter 2, I discuss man's relationship with nature and nature's inherent importance to humans. Chapter 3 reviews the historical integration of architecture and nature. Part I concludes with the evolution of the skyscraper form in chapter 4, which outlines the steps in creating the skyscraper's fractal derivative.

Part II concerns the various perceptual and cognitive mechanisms humans use in processing environmental data. The unique characteristics of natural forms are understood by the conceptual qualities that arise as a consequence of their geometry and man's cognitive structure. Chapter 5 provides an overview of the Gestalt principles of visual perception, its applicability to fractal forms, and in particular, the holistic nature of the fractal form. The following chapter reviews principles of perception and cognition and proposes that the perception of the fractal architectural form produces perceptual and cognitive associations to natural forms because of the presence of a fractal structure. Chapter 7 evaluates the concepts of universals and abstraction to explain the perceptual bridge between natural forms and fractal architecture. The concluding chapter of this section, chapter 8, provides a fractal paradigm of an abstract, modernist midrise building form that, owing to its generative nature, exudes an organic quality.

Part III begins with a discussion of alternative methodologies for utilizing fractal geometry to generate elements of architectural form. It then examines the relationship between science, art, and nature and, in particular, the scenario that proposes that the universe has a computational nature. Specifically, in chapter 9, I discuss the theoretical computational character of nature and the analogous quality of fractal architecture. Chapter 10 reviews uses of fractal architecture other than the direct generation of three-dimensional form. This is followed, in chapter 11, by a discussion of the confluence of turn-of-the-century art movements with fractal architecture. Part III concludes with an examination of the house building form in the context of two diametric philosophies on the relationship between architecture and nature.

PART I

Man, Nature, and Architecture

The Journey from Mathematical Monsters to the Key to Nature's Structure

Fractal architecture is an innovative direction in the design and development of architectural form, rooted in the principles that govern the geometry of natural form. Fractal geometry is a recursive mathematical derivation of form that possesses a self-similar structure at various levels of scale or detail and, if the number of recursions is large, results in a dense structure that challenges dimensional qualification. An understanding of the genesis, attributes, and principles of fractal geometry provides a foundation for comprehending the structure of natural forms. What began as a study of geometric "monsters" transformed over time into a fascinating key to understanding the structure of nature. The analysis of the characteristics of this structure serves as a springboard for applying these principles to architecture.

HISTORY OF FRACTAL GEOMETRY

Fractal geometry is part of a nonlinear revolution that has prompted the reevaluation of the nature of mathematics and science as well as reformulating philosophical thought. The predecessors of fractal geometry were based in a linear geometry developed by a Greek mathematician, Euclid of Alexandria. Euclid authored *Elements*, a textbook outlining a set of logical principles deduced from a small set of axioms to form what is known as Euclidean geometry. These principles describe a methodology of constructing geometric objects, including three-dimensional primitives, which were espoused by Plato as the building blocks of the universe. From 300 B.C. up through the nineteenth century, these

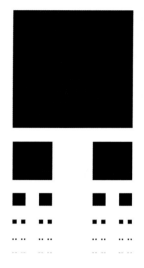

1.1a

1.1b

Figure 1.1. a. Cantor's Dust; b. Peano's Curve.

rules dominated mathematical thought. During the early 1600s, the French philosopher Descartes built on these tenets and introduced the concept that our universe could be quantified by the Cartesian coordinate system, in which three poles intersect perpendicularly, typically labeled as the x, y, and z axes. These are articulated with perfectly even gradations, providing the ability to locate everything precisely in space.[1] These clear and geometrically rigid axioms were embraced as they provided clarity in modeling system behavior and lifted it from the randomness of the universe, which was beyond understanding. The randomness within the human environment was seen as Nature's screen, used by her to hide her pure forms. These early philosophers could not conceive that calm equilibrium and turbulent chaos could be one within Nature's body and inseparably interlaced in the pure abstract harmony of a single mathematical equation.[2]

Nature, however, appears to have been playing a joke on mathematicians, asserts Benoit Mandelbrot, who is considered the father of modern fractal theory. Mathematicians may have been lacking in imagination, but Nature was not.[3] Beginning in the nineteenth century, a revolution in mathematical thought commenced, propelled by the discovery of mathematical structure that did not fit the precepts of Euclid, Descartes, or Newton. Mathematicians such as George Cantor, Giuseppe Peano, David Hilbert, Gaston Julia, Helge von Koch, Waclaw Sierpinski, Gaston Julia, and others created abstract forms that held clues to understanding nature in a visual sense[4] and provided glimpses into infinity. Although all these structures served as models for the complexity of nature, they were regarded with distaste as geometric aberrations, a pathological "gallery of monsters." These constructions, however, brought into question some of math's fundamental beliefs. During this period of crisis, these pioneers came in contact with bizarre shapes that challenged the prevailing concepts of time, space, and dimension.[5]

Cantor's Dust was formulated by George Cantor by taking a line segment, a one-dimensional object, and replacing it with two copies one third the length of the original placed at either end of the original line. The resulting figure appeared to be the original line with the middle third missing. The process was repeated on each of the remaining line segments, splitting each one into thirds and deleting the middle third. As you continue the process to infinity, it appears that you jump in dimension from the one-dimensional line to a series of zero-dimensional points or dust: Cantor's Dust (see Figure 1.1a).

1.2a

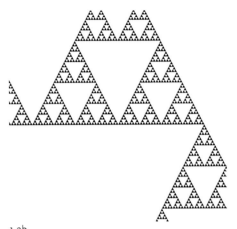

1.2b

Figure 1.2. a. Sierpinski's Gasket; b. Sierpinski's Gasket detail.

A similar but diametrically opposite construct was developed by Italian mathematician Guiseppe Peano when, in 1890, he invented the *Peano Curve* (Figure 1.1b). In this geometric object, a jump from one dimension to the second dimension is achieved in that a continuous curve of one dimension with no width or area could fill a region of space. Each time you repeat the process of substitution, you leave less space between the lines, and if you carry the process to infinity, theoretically, you fill the space. Cantor's Dust transformed a one-dimensional object into zero dimensions, whereas Peano's curve took a one-dimensional object and visually made a two-dimensional figure.

Waclaw Sierpinski developed one of the most recognizable fractal forms: the *Sierpinski Gasket* (Figure 1.2). The base object is a solid triangle that is replaced by three copies of the triangle scaled down to one-third of its original size. Each of the three copies is translated to one of the points of the triangle. The resulting figure is essentially the original triangle with an unfilled upside-down triangular hole in the middle. It is in fact a set of three scaled-down copies. The process is repeated again, resulting in each of the three solid triangles being replaced with a triangle with a hole, which is really a set of three copies of the previous object. The process is repeated as many times as you want, replacing each solid triangle with a scaled-down copy of the set of three solid triangles separated by an upside-down triangular hole (Figure 1.2). This process is theoretically continued to perpetuity. The fascinating part is that if you start to zoom in on a section of the Sierpinski Gasket, a structure will be revealed that appears very similar to the overall object: a triangulated gasket. Each time you zoom in on a section of a previously zoomed-in section, you will see the same similar triangulated structure—a visual glimpse into infinity.

After the burst of innovative mathematical inquiry in the years around the turn of the nineteenth century, research plateaued because of the arduous calculations involved in the generation of these new geometric shapes. Mathematicians spent days and weeks drawing by hand their experiments with the new visual universe. These initial drawings tended to be crude and inaccurate. The burden of hand calculations and graphic representation stymied research until the advent of computers.[6] With the introduction of computers, what took days and weeks could be done within seconds with pinpoint accuracy. The mathematical revolution picked up where it left off in the middle to late twentieth century. John Heighway continued research into iterative construction with *Heighway's Dragon* (1960) (Figure 1.3a).

1.3a

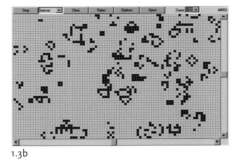

1.3b

1.3c

Figure 1.3. a. Heighway's Dragon; b. Conway's Game of Life; c. L-System.

Stanislaw Ulan and John von Neuman's 1940s research into crystal growth and self-replicating systems was developed by John Conway and Marin Gardener into the *Game of Life*, which was based on their theory of cellular automation (Figure 1.3b). Aristid Lindenmayer developed a formal language utilized to model plant growth called *L-Systems* (1968) (Figure 1.3c).

The primary figure in this mathematical revolution was Benoit Mandelbrot, who brought fractal theory to the forefront of scientific consideration. Mandelbrot acknowledges the work of his predecessors: "I rejoiced in finding that the stones I needed—as architect and builder of the theory of fractals—included many that have been considered by others."[7] In the late 1950s, Benoit Mandelbrot was a staff mathematician at IBM's Thomas J. Watson Research Center. His assigned task was research methodologies to eliminate noise that disrupted signal transmission. In his investigation he recognized a complex configuration of chaos and concluded that the technology that IBM was developing would not be able to contain it. Although he had no training in telecommunications, the structure of the noise was similar to the research Mandelbrot had done with cotton prices. Starting in the early 1950s, he researched commodities prices and concentrated on cotton prices because of the availability of pricing data from centuries of trading. During that time, the price of cotton behaved with a degree of consistency. The amount the price varied over centuries was similar to the amount it varied over decades, which was similar to the amount it varied over years. If magnified, the price of cotton during any particular duration of time held a similar pattern to that of the entire period of study. Mandelbrot termed this statistical equivalence *scale invariance*. In examining these curves, you see cycles within cycles within cycles; however, the embedding of each cycle is not simple. Each cycle has a certain amount of variation, and although the range of variation is consistent, the variation of a cycle within the variation makes predictability at every point in time and at every level of scale difficult.[8]

Other phenomena, such as river discharges, coastlines, and commodity and stock market prices, exhibit the same acutely cyclic structure. Mandelbrot developed a series of forgeries of the graphs of these chaotic phenomena. These phenomena fluctuate up and down in cycles in that they contain cycles within cycles within cycles. They are perfected by adding a random factor at each step that makes them aperiodic and more genuine. These charts were shown to experienced

1.4

practitioners of the various fields, who could not tell whether or not they were real (Figure 1.4).

Benoit Mandelbrot conceived what is considered mathematically as one of the most complex and beautiful objects ever created.[9] It belongs to a category of fractals known as *escape time fractals*, which are created by calculating each point on the complex plane, a modified Cartesian coordinate plane, by a large amount of iterations of the formula $x_{n+1} = x_n^2 + c$ and compared to a bounded circular area. Typically, all the original points, which never orbit beyond the bounded area, are colored black, and the remaining points are colored according to the iteration during which their orbits fall outside the bounded area. The Mandelbrot Set serves as an encyclopedia for an infinite number of fractals, most notably the various Julia sets. As with the Sierpinski Gasket, one of the most prevalent characteristics of fractals is the nested self-similarity. As you delve deeper and deeper into the details of the Mandelbrot Set under ever-increasing magnification, you find self-similar structures, mini Mandelbrot Sets, within a dizzying kaleidoscopic panorama of fantastic nested structures (Figure 1.5).

Benoit Mandelbrot noted that fractals have many features in common with nature's forms. He presented his theories in his revolutionary book *The Fractal Geometry of Nature*. He was able to take the gallery of monsters of his predecessors and develop a language of nature to "celebrate nature by trying to imitate it."[10] Concurrently with Mandelbrot's research, Michael Barnsley developed an alternate fractal construction, iterated function systems, which is used to model natural objects. For Barnsley fractal geometry was an extension of the classical geometry of Euclid and Descartes. It was a new language, and "once you speak it, you can describe the shape of a cloud as precisely as an architect can describe a house."[11]

Researchers have likened chaos theory, which describes the behavior of a number of natural dynamical systems, to fractal geometry. In studying the development of natural processes over time, we think

Figure 1.4. Mandelbrot forgeries.

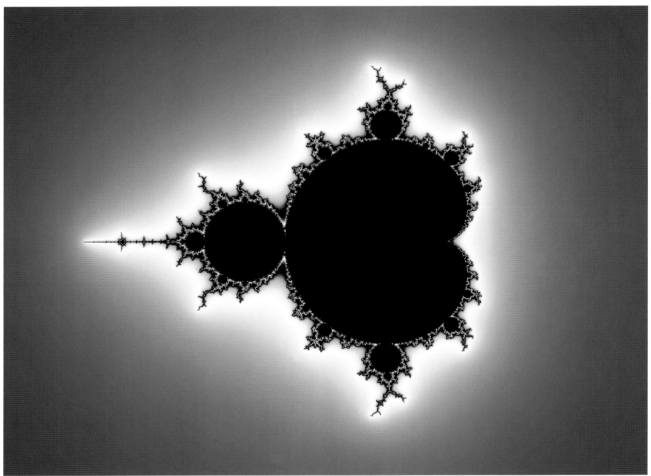

1.5a

Figure 1.5. a. Mandelbrot's escape time fractal; b–g. Successive levels of magnification of the Mandelbrot Set demonstrates the self-similarity of this infinite fractal, as the "mother set" appears at different levels of scale.

of it in terms of chaos theory. The structural forms that a chaotic dynamical system leaves in its wake are understood in terms of fractal geometry. The relationship of fractal geometry and chaos theory essentially awakens our understanding of natural equilibrium, harmony, and order. It offers a holistic and integral theory that understands the complexity of nature.[12]

FUNDAMENTALS OF CREATING FRACTALS

One of the most surprising and fundamental characteristics of fractal geometry is that complex forms result from a simple process. An essential element of that procedure that is responsible for this characteristic is the use of a feedback loop, a fundamental element of the exact sciences. The following process is explained in the book *Fractals for the Classroom* using the metaphor of a Feedback Machine

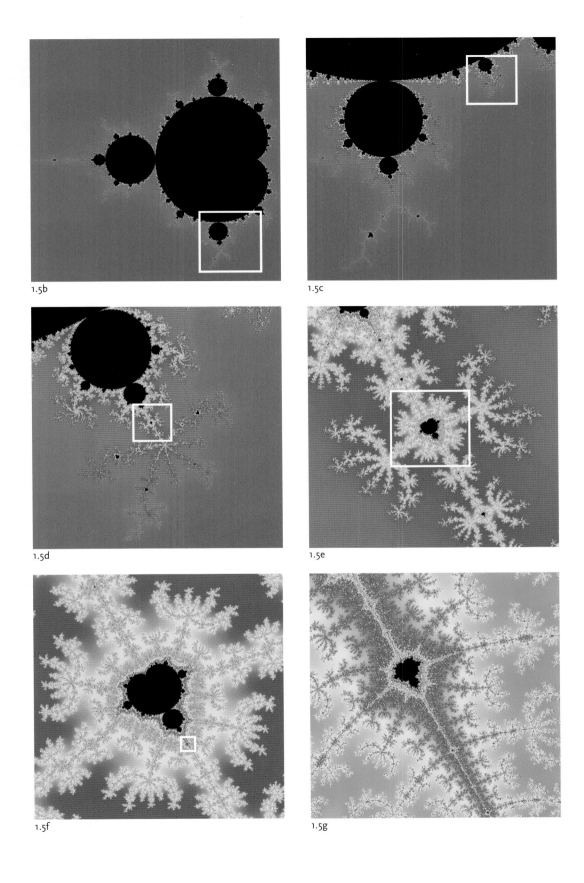

1.5b

1.5c

1.5d

1.5e

1.5f

1.5g

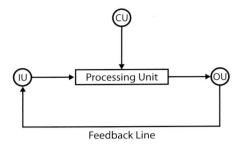

1.6

IU = Input Unit
CU = Control Unit
OU = Output Unit

(Figure 1.6). The Feedback Machine consists of three storage units (the input unit [IU], the output unit [OU], and the control unit [CU]) and one processor (the processing unit [PU]). The IU and CU are connected to the PU by input transmission lines while the OU is connected to the PU by an output transmission line. The OU is connected to the IU with the feedback line. The Feedback Machine is controlled by a clock that counts each processing cycle. The system starts with a preparatory cycle, during which information is loaded into both the IU and the CU. The information in the CU is transmitted into the PU. Once this operation is complete and the Feedback Machine is set up for processing, the running cycle commences. During the running cycle, the information in the IU is transmitted into the PU, which transforms the data based on the information received by the CU. The data are then transmitted to the OU, which transmits the information back to the IU through the feedback line, and one cycle is complete and registered by the clock. The system continues to run as many cycles as the clock is programmed to allow it to run.[13]

An intuitive example of the Feedback Machine would be video feedback, whereby a video camera as the IU looks into a video monitor as the OU, and whatever is seen in the camera's viewing zone is fed into the monitor. In this example, the camera and monitor electronics serve as the PU, and the variables of focus, brightness, and so on, provide the CU parameters. The variables that affect image generation are the rotation angle of the camera, the position of the camera, and the relation of the centers of each.[14]

The metaphor of the Feedback Machine is extended to the concept of a copy machine that has one lens with a reduction feature. If we put an image on the copy machine and specify a reduction factor of 50 percent, we obtain an image that is uniformly reduced by a factor of one half. The image is similar to the original, and the process used to generate it is called a *similarity transformation* or *similitude*. In a similarity transformation, if a rectangle is inserted as the input image, the output image is a rectangle. The only difference is the scale of image. The angles are the same, as are the proportional dimensions of the object.

Utilizing the Feedback Machine prototype, this output unit, which is a half-size copy of the original, can be inserted as the new input unit, and the resulting figure would be a half-size copy of it, or a quarter-size copy of the original image.[15] If this process is continued for a large number of iterations, or cycles of calculations, the image

Figure 1.6. Feedback machine.

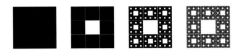

1.7a

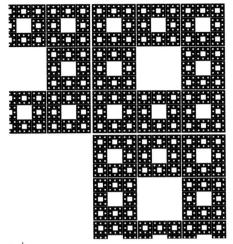

1.7b

Figure 1.7. a. Sierpinski's Carpet; b. Sierpinski's Carpet detail.

will eventually reduce to a point, or an *attractor*. The concept of an attractor is analogous to a marble rolling around a bowl. As time or cycles increase, the ball will gravitate to the attractor symbolized by the bottom of the bowl.

At a higher level of sophistication, the copy machine has multiple lenses and is known as a multiple reduction copy machine or MRCM. The MRCM has a dial for three variables: dial 1 sets the number of lenses, dial 2 sets the reduction factor for each lens, and dial 3 sets the location of the image from each lens within the overall configuration of the total image.

Each lens copies the image, reduces or contracts it by some factor, and places the resulting image somewhere on the page. The summation of all the various lenses' images can be inserted as the new input unit, and resulting figures would be the same proportional reduction of that image. This feedback line is the critical link in the system that takes the series of contractions of the initial image and reinserts them as the new input image.

As an example, we will start with a solid square as the initial image. The MRCM has eight lenses, each programmed to reduce the image to 33 percent of the original size and to translate the image to the outside edges of the original image, resulting in a square torus as the output unit consisting of eight smaller squares. If we transmit this image into the input unit module and run the MRCM again, the resulting image will be a square torus consisting of eight square sub-toruses with a total of $8 \times 8 = 64$ squares each $0.33 \times 0.33 = 0.1089$ the size of the original square. If we again transmit the image to the input unit and run the MRCM, we obtain a square torus consisting of eight subtoruses, each of which consists of eight sub-subtoruses with a total of $8 \times 8 \times 8 = 512$ squares each $0.33 \times 0.33 \times 0.33 = 0.035937$ the size of the original square (Figure 1.7).

In a simple Feedback Machine with one lens, the image progresses to one point, the attractor, as the number of cycles increases. In the MRCM, as the number of cycles or iterations increases, the image crystallizes toward one unique final image as the attractor. In the preceding example, the unique image is the Sierpinski Carpet. In examining the Sierpinski Carpet, you will note a high degree of self-similarity. Each area you zoom in on is highly similar to other areas and to the whole.

The next level of sophistication is to permit the lenses of the MRCM to reduce the input image by different factors for each of the three directional vectors x, y, and z. A lens can be configured to reduce the width by 50 percent, the depth by 25 percent, and the height by 33 percent. In a similarity transformation, the angles and proportional distances are maintained, while in the instance in which the scaling factors are different, that is not the case. These transformations are termed *affine linear transformations*. At this level of the MRCM, not only is scaling by different factors permitted but rotation, shearing, reflection, and translation are all permissible affine linear transformations.[16] In studying an image derived from this MRCM, you will note that the hallmark characteristic of self-similarity is still strongly present but in a different, more interesting manner. It is not a straightforward scaled-down image but rather one that is also rotated, translated, sheared, and so on, giving it a more unique identity but preserving its self-similar traits. Technically speaking, only when the transformation is a similitude is the resulting fractal form self-similar. When the transformation is affine, the resulting figure is self-affine. As you look around the natural world, you will rarely if ever find a technically self-similar form, but you will consistently find self-affine forms. You consider these forms, however, as self-similar, and for the purposes of this book, self-affine forms will be considered self-similar.

As you can imagine, the spectrum of compositions that can be developed from the combination of the various variables is vast. A particular set of affine transformations iterated a number of times generates a unique geometric figure or attractor. The key in fractal design is finding the right set of transformations to produce a satisfying form.

This highest level of sophistication of the MRCM provides the full power necessary to model natural phenomena. Living natural forms grow at various rates or according to allometric growth. At first a child grows proportionally, but after a few years, the ratios shift so that the height grows faster than other areas such as the size of the head and legs. A baby's head is unduly large and its legs disproportionately short. After the primary growth process is complete, the ratios come back in line.[17] According to D'Arcy Thompson, living organisms and their growth are so complex that strictly proportionate growth, or similitudinal growth, is not typical; rather, typical growth patterns exhibit more affine-like transformations. The branch of a tree is not a perfect copy of the trunk. In addition to being smaller, it is rotated and skewed in space. To model natural systems, you need the extensive array of possibilities that this level of MRCM provides. This type of MRCM is known as an *integrated function system* or IFS.[18] In IFS terminology, the input unit is termed the *seed shape* and the clock unit is an *iteration*.

There are two ways to develop natural fractal forms using an IFS. One method is termed the *stem and branches* technique. You start by sculpting a seed shape that resembles the stem or trunk and then use the various affine transformations to arrange copies of it as the first level of branches. The natural form grows outward from a thin beginning in the same way that many trees and bushes branch out step by step. The second methodology is termed the *trace and tile* or *collage* technique and is generally attributed to Michael Barnsley. The collage technique is considered the golden rule in fractal design.[19] Using this method, you take a seed shape that approximates the general size of the final form and then, using affine transformations, cover the seed shape with copies of itself. In nature these forms are seen in leaves and other plants that unfurl partially formed and then differentiate as they develop. In the natural world, you will find many forms that utilize a combination of both techniques.[20]

A general methodology for fractal design consists of the following steps:

1. Determine the limits or number of iterations appropriate to give the level of self-similarity.
2. Determine the relationship between one level of scale and the next.
3. Create a seed shape to approximate either the smallest (stem and branches) or largest (trace and tile) level of scale.
4. Use affine transformations to place copies of the seed shape to provide the structure of scaling.
5. Run the IFS and observe the results after each iteration.
6. Adjust the affine transformations based on your observations and run the IFS again.
7. Repeat step 6 until you achieve a satisfying fractal form.[21]

If you completely cover the seed shape with copies of itself without any overhangs, indentations, or holes, the fractal form will look very much like the seed shape. If you structure the affine transformations to form overhangs, indentations, holes, and other differentiation techniques, they will continually spread through the composition at each level. One of the keys to fractal design is the anticipation and control of these features, which articulate the structural relationships that provide the inherent aesthetic value.

CHARACTERISTICS OF FRACTAL FORM

Fractal forms exhibit certain essential qualities that make them unique and pique human interest and appreciation. These qualities are interwoven, reinforcing and supporting each other. Among these qualities are the following:

- self-similarity
- holism
- structure
- generative quality
- dimension
- organizational depth
- recursive/nested quality
- geometric diagram

In looking at the natural forms around you, one notes that despite the tangles, twists, and other irregularities, they exhibit patterns whereby one section of the shape looks like other parts of the shape and like the whole. This concept of *self-similarity* is readily apparent as an extension of the elementary geometric principle of similarity. It is the underlying theme in all fractals, varying to the degree it is exhibited from fractal to fractal. The precise definition of similarity is mathematically transformed to one of affinity when applied to natural forms. A cauliflower, which is a treasure trove of what one considers self-similarity, is obviously not a group of similitudes but rather a group of affinities that contain the essential organizational structure of the whole and, by definition, the surrounding parts and that give them a little twist, a little bit of a skew. You do not consider the subtle distortion but inherently recognize the interwoven set of relationships of similarity between each part: the sub-subwholes, the subwholes, and the whole.[22]

The small variations do not detract from the interest in the configuration but rather enhance it. Strict self-similarity drifts toward tedium while affinity provides the tension between self-similarity and independence, increasing the interest. By applying IFS to geometric or abstract objects, the configuration produced exhibits an organic nature. The organic quality can be traced to the self-similarity within the form inherent to its generation by IFS. This concept is fundamental to its application to architecture.

Holistic unity is a dominant characteristic of nature. This unity is based on a plan or concept that determines the structure of the parts and controls their growth and form. This holistic structure is inherently characterized by Aristotle as "the whole is more than the sum of the parts." For Goethe and Alberti, this was a chief characteristic of the organic design they strove for.[23] Christopher Alexander, in his *Nature of Order* volumes, has as a foundation the concept of wholeness that he finds prevalent in nature. Nature achieves this wholeness in a series of structure-preserving transformations that interlink with each other and reinforce the perception of the whole.

Inherent to the application of IFS to generate fractal forms is this holistic quality. Owing to its recursive, interconnected and iterative character, changes to one part are reflected throughout the entire form. The degree to which the change is apparent is dependent on the number of iterations executed. The more iterations that are performed, the more the structure is embedded, and hence revisions to that structure will become apparent to a greater degree.

One principal misunderstanding of fractals and their application to architecture is that the simple repetition of forms at different scales suffices to make a design fractal and therefore provide it with an elusive organic quality. In an extremely superficial analysis, one might draw the conclusion; however, this idea is empty of any understanding on the nature of fractal structure. The repetition of shapes at various levels of scaling that gives the object the quality of self-similarity is the result of a series of transformations. The initial set of transformations acts as the blueprint or *structure* establishing the form going forward. This structure is reinforced and enhanced with each successive iteration. In Figure 1.8, you can see the Sierpinski Gasket formed with three different geometric objects: a triangle (Figure 1.8a), a rectangle (Figure 1.8b), and a circle (Figure 1.8c) as the input unit or seed object. As the iterations increase, the awareness of the seed object decreases and the perception of the structure of the transformations increases. The structure of the transformations can be thought of as the nature of the relationships between the parts and between the parts and the whole. Each of the three instances results in the same final image or attractor of the prescribed set of transformations independent of the seed object's shape.[24] The congruence of the resultant objects arises from each of the examples having the same prescribed set of transformations.

This concept of structure is essential to the transposability of fractal geometry to architectural form. A structure is a perceived set of relationships.[25] The abstract understanding of structural features is

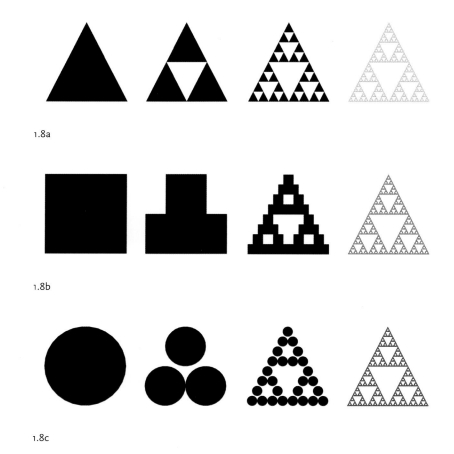

1.8a

1.8b

1.8c

Figure 1.8. a. Sierpinski's Gasket triangle seed shape; b. Sierpinski's Gasket rectangle seed shape; c. Sierpinski's Gasket circle seed shape.

the basis of perception and the foundation of cognition. Thinking is focused on the structural relationships as opposed to the placeholder objects, in this example, the square, circle, and triangle. Christopher Alexander developed the theory of living structure as the organizational basis of nature. This concept of living structure is the source of wholeness and is related to the perception of life. It is a configuration of elements that resonates with humankind's fundamental emotional and cognitive components.

Until recently, there has been a chasm between man-made artifacts and natural objects. The man-made objects are divorced from the process that created them, while the natural objects reflect this process. In biology the composition of an organism is inseparable from the process that creates it. D'Arcy Thompson believed that the origins of biological form can only be understood as a product of its growth process.[26] This *generative* quality is articulated in the fractal form expressing the process that created it. The fractal form is derived from the multiple iterations of simple transformations that with each iteration reinforce and strengthen these relationships and, in doing so, increasingly express the generative process that created the fractal form. The development of creating fractal form through the IFS is inherently expressive of its generative process.

In classical geometry, objects have a whole number *dimension* reflective of their place in the Cartesian universe. Cubes, spheres, and other solids are three-dimensional; squares, circles, and triangles are two-dimensional; lines are one-dimensional; and points have zero dimension. As researchers learned around the turn of the century, there exist geometric objects that appear to span dimensions. Cantor's Dust strides the dimensions of one and zero, while the Peano Curve bridges the first and second dimensions. A classic fractal query asks, "How long is the coast of Britain?" If you measure the coastline using a measuring stick of two hundred miles, you will get a certain measurement, but if you perform the same measurement using a smaller measuring stick, you will get a higher number. This is because with a smaller measuring stick, you can get into more of the nooks and crannies of the coastline. A fractal dimension of an object is a measure of its complexity at all scales and is typically higher for fractal forms than for the object's classical geometrical dimension. It involves calculating the logarithmic relationship between the measurement unit and the object's measurement.

Inherent to the composition of a fractal form is the characteristic of organizational depth. *Organizational depth*, a hallmark of complexity, is the transformation of deep structure into the form of the composition in the same way that nature displays its organizational depth in its forms. Organizational depth describes the manner in which the structure is brought together. These compositions that display organizational depth are abundant in linkages between the parts and display a high degree of self-similarity and nested structure. The linkage of these nested hierarchies indicates the degree of organizational depth and hence the resonance of the composition.[27]

Related to organizational depth is a fractal's *recursive and nested* qualities. Because an IFS fractal's elements are composed of the previous iterations' composite structure, that previous iteration is nested within the other. The degree to which the fractal iterates determines the amount of recursion that occurs. The richness of an IFS fractal is a function of this recursive and nested quality coupled with the fractal's self-similar qualities. Each of these elements reinforces and enriches

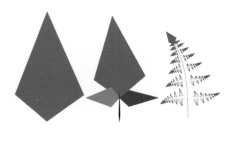

1.9

the other and provides the basis of the archetypal fractal quality of self-similarity at all levels of scale.

Researchers such as D'Arcy Thompson have speculated that nature's forms are derived from the forces acting on them. In art, Rudolph Arnheim has similarly theorized the configuration of works of art as constellations of visual forces. If we take many of the fractal qualities present in nature's forms and abstract them to their essence as a *geometric diagram* of those forces, we will be able to transpose those constellations of forces present in nature's fractal structure to architecture. Christopher Alexander has referred to these as "schemata for living structure."[28] Related to the determination of fractal structure, fractal forms display a geometric diagram of order that strikes a chord in our gestaltian perception that denotes an organic wholeness. There occurs a reverberation between our perceptual construct of fractal structure and the geometry of nature that connects us to the greater forces in the universe.

NATURE'S FRACTAL STRUCTURE

Ernst Haeckel, an eminent German biologist who mapped the genealogical tree that related all life-forms, maintained that nature is structured by fundamental internal laws of growth and metamorphosis.[29] These laws constitute a higher plane of lawfulness and set boundary conditions under which the subsidiary level of organic life is controlled by biochemical laws. The chemical processes as a medium for life processes are determined by the principles of a higher order, the laws of nature.[30] One result of these laws of nature is the concept of self-organization. In a typical process, the chaotic behavior of billions and billions of molecules reaches a tipping point and alters their behavior and spontaneously synchronizes them into a self-organized system. The system's dynamic equilibrium resulting from the interactive exchange of information is more than the sum of its parts. The dynamic process of self-organization causes the fractalization of matter whereby the system acts as a whole and cannot be dissected without causing the degeneration of the entire structure. When a chaotic process has generated a form, a fractal character is the basis for that form. It has been hypothesized that the fractal structure of natural forms enhances their sustainability.[31]

The basis for intricacy in fractal forms is the concept of a simple rule or law of nature, which, when iterated over and over again, produces complex structures. Researchers have concluded that this process is

Figure 1.9. Barnsley fern
Figure 1.10. a. Mountain formation generated with fractal geometry seed shape; b. Mountain formation generated with fractal geometry iteration 1; c. Mountain formation generated with fractal geometry iteration 2; d. Mountain formation generated with fractal geometry iteration 5.

1.10a

1.10b

1.10c

1.10d

also responsible for the nested intricacy found in nature.[32] The classic example of the fractal structure in nature is the Barnsley fern, utilizing the collage technique of fractal modeling. Referencing Figure 1.9, the seed shape is a quadrilateral that approximates the overall shape of the fern. From this seed shape, four copies are made and transformed in various ways. One copy is extremely compressed in all axes to form the stem of the fern and is placed to slightly protrude past the bottom of the seed shape. The next copy is slightly reduced and placed so the top of it approximates the top of the seed shape and overlaps the stem copy. The third copy is scaled down to form a shape between the first and second copies, rotated to the right in the range of 90 degrees, and transformed to the middle of the stem, which is also the base of the seed shape. The last copy is transformed similarly to the third copy at a slightly different scale and is rotated to the left rather than the right. These sets of transformations are considered the fractal blueprint of the fern structure.

The next iteration clearly reveals the process for modeling this natural structure. The first copy, which is the stem, is hardly affected visibly because of the severe nature of the compressive scaling used to transform it. The second copy at the top demonstrates the process as its stem extends the first copy acting as a stem and from that sprouts three copies of the initial set of transformations, all further scaled down to fit within the shape of the initial second copy. This set of transformations illustrates how the process marches its way up to the top of the fractal tapering as it rises. The rotation of the third and fourth transformations replaced with rotated, scaled-down copies of the fern's fractal blueprint displays the articulation of the branching structure. The next iteration further reveals the fern's expressive structure as the second copy rises to the top, leaving in its wake the branching of its third and fourth copies, while the third and fourth copies further develop the nested branching structure. A comparison of the fractal fern, iterated a number of times, with a real fern reveals a remarkable equivalence (Figure 1.9).

In Figure 1.10, fractal geometry is used to generate a mountain formation. By viewing the multiple iterations of the process, you can see how fractal structures develop irregularities, crooks, crannies, and crevices within crevices. This characteristic is responsible for the illusion that makes it seem as though what would be a two-hour hike to scale the summit from the base actually takes all day, as you climb up and down, in and out of the crevices of the mountain.

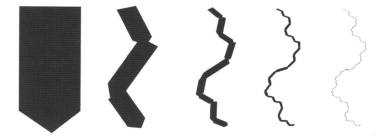

1.11

Water frequently forms fractal structures because of its behavioral nature to act similarly at different levels of scale.[33] Oceans are made up of waves, which are made up of smaller waves, which in turn are made up of even smaller waves.[34] Figure 1.11, modeling a winding river, indicates the levels of scale relationship as the iterations increase. As the model develops, the river takes shape as if you are getting farther and farther away. You start with the initial iterations as if you are just above the river, and after many iterations, it appears that you have a atmospheric view of a river winding its way through the countryside.[35] Fractal modeling has been used in the evaluation of the Gulf Stream.[36]

Star field patterns were modeled by Fournier using the path blazed by Cantor when he created Cantor's Dust. Whereas Cantor hopped between the space between one and zero dimensions, Fournier applied fractal modeling to the third-dimensional universe. Although it is overly regular, Fournier's universe provided the basis for others to develop theories of a hierarchical universe where stars and other celestial objects are ordered in an ascending cascade self-generated from a uniform gas.[37] This universal structure displays self-similarity within a range of scales.[38] The nonperiodic orbits of heavenly bodies have been modeled by fractals and used by researchers to analyze their draw to strange attractors.[39] In Figure 1.12, the classic spiral form of a galaxy is modeled.

Benoit Mandelbrot discovered the fractal geometry of nature through simulations of commodity pricing. Since that time, investment banks have used fractal modeling to simulate the patterns of economic indices as well as other financial instruments. These studies reveal the market's tendency for persistence of memory, both on a short-term and long-term basis, on every scale from hourly fluctuations to trends that extend over centuries. The analysis of the markets using this tool

Figure 1.11. River formation generated with fractal geometry.

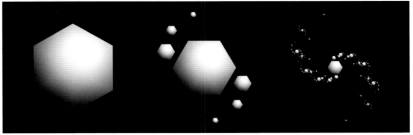

1.12

indicates fractal behavior occurring before changes in the marketplace.[40]

Fractal geometry has been cited in the analysis of physiological form. Benoit Mandelbrot deemed the human lung as being "of excellent geometric design," which in Mandelbrot's world means quintessentially fractal.[41] Our circulatory, respiratory, and urinary systems and liver structure exhibit a fractal branching structure.[42] The graphs of physiological processes such as heartbeats and brain waves have fractal characteristics. Fractal rhythm analysis is utilized in the analysis of certain physical conditions such as schizophrenia, forms of epilepsy, asthma, hyperventilation, and arrthymia.[43] The unique folding characteristics of mammalian brain geometry are beyond classical geometry but embrace the space-filling characteristics of Peano Curves and fractal geometry.[44]

Dr. Bruce Lipton, a noted anatomist and cell biologist from the University of Virginia, has noted in the evolution of the human cell structure that there exists a "fractal ladder" that is responsible for achieving higher consciousness of each succeeding level of development. Extending the trajectory of this research, where cells interact fractally to form humans, humans interact fractally to form humanity, humanity interacts fractally to form the next rung on the universal consciousness, and so on, a unique new fractal perspective sheds new light on the concept that we are created in the image of God.[45]

Similar to those found in the Mandelbrot Set, fractal structures have been found in the simulation of various physical, chemical, and electrical phenomena such as soot aggregation in chimneys, the structure of lightning, and zinc deposits in electrolytic experiments.[46]

As indicated previously, a common household vegetable, cauliflower, is a prime example of fractal form. As you peel off a branch and examine it, you see you have a structure that is smaller but extremely similar to the larger piece of cauliflower. Repeat the procedure taking a branch from the piece you broke off, and again you witness self-

Figure 1.12. Galaxy formation generated with fractal geometry.

similarity at a different level of scale: the hallmark of a fractal configuration. A not-so-common household vegetable, Romanesco broccoli, exhibits an apparent and beautiful self-similar spiraling organization. Classic fractal compositions are associated with the structure of trees. In Figures 1.13 through 1.15, we have an oak tree (Figure 1.13), a pine tree (Figure 1.14), and a maple tree (Figure 1.15), respectively, each with its blueprint initial iteration, ensuing iterations, and blooming fractal form. As you can see, the fractal prototypical organization produces tree forms with their distinctive compositions.

THE FRACTAL PHILOSOPHY

At some point of time, when you embrace the principle of self-similarity as a fundamental characteristic of nature, you will reflect on the philosophical implications of this concept. In grasping the element of interconnectedness of nature, it undoubtedly has profound implications on your idea of your relationship with nature and other fellow humans. "When you grasp fractal geometry your perception of the natural world will be fundamentally changed. You will look at flowers, trees, clouds, mountains, streams of water, the distribution of stars and the form of the universe in a new light."[47] When you acquire fractal awareness, you see the world in a different light. Instead of observing the world with a reductionist viewpoint, where things are separate and distinct, you perceive and understand the world as a resonance of a greater whole.[48] This philosophy is augmented by scientific principles developed by Albert Einstein and Ernst Mach, in which the mass of a body is not an intrinsic property but a derivative of the mass of the rest of the universe. Particle physics supports the concept of one particle as a reflection of and derived from other particles.[49] This new perspective draws you to the Gaia hypothesis first developed by British atmospheric chemist James Lovelock in the late 1960s. In this theory, the world is viewed as one organism, where Gaia acts as Darwin's natural selector. The variables of the earth, such as global temperature, the makeup of the gases in the atmosphere, and the oceans' composition of salinity and alkalinity, are influenced and regulated by the biota.[50] The appreciation of this hypothesis is amplified as we better understand the effects of human behavior on the environment and the consequential effects of the environment on human behavior.

In viewing a natural phenomenon such as a waterfall, you are enthralled by the energy and intricate organization of the self-generated geometric composition. A similar feeling is engendered when you

Figure 1.13. a. Oak tree form produced with fractal geometry seed shape; b. Oak tree form produced with fractal geometry iteration 1; c. Oak tree form produced with fractal geometry iteration 4.

Figure 1.14. a. Pine tree form produced with fractal geometry seed shape; b. Pine tree form produced with fractal geometry iteration 1; c. Pine tree form produced with fractal geometry iteration 4.

Figure 1.15. a. Maple tree form produced with fractal geometry seed shape; b. Maple tree form produced with fractal geometry iteration 1; c. Maple tree form produced with fractal geometry iteration 4.

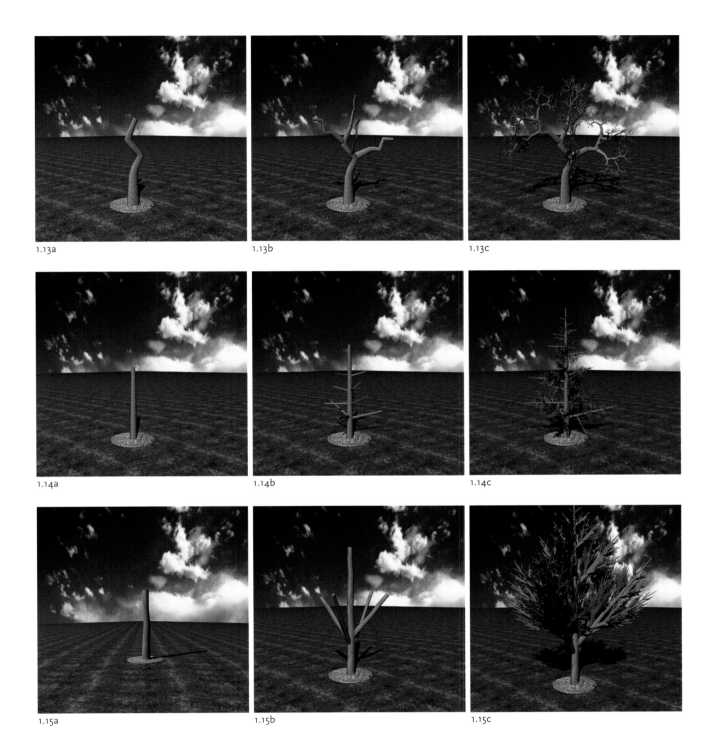

1.13a

1.13b

1.13c

1.14a

1.14b

1.14c

1.15a

1.15b

1.15c

look at a rose in full bloom or a sea of sunflowers swaying in the breeze. Consciously or subconsciously, these natural wonders strike a chord within us as being beautiful and connect us with universal principles. Fractal geometry provides a bridge allowing us to utilize these principles in architecture.

SUMMARY

Fractal geometry has evolved from a mathematical curiosity to a possible key to understanding the natural world. The basic processes underlying a category of fractals known as iterated function systems are surprisingly simple but produce incredibly complex natural forms. The repeated iterations of simple rules of formation create the vast array of complex structures of nature; hence the fractal credo can be summed up as "simplicity equals complexity."

CHAPTER **2**   # The Human Desire for Nature

In the previous chapter, the connection between fractal geometry and nature was established. Fractal geometry, by replicating the processes of morphogenesis, can create forms that possess the inherent characteristics of natural structure. Given this association, we must examine the relative importance of nature to humans to judge the significance of the relationship to fractal geometry.

THE HUMAN AFFINITY FOR NATURE

By observing your home, work, and leisure environments, the importance of nature is apparent. Can you look very far without seeing a natural object, material, or depiction of a natural scene or form such as a household plant (Figure 2.1)? In a study by Csikszentmihalyi and Rochberg-Holation, approximately 50 percent of the eighty-two families surveyed stated that plants were one of things in their homes most important to them. They noted that plants embodied their personal values to a higher degree than other objects in their home.[1]

On a weekend, this desire to develop one's natural environment is on full display at your local garden center. You see scores of people come there to spend considerable amounts of time, money, and effort to beautify their surroundings with natural objects. Trees, shrubs, plants, flowers, grass seed, and fertilizer are purchased, transported, and installed because of the high value universally placed on their utility to provide pleasure and satisfaction.[2] Evidence of the value of nature is further demonstrated by the willingness of people to spend money

2.1

Figure 2.1. Household plants.

for a paramount view of a scenic vista such as a water view, expend resources of time to travel to exceptional natural environments, or endure physical hardships to experience natural surroundings. These value judgments cannot be accounted for by the usual incentives of sustenance, money, status, or sex and have to be attributed to a deeply rooted human affinity.[3] A significant finding of a number of studies on the effect of natural environments is the degree of cross-cultural similarity in values associated with nature. A considerable number of the international participants endorsed the values associated with animals, plants, and open spaces.[4] The universality of value for the spectrum of nature denotes its intrinsic aspect relative to humans.

This high value is further exemplified by the real estate value placed on locations with scenic vistas and proximity to coastlines and lakeshores.[5] In general, tourists are attracted to areas with spectacular natural wonders such as the Grand Canyon, Victoria Falls, the Andes and Alps mountain ranges, and the national parks of Yellowstone, Yosemite, and Sequoia and Kings Canyon (Figure 2.2).

Biophillic researcher Stephen Kellert has noted the following trends in people's experience of nature:

- More Americans visit zoos and aquariums each year than attend all professional baseball, basketball, and football games combined.
- A majority of Americans annually watch at least one nature-related television program.
- Visits to national parks have soared, with more than 400 million visits occurring annually.
- Ecotourism has become one of the fastest growing segments of the international travel industry.
- Three million people participate in whale-watching trips each year, an activity virtually unknown fifty years ago, when these creatures were being slaughtered to extinction.[6]

In most human environments, ranging from the simple home with its garden to a thriving metropolis, there exist provisions for an explicit natural refuge. The worldwide phenomenon exists of establishing parks, gardens, and protected wilderness because of their perceived physical, psychological, and spiritual benefits. The physical and mental benefits of contact with these explicitly natural environs include rest, relaxation, and restoration from illness; spiritual renewal; contemplation; and self-reflection. Trees, bushes, and plants have stress-reducing and restorative

Figure 2.2. a. Grand Canyon; b. Victoria Falls; c. Andes Mountains; d. Yellowstone National Park; e. Yosemite National Park.

2.2a

2.2b

2.2C

2.2d

2.2e

benefits for both children and adults.[7] Natural surroundings such as a park or garden or even a view of a natural setting strengthen cognitive awareness, memory, and general well-being and alleviate depression, boredom, loneliness, anxiety, and stress.[8] It is thought that the ability of natural surroundings to replenish our concentration arises from their characteristic straddling of the stimulation threshold, neither overly exhilarating nor uninteresting. This quality contributes to the belief that natural surroundings are the most advantageous places for achieving restorative objectives.[9] These stress-reducing effects are manifested in physiological indicators of a reduction of blood pressure and an improvement in muscle tension. This research has been noteworthy and consistent in its conclusion of the restorative, healing, and physiological effects of park-like environs, especially those with savanna-like characteristics such as water features, meadows, colorful flowers and bushes, and healthy full-grown trees with impressive canopies.[10]

When you visit someone in a hospital, you frequently bring flowers to brighten the patient's setting and consequentially his or her emotional mind-set. The presence of natural objects in a room, views of natural settings, and exposure to gardens were the most widely sought preferences by hospital patients. Patients recovering from major surgery with outdoor views had significantly better recovery rates and substantially lower requirements for medication than patients whose view was a brick wall.[11]

Business environments are similarly enhanced by exposure to natural forms. Job stress is reduced and emotional well-being enhanced by simple viewing of nature. Research on U.S. workers found that those with window views had less frustration and a higher level of physical and mental health than those without. A before-and-after study of a major central Michigan furniture manufacturer's move from a location with minimal natural amenities to one with "green" features revealed substantial improvement in work performance, job satisfaction, heath, and relaxation among workers.[12]

There has been exploration on the correlation between property values and open space in two northeast housing tracts. In two architecturally identical developments with the only difference being the amount of trees, grass, and other vegetation, the results indicated that residents in the development with appreciably more greenery had higher levels of well-being, both emotionally and physically; better stress and conflict management capabilities; and an increase in cognitive functioning.[13]

Another study concerning eighteen neighborhoods around New Haven, Connecticut, involved the assemblage of a little fewer than one hundred major biophysical and socioeconomic variables. Environmental quality was indicated by species diversity, biomass, chemical pollution, native versus nonnative species, and so on. While residents were not cognizant of environmental measures such as hydrological flow, they were aware of prominent landscape qualities and ecological practices that derive from aspects of environmental quality. In particular, clean, vibrant water features, plentiful parks and open spaces, mature trees, and beautiful roads were appreciated. Residents' "environmental affinity" was a strong indicator of environmental conditions present in the neighborhood. Another noteworthy prognostic variable was the relationship between the diversity of native tree species to socioeconomic conditions and environmental perceptions. These measures of environmental affinity and diversity of tree species were independent of income and educational levels. In general, neighborhoods with healthy natural environments have an increased affinity for their ecosystem and a higher quality of life, while those areas with a poorer-quality natural environment are less emotionally involved with the ecosystem and have a lower quality of life. The healthier natural environment inspired residents to become attached to and care for it, which in turn increased the quality of the environment and residents' satisfaction with their efforts, resulting in rising perception of their quality of life.[14] Research that inquires of participants an accounting of their favorite places produces a predominance of natural settings.[15]

The enduring popularity of these natural settings is frequently attributed to their aesthetic qualities. This experience of natural beauty is cited as a source for mental and physical benefits, including stress relief. This phenomenon has been tied to a universal human inclination that results in adaptive intellectual benefits, including curiosity, creativity, increased exploratory drive, an increased capacity for problem solving, and the recognition of symmetry and harmony. Environmental psychologists Rachael and Stephen Kaplan theorized that the physical and mental benefits bestowed by garden- and park-like surroundings are derived from four factors: coherence, complexity, mystery, and legibility. One of these characteristics, coherence, is fundamental to the transposition of fractal geometry to generate architectural form. According to the Kaplan research coherence is the human awareness of and capability to recognize and derive the symmetry, order, and organization of nature's forms.[16] This capacity imbues the observer with a cognitive template derived from the configuration of the natural form and correlated with intrinsically positive associations. When this template is transposed to an observed artifact, such as a building formed by fractal geometry, because of its similar structural relationships to nature, unconscious positive associations are conveyed.

BIOPHILIA

The human affection for nature as a primary source of mental sustenance has been attributed to its evolutionary hardwiring into the human brain. Biologist Edward Wilson first theorized and subsequently elaborated on his theories through research with Stephen Kellert that humans have a genetic tendency to focus on life and affiliate with other life-forms. Subsequent studies have provided support for this hypothesis. It theorizes that we have inherited a predisposition to respond to the natural environment in certain ways such as emotional reactions. On the basis of a primary quality of an innate inclination toward nature, this theory has been termed *biophilia*.[17]

Biophilia has manifested itself in conventional dreams and people's responses from childhood onward through adult life. It flows through cultures in repetitive patterns of society, as noted in anthropological studies. The preference for natural settings over urban surroundings as well as other cultural expressions appears preliminarily detached and unrelated, but there is a simple reality to instinctive archetypes that guide the experience of ordinary people.[18] Although the genetic predilections have some variability according to cultural extremes, there appears to be sufficient evidence to validate the premise. These biologically based emotions are marked by the rapidity and certainty with which we react to certain animals and foliage.[19] Contact with animals, scenic vistas, close interaction with flora, and even pictorial or electronic surrogates produce physiological reactions such as reductions in our systolic pressure and inhibit adrenals from secreting adrenaline.[20] While people may prefer the urban environment for culture, commerce, and ease of transportation, when they want to relax and rejuvenate, they are drawn toward natural settings such as parks or beaches.

In the book *The Biophila Hypothesis*, Edward Wilson and Stephen Kellert outlined biophilia's basis on the following assertions:

- It is an inherent biologically based condition.
- It is an element of the human genus's evolutionary legacy.
- It is related to human competitive advantage and genetic fitness.
- Its implementation fosters individual meaning and personal fulfillment.
- On a subconscious self-interest basis, it is responsible for human moral and ethical ecological mores.[21]

These genetic tendencies can be diminished or augmented by a number of factors. As it is genetically based and genes can be mutated and changed over generations, human gene lineages can have varying degrees of genetic predisposition toward nature. Children's environments—in particular, their learning environments—condition the expression of their genetic penchant for biophilic values. The number of environmental triggers in the form of biodiversity within habitats, personal hands-on contact with other forms of life, and the degree of oral and written traditions involving plant and animal narratives also work to suppress or enhance biophilic values.[22] The degree to which biophilic values are incorporated into personal identity extends beyond bodily and material sustenance to embrace aesthetic, intellectual, and spiritual meaning and fulfillment.[23] Biophilia is an expression of a biological need integral to the human developmental process and essential to physical and mental growth, ignored at one's peril.[24] This phenomenon of nature's capacity to provide meaning and fulfillment and to augment and broaden life experience occurs at both individual and societal levels.[25]

A central element of biophilia is that it has a genetic basis. The genesis of the evolution of the human brain began millions of years ago in a biocentric world quite different than our current technologically based way of life.[26] Man, confronted daily by predators, struggled to find safety and sustenance to survive. A hunter-gatherer party witnesses one of its members, bitten by a snake, suffer considerably and die. The other members observe the lethal effect of the event, altering their behavior through vicarious conditioning to enhance their ability to stay alive. The humans that embed this information to the point that it controls their behavior increase their chances of survival, and those who do not diminish their chances.[27] Human physiology is constructed of countless cells that communicate across their membranes by means of chemical surges and electrical impulses that occur too rapidly to be comprehended. As the cerebral cortex evolved, it relied on tricks to enhance the speed of computation and to increase the size of its memory. Operating on the principle of maximizing information while expending the minimum amount of energy, it utilized analogy and metaphor to sort the chaotic panorama of sensory input into categories and hierarchies for rapid access.[28] The archetypical episode of the predatory fatal snake bite is absorbed by the human chemical machinery, mutating its inheritable composition.

A subordinate primate relinquishes its feeding place to a dominant one. The monkey with the superior genes gets fed and breeds, while the one with inferior genes does not and perishes. Primordial humans, like the predators they feared, were survival machines bonding self-preservation to their genetic determinants. Each organism is inherently self-projecting, pushing its self-development and self-defense as the essence of its biological composition. It does not act selfishly but for its own sake to protect its perceived intrinsic worth. The inherent relationship of genotype to phenotype synthesized the mind's coping mechanisms to evolve to enhance its survivability. A certain genotype stimulates a behavioral response that enhances the individual's survival and reproductive probability. Consequently the genotype extends through the culture as those without the genotype diminish, increasing the frequency of the response. This biocultural evolution guided the development of primitive culture through hereditary learning propensities amplified by the spread of the associated genetic configuration through natural selection. This gene-culture evolution is a probable explanation for the inception of biophilia.[29] Biophila has augmented to confer on humans who have a broad affiliation for life and lifelike processes distinct advantages in their human evolutionary struggle to adapt, persevere, and flourish as individuals and as a species.[30] As time has marched on, evolutionary Darwinism has transformed this trait from an advantage to a fundamental human attribute.

The prevalent use of animal symbolism is substantiation of our biophilic integration, as animals take on human qualities and humans take on animal qualities, reflecting societal relationships and social order. We worship the bee, whose main concern is for the group; malign the pig for its greed; and fear the nocturnal bat as the forbearer of evil. This phenomenon is universal and time tested, attesting to the deep significance of this segment of biophilia. Remnants of the ancient beliefs of our ancestors are inextricably woven into our evolutionary psyche, tying us to our animal kin emotionally and psychologically.[31]

Biophilic responses can be established in the aversion most Western people inherently have toward snakes (Figure 2.3). The general theory was demonstrated in research on rhesus macaques, the large brown monkeys of western Asia. When adult rhesus macaques see a snake of any kind, they respond with a generalized fear response common to their species. This is also true of rhesus macaques raised in the laboratory without any previous experience with snakes. They respond in a similar but weaker manner as those macaques brought in from their natural habitat.[32]

The effect that snakes had on the mental development of Western humans can be traced to primitive man's experience that snakes are a major source of injury, sickness, and death. The prehistoric humans who possessed this genetic propensity flourished, while those without it perished. This recognized awareness of snakes assimilated into the brain's structure gave rise to its presence in dreams and psychoanalysis. The mind works to create symbols and fantasies from powerful

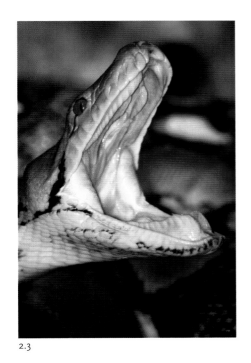

2.3

Figure 2.3. Snake.

35

2.4

embedded images utilizing the cognitive path to form those images. Cultural mores, developed from the collective cognitive interpretation of human experience, transform the reptilian snake into the virile serpent epitomized as the representation of evil in the Garden of Eden (Figure 2.4). This conversion is the result of the mind's coping mechanism of utilizing biases to efficiently process sensory information. The summation of these biases, which genetic and physiological research consider biological in nature and built into the human sensory and cognitive architecture, composes what we term *human nature*.[33]

A particularly compelling example of the consequence that biophilia has imposed on human cognition is habitat selection. Research has studied the prevailing primal habitat in which the brain evolved. Utilizing innate feelings, primitive man chose his habitat through the orientation devices and learning experiences integrated over generations.[34] Habitats were selected based on their ability to evoke emotional states that were positively associated with survival and expected reproductive success. The learning rules utilized to discriminate potentially dangerous sites from more nourishing ones were deeply embedded in the brain and the genes that produced it.[35]

Primal man gravitated toward savanna-like environments because of a number of advantageous features. Savannas such as the one pictured in Figure 2.5 offered abundant plant and animal resources for ground-dwelling humans. With their clear views and vantage points, cliffs, hills, and ridges offered surveillance of the outlying area to detect predators and rival bands. The scattered groupings of trees offered shelter and protection. The presence of water presented a natural defense against intruders and supported sources of nourishment in the form of fish and edible plants. The presence of edible matter was marked by the presence of flowering plants. In comparison to the other prominent environmental setting, rain forests, savannas were better suited for human habitat. While rain forests have a higher degree of biodiversity, their biomass productivity is lower than that of savannas. A rain forest's biodiversity is concentrated in the forest canopy out of the reach of the ground-dwelling primitive man. Its environmental advantages did not translate a competitive survival advantage for primal man. Rain forests have significant drawbacks for human habitation, including a higher degree of spatial enclosure, an increased likelihood of encountering close hidden threats, and a higher probability of

Figure 2.4. Garden of Eden serpent.

2.5

Figure 2.5. Savanna.

becoming infected with diseases that are not present in drier savanna environments. These factors coalesce to form an environment that has significantly less potential for safety than savannas.[36]

Research has concluded that humans posses a predisposition towards environments with savanna or park-like qualities inclusive of openness with relatively uniform grass cover, colorful flowering plants and groupings of trees. Other studies have determined that North American, Asian, and European adults consistently preferred environments that were savanna- or park-like.[37]

Humans' genetically based tendency toward park-like environments is apparent in landscape design. Urban dwellers or those in unremarkable natural settings exert considerable time and energy to transform their surroundings to include savanna-like elements or journey to park-like settings to receive their "savanna gestalt." They yearn to incorporate the qualities that correlate with their evolutionary concepts of safety and sustenance. At Pompeii, the ancient Romans incorporated formal gardens next to most functional structures, and ancient Japanese gardens similarly stress the orderly arrangement of garden elements such as trees, shrubs, open space, and water elements.[38] These elements carried forward through history and can be

37

2.6a

2.6b

Figure 2.6. a. Pompeii formal garden; b. Gardens of Versailles; c. English house garden.

confirmed by walking the formal gardens of any palace grounds or strolling through a simple English house garden (Figure 2.6). These ideals are reflected in the valuation of real estate, where locations close to bodies of water or possessing water views are highly valued, or in Manhattan, where there is a positive relationship between proximity to Central Park and real estate value.

2.6c

BIOPHILIC VALUES

Biophilia is produced from a complex set of learning rules that mold feelings across the emotional spectra emanating in a series of values. The following values vary in content and intensity among individuals and groups within limits imposed by man's evolutionary biological constitution:

- *Utilitarian* values view nature for its physical benefits such as physical, material, and commodity advantages for human sustenance, defense, and safety. As science develops technology to further utilize the natural qualities, such as the use of ethanol as a gasoline additive, this value is enhanced. Interacting with nature also provides mental benefits such as feelings connected with nurturing a living entity and the connection to a greater whole.
- *Dominnistic* values reflect the desire to master and control nature. The expression of this value results in a range of needs from satisfying the emotional desire to be independently safe and secure to coping with challenges and adversity.
- *Naturalistic* values reflect some of the most ancient motivating forces in the human relationship with the natural world. The satisfaction gained in direct contact with nature as a source of diverse stimulation provides an increased sense of awareness

and attentiveness, curiosity, an enhanced sense of creativity and imagination, and peace of mind. Studies have consistently found stress mitigation to be one of the most expressed benefits of contact with nature.

- *Scientific* values, which have occurred throughout time and across cultures, regard nature as understandable through exact study and methodical inquiry. This ranges from reductionist inquiry focusing on the constituent elements independent of their integrative nature to the emphasis on the interconnectivity and interdependence of the natural elements. The intense and deep examination of nature often results in profound appreciation of the breadth and beauty of nature's complexity.

2.7

- *Symbolic* values are reflected in the anthropomorphical use of nature as a methodology to facilitate communications and ideas. The sights, sounds, and sensations of nature have been symbolized through imagery, language, and metaphor to be used in myth, fairy tales (Figure 2.7), legends, and stories as a means to confront basic human developmental issues such as identity, conflict, and desire. The symbolic use of nature enables these complex issues to be confronted in an endurable, nonthreatening way.

- *Aesthetic* values reflect some of most powerful appeals of nature to humans. Natural beauty responds to a number of inherent human needs and capacities. Humans are programmed to recognize and respond to harmony, symmetry, balance, and elegance. The adaptive value of observing natural beauty is associated with derivative feelings of tranquility, peace of mind, the sense of well-being, and, in many cases, a feeling of the sublime. The intensity of the feeling varies but the occurrence does not. Research has confirmed human preferences for natural design and patterns, and studies have found the aesthetic value of nature to be consistent across cultures. Additional research has linked the aesthetic preference for certain landscapes to the evolutionary preference for savanna-like qualities.

- *Humanistic* values mirror the significant emotional attachment people have to elements of the natural world. This value is most common with domesticated animals and is expressed as "love" for the object of affection. It fosters the capacity for giving and receiving affection, forming cherished and companionable relationships, and fostering cooperation and trust. The therapeutic value of domesticated animals has been documented in a number of studies.

Figure 2.7. Fairy tales and nature.

- *Negativistic* values are based on the antipathy, fear, and avoidance of nature accompanied by feelings of awe and respect. This value is usually associated with primitive feelings associated with spiders and other biting and stinging creatures as well as powerful natural phenomena such as tornados and tsunamis. The ability of nature to motivate and confront physical and mental growth probably requires an element of fear.
- *Moralistic* values develop strong feelings of affinity, ethical responsibility, and reverence for nature. This mind-set results from a fundamental belief in the reciprocity between humans and nature and a consequential link between human identity and the natural world. This feeling of belonging to a universal continuum occurs across cultures and spiritual orientations. Science has endorsed this conviction as the genetic code has been found to have a high degree of similarity in most creatures.[39]

These values interact to form three general responses to peaceful natural environments: liking/approach responses, restoration or stress recovery responses, and enhanced high-order cognitive functioning. Liking/approach responses are associated with the desire for elements common to savannas or parks grounded in the genetic evolution of the human brain. Certain broad classes of natural elements such as water, green flora, and colorful flowers are preferred over modern synthetic constructs. Research has confirmed the biophilic hypothesis of human aesthetic preference for landscapes as diverse groups and cultures have endorsed reassuring natural environments.[40] Restorative responses were shaped by the hostile nature of primitive man's environment. To survive, man was subjected to stressful encounters, including threats from predators and antagonistic encounters from other groups relating to instituting dominance hierarchies and social order. These daily challenges provided for a grueling existence. In the selection of habitats, primitive man was drawn toward those settings that provided restorative capacities for the recharging of physical energy and the attenuation of stress responses. Man retained this genetic profile to respond to unthreatening natural settings with feelings of mental restoration and stress mitigation. Studies have persuasively concluded that leisure activities in natural environments are important for people to cope with stress. Most investigations on urban parks have determined that restoration from stress is a key apparent benefit of these settings. Exposed to savanna- or park-like settings, people describe being in states of relaxation and peacefulness. A sampling of students in San Francisco confirmed that a large majority of them sought natural environments when they were under stress.[41]

The effects on high-order cognitive functioning involve integrating diverse material or being able to correlate previously unrelated information resulting in creative problem solving. The advantages of this activity accrued to creative prehistoric individuals who prospered in the natural selection evolutionary process. Humans' emotional state has a profound effect on virtually all aspects of cognitive activity. By enhancing their emotional state through stress-relieving environments, humans facilitate remote associations, integration of material, and the perception of relatedness among different materials. Inheriting this genetic disposition, they are able to enhance creative intellectual thinking while in serene natural locations. Anecdotally, it has been reported that a number of Nobel Prize–winning ideas transpired during walks in peaceful, park-like environments.[42]

THE HUMAN CONNECTION WITH NATURE

Although taken for granted, the recurrent connection with natural forms is a fundamental requirement for human physical, mental, and moral welfare; personal development; and productivity.[43] This canon explains the consistent appearance of nature and natural forms in society, revealing itself in cultural preferences, creations, and constructions. It emerges in the way we choose materials, the decorative motifs we use, the recreational choices we make, the places where we want to live, and the literary devices we use.[44]

Howard Searles, a renowned psychologist, studied the effect of nature on normal development and for schizophrenic patients. He concluded that there was a fundamental kinship between humans and their natural surroundings that comprises the framework for identity formation and emotional and mental development. Nature constitutes one of the most fundamental elements of human psychology owing to a conscious or unconscious conviction of the transcendental relationship with nature.[45]

As an example, trees are a consistent biophilic element that is embedded in human awareness on different levels. The naming of streets after tree types signifies the degree to which this element is entrenched within human significance. They are viewed as an integral component of the resident's property, the neighborhood, and the greater metropolis.[46] Trees are valued for their habitat for animals such as birds and squirrels; their provision of shade and filtered light; their mental benefits associated with the gentle swaying and rustling of their branches and leaves; and their graphic representation of the yearly cycle by the appearance, coloration, and disappearance of their leaves.[47] These values are confirmed by the correlation of trees with property values, which contribute to the residents' self-perception.[48] In scientific surveys on residents' attitudes toward trees, respondents frequently utilized pronouns preceding the identification of the type of tree, that is, "our oak tree" distinct from others in the neighborhood.[49]

Trees' historical value is exhibited by the common practice of the planting and dedication of trees for memoritive occasions such as the birth of a child, in honor of a deceased relative, or to celebrate a marriage. Often there is an obligation on the part of the planter to nurture the tree and guard its health as the fate of the tree and the dedicatee are believed to be intertwined.[50]

The spiritual characteristics associated with trees are exemplified by the historical idea of sacred groves, which are prevalent in countries such as India. In these sanctuaries, largely undisturbed spaces are recognized as places where deities or guardian spirits reign, and people commune with them and the other spirits of nature and experience the mental and physical benefits of nature.[51]

The noted psychoanalyst Carl Jung utilized the metaphor of the tree for the course of human life. The tree operates as an archetype or part of the collective unconscious common to humanity. The roots of the tree symbolize genealogy, the trunk represents evolving personal identity, the branches those characteristics and traits that connect to the environment, and the fruit the creative products of an individual life.[52] The tree appears in our literary lexicon due in part to its vertical orientation that is similar to the orientation of humans and unlike most other natural forms. Altman observes that the image of a tree has the ability to raise human consciousness through its association with values of permanence, stability, trustworthiness, fertility, and generosity.[53] The tree is conventionally utilized as an organizational device to trace lineage.

ENVIRONMENTAL IDENTITY

As discussed earlier, there is a fundamental human connection with nature embedded within every human's physical and cognitive makeup. That basic core relationship varies to an extent from person to person and is further modified by a person's experience with nature. These factors contribute to the formation of a person's identity relative to nature. Identity is a self-constructed dynamic organization of beliefs, desires, drives, and abilities. It is linked to the idea of self-concept in that both are self-generated, but whereas self-concept is restricted to cognitive variables, identity includes an emotional component.[54] Identity involves beliefs of who we are and who we want to be.[55] On the basis of factors such as gender, race, social class, occupation, ethnicity, and nationality, it is a function of the experiences of ourselves and other people encountered across a life span such as the integration of childhood memories into adult self-images.[56] These perceptions are further mediated in part by cultural symbols, ideas, and visions.[57]

Identity can be thought of as a self-organized configuration of self that can be structured hierarchically in multiple ways, depending on the context of the situation. The multiple ways of organizing this hierarchy correspond to our multiple identities. When I am focusing on myself as distinct from others, I focus on issues that affect me individually, emphasizing my own personal goals, interests, and welfare. When I reorient myself to the hierarchy of self toward myself as a member of a group, I emphasize myself as a member of that group, focusing on the issues that affect the welfare of the group.[58]

One aspect of a person's identity is his or her environmental identity, which is shaped by cultural worldviews and religion to transmit broad beliefs on causality, humanity, ethics, the universe, and appeals to the intrinsic value of nature. This facet of identity can be similar to other collective identities, inherently giving a sense of connection and being part of a larger whole.[59] Environmental identity is the sum of one's perceptions and evaluations regarding nature and their impact on daily circumstances.[60] This aspect of identity relates to how we see ourselves in relation to the natural world and entails a sense of connection to nature. It is premised that nature and the environment have meaning and significance for people, creating a link between identity and nature that psychologists believe is fundamental to human emotional, cognitive, and personal well-being.[61] It has a relative nature in that the personal importance of nature competes with other facets of identity. This is exemplified by the sometimes competing objectives of ecological action versus economic consequences in formulating strategic plans: for example, the decision to chop a tree down for Christmas despite having contradicting values regarding its natural value.[62]

Environmental identity is developed in part because of anthropomorphic reasoning and its counterpart, physiomorphic reasoning. In *anthropomorphic reasoning*, we interpret natural phenomena in terms of ourselves and our personal experience, whereas in *physiomorphic reasoning*, we draw on our experience with nature to understand ourselves. These two reasoning methodologies are reciprocal components of the same progression metaphorically mirroring and reinforcing each other. These are examples of an epistemological process termed *subjectification*, where by attaching meaning to an object, the object and self are established in a unique and intertwined relationship.[63]

CHILDHOOD AND ENVIRONMENTAL IDENTITY

These learning methodologies start in childhood ego development when, as infants, we confront the world and discover how to transform an apparently chaotic, uncontrollable natural environment into a world experienced as a harmonious extension of ourselves.[64] Children utilize nature and natural objects to interpret themselves and experiences with other people.[65]

From infancy onward, we are drawn toward natural creatures "like moths to a porch light," as evidenced by a toddler's fascination with a puppy or kitten.[66] As children progress, they utilize transmorphic reasoning to move past minor differences between themselves and nature and focus on salient aspects to develop isomorphic relationships with nature where it is compared directly with humans, establishing equivalency in moral terms. Studies have confirmed the embedment of nature within children's identity. In a Houston study, 84 percent of children stated that animals were a significant part of their lives, similarly to plants at 87 percent and parks or open spaces at 70 percent. In another study, children believed that polluting a bayou would be objectionable if harm occurred to birds (89 percent), water (91 percent), insects (77 percent), or the view (93 percent).[67] Research indicates that children's moral reasoning concerning natural objects spans across cultures because of the universal and invariant aspects of nature that foster children's environmental identity.[68]

As children reach adolescence, identification with nature through these psychological mechanisms diminishes. This is due to a number of possible reasons such as the development of a more hierarchical concept of life or the concern with place in society and social identity. As adolescents mature into adults, the facet of their identity associated with nature reasserts itself in the form of environmental activism, greater recognition of nature's facets, and a rise in the valuation of nature's experience.

PLACE IDENTITY

The ongoing association with natural surroundings that results in a secure, satisfying, and pleasing experience results in *place identity*: a profound, positive, emotional bond to that environment.[69] This sense of a secure and satisfying connection with one's environment has been termed a *spirit of place* independently by biologist Rene Dubros and landscape architect Frederick Olmstead. This phenomenon converts the inanimate landscape into a living entity within personal identity instilled with a uniqueness and spirit. The characteristics of a "spirit of place" include an increased consciousness of familiar settings; a bonding based on shared experience; and the repeated reinforcement of customs, habits, and rituals. What makes a place extraordinary is the unique integration of culture and nature. It is a place of human significance reflecting personal mores in continuous, recursive contact with the natural environment. The spirit of place, a sense of an enduring relationship, and connection to a particular place are also termed having "roots." The desire to have roots has both social and biological meaning and is a fundamental but unappreciated facet of human existence.[70]

CULTURE AND ENVIRONMENTAL IDENTITY

An environmental identity is a significant part of the full identity of primitive, indigenous cultures. In these cultures, there is an intimate connection with the environment. Communing with nature and awareness of its sensations, characteristics, and signs is a fundamental underpinning of their society. This environmental identity fosters the concept of Gaia and the great flowing continuum where we are an extension of a greater universal whole. This strong form of environmental identity arises from the society's dependence on nature for its nourishment and security. Steven Kellert and Edward Wilson studied a group of New Guineans whose culture was formed based on native plants and animals. Their strong environmental identity was fostered by the direct economic utility of natural materials and foods.[71] This orientation influenced their process of form making. In modern or self-conscious culture, the artist is the force in the design process. In the un-self-conscious culture, the artist is the agent of change or the conduit for the forces of design. This process of form generation consists of incremental change to adapt existing forms to changing environmental conditions. This process is constrained within the traditions that developed over time from the environmentally oriented culture and work as the governing structure to the process. The procedure is analogous to a natural self-organizing process by which incremental change is implemented through a feedback loop until an equilibrium condition is reached. As with nature, forms of great complexity and coherence are generated.[72] Examples of indigenous fractal architecture are noted in *African Fractals,* by Ron Eglash, in the African city of Logone-Birni and in the village of stone buildings in the Mandara Mountains, both in Cameroon, as well as in a Ba-ila settlement in southern Zambia.[73] Rather than being a conscious imitation of nature, these structures emerged from the local culture, in which recursion is a fundamental characteristic. The recursive cultural orientation gives rise to an un-self-conscious fractal aesthetic exhibited in the design of its artifacts and structures.

AN AESTHETIC APPRECIATION OF NATURE

A plethora of nature's works have been judged as the epitome of aesthetically pleasing forms. Immanuel Kant, one of the most influential thinkers of the Enlightenment, engendered a theory of aesthetic qualities. The purpose of the theory was to identify the nature of the pleasure underlying the aesthetic judgment of nature, the character of the pleasure, and the psychological processes that create the feeling of gratification. This process is inherently subjective and is centered on an object's capacity to provide contentment or discontentment in a person with normal perceptual and cognitive abilities. In Kant's theory, there is an initial judgment of taste or free beauty regarding the object's form such the quality of its boundaries and the articulation within its margins. Second, there is a judgment on the perceptual expression of any element of an object's material such as its sensual qualities of sound, smell, taste, or color. Last, there is a conclusion on the suitability of the object to stimulate the conclusion that the object's quality is far greater than that of normal perception. This process of evaluating an object's beauty is produced by the interaction of two cognitive powers. In perception, imagination connects and arranges the information provided by the senses to form an accurate representation of the observed entity, while understanding unifies the assemblage of sensory information by placing it in the category of what the object is. The sensory data of flowing curvilinear shapes, brilliant colors, and a beautiful scent are synthesized into a flower in full bloom. For Kant the phenomenon of experiencing beauty is the sensation experienced when the two cognitive powers interact in free harmonious play. A beautiful composition is one that imagination would create if at play under the singular limitation of conforming to the type definition in understanding. When someone sees a beautiful form, understanding only has to perform the minimal exercise as a monitoring function. Given this nominal expenditure of its energy, it is at ease in the presence of a beautiful object, enabling it to interact with imagination effortlessly. Kant's idea of beauty is characterized by this recursive play of imagination and understanding mutually accelerated and enhanced by their reciprocal harmony. In natural forms characterized by a fractal configuration, the part-to-whole association unifies the variety of subforms and parts, and the elements manifestly appear to belong with each other and within the whole. When natural compositions exhibit this wonderful array of unity and heterogeneity, understanding's task of imposing harmony is particularly minimized because the nature of its beauty is its unity. This enables imagination and understanding to impose fewer impediments on the other's activity, quickening their interactive dance to the point that they operate together and produce a feeling of delight.[74]

Nature can be appreciated aesthetically as art and as nature. Aesthetic judgments of natural beauty can be conceptualized as a response to the properties of the entity. The nature and arrangement of its components or the interrelationship of its elements render the object as inherently gratifying. Environmental formalism is a model of formalistic aesthetic appreciation of the natural environment based on the aspects that constitute the form of an object, and the aesthetic value of an entity is determined by these formal qualities. The perception of a natural object comprises its contours, patterns, and designs. These form elements are manifested in the sensory qualities of its lines, colors, and textures, whose assemblage generates the object's perceived form. This assemblage can be characterized by its formal qualities such as harmonious or disorganized, balanced or unbalanced, clear or perplexing. Environmental formalism suggests that you should view the elements of the natural environment, such as water, trees, plants, hills, mountains, and valleys, from an abstract perspective to derive the form elements of nature. By focusing on the lines, colors, textures, and their relation to each other and to the whole, you can ascertain its beauty. Nature is characterized by harmonious, balanced, and integral forms and the assimilation of a variety of forms into the greater whole by the same characteristics of the individual elements. This aesthetic quality is generally considered to be intrinsically appealing and consequently gives rise to an enduring affection by humans for nature.[75] The intrinsic appeal of nature is embodied in its mystifying structure of form, a secret unlocked by the advent of fractal geometry.

This model of aesthetic appreciation is limited in that it cannot accurately evaluate the loss of aesthetic value to the natural environment by inherently disharmonious man-made artifacts such as power lines transversing a picturesque valley. The power lines' aggressive, expressive nature is in conflict with the tranquil communicative qualities of the natural environment. An alternative model of aesthetic appreciation values nature in terms of its informal expressive qualities such as serenity, majesty, delicacy, gracefulness, and somberness. The range of human emotions, ideals, and attitudes felt in the experience with a natural object is associated with that object to the point that the object is seen as expressing those emotions. Humans associate the desert with its austerity, flowers with gracefulness, a meadow with tranquility, and a threatening sky before a storm with trepidation to the point that they do not separate the object from its characteristic.[76]

These models are enhanced by the consideration that the knowledge that an object is natural influences and is integral to the emotion we feel toward it.[77] If we were to view an object we believed was natural only to find out it was an artificial replica, our interest would most likely diminish. The aesthetic appreciation of nature consists in the disinterested pleasure in its form and that it is natural and a result of natural forces. The delight in hearing a bird's song is significantly derived from it emanating from a living creature as an expression of life and vitality.[78] The question arises on the generative force that manifests itself in the purposiveness of nature's beautiful forms, leading to an inquiry within ourselves and the ultimate purpose of our existence. The pleasure derived from the knowledge that the object under consideration is natural and alive is concordant with our morality and engenders a sense of belonging to it.[79] This connection involves a tender love and respect for natural objects owing to their uncoerced life, its existence through itself and according to laws of a higher order.[80]

A number of formal models of aesthetic appreciation based on these two general categories have been devised:

- The object model maintaining nature's aesthetic appreciation should be based on the sensuous design qualities of the object considered as well as its abstracted expressive qualities.

- The landscape model argues that nature should be appreciated aesthetically as a momentous landscape viewed from a specific point and distance and concentrating on its aesthetic qualities of color, shape, and form viewed at a distance.
- The natural-environment model focuses the aesthetic appreciation of nature on its natural characteristics. It holds that the sensuous experience of nature should be prioritized instead of operating in the background.
- The arousal model is analogous to the natural-environment model and considers the aesthetic experience of nature as derived from the quality of the emotional response to nature.
- The acentric natural aesthetic model holds that nature is a hierarchy of unknowability. As one level of this hierarchy is understood by science, that knowledge reveals the next layer of mystery in a fractal structure where each level renders as much detail and complexity as the preceding level. This process goes on infinitely as nature is infinitely deep in its complexity.[81]

Aesthetic appreciation is altered by the extent of knowledge you have of the natural phenomenon. Different levels of understanding give rise to thoughts, emotions, and images that would not necessarily be presented. At a shallow level of understanding, you can identify a cloud as cumulonimbus and have a certain level of appreciation. At a higher level of understanding, you note the anvil top and irregular underside and comprehend that it is a thundercloud. You grasp the powerful forces at work and it transforms your aesthetic experience. It is essential that the nature of this additional knowledge transforms the essence of the understanding and perception of the phenomenon. When you were young, the Milky Way was a light, permeable shear. With additional knowledge, you comprehend it as an exceptional accumulation of stars, and at an even higher level of understanding, you realize it is the heart of our galaxy, marking your place within it and within the universe.[82]

NATURE, THE SUBLIME, AND GOD

When we consider the night sky with this higher level of understanding, we are confronted with its immensity: the immensity of the universe, the immensity of the distance of the objects we see, and the comprehension of the relative immensity of the space-time phenomenon confronting us.[83] The awareness of the expansive nature of the natural event being considered kindles a complex mental state interweaving a sense of awe at the majesty of the phenomenon with a sense of vulnerability and insignificance. This mental state, which unifies the dualities of positive and negative emotions, is known as *sublime*.[84] It is evident in the power of a typhoon, a tsunami, an earthquake, a bolt of lightning, the turbulent sea, and the splendor of a towering waterfall. It is conveyed in natural objects such as mountains, which, in addition to their characteristic vastness, also present nature's infinite and eternal quality. Where the mind reflects on the beauty of a flower in peaceful contemplation, nature's sublime phenomenon agitates or stimulates the mind. It struggles to understand the immense and infinite character of nature.[85] For Immanuel Kant, the aesthetic estimate of an object of this magnitude involves the fractal conceptualization of the parts preceding and acting as a representation of the whole.[86]

Owing to their inherent characteristics, the contemplation of sublime works of nature inevitably causes humans to reflect on God. Research has demonstrated that environmental values have strong religious and moral implications.[87] An important element of this conviction is the concept of life associated with natural objects, which is fostered by anthropomorphic reasoning. The right to life is considered a basic property common to both nature and humans.[88] Other studies have noted the indescribably deep, spiritual attachment people have to trees and that the spiritual dimension of trees expresses the beauty of life and God's work, which nurtures the soul.[89]

Nature is the principal unrelenting and continuous manifestation of God, cosmogenic truth, and universal intelligence that humans experience. This association is responsible for the perception of nature's intrinsically religious value. Spiritual development is an essential human drive. The contemplation of nature feeds into this drive by providing a gratifying medium to God. For people such as Rudolf Steiner, who learned "to see God in nature and nature in God," it is a source of spiritual nourishment.[90] The essence of God and the essence of nature are the components of a duality on the surface of which is the physical form of nature with God concealed behind it.[91]

SUMMARY

By studying natural phenomena, we endeavor to reveal hidden laws and truths. Nature is considered the artifact of God, and it is through it that we can come to know God. Nature is conceived as being designed by God and is expressed through its inherent order. The unveiling and use of the fractal generative principle of this inherent order is postulated to connote similar associations. By using fractal geometry to generate architectural forms, the same geometrical structural principles that engender universal and cosmological associations in natural forms should unconsciously be applied to some degree in man-made artifacts generated by the same geometric principles. For Rudolf Steiner, in these archetypal structures we would create "larynxes through which the gods may speak to us."[92]

CHAPTER **3**   **Nature's Order and Its Architectural Embodiment**

3.1.

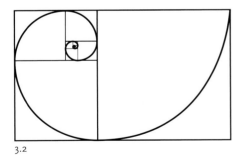

3.2

Figure 3.1. Archetypal natural form.
Figure 3.2. Logarithmic spiral.

The association with nature has been demonstrated to be an essential human requisite affecting our mental, emotional, and consequently our physical health. This relationship is rooted to some extent in man's perception of aesthetically gratifying archetypal forms that are harmonious with embedded analytical constructs. The characteristics of these mental concepts are established on certain principles of order. Artifacts based on these principles should invoke associations and emotional reactions similar to those experienced with nature. Utilizing natural forms has been a fundamental device of architects through history. As science has revealed a deeper understanding of natural morphological processes, we are able to go beyond the heretofore application of natural motifs and imitative forms to utilize the derivative processes of natural forms.

An archetypical configuration in nature is the golden ratio of 1.618. It occurs when the ratio between the sum of two quantities and the larger of the two quantities is equivalent to the ratio between the larger and smaller quantity of the sum or $a{:}b = b{:}(a + b) = 1.618$. When you graphically utilize the golden ratio in the relationship of rectangles, you create a series of radiating rectangles that possess the fractal quality of self-similarity. When you connect the equivalent points on the radiating rectangles, you form a logarithmic spiral (Figure 3.2), which is prevalent in nature. It presents itself in a cascade of similar shapes from the shell of a snail to the pattern of pine cones and sunflowers to the overall geometry of galaxies (Figure 3.3). A related concept is the Fibonacci

3.3a   3.3b   3.3c

sequence, which consists of a series of numbers that are composed of the addition of the two previous numbers: 1:1:2:3:5:8:13:21:34:55. . . . The Fibonacci sequence is associated with the distribution of elements in natural forms such as the configuration of florets in sunflowers.

Three geometric derivatives of the golden proportion—the Golden Section, the related Divine Proportion, and Golden Rectangles— have been utilized extensively in determining the configuration of architectural elements and form. The Golden Section appears to have been a governing factor in the design of the Pyramids at Giza and the Parthenon at the Greek Acropolis (Figure 3.4) and was used extensively at the Great Mosque at Kairouan. Its comprehensive use is attributable to the perceptual satisfaction of its proportions. The Golden Section has been used as a characteristic geometric organizing principle in Gothic and Renaissance architecture. Applied in plan, section, and elevation, it controls the configuration of spaces, the vertical relation of spatial elements, and the distribution and proportion of façade components.[1] Le Corbusier, advocating the extension of the Golden Section from its use in Leonardo Da Vinci's Vitruvian Man, based his architectural proportioning system, Le Modular, on it. He utilized Le Modular in his work on the belief that the rhythms generated by it resound in man because of an organic interconnection.

3.4

NATURE'S SYMMETRY

An aspect of nature that is readily apparent is its symmetrical proper- ties. At an obvious and elementary level, many aspects of nature are structured with various degrees of linear, radial, and plane symmetries. Looking in the mirror, you note that humans are one of many nature's creatures that possess bilateral symmetry, or *reflection symmetry,* about

Figure 3.3. a. Pine cone; b. Snail shell; c. Sunflower.
Figure 3.4. The Golden Rectangle and the Parthenon.

3.5a

3.5b

3.6

Figure 3.5 a. Starfish; b. Flower with radial symmetry.
Figure 3.6. Bee honeycomb.

the vertical axis. Drawing a hypothetical line down the middle of the front of your body, the left side is an approximate reflection of the right side, as it is for butterflies, beetles, dogs, cats, and on and on. Other types of linear symmetry are reflection symmetry about the horizontal axis, *translation symmetry* (simple repetition of shapes separated by a consistent amount or translation), *glide reflection symmetry* (reflection of a shape with a translation), and *rotational symmetry*. *Radial symmetry* is rotational symmetry about a fixed point and is classified whether each element is symmetrical as in dihedral symmetry (D) and is termed cyclic symmetry (C). Each of these classifications is further distinguished by an integer indicating the number of rotations about the central point that is required to rotate through each element and return to the starting point. Classic cases are the starfish, which exhibits D5 radial symmetry (Figure 3.5a) as each element is symmetrical about a central axis and there are five arms or rotations. Snowflakes typically exhibit D6 symmetry, jellyfish present D4 symmetry, and flowers (Figure 3.5b) exhibit various degrees of radial symmetry, both cyclic and dihedral. Symmetry also occurs in the plane and is known as *wallpaper symmetry*. This aspect of symmetry involves reflections, rotations, translations, and glide reflections of symmetrical and non-symmetrical fundamental regions to form one of seventeen patterns. The classic example is the bee hive honeycomb (Figure 3.6), where a hexagonal fundamental region is translated in one of two directions to tile the plane. Owing to its geometric economy, hexagonal symmetry is a prevalent configuration in nature.

D'Arcy Thompson, in his seminal work *On Growth and Form*, noted that natural structures were consistent with a set of production rules and proportional geometries as if their form was a result of function times economy.[2] In the eighteenth century, French philosopher and mathematician Maupertius echoed this concept when he theorized that the evolution of a dynamic system is organized according to the principle of minimum energy consumption. The branches of a tree are angled to permit the most efficient flow of sap or to require the least amount of energy to distribute sap, and the subbranches' characteristic levels of scale are based on the same principle albeit to a lesser extent. This principle was extended by physicist Max Planck as indispensable to modern quantum theory.[3] It is postulated that its application is at the heart of the explanation of why fractal geometry accurately models natural forms. The structure of the whole organism is often reflected in every part because of the proposal that corresponding forces act on each part in a hierarchical scaling structure. The forces that shape the branch shape the subbranch that shapes the twig.[4]

FORM AND FUNCTION IN NATURE

There has been an increasing realization that the forces and processes that are active in nature's morphology are a central component of the aesthetic appreciation of nature.[5] Scientists such as Adolf Portman conjectured that the organization of the functional apparatus of natural entities affects form by following independent rules.[6] This can be seen in the factors that determine the variables of a bird's shape, the feathering type, the shape of the beak, the length of the neck, and the shape of the wing. The type of flight that is characteristic of the relation of wing size and shape to the body is evident in the short-wing typology of maneuvering birds (Figure 3.7a) versus the larger wing type of soaring birds (Figure 3.7b). This orientation toward the derivation of form is directly in line with the modernist creed that form follows function. Le Corbusier properly concluded that there are natural forces in nature that generate forms based on fitness of purpose and according to laws of economy. He believed this was a universal principle that causes the qualities of harmony, order, and balance present in the natural world. By utilizing these forces in architecture, he believed it would put man in greater contact with the universals that govern existence.[7] Nature's universals are unveiled to man through its apparent order. The appreciation of nature is to an extent the conscious or unconscious appreciation of this order imposed on the object by intrinsic and external forces.[8]

NATURAL COMPLEXITY

The concept that apparently simple systems in nature reveal vast complexity can be observed by analyzing the single natural entity and the relationships between its parts and by examining the totality of these relationships in the abundant number of forms in nature.[9] Natural forms are characterized by the organizational depth in which the array of parts are brought together. Nature is rich with compositions abundant in linkages and a high degree of redundancy characteristic of the form of scale symmetry found in self-similar configurations. The degree of nested subsystems within and comprising the overall structure and their linkages reveal a dimension of how highly organized the organism is.[10] Researcher Grant Hildebrand has examined certain paired elements the human affinity for nature present in significantly

3.7a

3.7b

evocative building and landscape designs. He noted that the presence of order and complexity in these environments provides the source for their resultant human proclivity. Order is the human observation of pattern, structure, and organization, whereas complexity is a consequence of a perceived lack of apparent order. Successful environments, whether created by nature or man, contain complexity and order in dynamic relation to each other. This complementary relation stems from their inherent dualism, where order without complexity results in monotony and complexity without order is difficult to organize and interpret—and is actually resented.[11]

COSMOGENESIS AND UNIVERSAL ORDER

Advances in science have reinterpreted complexity as the basis of a new view of cosmogenesis. The search for order in the universe is a venerable endeavor that has been attempted since the beginning of time. A Cornell researcher, John Gowan, noting the repeating patterns, cycles, and processes of natural phenomena in nested self-similar hierarchies throughout nature, has developed a fractal algorithm as a cosmic ordering principle (Figure 3.8). The fractal structure of this model is postulated as the simplest, most economical method of constructing a universe. As with the principle of resonance, the elaboration of a fractal structure is premised on the least energy or least resistance principles first championed by Maupertius. The matrix structure is divided vertically into three realms, and each realm is segregated into four levels in an ascending hierarchy: microphysical (particles, atoms, molecules, RNA), biophysical (cells, organisms, species, Gaia), and astrophysical (star, galaxy, universe, multiuniverse).

Figure 3.7. a. Maneuvering bird; b. Soaring bird.

57

	4 Conservation Laws Connected in Triplets = Cosmos 3 Particle Classes x 4 Forces				
	Gather (Unit)	Repeat (Pair)	Share (Group)	Transform (Emergent Unit)	
(level)	MICROPHYSICAL REALM (3 families of 4 particles; 3 quarks x 4 charges)				G A T H E R
Particles, Baryons	Light "Big Bang" "Higgs Cascade"	Electric-Magnetic; Space-Time; Matter-Antimatter	Baryons, Gluons; 3 Quarks, 4 Charges (flavor, color, electric, spin)	Symmetry-Breaking; Leptons, IVBs, Higgs; Neutrinos, Mesons; Baryons: Hydrogen Atom	
Atoms, Elements	Baryons, Hydrogen Atom	Nucleon Pairs; Quark Pairs; Lepton Pairs	Alpha Particle (Helium Nucleus); 4 Nucleons Each of 3 Quarks; Carbon: 3 Alpha Particles	Periodic Table Elements; Atomic Nucleus; Electron Shell	
Molecules Crystals	Atoms, Heavy Elements	Atomic Pairs (H2); Charge Pairs; Spin Pairs; Magnetic Pairs	Carbon: Tetrahedral Bonding; 4 Bonding Sites in 3rd Shell; 1S2, 2S2, 2P2; Water: Tetrahedral Bonding	Molecules; Organic Polymers: Crystal Growth and "Cloning"	
Chemical Systems RNA	Organic Polymers, Crystals	Base Pairing; RNA/DNA: AT, CG; Double Helix	Metabolic RNA/DNA: 4 Nucleotides Each of 3 Chemical Groups	Chemical Systems; RNA/DNA: Replication; Competition, Evolution	
(level)	BIOPHYSICAL REALM (DNA: 4 nucleotides each of 3 chemical groups; 4 nucleotides code in triplets;)				R E P E A T
Cell (Life)	Chemical Systems RNA	DNA: Reproduction; Genetic Replication	Genetic Code; 4 Nucleotides Code in Triplets; Nucleus, Organelles	Cell: Collective System Identity: "Life"; "Self", Membrane	
Organism	Cell	Cell Division: Mitosis-Meiosis	Specialized Organs: Chromosomes, Gonads	Organism: Collective Cellular Identity; Skin	
Species	Organism	Sexual Reproduction; Male-Female	Population Genetics; Social Organization; Specialized Professions	Species: Social Identity; Closed Genome	
Gaia (Planet Earth)	Species	Speciation; Tetraploids, Hybrids	Ecosystem Mutualisms; Bio-geochemical Cycles; 4 Seasons of 3 Months	Gaia: Earth-Life Unity, Common Descent, DNA; Atmosphere; Gravity	
(level)	ASTROPHYSICAL REALM (gravitation: 4 third-order equations; Kepler: 3 laws in 4-D)				S H A R E
Star	Planet	Earth-Sun Earth-Moon	Planetary System: Kepler's 3 Laws of Planetary Motion in 4-D; Central Sun	Star: Energy and Light; Nuclear Fusion; Gravitational Orbits	
Galaxy	Star	Binary Stars; Sun - Jupiter	4x3 Nucleosynthetic Pathway: Main Sequence Stars; Galactic Structure: Spiral Arms, Nucleus, Central Black Hole	Galaxy: Star Nurseries; Supernova Generations; Heavy Element Creation: Disperse, Mix, Recycle	
Universe	Galaxy	Galactic Pairs; Andromeda- Milky Way	Gravitation: Four 3rd Order Equations; Galactic Clusters and "Foam"; Central Massive Galaxies	4-D Universe: Electromagnetic Energy; Space and Time; Particles, Charges, Forces	
Multiverse, First Cause	Universe	Universe Pairs: Antiuniverse (Antimatter)	Multiverse: Big Bang; Beginning of Universe; Trinity; Tetragrammaton; 4 Conservation Laws in Triplets	Multiverse; First Cause; Quantum Origin? Physical Constants	

Each level is a composite of the preceding level. Horizontally, each level is separated into a four-part algorithm at increasing levels of complexity. Starting with a simple input entity, it transforms into an initial stage of bifurcation reflecting the universal interactive dyad or apposition of polarities (proton-electron, male-female), advancing to an organizational structure acting through groups of dyads and then finally to a stage of chaotic transformation resulting in a new emergent unit. At this point, the algorithm's fractal nature is manifested as the emergent unit from this level becomes the input entity of the next level. This transformational fractal structure presents an intuitive resonant universal order of nature.[12]

The universe is characterized as being fundamentally adaptive and self-organizing. It is perpetually reaching new levels of self-organization, adjusting to environmental variables. Articulated by physicist David Bohm, the universe enfolds an "implicate order," the ultimate basis of natural order and unifying principles of the universe, and unfolds the explicit order we perceive in natural forms.[13] The enfolded natural order from which natural forms unfold is by definition intrinsic and not imposed from outside. The unfolding of natural order within the perception of "living structure" and the presence of the quality of "wholeness" are fundamental to the thesis Christopher Alexander presents in his *Nature of Order* series.

THE WHOLENESS OF LIFE AND THE HUMAN AFFINITY FOR ORGANIC FORM

The precedent condition in the *Nature of Order* essays is the concept of life. Every form has a measure of order and a degree of life. Life exists as a general condition that is present to some degree in every physical entity, whether organic or inorganic. It is a quality distinct from the biological definition of life. It exists in every entity in space, in clouds, trees, rocks, concrete, flowers, buildings, water, and on and on. Every region of space has an interconnected degree of life that has some definition and, to an extent, quantification. Like the living vibrant grass lawn it separates from the road running alongside, the inert concrete curb has life that is integrated with the life of the lawn to form a harmony in the interaction of man and nature.[14] Some entities in space have much life; others have less. The degree of life in a clear mountain lake (Figure 3.9a) is higher than in a stagnant, polluted pond (Figure 3.9b). It is higher in the roaring fire in your fireplace than in the smoldering embers of its aftermath.[15] In *Growth*

Figure 3.8. Gowan's fractal algorithm.

3.9a   3.9b

3.10

Figure 3.9. a. Mountain lake; b. Stagnant pond.
Figure 3.10. Flower's pentagonal symmetry.

and Form, D'Arcy Thompson noted that the waves of the ocean, the rainbow after a storm, the shapes of the clouds, the brilliant colors of a sunset manifest their intrinsic harmony and excellence, their life. It is inevitable that the physical sciences cannot fully explain the order and hence life that reigns throughout these manifold phenomena, an order more characteristic in its totality than in any of its individual phenomena.[16]

This experience of life is fundamental to our humanity and enables us to feel the world more deeply through the profound universal attributes emanating from the intrinsic quality of the object.[17] The gathering of flowers in the vase in the middle of the table forms a center that animates the surrounding space with its life. Within the domain of the space, the placement of the bouquet of flowers wakes the surrounding space by establishing connections between the emergent life of the flower configuration and the other objects in the space.[18] To an extent, its life is generated by nature's unique relationship with its genus's expression of "ornament." In nature, there is nothing that can be identified as pure ornament without function, and functional systems in nature are typically beautiful in an ornamental sense. Nature does not distinguish between ornament and function.[19] The beautifully colored petals in Figure 3.10, which form a pentagonal radial symmetry, have a function intrinsic to the flower. Human cognitive processes comprehend the pattern as a whole with an intuition essential to the energy of the phenomenon generated by its ordered structure.[20]

The emotional quality of life that is projected by humans results

3.11

from the perception of wholeness emanating from the spatial configuration and its constituent parts. This configuration is the fundamental characteristic of organic form. The unity of all of the parts into one indissoluble whole whose coherence is greater than the sum of its parts results in the perception of that form as being organic. The attributes of an interpenetrating structural hierarchy of levels in which every part is made up of preceding levels of the hierarchy and each is part of the whole signifies the organic. The resultant unfractionability is the center of perceivable wholeness. The perception is, on a macro level, analyzing the spatial environment as a whole and the constituent relationships within it, on a succeeding, descending microhierarchy of the components that make up the spatial environment and the elements that form those components. Christopher Alexander believes that the process that generates the quality of wholeness is founded in the biological processes that create natural life-forms.[21] Nature, left to its own devices, generates configurations that espouse the qualities of wholeness through the structure of their form. These "structural" qualities appear in a wide variety of natural systems and phenomena and are termed by Alexander as *living structure*. Structure is the relationship of a class of qualitative elements that characterize "wholeness" within each natural form, between discernible and distinct natural entities, and within the natural environment." Living structure is generated by a series of recursive structure-preserving transformations applied to

Figure 3.11. Flower's beauty.

3.12

this structure. The structure that is preserved is the presence and inter-relationship of these qualitative elements, which espouse the quality of wholeness and generate the perception of "life." Each set of recursive transformations is discernible and is resultant from the previous state of the organism. They reinforce and amplify the structural relationships that form its living structure.[22] The metamorphic process generating living structure is the unfolding of nature's order. The conscious or unconscious perception of this vital substrate underlying all matter satisfies the intrinsic human need to be connected to the world and universal truths. This fundamental connection is the basis of the restorative effects and contemplative effects that attract humans to natural environments and the affinity people express for nature's forms (see Figure 3.11).

FRACTAL GEOMETRY, LIVING STRUCTURE, AND WHOLENESS

Alexander's characterization of structure and living structure is indistinguishable from the definition of the processes that create fractal geometry. In particular, the generative characteristic of recursive structure-preserving transformations is the essence of fractal geometry. As we examine more detailed aspects of wholeness and living structure, we will find additional corresponding properties attesting to fractal geometry's validation as a generative tool to create forms

Figure 3.12. Field of sunflowers.

endowed with the qualities that engender feelings of living structure, wholeness, and life.

One of the underpinnings of the concept of living structure is that wholeness springs from a defined system of centers that perpetuates the organizational structure. Wholeness exists within space as a neutral quality that is increased or decreased by the quality of the entities that exist within it. These centers and the interplay between them and the linkages that result from that interplay create living structure, which emanates the quality of wholeness and arouses the emotionally based perceptions of life.[23] The totality of the physical environment throughout its hierarchical scale is perceptually constructed of centers in varying degrees of distinctness and overlap. Mountains, rivers, roadways, trees, buildings, flowers, windows, lakes, and so on are all part of one continuous integral system. These entities and their relationships of interaction interlock with and influence other centers, forming varying degrees of coherence.[24] The stronger the organization of a center, the greater is its capacity for creating and maintaining relationships with other centers, resulting in a higher degree of wholeness.[25]

The concept of centers and their linkages is fundamental within the natural world. The heterogeneous makeup of space results in evolving delineations of systems differentiation. The aggregation of this layered, interlocked progression of centers and relationships

63

3.13

3.14

Figure 3.13. Levels of scale.
Figure 3.14. Strong centers.

produces a complex but wonderfully coherent environment for human habitation. The flower is one of the most universally beautiful forms because of its radiating wholeness extrapolated from the living structure generated by its field of centers. This can be most readily seen with a sunflower, where its centeredness is created by the organization and interplay of its centers. They are centers owing to the strength of their configuration, which generates a higher degree of centeredness. The circularity of this phenomenon is at the heart of understanding the production of wholeness and life. It manifests itself, moreover, in a group of sunflowers and climaxes in a field of sunflowers. A field of sunflowers slowly waving in the breeze is a collectively beautiful manifestation of natural beauty generated by nature's order (Figure 3.12).

PROPERTIES OF NATURAL ORDER

In the *Nature of Order* series, Christopher Alexander identifies fifteen properties or structural characteristics of natural systems that establish order within nature. These properties occur continuously in nature in part because they are the basis for the recursive structural transformations. They are the qualities that form the connections between centers, act to reinforce centers, and form larger centers.

- *Levels of Scale.* This property comes logically from the manner in which the natural organism brings itself to order. The appearance of this property is one of the most widespread characteristics of natural systems. A purposeful order is demonstrated by the presence of functional coherence at different stages, resulting in recognizable hierarchies within the configuration. The presence of a continuous scale hierarchy of functional structure is so pervasive throughout nature that it is a fundamental cognitive property of organic form (see Figure 3.13).[26]
- *Strong centers.* Not to be confused with the macro concept of centers as perceptual organizers of natural environments, many natural self-organizing organisms utilize centrally driven processes as generative methodologies. The generative force radiates outward in spatially symmetric force field arrangements and is characteristic in physics, biological life-forms, and molecular configurations (see Figure 3.14).[27]
- *Boundaries.* When different systems are spatially proximate, a boundary or zone of interaction frequently forms for functional separateness or transition. The boundary can be substantial,

64

3.15

developing as a distinct entity with its own discernible shape, properties, and characteristics. It functions both as a transitional device separating the adjacent phenomenon and as a unifying force between itself and each adjacent condition.[28]

- *Alternating repetition.* In most natural systems, repetition occurs in an alternating composition rather than as simple repetition. The initial repeating units alternate with a subsequent set of repeating elements. Both arrays of repeating units have centers and coherence in their own right, with their own distinct sequence and constancy. The alternating rhythms interlock in counterpoint reinforcement of each other.[29]

- *Positive space.* This property is the result of the perception of the internal coherence of the self-organizing principle of the organism. The internal wholeness of the organism radiates to manifest itself not only in its physical form but also in the space between its components. Each element of space has character, and as opposed to empty banal space, the space affected by radiating wholeness of an adjacent organism is positively charged.[30]

- *Good shape.* As noted by researchers and writers such as D'Arcy Thompson, throughout nature, there is widespread occurrence of shapes that are judged to be beautiful. This quality is a consequence of some of the other properties articulated by Alexander, which fuse to form a perceptual amalgamation with its own observable distinction. Good shape is derived by the recursive aggregation of elemental geometric shapes, frequently curvilinear, with their center properties forming minor centers through the recursive process.[31]

- *Local symmetries.* Symmetries occur in nature because of the natural generative forces being controlled by the principles of minimum energy and least action. There is no reason relative to the governing action of these principles to deviate from the symmetry to develop an asymmetry. These symmetries, generated in layers nesting sub-subsymmetries within subsymmetries within symmetries, are widespread through a number of natural systems (see Figure 3.15).[32]

- *Deep interlock and ambiguity.* The presence of adjacent systems interacting along large surface areas relative to their volume produces a high degree of interrelating connections or deep interlock. The resulting perceptual quality is ambiguity, where a subsystem can be observed to belong to either of the two perceptually over-lapping systems.[33]

- *Contrast.* A significant relationship that provides mutual

Figure 3.15. Local symmetries.

3.16

reinforcement is the positioning of opposites. An exclusive unity is created by the bond generated from the centers of discernible opposites stronger than many other perceptual connections. Contrast is the characteristic that creates the energy of the tie between the two opposites.[34]

- *Gradients.* As a system's generative force varies, the physical manifestation of that force also varies systematically. Each level of gradient forms a center that relates not only to the precedent condition of the force but also to the antecedent condition strengthening the center of both conditions and the components of the gradient.[35]

- *Roughness.* Perceptual irregularity is one of the hallmark characteristics of natural structures. Organic form is an interplay of the self-generating forces within an organism and the environmental conditions and constraints. The environmental factors overlay the organisms' predestined form, twisting, gnarling, and distorting it and producing the roughness characteristic of nature. This attribute enhances wholeness by increasing the diversity of subwholes all under the interlocked relationship with the whole of the generating force.[36]

- *Echoes.* The generating forces in nature produce geometric forms that have characteristic angles and proportions. As the generative force occurs at various scales throughout the organism, the repeated appearance of these angles and proportions is echoed throughout the organism. The resemblance of these subforms produces a morphological character in tune with wholeness (see Figure 3.16).[37]

- *The void.* As nature spreads its generative principles through the wholes, subwholes, sub-subwholes, and so on, the energy radiates and intensifies. At the center of the generative whole is the stability of the larger whole, or the void. The absence of high energy fulfills the psychological requirement for calm at the center of the force.[38]

- *Simplicity and inner calm.* The fractal mantra is that great complexity comes from the compound iteration of simple rules. As a product of the principles of minimum energy and least action, natural configurations are inherently the simplest expression of nature's generative force. There are no extraneous or unnecessary pieces, nonetheless leaving structures of great beauty and intricacy, emanating inner calm from their simplicity.[39]

- *Nonseparateness.* This property reiterates the organic principle that each part of an organism is inseparable from any other because

Figure 3.16. Echoes.

66

each part is connected and interrelated to a whole that is more than the sum of its parts. The removal of a part removes not just that distinct part but part of everything else and a portion of the essence of the whole.[40]

These fifteen properties of natural systems, which generate order that produces wholeness and life, are predominantly characteristics of fractal structures. A fractal configuration has *levels of scale* because of its recursive iterations of geometric transformations. The initial set of transformations creates the strong attractors toward which the contraction mappings are drawn. These strong attractors form *strong centers*, which, while retaining their own attraction, radiate the same geometric configuration in each successive iteration, exponentially increasing the subcenters. The radiating of the fractal structure with its set of linkages and associations *positively charges* the spaces around and between each of the parts. *Deep interlock and ambiguity* are inherent in the nature of linkage and connection between the parts and subparts of a fractal structure. Each of these centers and successive subcenters anchors a set of *local symmetries* about a scale, in addition to other geometric symmetries inherent in the initial set of transformations. The presence of the local symmetries in recursive descending hierarchical levels of scale generates *echoes* of the whole within each part. This creative process has recurrently produced natural forms that have inherent *good shape*, which emerges through the degree of *roughness* imposed by the environment. This form, in which each element is essential in a part-to-whole-to-part relationship, *cannot be separated* and radiates *inner calm in the simplicity* of this relationship.

Alexander reaffirms the human substrate that provides the connection between our cognitive, psychological, and emotional needs and the natural environment. This connection is consciously or unconsciously centered on the order we perceive in the natural world. This order coalesces in a perception of wholeness that emanates life."[41] Alexander notes that these fifteen properties consistently appear throughout that spectrum of natural structures and environments at many levels of scale. The properties' role appears to be as centers of distinct natural functions that through their linkages and relations form the coherence of nature's system. They maintain the integrity and viability of the system through their mutual support and intensification. The convergence of the perceptual properties and underlying philosophical underpinnings of *Nature of Order* and fractal geometry are too evident

3.17

to disregard. This convergence further reinforces the case for fractal geometry as the generative mechanism to produce structures that invoke responses similar to those brought about by exposure to nature.

Nikos Salingaros echoes Alexander's theory of utilizing the order in nature or its "structural" relationships as a basis for the generation of architectural form. One of the principal characteristics of nature's structural relationships is the presence of levels of scale that govern the subdivisions within each natural structure and a lattice of perceptible hierarchical linkages between a structure's elements.[42] The discernment of this matrix of linkages gives rise to an emergent property inherent to that form and perception of beauty.[43] Salingaros develops a methodology to quantify the "architectural life" of a building as the product of the structure's architectural temperature and the architectural harmony. *Architectural temperature* relates to the character of the design elements such as color hue, presence of contrast, and degree of curvature. *Architectural harmony* is based on the visual organization of the artifact such as the presence of symmetries and, in particular, self-symmetry.[44] For Salingaros, fractal structures have an abundance of architectural life owing to a high architectural temperature and high degree of architectural harmony.[45]

NATURE'S FORM IN ARCHITECTURE

The impact on nature and its order has influenced man throughout history to embed it in the artifacts and environments created by them. The designs of ancient Egyptian temples were based on that culture's

Figure 3.17. The Pantheon.

3.18

relationship with nature and the cosmos. They believed that the divine was present in nature and used mathematical models based on astrological study to design their temples. Rudolph Steiner deduced that the genesis of the palm or acanthus motif, used extensively in ancient architecture, was the union of opposing life forces of earth and sun. Early humans were bound to the earth, represented by lines of gravitational force curving up to a point representing man, and were vitally connected to the sun, represented by the sun's rays streaming to a point. Egyptian architects utilized a natural form, the palm, to metamorphically represent man's place in the cosmos with the union of the bud and the palm leaves. This extensively used motif sprung from the perception of the essence of the relationship between humanity and nature. This motif was eventually developed in relief as the acanthus leaf, which was utilized in Corinthian capitals.[46]

The Greek temple provides the point of departure for two different trains of thought on the nature of architecture and its relation to nature, represented by the work of Le Corbusier and Frank Lloyd Wright. The Greek temple architecture of primary forms constituted the purity of place where gods resided. The dwelling place of the gods was inserted within the natural world and the world of human activity, uniting man with the spiritual world.[47] Greco-Roman classicism was the basis for the influential work of Le Corbusier, who believed that the ideal relationship of artifact and nature was the juxtaposition of the clear clarity of architectural form with the veiled purity of natural law, both springing from the same universal point.

Figure 3.18. Hindu temple.

69

3.19

The Pantheon in Rome expresses the continued integration in Roman architecture of our innate need to be connected to the cosmos and understand our place within it (see Figure 3.17). The circular array of coffers lining the interior of the cupola, diminishing in size as it rises to the shaft of light streaming through the opening at the apex, clearly represents the universe and the presence of God.

The most dramatic example of organic architecture is the structure and articulation of Hindu temples (see Figure 3.18). These structures, though they may not be formally fractal structures, exhibit all the perceptive qualities of fractals in the nesting of the overall shape within its constituent form elements and articulation of those elements. The Hindu temple form was an expression of the fundamental beliefs of the Hindu religion and the archetypes that supported it. One of the

Figure 3.19. Interior of a Gothic church.

3.20

3.21

Figure 3.20. Borromini's Sant'Ivo alla Sapienza.
Figure 3.21. Gaudi's Sagrada Familia.

words for temple, *vimana*, literally means a well-proportioned, finely organized, harmonious whole. Fractal-like self-similarities in nature were embedded in their philosophical views and sense of oneness. Intuited recursive geometry was utilized to reflect these views in Hindu temple architecture. The mountain is an archetype in the Hindu universe epitomizing the center of the universe, with the vertical lines of its form leading up to supreme points of transcendence. The Hindu temple's fractal form expressed the fundamental Hindu experience of the infinite through reintegrating the part to the whole.[48]

Advances in structural building technology affected the form of Gothic architecture along the organic form-generating principles of least energy and minimum action (see Figure 3.19). Utilizing the pointed arch and flying buttresses, the thick, bulky masonry walls of Romanesque architecture gave way to a light, skeletal, sculptural structure. Walking down the aisles of a Gothic cathedral, you experience the ribbing of the column shafts radiating into intricate fan-vaulting tracery as if it were a tree-lined path with a canopy of branches and leaves. The decorative carvings employed throughout Gothic architecture, such as crockets and green men, reinforced man's connection with nature. The vibrant structure and intricate, billowing articulation of Gothic architecture conveyed an organic feel and a sense of life.

The fundamental canon of organic architecture was espoused by Renaissance architect and theorist Leon Battista Alberti when he derived the principles of organic unity and applied them theoretically to architecture. For Alberti, beauty was a quality perceived by an innate faculty that appreciated the unity that was present in nature. Beauty was derived from the skillful and elegant connection of the constituent parts based on a concept of the whole that determines the structure of the parts. Alberti termed this concept *concinnitas* and considered it the defining mechanism to harmonize architecture with universal truths. Architectural beauty depended on the integration of number, outline, and position dictated by *concinnitas* to form a structure.[49]

The Baroque period in architecture was a forbearer of the curvilinear features of the organic architecture first explored at the end of the nineteenth century. Churches such as Sant'Ivo alla Sapienza by Francesco Borromini exhibited organic aspects in their exteriors, in the latter case, in the form of a striking spiral spire and a flowing, undulating space that feels organically alive (Figure 3.20).

Inspired by John Ruskin, who advocated nature as the source of form epitomized in Gothic architecture, from Ferdinand Moser's

Ornamental Plant Studies from the Sphere of Native Flora and Owen Jones's *The Grammar of Ornament*, which derived ornament from plant forms, Art Nouveau was born. Art Nouveau was a movement that, unlike previous architectural styles that utilized natural elements in predominately appliqué techniques, integrated organic form in totality as functional components in addition to the extensive use of floral motifs. Art Nouveau was characterized by curvilinear forms with the structural integrity of Gothic architecture, epitomized by the entrances to the Paris Metro stations by Hector Guimard, the structural and decorative ironwork by Victor Horta, the stylized floral motifs and ornamentation of Charles Renee Macintosh, and the Eiffel Tower by Gustav Eiffel. The new organic form was dramatically exhibited in Barcelona in the work of Antonio Gaudi. Demonstrated in buildings such as the Casa Mila, undulating façades, organic structure derived from observation of nature and empirical studies with weights and string, and employing curvilinear organic forms to define a rooftop garden, the public was introduced to a new architectural paradigm. Gaudi's work is epitomized by his unfinished masterpiece Sagrada Familia (Figure 3.21), which exudes a vibrant life through its organic structure and articulation. Gaudi's biomorphic form was continued with Erich Mendelson's expressionist Einstein Tower in Potsdam, which Albert Einstein himself termed "organic," and Friedensreich Hundertwasser's colorful, undulating, spiraling Waldspirale.

Organic architecture was promoted by the theoretical dissertations of two influential architectural philosophers, Hugo Haring and Rudolf Steiner. Hugo Haring abhorred the imposed geometric rigidity of established building form and espoused the idea of *Gestaltung*, or form making, in which the form unfolds from its function. His thesis repelled pure platonic geometry for the curvilinear shape of natural forms due in part to the ability of their expression to generate positive emotional reactions. Rudolf Steiner was heavily influenced by the theories of Wolfgang Goethe, an influential German writer, philosopher, and scientist who coined the maxim of "architecture as frozen music."[50] For Steiner, the creation of significant works of art and architecture is dependent on the ability to discern the order, harmony, and meaning of nature. The exalted works of architecture are at the same time the most sublime works of nature. Beauty was a manifestation of the hidden laws of nature that the architect brings forth in the expression of their buildings.[51] By applying the hidden laws of nature, forms emerge slowly and transform according to the same

3.22

3.23

rules that govern natural structures. Steiner applied the concept of morphological development to architectural design by concentrating on the unity present in the structural relationships of natural forms.[52]

Louis Sullivan mirrored Gaudi's work, albeit in a structurally rectilinear form. In his publication *A System of Architectural Ornament*, Sullivan documented a process of integrating the articulation of natural form within a geometrical substructure. Inspired by the conception of nature's forms from the functions they perform, Sullivan formulated the axiom "form follows function" to be applied to architecture. In his essay "Tall Building Artistically Reconsidered," he outlined the principles of his organic design philosophy, which expressed the structure by articulating it with his geometrically controlled natural forms and composed the overall form of the building unique to itself (see Figure 3.22).[53] Sullivan's legacy was carried on by Frank Lloyd Wright, who is, through his work and writings, considered the father of American organic architecture. A Wright protégé, Paolo Soleri, championed the concept of *arcology*, which integrates architecture with ecological principles.

Organic architectural form continued with the work of Kendrick Bangs Kellogg, whose work, such as the Yen House and High Desert Home, radiates biomorphic form, and Frank Gehry, whose signature architectural design, epitomized in the Bilbao museum project, has thrust organic expressionist design squarely into the public's consciousness (Figure 3.23).

These periods in architectural history have utilized natural forms in various ways, verifying their fundamental importance as a human value and connection to collective values. Paolo Portoghesi, in his publication "Nature and Architecture," examined archetypes in nature that have been utilized in the full spectrum of possible applications from decorative appliqué to emulation of form to its use as a conduit to universal principles:

- *The skeleton*. The skeleton is a basic natural concept that permeates through human, animal, and plant species as a requisite structural homology. Gothic architecture was the first meaningful celebration of the beauty of the structural skeleton. Modern architecture represented by the International Style attempted to purify architecture by exhibiting the structural skeleton. Skillful use produced wonderful architecture, but frequently, unskillful application gave us banality. Currently architects such as Calavantra

Figure 3.22. Louis Sullivan.
Figure 3.23. Gehry's Bilbao museum.

3.24

3.25

Figure 3.24. Calatrava's Lyon Air Terminal.
Figure 3.25. Taut's Glass Pavilion.

(Figure 3.24) have reintroduced the Gothic notion of structural skeleton as an art form.[54]

- *The womb.* The concept of a womb has been utilized by architects to provide a sense of security and comfort to the users of an architectural space. The concept of a home is essentially a womb securing the inhabitants from the outside world. Through the hierarchy of spaces and the presence of a fireplace, Frank Lloyd Wright provided the emotional reassurance of the womb in the design of his houses. Interior courtyards provide a similar facility, trading openness, fresh air, and light for a diminished sense of security.[55]

- *The mountain.* As indicated previously, Hindu temple design is directly related to the essential role a mountain plays in the Hindu religion. The mountain archetype is apparent in Mayan architecture, the pyramids of Egyptian architecture, and the cupolas that grace the cityscape of Rome.[56]

- *Geomorphism.* The characteristic trait of geomorphic architectural form is curvilinear lines of flow shaping the form of the building as water molds natural rock masses. Antonio Gaudi pioneered this prototype in his classical structures in Barcelona, and it is characteristic of the work of Frank Gehry.[57]

- *Crystals.* The geometric purity of crystals has been a source of inspiration for centuries. It served as an ideal for church design in the Renaissance, the inspiration for Bruno Taut's Glass Pavilion (Figure 3.25) at the Cologne Werkbund Exhibition, and the structural basis of the work of Buckminister Fuller. With the advances in building technology, the crystalline form has experienced resurgence, as seen in Denis Laming's Kinemax at Futuroescope, Peter Eisenman's design for Church for the Year 2000, Rem Koolhaus's library in Seattle, and Daniel Libeskind's design signature.[58]

- *The shaft.* The longitudinally oriented natural forms occurring in trees, plants such as bamboo, and the stems of flowers has been allegorically employed in the piers of Gothic cathedrals and has been characteristic of the loggias of Venetian architecture. This concept is central to the classical skyscraper base-shaft-crown morphology.[59]

- *The branch.* The tree is a quintessential natural form that humans intrinsically value. The ribbing that arises from the column shaft in Gothic architecture rising up to the intricate fan vaulting

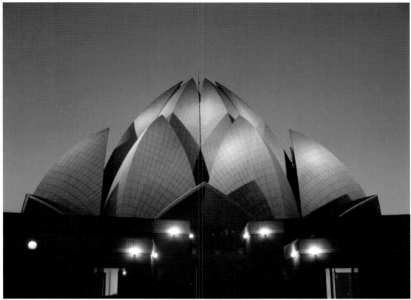

3.26

undoubtedly metaphorically inspires the inhabitants. Antonio Gaudi utilized this structure as the interface between the columns and floors of his work at projects such as Parc Guell.[60]

- *The inflorescence.* This is a natural reproductive system structure based on flowers arranged about a vertical axis. This has manifested itself in Renaissance architecture such as the cupola of the chapel of the Holy Shroud in the Duomo in Turin through the expression of punched windows in the architecture of Frank Gehry, exemplified in his Fred and Ginger building in Prague. Many vertical radial religious towers, such as minarets, also use this as an expressive device.[61]

- *The flower.* The ideal model of centrality and frontality is embodied in the inspiration of the flower. The Bahai temple in Delhi, shown in Figure 3.26, is modeled after a partially opened lotus flower, which symbolizes purity and peace. The Sydney Opera House has a similar architectural expression and has long been an Australian tourist attraction.[62]

- *The stars and the light.* Since the beginning of time, man has been captivated by the cosmos, represented by a star-filled sky. The construction of many ancient temples was influenced by identification with the universe and the movement of its heavenly bodies. The crossings of churches are frequently marked by domes whose interiors mimic the heavens. The human response

Figure 3.26. Bahai temple.

to the dramatic shaft of light streaming through the oculus of the Pantheon in Rome confirms its significant allegorical value. The use of light in the Hagia Sophia similarly raises the experience of the architectural space.[63]

- *Radii.* Outward radiation from a central point is one of the most common morphological configurations in the plant genus. The classic rose window has asserted its prominence in human architectural perception based on this configuration. The Chrysler Building in New York, with its radiating spires rising to a dramatic central spire, dramatically crowns this architectural monument in an organic morphology.[64]

- *Spiral.* The spiral geometry is embedded in the human psyche as one of the most elegant of nature's configurations, presenting itself in diverse forms as shells, flowers, and plants. Signifying its importance, ancient man utilized the spiral as the derivative force in the creation of the ziggurat. Frank Lloyd Wright employed it similarly in the design of the Guggenheim Museum in New York. It has been utilized to form the geometry of spires on notable buildings such as Sant'Ivo alla Sapienza.

Historically, man has incorporated in his architecture the beauty he perceives in nature and the order present in natural forms simply in a decorative appliqué or at best as an imitation of its form. During this time, man has sought to unlock the key to the natural principles that give rise to organic form. This unrelenting quest has perpetuated through recorded time because of the certainty that universal harmonies present in nature's order with which we are in sync can be attained in architecture, producing an emotion similar to the emotion we experience when confronted by natural beauty.[65] Rudolf Steiner held that the profound mysteries of the universe are expressed to us by the emotion we feel when we see an object of beauty. For Steiner, the basis of artistic conception is found in a state of consciousness that existed before recorded time and that we seek these primordial forces of knowledge, which are the origins of artistic form and design and which sprang from the human soul, not from the imitation of external phenomena. Using Goethe's phenomenological method, the artist or architect deeply dwells on the natural phenomenon to sense its inner principles or the lawfulness of its dynamic forces. For Goethe, though the "what" is important, the "how" or the way the phenomenon is formed is the primary focus of attention. Art and architecture allow these principles to express themselves through man's artifacts. The artistic organization of perceptual phenomena reveals the inner principles or nature's laws expressed through architecture. This translucency has an inherent beauty arising from the revelation of the deeper precept.[66] Goethe's philosophical conviction immersed in scientific inquiry led Steiner to an organic architecture embodying the biological theories of plant morphology.[67] The expression of nature's underlying laws was through proportion and symmetry to structure a unity characterized as an organic whole.[68]

BIOMORPHIC FORMS VERSUS FRACTAL ARCHITECTURE

With advances in building technology and the influence of computers on the design process, a new world of architectural form has opened up. These advances permit the use of more biomorphic forms that incorporate free-flowing curves in any or all the traditional axes. There is an architectural school of thought that believes philosophically that psychological and emotional benefits derived from an organic architecture can be achieved with the use of biological forms. Biomorphic forms integrate with the world of nature that envelops it and appear to be products of it. These forms are very interesting and are a further step toward the integration of architecture and nature. They are still, however, just another step in the historical integration of man with nature by imitation of natural forms that occurred from ancient civilizations through Gothic architecture and Art Nouveau. Although they engender emotions consistent with natural beauty, they fall short in the same way as when we learn that an object we believe is natural is actually man-made. The significant difference between architecture based on biomorphic forms and architecture based on fractal geometry is that biomorphic forms are imitations of nature, whereas fractal architecture utilizes what appears to be the same generative processes that nature uses, which inherently bestows on it the same emotive properties.

ORGANIC ARCHITECTURE

Natural structures from molecules to flowers to mountains have evolved over billions of years, producing forms that are highly functional and efficiently simple. Through their generative processes, they represent an elegant equilibrium of form and force.[69] These structures form cognitive archetypes of the natural world for humans. The utilization of their generative principles in the development of architectural forms that exhibit morphologically similar structural qualities should engender the same cognitive association. In *Building for Life*, Stephen Kellert discussed biomimicry as a path to organic design and biophillic architecture. For Kellert, organic design fosters direct, indirect, or symbolic experiences of nature through various means, including forms that mimic natural processes and accord with an archetypal image of the natural world.[70] Psychologist Judith Heerwagen has attributed the presence of fractal characteristics as a biophilic design feature that engenders positive emotions based on an affinity for nature.[71]

A fundamental character of organic design is that it is generated by a process of self-organization. Natural forms are a result of a self-generative process unique to their species. These processes are derived from the hidden laws of nature, manifesting themselves in the form produced by them. In their evolution, these processes adapt through mutation to certain environmental factors. Similarly, in utilizing these processes, the designer has the opportunity to adapt the process to better attain his or her aesthetic goals. For a building to achieve the essence of an organism, it must be the result of similar self-organizing processes such as fractal geometry. The characteristics we perceive as organic are a result of these natural processes in which the forms emerge and transform.[72]

Organic architecture is characterized by rhythms arising from polarities such as coherence and complexity and inherent structural configurations.[73] The composition initially presents complexity as the unity revealed, while pleasing, is intuited and not fully understood. As the part-to-whole-to-part relationship is examined, an innate lucidity in the relationships is discerned. These relationships span levels of scale from the configuration's structure generating a cascade of cognitive interplay and association. These qualities operate in cognitive syncopation, inducing a cognitive rhythm and a consequential perception of life.

The most defining attribute of organic design of which the aforementioned qualities are subsets is its holistic nature. In organic design, derived from the part-to-whole-to-part organizational schema, each element exists within and in accordance with the whole. Depending on the level of emergence, if that element is changed or deleted, each part of the aggregate whole as well as the organic whole is changed.[74] The historical proponents of organic architecture, Alberti with *concinnitas*, Goethe with *Urpflanze*, Wright with integrated space, and Le Corbusier with harmonies, have all focused on this quality as the defining tipping point of organic design. The purposeful unity of an organism through the perception of its holistic order gives voice to its inherent phenomena and the source of its aesthetically persuasive power.[75,76]

Patterns appear in nature, reoccurring in successive generations and across species. The geometry of the golden ratio is expressed as the guiding principle in the growth of shells and the distribution of leaves. The rhythm present in natural forms has been attributed to geometric laws. Le Corbusier sought in geometry the universal laws responsible for the natural rhythms that produced the feeling of harmony.[77] The geometry that serves as the basis for a significant degree of natural morphology is fractal geometry. Its fundamental character embodies the organic design characteristics of self-generation, the polarity of order and complexity, and holism. It use in the generation of architectural form is the bridge between human artifact and the natural environment.

SUMMARY

The human appreciation of nature arises in part from the order that is perceived when viewing natural forms. This order is exhibited in various symmetrical structures and relationships. The most significant of these attributes is self-symmetry, which is the identity characteristic of natural forms. Throughout history, man has strove to incorporate nature within his architecture, reflecting its significance. To date, it has mostly consisted of the appliqué of nature's motifs or imitation of natural structures. With advances in the understanding of fractals, we can restructure architectural form creation to incorporate the generative structure of nature and truly integrate nature into architectural edifices.

CHAPTER **4**   **Skyscraper Form and Its Fractal Derivative**

Up until the late nineteenth century, because of structural considerations and the difficulty people have in climbing a large number of stairs, buildings rarely rose above five stories. With technological developments in steel, reinforced concrete, elevators, and water pumps, architects were able to break this barrier and design buildings of ten stories or more, giving birth to the skyscraper form. Before the implementation of structural steel framing, buildings relied on load-bearing masonry construction, which has a practical limit reached with the Chicago's Monadnock Building in 1891 and Philadelphia's City Hall in 1901. With the realization of structural steel technology, buildings could be erected many stories higher as well as permit the design of innovative forms. Structural steel was first utilized in the Crystal Palace and the Eiffel Tower. Employing structural steel framing inspired a reconsideration of the exterior wall of the building, from the hulking masonry expression to the concept of the exterior wall as a skin or curtain, leading to the idea of a curtain wall. This new exterior wall paradigm was first fully utilized in the Hallidie Building by William Polk in 1917.

Once it was technically feasible to build structures that were higher than ever before, practical considerations, such as transporting people up to those floors, had to be addressed. The first elevator was made by Elisha Graves Otis in 1852 and was introduced at the world exhibition at Manhattan Crystal Palace. It was first used in the Haughwout Building in New York in 1857. The elevator not only permitted higher

4.1

4.2

Figure 4.1. New York Tribune Building.
Figure 4.2. Home Insurance Building.

stories to be built because people no longer had to walk up but it also turned the value of real estate within buildings upside-down. Prior to the elevator, lower floors were more valuable because of ease of access. With the introduction of the elevator and the erection of taller buildings, the lower floors were considered less desirable because of their proximity to the dankness of the streetscape, whereas the higher floors were light filled and had marvelous views.[1]

The development of mechanical systems in concert with other construction developments provided the third aspect of building technology to contribute to the skyscraper building form. Early buildings were heated through the use of fireplaces, and later a boiler in the basement would heat water, which would be pumped up to radiators on the floors above. Eventually, a system of metal ducts was implemented that would carry air that was either heated or cooled from either a central plant or a group of satellite units. Storage tanks at the tops of buildings supplied water for plumbing and fire protection.

These technological developments provided a solution to the increased concentration of people and commerce in cities such as Chicago and New York at the end of the nineteenth century and contributed to a real estate boom. Corporations of the Industrial Age and related companies such as stock exchanges sought to locate in central urban areas. The increased height in buildings not only provided increased real estate value but was a source of prestige. Architecture as a language for commercial communication was first implemented with the construction of the New York Tribune Building, built across from City Hall in 1875 (see Figure 4.1). The building was capped with a clock with the word *Tribune* above it. When a person looked up to see what time it was, the person consciously or subconsciously embedded a positive connotation toward the Tribune Company.[2] Similar to the perception of royal palaces and religious edifices of history, the skyscraper is a symbol of individual and corporate prestige. This also applies to the inhabitants of the buildings as well as the owners of the structures. The presence of the skyscraper form across the skyline in all major cities plays an important role in the identity of the city.

The first skyscraper, a term borrowed from the terminology of sailors used to denote the tallest mast of a ship, is generally considered to be the Home Insurance Building in Chicago, designed by William LeBaron Jenny in 1885 (Figure 4.2). The initial flurry of skyscraper construction occurred in Chicago and New York. In New York, buildings were generally built out to the property line and straight up to

4.3

4.4

Figure 4.3. Hugh Ferris renderings.
Figure 4.4. Reliance Building.

maximize square footage. With a more international presence, the structures in New York incorporated stylistic tendencies and ornamentation from previous historical periods. Influences from Greek, Romanesque, Gothic, Queen Anne, and Renaissance periods were embedded within the New York skyscraper form in such structures as the Heckscher Building and the Woolworth Building. The Chicago aesthetic was less ornamented and more expressive of the structure of the building.

Two developments that shaped the archetypal skyscraper form were the New York Zoning Resolution of 1916 and the development of the Chicago School of architecture, as represented by the theories of Louis Sullivan. With the explosive growth of skyscrapers, their effects on the light and air reaching the streetscape were being felt and debated. The issue appeared to come to a head with the announcement in 1912 of the construction of the new Equitable Life Assurance Company headquarters at Park Row in New York City. The structure was to occupy the entire plot, contain over a million square feet, and rise straight up from the property line to become the world's tallest building. To preserve light and air and not limit the height of the building, the New York Zoning Resolution of 1916 required buildings to be set back after a certain height, resulting in a wedding cake form that was captured by Hugh Ferris in a number of classic charcoal renderings shown in Figure 4.3. The success of the New York City zoning law resulted in cities enacting zoning regulations that stipulated setbacks to permit light to reach the street level.

At the end of the nineteenth century, the Chicago School was creating a new aesthetic, as expressed in the construction of the Reliance Building 1895 (Figure 4.4), the Fischer Building in 1896, the Auditorium Building in 1889, and the Old Colony Building in 1894. The Chicago aesthetic emphasized the structural simplicity that reflects an affinity for organic forms. In his treatise "The Tall Building Artistically Considered," Louis Sullivan outlined his theory on the expression of skyscraper form, which he believed needed to exhibit the quality of loftiness. He put forth the three-part division of the structure, starting with a base consisting of a few floors that is treated "in a more or less liberal, expansive, sumptuous way," above which is a series of office floors based on the characteristics of an office cell repeated horizontally to form the floor and then vertically to form the central element of the composition. At the top is the "attic," with the power of a solid wall provided by "its dominating weight and character," a statement that

4.5

4.6

Figure 4.5. Empire State Building.
Figure 4.6. American Radiator Building.

the succession of office tiers has come to an end. Through examples of the classic column form; trinities in nature and art; the logic of a start, middle, and end; and organic examples in nature, Sullivan confirms the correctness of the three-component configuration of his skyscraper form. He further states, similar to structures in nature, that this aesthetic generates its form from its function, or as classically expressed, "form follows function."[3]

The synthesis of zoning laws that stipulated setbacks to permit light and air with the Chicago aesthetic has produced the archetypal skyscraper form. This is exemplified by buildings in New York such as the Empire State Building (Figure 4.5), the Chrysler Building, 40 Wall Street, the American Radiator Building (Figure 4.6), the General Electric Building, and the Carlyle; and by Chicago's Board of Trade Building, Tribune Tower (Figure 4.7), and 333 North Michigan Avenue.

GENERATING THE FRACTAL SKYSCRAPER FORM

In the generation of a traditional skyscraper form through fractal geometry, we utilize the collage technique. In this method, the initial step is the establishment of a seed shape (Figure 4.8), which approximates the mass of the final form. By making copies of the seed shape and through affine transformations, these copies are scaled, rotated, and translated to form a matrix of relationships, the totality of which is different than the simple form of the seed shape. Although you can utilize any shape of any size as a seed shape, there is certain logic in utilizing a rectangular slab that approximates the volume of the possible building area. The use of a Euclidian object such as a rectangular slab as the seed shape is appropriate relative to commercial construction practices and urban considerations but is anathema to many devotees of organic architecture. They hold that organic architecture should be based on biological forms, which are rooted in curvilinear shapes. Though there are certainly a wealth of architectural applications based on biological forms, this does not preclude the application of organic architecture's principles of fractal geometry within a Euclidian framework. The important factor is the human perception of the "structural" relationships of the elements to the whole, the elements to other elements, and the consideration of the whole based on these relationships.

The process of generating a skyscraper form based on fractal geometry commences with a seed shape consisting of a slab 175 feet in width and length and 600 feet in height and located at the coordinate position 0,0,0. These dimensions are appropriate for a midtown site in a major city for a fifty-story office building. After you have generated the slab, it is important to take note of the pivot point, which is currently at 0,0,0. The pivot point is the point where translations, scaling, and rotations take place. It is the object's local coordinate center. At the end of each iteration, it is essential to restore the location of the pivot point of the new seed shape so that it is the same as the initial location. All of the initial translations are from the original pivot point location of 0,0,0. As the copies are added together, the pivot point moves typically to the average location of their pivot points, which is different from the initial location. The next iteration's set of copies are translated from this point, and if it is not from the original pivot point, all subsequent transformations will be offset by the amount of the deviation from the original pivot point.

- A typical base will be set out to the edge of the property and has an element of repetition to establish a cadence with the street. To achieve this, four copies of the seed shape are made, each with a length and width of 60 percent of the seed shape and a height of 25 percent of the seed shape. Each is placed on a diagonal vector derived from a distance of 52 feet from the pivot point in both the x and y vectors relative to each quadrant of the x-y plane. The four copies of iteration 1 are illustrated as white transparent boxes in Figure 4.9a.

- The shaft is a made up of two components, the first developed by generating a smaller copy of the seed shape scaled down 98 percent in the x axis, 98 percent in the y axis, 85 percent in the z axis and is shown in green in Figure 4.9b. The second component, depicted in red in Figure 4.9b, is another copy of the seed shape scaled down 90 percent in the x axis, 90 percent in the y axis, 98 percent in the z axis and is rotated 45 degrees about the z axis. The rotated element gives the composition a vertical emphasis, and the unrotated component anchors the shaft and provides the shoulders of the shaft.

- The capital is composed of five elements, the first being a central cube that is a copy of the seed shape reduced 80 percent in the x axis, 80 percent in the y axis, 20 percent in the z axis, and translated along the z axis approximately 500 feet. It is shown in

4.7

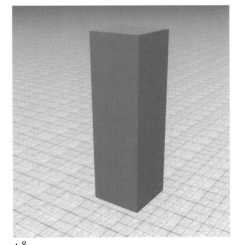

4.8

Figure 4.7. Chicago Tribune Tower.
Figure 4.8. Traditional skyscraper seed shape.

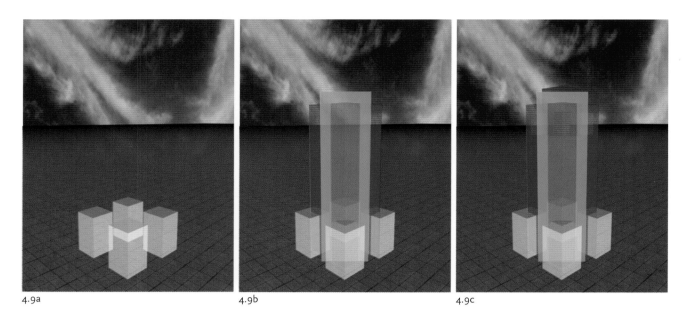

4.9a   4.9b   4.9c

Figure 4.9c in blue. The shoulder corners of the unrotated green portion of the shaft each receive an accent that bisects the rotated shaft's diagonal. This is achieved by making four copies of the seed shape scaled down 40 percent in the x axis, 40 percent in the y axis, and 10 percent in the z axis, which are translated 52 feet in both the x and y vectors relative to each quadrant of the x-y plane, and then translated approximately 500 feet along the z axis. These are shown in gray in Figure 4.9c.

- Added to the overall form are a series of vertical accents, shown in black in Figure 4.9d. These elements are copies of the seed shape that are scaled down by 87.5 percent in the x axis, 85 percent in the y axis, and 40 percent in the z axis. These are then translated by a horizontal vector composed of 57 feet in the x axis and 87 feet in the y axis to each quadrant of the x-y plane and then translated vertically 133 feet.

All the copies of the seed shape that constitute the base, shaft, and capital of the traditional building form are synthesized together to form the new seed shape. The initial seed shape is deleted and the new seed shape is iterated a second time, utilizing the new seed shape according to the same generative rules used to compose the set of components.

- In Figure 4.10a, the four white components are shown. Every one of these is an obvious copy of the new seed shape, each with the

Figure 4.9. Traditional skyscraper, iteration 1.

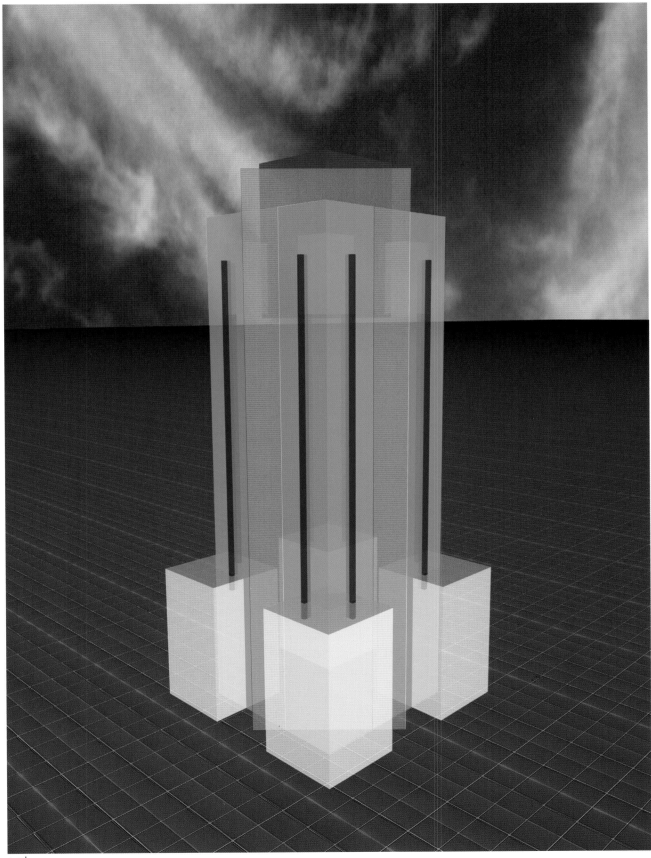

4.9d

4.10a   4.10b   4.10c

various subcomponents clearly indicated. The subset of white elements starts to form a rhythm at the street level, which is a desired pedestrian experience.

- In Figure 4.10b, the green element is inserted with its white subcomponents fusing with white elements. Figure 4.10b also illustrates the addition of the rotated red shaft component. The white subcomponents of the red component insert a major angled element within each façade of the base section, providing a defining element that reorganizes the composition of the base. This defining element continues up through the shaft as the corners of the rotated copy of the seed shape protrude through the green element of the shaft.

- The major portion of the capital, the blue element, is added in Figure 4.10c. Its various subcomponents start to articulate the crown of the composition. The four gray components of the crown section that sit on the shoulders of the green element are shown in Figure 4.10c. A large portion of these components remains buried within the other elements. As the composition is further iterated, each of those elements shrinks toward its attractor by virtue of the fact that they are scaled-down copies of the seed shape. As they recede, the elements translated to a fixed position emerge.

- In Figure 4.10d, the black accent elements are added. Within each of these parts, you can see the subcomponents articulated, illustrating the breadth of self-similarity throughout the overall composition.

Figure 4.10. Traditional skyscraper iteration 2.

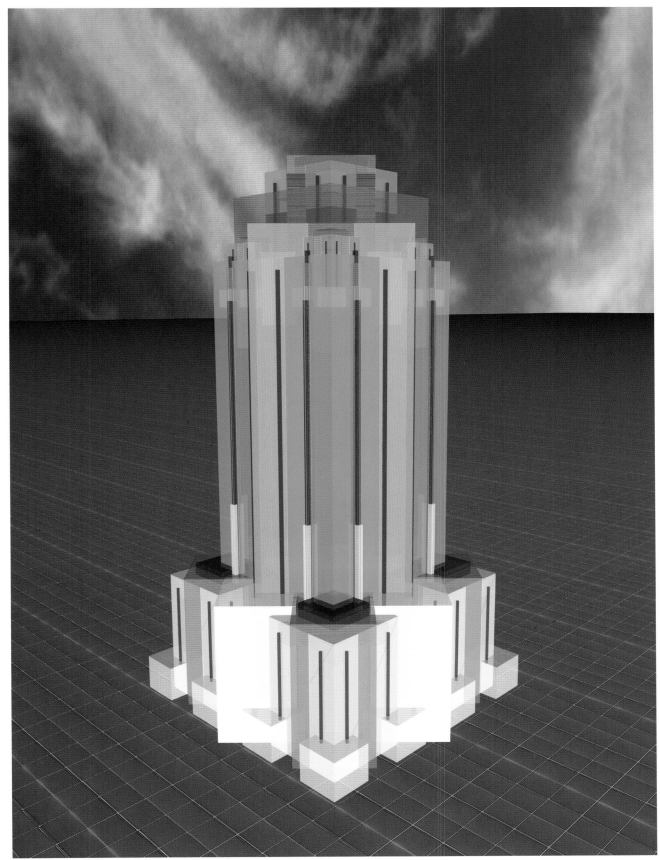

4.10d

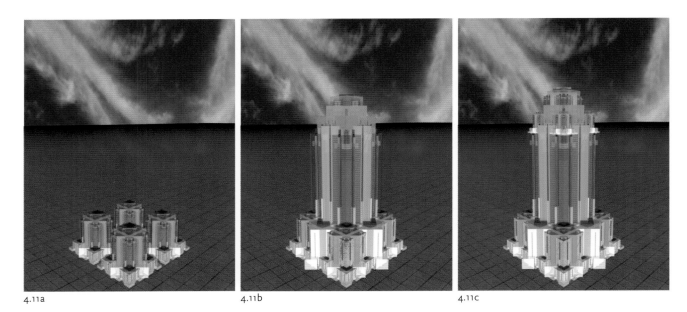

4.11a   4.11b   4.11c

As with the conclusion of the first iteration, all these elements are fused together to form the new seed shape. This new seed shape serves as the basis from which the generative rules are applied to form the elements of iteration 3.

- The four white elements of iteration 3 that compose a significant portion of the base are shown in Figure 4.11a. All the elements are further articulated; most notably, the inclusion of the rotated shaft element reinforces and strengthens the pedestrian rhythm.
- Figure 4.11b illustrates the green element of iteration 3 and the red element. Both elements further articulate not only the shaft but also the base and crown.
- The five components that constitute the capital are shown in Figure 4.11c. They provide a highly detailed organic crown to the composition.
- The vertical ribs are added in Figure 4.11d, reinforcing the vertical emphasis already present and whose close examination provides a source for self-similar details within the form.

In examining the images, you can see that many of the components are submerged within other elements. As the elements are further iterated, they contract toward an attractor because the scaling factors are less than 100 percent. As they contract, the elements that have been translated to specific positions emerge. This phenomenon is evident in the comparison of the various iterations in Figure 4.12.

Figure 4.11. Traditional skyscraper, iteration 3.

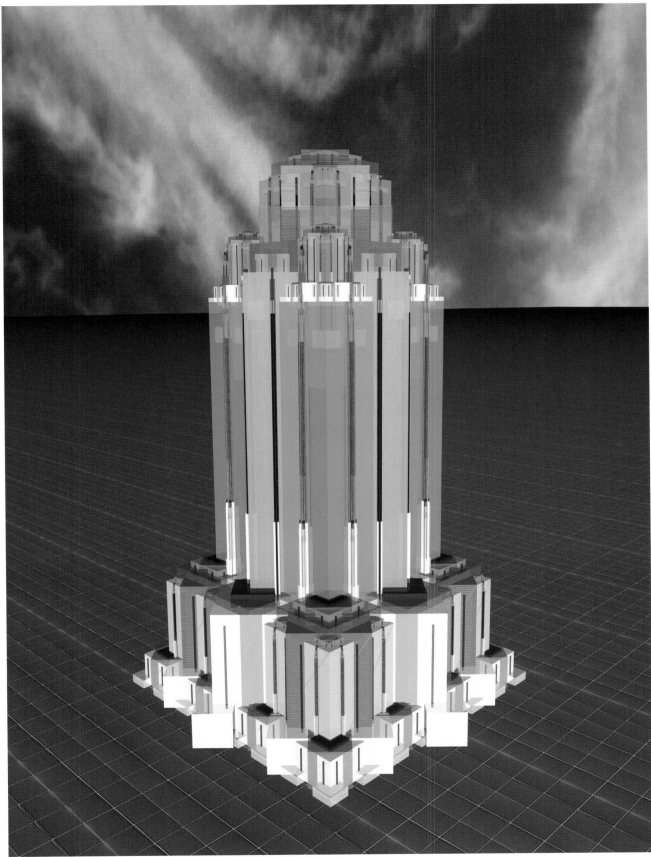

4.11d

4.12a

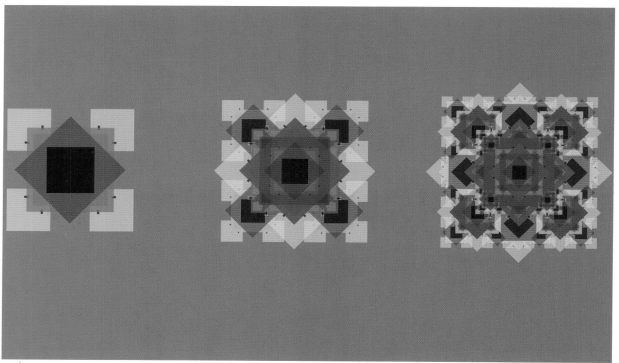

4.12b

Figure 4.12. Comparisons of the iterations; a.
Front façade; b. Plan.
Figure 4.13. Fractal form with an opaque
material; a. Corner perspective;
b. Front perspective.

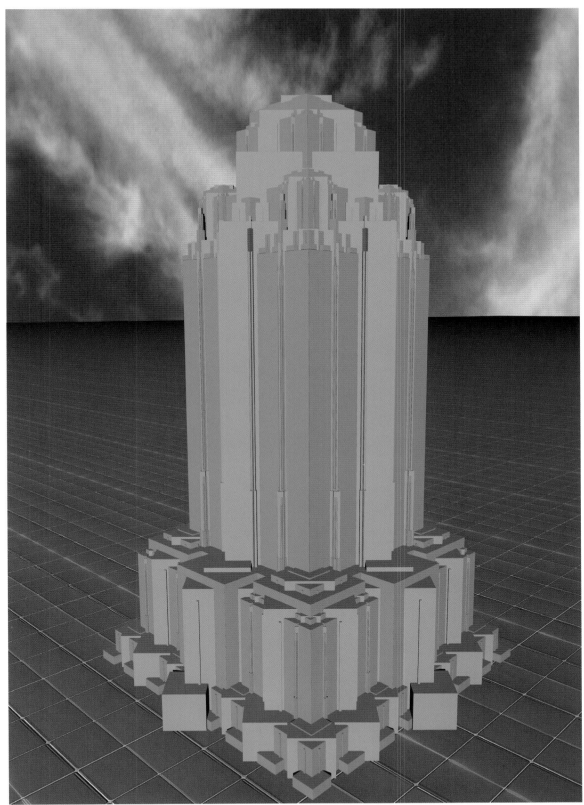

4.13a

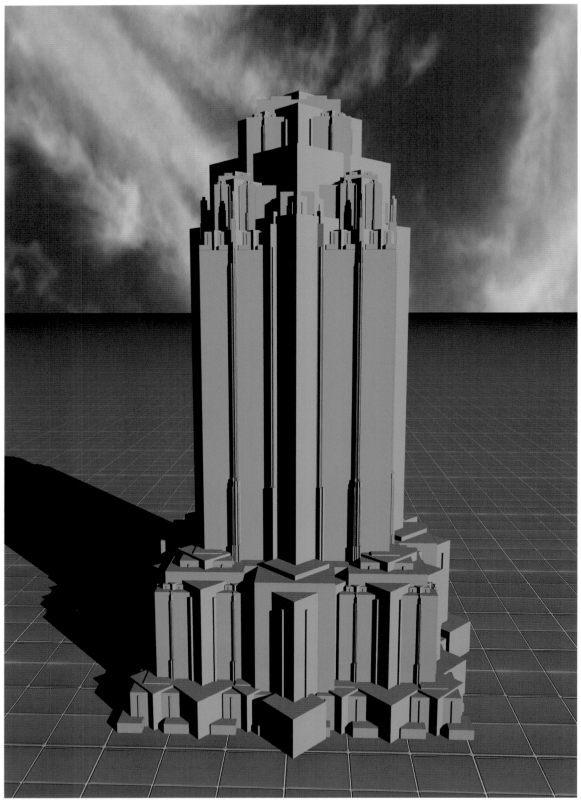

4.13b

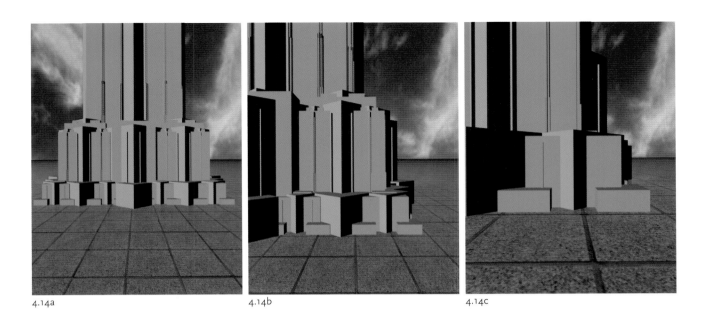

4.14a   4.14b   4.14c

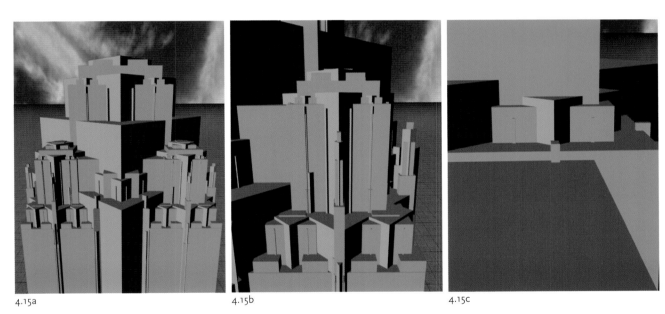

4.15a   4.15b   4.15c

Figure 4.14. Archetypal fractal characteristic of
similarity of form at different levels of scale at
base.
Figure 4.15. Archetypal fractal characteristic of
similarity of form at different levels of scale at
capital.

The unfolding of the organic form increases exponentially as the form manifests an identity. Figure 4.13 depicts the fractal form with an opaque material instead of the translucent material that was utilized to show the internal relationships. This group of images shows the form as it would be perceived in the normal course. Figure 4.14 illustrates the archetypal fractal characteristic of similarity of form at different levels of scale present in the elements at the base of the building. Figure 4.15 similarly shows this characteristic cascading of fractal structure through the elements with the crown of the building.

ART DECO

Skyscraper styles have evolved over time, but one of the most enduring and prevalent styles has been Art Deco. Originating in France through its introduction at the 1925 Exposition des Arts Decoratifs et Industriels Modernes in Paris, the Art Deco movement spread throughout the world and created a number of distinctive architectural buildings in the 1920s and 1930s and is an enduring influence on architectural design even to this day. Its distinctive elements of form and its streamlined and geometric characteristics were influences from the industrial design of the period as well as from other predecessor and concurrent architectural expressions such as Dutch and German Expressionism, Bauhaus, DeStijl, International Style, Chicago School, and Frank Lloyd Wright.[4]

The Art Deco period is generally classified into three periods: Zigzag Moderne, characterized by highly decorative façades utilizing stylized geometric ornamentation influenced by previous historical periods; Classic or PWA Moderne, distinguished by a more stripped down but distinct monumental aesthetic reflecting the austerity of the Depression; and Streamline Moderne, which simplified ornamentation to pure lines and a clean look. An apparent influence that helped shape the streamlined aesthetic was the work of Italian Futurist Sant'Elia. Although he was killed in World War I, he produced a volume of renderings depicting significant buildings for a futuristic city called Cittia Nuova.[5] The influence of the Futurist movement as well as the austere expressions of the Bauhaus and DeStijl movements contributed to restructuring the Art Deco vocabulary to fit the economics of the Depression. The characteristics of this period included the use of horizontal lines and pronounced stepped vertical elements.

Generating a Fractal Art Deco Skyscraper Form

Again implementing the collage technique, an architectural form representing the Art Deco period is generated utilizing fractal geometry. A seed shape is used that approximates the final mass of the building: 160 feet wide, 120 feet deep, and 320 feet high. The overall form consists of a base of intermingled elements that produces a layered mass similar to that of a mountain. From this base, articulated elements rise.

- The base consists of four elements, two of which provide articulation and character to the form's pedestal, the other two acting to form the required bulk. The first two elements of iteration 1 are depicted in white translucent material in Figure 4.16a. Each is a copy of the seed shape scaled down by 33 percent in width, 90 percent in depth, and 30 percent in height. Each is rotated either clockwise or counterclockwise 90 degrees about the *y* axis and then translated 25 feet vertically and 9 feet horizontally in the direction of its rotation. The other two elements that form the base are depicted in blue in Figure 4.16b: one a copy of the seed shape scaled down by 75 percent in both width and depth and 50 percent in height, and the other scaled down 95 percent in width, 85 percent in depth, and 40 percent in height.

- The main vertical element that forms the shaft of the skyscraper form springs from this base and is shown in gray in Figure 4.16c. It is a copy of the seed shape contracted to 95 percent in width, 85 percent in depth, and 90 percent in height. On both sides of this main shaft element are two components shown in red in Figure 4.16d. They are copies of the seed shape reduced 35 percent in width and depth and 80 percent in height, translated 50 feet horizontally either left or right and then rotated either clockwise or counterclockwise 90 degrees about the *z* axis so the side façades will reflect the front façade.

- On top of the shaft elements, an additional copy, shown in green in Figure 4.16e, is created scaled down to 15 percent in width and height and scaled up 15 percent in depth, rotated 90 degrees about the *z* axis, and translated vertically 207 feet.

- This assemblage of interrelated elements constitutes the basic mass of the form. A vertical element is attached that consists of a copy of the seed shape contracted to 5 percent in width, 86 percent in depth, and 80 percent in height and translated vertically 35 feet. Ten horizontal elements are added, each of which consists of a

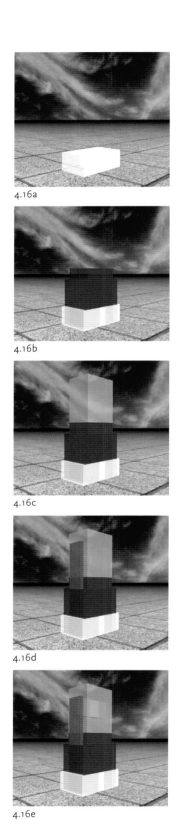

4.16a

4.16b

4.16c

4.16d

4.16e

Figure 4.16. Art deco skyscraper, iteration 1.

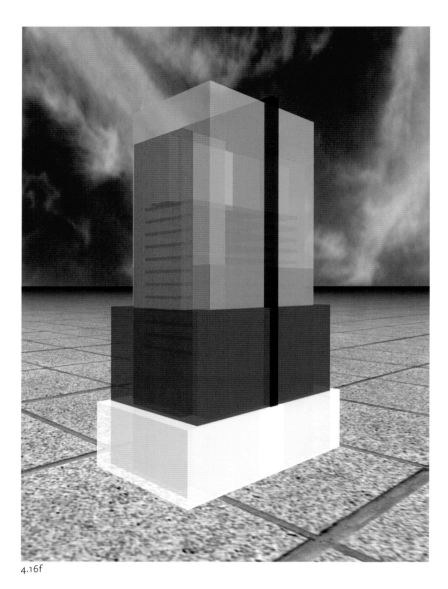

4.16f

copy of the seed shape reduced to 76 percent in width, 46 percent in depth, and 95 percent in height. Each element of this group of ten horizontal elements is interspaced by 10 feet vertically to form a horizontally oriented element that is translated vertically by 95 feet to stretch from that point to a point 205 feet vertically. This group of vertical and horizontal elements that serves to articulate the form is shown in black in Figure 4.16f.

The amalgamation of these eighteen elements forms the new seed shape to which the same set of transformation or generative rules is applied. As with the previous architectural form, certain elements are covered by other elements during the initial iterations

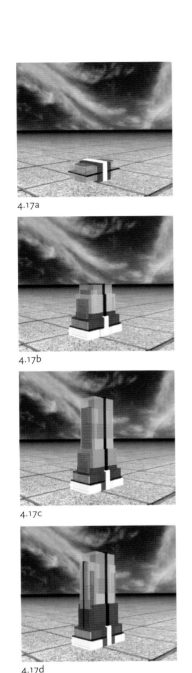

4.17a

4.17b

4.17c

4.17d

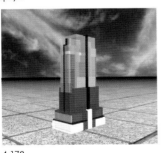

4.17e

Figure 4.17. Art deco skyscraper, iteration 2.

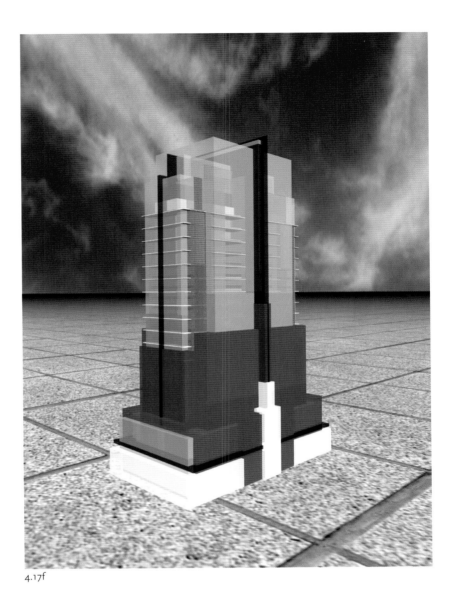

4.17f

that emerge as you continue the iterations. These elements are typically ones that are translated to fixed positions, and as the elements that cover them contract to their attractors or ultimate points of contraction, they are uncovered. The phenomenon of attraction to a point comes from the generative rules, which contain a contraction mapping in the scaling factors that are less than 100 percent. As you continue the iteration and the related scaling, the element shrinks to a fixed point.

- In Figure 4.17a, the two white elements are shown. The orientation of these components is made clear by the next level of articulation of the fractal structure within them. The contribution of these elements to the horizontal emphasis of the base and vertical prominence at the entrance is evident.

- Figure 4.17b shows the other elements that comprise the remainder of the base, which counterbalances the white elements by partially overlapping them with a more vertical emphasis.

- Figure 4.17c depicts the addition of the gray element, which encapsulates the upper portion of the blue base elements in a singular shaft section.

- Figure 4.17d adds the red elements, which show their rotated orientation by their black vertical accent. These provide significant vertical elements to the shaft in a traditional skyscraper stepping format.

- Figure 4.17e inserts the green module at the top of the structure. The majority of this element is still immersed in the gray element, but its red subelements protrude and adjoin the base red elements.

- Figure 4.17f adds the black vertical and horizontal accent components. The horizontal ones are still immersed in the red elements, but the vertical portion starts to articulate the strong frontal vertical emphasis.

These elements, which start to show the increased articulation of structure, are fused together to form the seed shape for iteration 3.

- Figure 4.18a depicts the white components of iteration 3. These elements in general have their vertical stress further emphasized. Because these elements are rotated 90 degrees, this emphasis is revised to a horizontal orientation.

- Figure 4.18b incorporates the two blue elements of the base. Their vertically reduced copies of the new seed shape provide a sequence of layered setbacks to the base section of the form. The articulation of the horizontal ribs provides a connection of self-similarity with the black horizontal elements.

- Figure 4.18c adds the gray element to the composition, which envelopes the upper part of the base section and carries the layered setbacks up into the shaft.

- The red components are added to the sides of the shaft in Figure 4.18d. They raise the threshold of the capital, provide a vertical emphasis to the side elevations, and because of their red subcomponents, reinforce the vertical emphasis of the shaft in the front and rear façades.

- In Figure 4.18e, the green component is incorporated into the composition. It serves as a horizontal counterpoint to the front

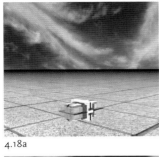

4.18a

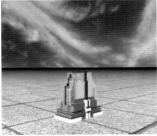

4.18b

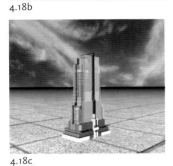

4.18c

4.18d

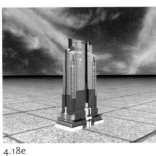

4.18e

Figure 4.18. Art deco skyscraper, iteration 3.

4.18f

vertical element and continues the flow of the red side vertical components.

- The vertical and horizontal black elements are inserted in Figure 4.18f. With the addition of the black vertical part, the central vertical becomes an interesting series of setbacks that carries the eye up to the crown.

The final fractal form is depicted in Figure 4.19 with the color coding removed. The self-similar characteristics are observable particularly in the distribution of the shaft, with the vertical accent throughout the structure. It is also present in the horizontal accent elements that are perceivable at a smaller scale at the corners of the shaft meeting the

101

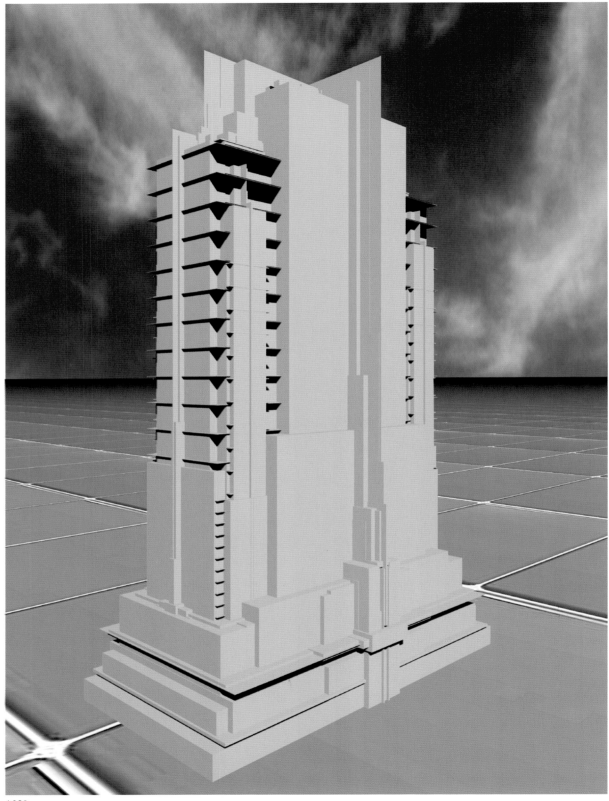

4.19a

Figure 4.19. Final form of art deco skyscraper; a.
Corner perspective; b. Front perspective; c. Side
perspective; d. Cascading level of detail.

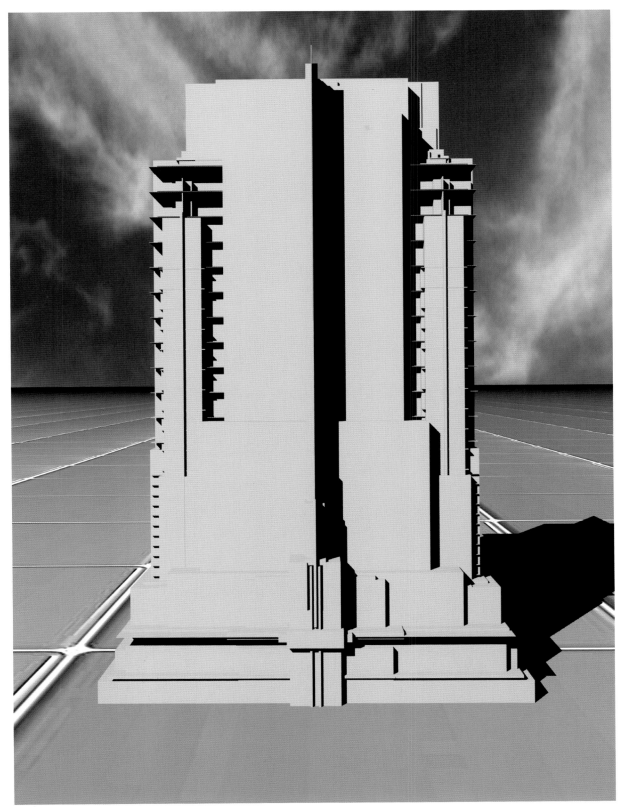

4.19b

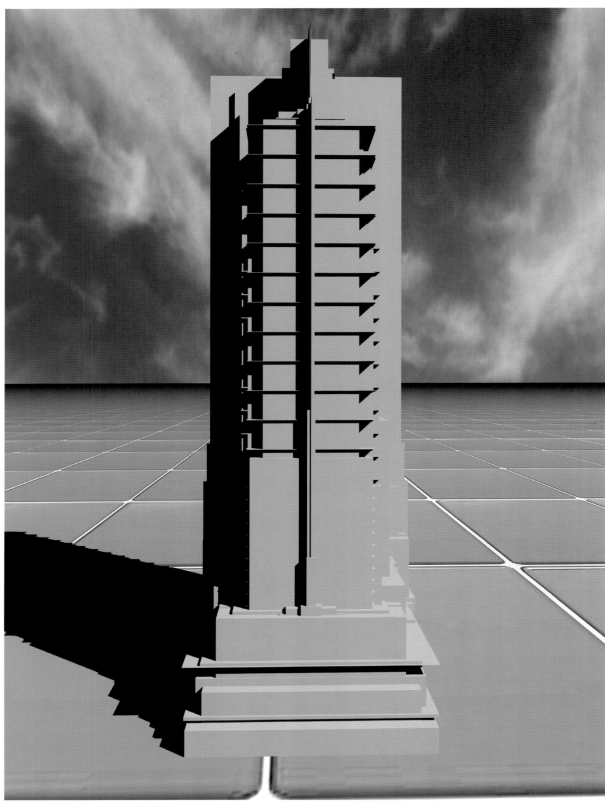

4.19c

4.19d

base. Figure 4.19b shows the front elevation, where the vertically ac-cented shaft element is repeated on either side of the main element. It is also perceived embedded horizontally within the base. Figure 4.19c illustrates the side elevation, which clearly shows the frontal shaft form that is a result of its 90 degree rotational transformation. Figure 4.19d is a detailed view of the top of the building, where the green crown element meets the red side shaft elements, all of which are rotated 90 degrees about the z axis. The green element has been increased in its depth dimension by 15 percent prior to its rotational transformation, which accounts for its pronounced vertical element.

FRANK LLOYD WRIGHT AND THE SKYSCRAPER FORM

Frank Lloyd Wright's skyscraper forms consisted mainly of two types: the urban block and the tower form.[6] He had only two high-rise proj-ects constructed, which were of the tower typology: the tower at the Johnson's Wax complex and the Price Tower. The Price Tower was the materialization of the skyscraper prototype Wright developed for a project at St. Mark's Square in New York City. Wright was an ardent proponent of an organic design philosophy in which the parts reflect the whole and in which variety can be achieved within the unified whole. According to the National Building Museum, Wright approached the design problem of St. Mark's with the intention of achieving a Goethe-ian *Gesamtkunstwerk* or total work of art.[7]

The Price Tower was commissioned by Harold Price, the owner of the Price Company, a local oil and gas business. The original program was for a three-story headquarters for his company but developed into a nineteen-story icon of Wright's design philosophy. Wright shunned the Chicago School of skyscraper expression and chose the organic archetype of a tree to generate the basis of the building's form. Rooted in the ground by the foundation, the trunk of the tree springs up from the ground through the void of the lobby that emphasizes the floors, which are cantilevered above it. At the lobby level, there is a compositional "rudder" that serves to anchor the dynamic rotational composition of the floors above.[8] The trunk continues up through four elevator shafts, from which the floors are cantilevered and spread out like branches of the tree. In plan, the series of four main branches on each floor consists of an apparent shear wall forming the main axis of the pinwheel mechanism and extends from the elevator core to a exit stairwell at the perimeter. The trunk reaches the top, where the

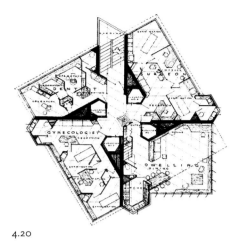

4.20

shear walls extend up to form a crown that echoes the organizational device of the plan and reaches for the sky.

Wright utilized the pinwheel as the plan's generating mechanism in a number of his projects, including St. Mark's (Figure 4.20). The pinwheel device produces a series of rotationally similar groupings and is characteristic of Wright's late housing parti. The site of the Price Tower has considerable space around it, which is conducive to observing the form whose rotational composition produces a spinning spatial vortex.[9]

The pinwheel configuration is generated by two overlapping square grids rotated 30 degrees, one clockwise and the other counterclockwise, on top of an unrotated grid. The rotated grids are the ordering mechanism that places the four arms of the pinwheel, in which each arm consists of an elevator and stairwell and a connecting corridor. Within each quadrant of the pinwheel, the residential and commercial spaces are structured by the unrotated grid with two end walls resting against two of the pinwheel arms. The rotational geometry evident in the Price Tower recalls aspects of Wright's decorative designs and invoked a dynamic quality to the composition of identical units and overcame the monotony of the simple repetition of similar units.[10]

The resulting architectural form is a dynamic, integrated example of organic form that Wright strove for.

Generating a Fractal Wright Skyscraper Form

The fractal Price Tower model consists of assembling elements at the top and bottom of the composition, a group of stacked horizontal elements that make up the floors, and groups of components that compose the vertical elements. The groups of elements are transformed copies of a rectangular prism seed shape.

- Figure 4.21a shows two groups of eight elements each, in red, that make up the base and the top of the building. The bottom group is composed of eight elements, seven of which are copies of the seed shape that are scaled down and rotated to form a group of vertical fins rotated 45 degrees about a central axis. The eighth element is a scaled-down and skewed copy that creates the anchor to hold the group of pinwheel-structured elements. The upper group of eight components has a similar pinwheel structure but with a central cube and an offset cube anchoring the pinwheel group. There are also two skewed elements that are a continuation of a group of vertical elements.

Figure 4.20. Plan for the Price Tower.

- The shaft of the Price Tower consists of bands of horizontal mullions and glass interspaced with alternating bands of reinforced concrete and terra cotta, illustrated in Figures 44.21b–4.21d. Each band is a synthesis of a simple vertically scaled-down version of the shaft and a skewed copy that is scaled down in length and width as well as height. The concrete bands, shown in white, are added in Figure 4.21b, the glass is depicted in light gray in Figure 4.21c, the terra cotta is added in black in Figure 4.21d, and the horizontal window mullions are added in dark gray in Figure 4.21e.
- Extending from the base and transversing the height of the shaft and, in some cases, through the crown of the structure is a series of skewed elements that form a vertical accentuation that is a counterpoint to the strong horizontal emphasis of the concrete, terra cotta, and mullioned glass bands. The two sets of elements are shown in blue in Figure 4.21f and green in Figure 4.21g.

All these elements are fused into a new complex seed shape that is iterated again according to the same generative rules.

- Figure 4.22a shows the base and crown sections derived from iteration 2. Each of these has a significant horizontal emphasis interspersed with vertically orientated groups of elements.
- Figures 4.22b–4.22e show the various elements of the shaft, reinforced concrete, terra cotta, glass, and metal mullion incorporated into the model. As with the base and capital sections, these have a pronounced horizontal emphasis with vertical elements acting as counterpoints to this overall compositional direction.
- Figures 4.22e and Figure 4.22f add the vertical elements, which, within each one, have the same horizontal emphasis with counterbalancing vertical components.

Figure 4.23 shows iteration 2 with the elements rendered in material that more closely approximates the materials used and a photograph of the actual Price Tower from a similar viewpoint. Figure 4.24 depicts the rendered iteration 2 from an aerial perspective.

The Price Tower was a singular achievement in Wright's career in that it was one of the two skyscrapers he built, but moreover it possesses the elusive organic quality for which architects have been searching for centuries. It cannot be just a coincidence that his choice of

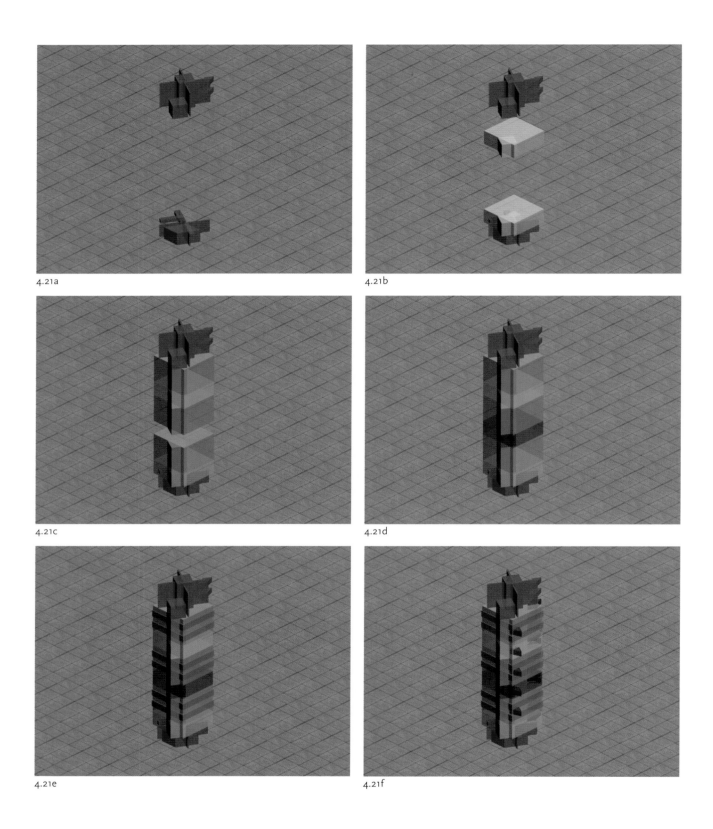

4.21a

4.21b

4.21c

4.21d

4.21e

4.21f

Figure 4.21. Wright skyscraper, iteration 1.

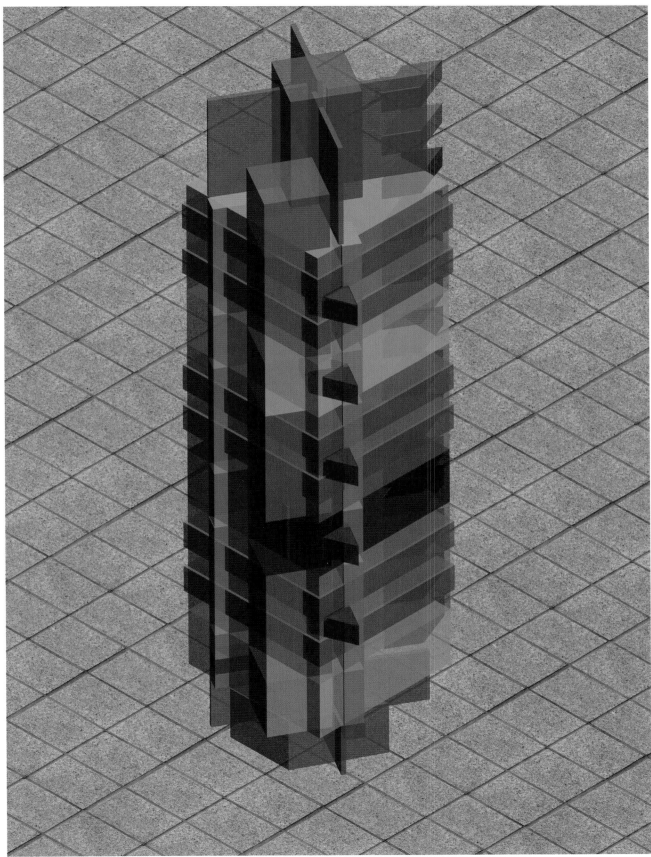

4.21g

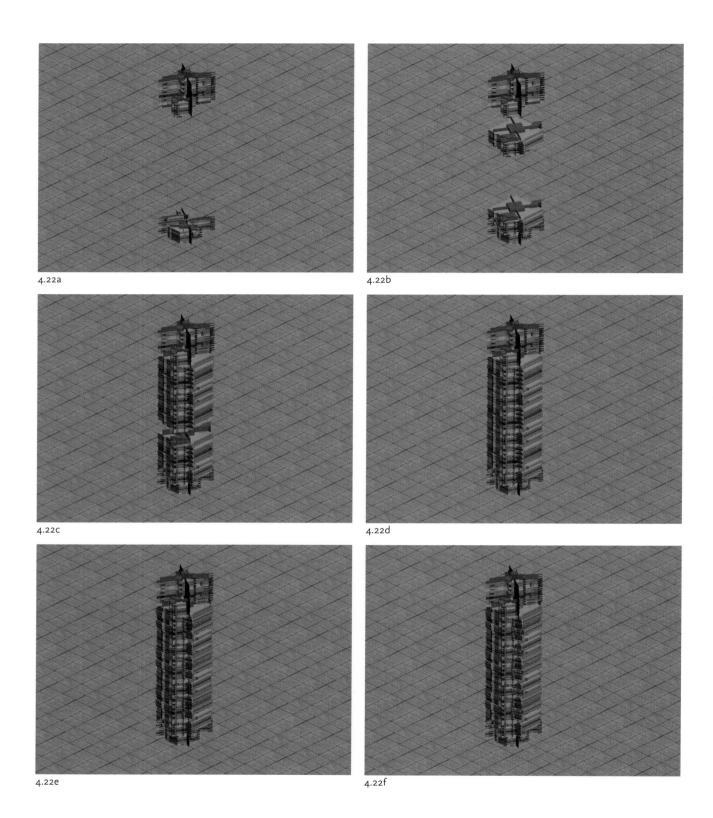

4.22a

4.22b

4.22c

4.22d

4.22e

4.22f

Figure 4.22. Wright skyscraper, iteration 2.
Figure 4.23. *(Overleaf)* a. Wright skyscraper,
iteration 2, with the elements rendered in
material that more closely approximates the
materials used; b. Photograph of the actual Price
Tower from a similar viewpoint.

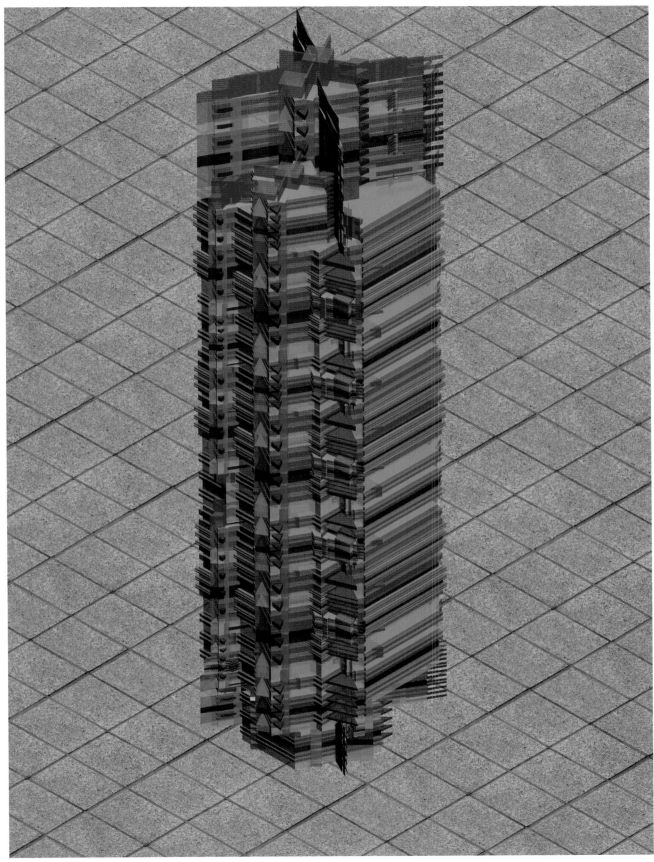

4.22g

4.23a

4.23b

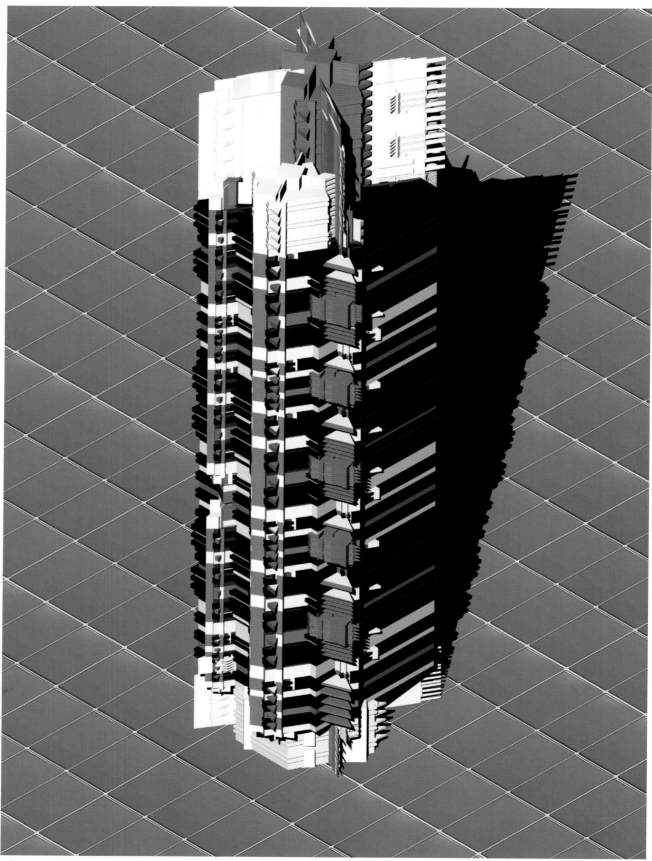

4.24

architectural metaphor, the tree, is an integral reason why the Price Tower achieved an organic quality. His composition integrates a masterful counterplay of vertical/horizontal and light/dark within his classic pinwheel spatial torsion, producing a form that has not been rivaled since its inception. The fractal derivative of this form overlays the organic quality of self-similarity to this composition. In addition to embedding the structure of the whole within each of its constituent parts, the fractalization of the Price Tower revises the regular rhythm of the horizontal striations of reinforced concrete, terra cotta, and mullioned windows into a fractal rhythm that recalls the principles of Cantor's Dust.

SUMMARY

The skyscraper form is a classic architectural structure that will proliferate as population density increases in urban areas. Because of its vertical orientation, the skyscraper shape correlates with the human perception of natural structures such as plants and trees. By utilizing fractal geometry to generate the skyscraper form, the correlation with natural form is extended by creating structures that possess the evocative nature of organic form. The interrelationships of the building's elements at various levels of scale generate the hallmark character of nature: self-similarity. Embodying the characteristics of natural form, these structures evoke inherent positive reactions that are magnified when considering the scale of the edifice.

Figure 4.24. Rendered Wright skyscraper iteration 2 from an aerial perspective.

PART II

Nature and Human Cognition

CHAPTER **5**   # Gestalt and the Wholeness of Fractal Structure

Chapters 2 and 3 of this argument for the utilization of fractal geometry to generate architectural form demonstrated that humans cherish nature on a perceptual, intellectual, and emotional level. The exposure to certain natural surroundings fosters significant mental and physical health benefits. Our affinity for nature is, to a considerable extent, channeled through the order we perceive in natural environments. The methodology in which nature's order strikes a chord in our cognitive structure is particularly attuned to the principles of fractal geometry. Man-made artifacts, such as architecture, that are structured according to the principles of fractal geometry should provoke a similar cognitive and emotional reaction through association and transposition. In addition to the correlative link between nature and forms structured by fractal geometry, a theory on man's perceptual mechanism, gestalt psychology, provides further evidence for man's inherent affinity for forms organized according to fractal geometry.

ORIGINS OF GESTALT PSYCHOLOGY

Gestalt psychology is a premise that postulates that the operational principle of the brain is innately holistic, with self-organizing tendencies to construct whole forms instead of the perception of a collection of parts. The genesis of Gestalt psychology, like many breakthroughs, is credited to a romantically seminal event, in this case, a fateful vacation trip aboard a train. A young Czechoslovakian psychologist, Max Wertheimer, came on an idea while watching flashing lights at a railroad crossing and seeing that they resembled lights around a theater marquee. Inspired by the revelation, he got off the train and bought a motion picture toy called a zoetrope. In a zoetrope, a series of sequenced pictures are placed within the interior of a barrel. Spinning the barrel and viewing the sequence through a slit, an illusion of movement is produced similar to a motion picture. Wertheimer made his own picture strips of simple abstract horizontal and vertical lines instead of identifiable objects. By varying the linear elements, Wertheimer investigated the conditions that caused the illusion known as *apparent movement*, or the *Phi phenomenon*. Apparent movement is generated by the dynamic interrelation of the elements rather than the simple sum of the individual elements.[1] The perceptual experience exists as fields of interacting dynamic parts ordered by the internal organizing structure generated by the perceiver.

One of the roots from which gestalt principles appears to have sprung from, is Wertheimer's cultural background. German philosophical tradition was significantly influenced by Immanuel Kant, who held that perception was a unifying act not based on simple association. There is not a one-to-one correspondence between the receipt of stimuli and the mind's perception. In the act of perception, the mind organizes the mosaic of stimuli received by the senses. This interaction between the mind and the stimuli is the experience of consciousness.

Wertheimer's ancestors were influenced by the holism movement of Eastern Europe before 1900. In this society, the fabric of social and cultural heritage integrated the pursuit of knowledge for its own sake and the idea of the "organic whole." This worldview was based on a dynamic with interdependent, interacting parts that characterized the world from family to community to the organization of the universe. This holistic cultural environment in all probability intimately influenced Wertheimer.[2]

Wertheimer was also influenced by the reading of Spinoza and the holistic philosophical conviction that unites nature and the universe. In this philosophy, the universe is a complex whole where apparent contradictions, inconsistencies, and irregularities become clear as complements and enrichments instead of discrepancies. The whole is made up of the interaction of complementary interdependent parts. Each of these components, while seen as part of the whole, retains a distinct and working uniqueness. This set of relationships between the parts creates a field of reciprocally functioning forces producing a dynamic equilibrium.[3] These characteristics of Spinoza's philosophy are consistent with the tenets of Gestalt theory and appear to have contributed to the formation of Wertheimer's intellectual foundation.

Wertheimer, although credited as one of the founders of Gestalt psychology along with Kurt Koffka and Wolfgang Kohler, built on the research of Christian Von Ehrenfels and a reaction against reductionism that considered the whole no more than the sum of its parts. The response to reductionism postulated that the whole is equal to the sum of its parts, and Ehrenfels proposed that the whole is somehow more than the sum of its parts. The whole is equal to the sum of its parts plus another element, its gestalt quality.[4] In 1890, Ehrenfels published a significant paper, "On Gestalt Qualities," in which he documented his theory by utilizing examples such as a melody still recognizable when played in different keys, even though none of the notes are the same. Ehrenfels contended that if a melody and the notes are so interdependent, then the whole is not just the sum of its parts but a collaborative "whole effect" or *gestalt*. He extended his analysis to abstract qualities such as angularity and squareness and concluded that these attributes are conveyed by a range of elements.[5] Wertheimer built on this theory and asserted that the whole is entirely different from the sum of its parts and is a priori to the parts. Wholes are separate integrated systems with an inherent structure unique to the whole, which determines the nature of the parts.[6]

Wertheimer performed experimental psychological research with Frederich Schuman, in particular, studies of visual space perception. It was in this laboratory that Wertheimer met and collaborated with Wolfgang Kohler and Kurt Koffka to become the first principal Gestalt psychologists.[7] Schuman published a paper with a number of compelling findings that anticipated Gestalt psychology. Among these findings are that incomplete figures can be perceived as complete; nearness among visual elements organizes groupings into larger wholes; and attention may either join parts of a figure into a whole or emphasize a part so that the perception of a whole becomes secondary, and properties of figures, such as grouping and organization, have their origin in both how the brain functions and the stimulus properties.[8]

JOHANN WOLFGANG VON GOETHE AND GESTALT'S PHENOMENOLOGICAL METHOD

Wertheimer, Kohler, and Koffka all studied with Carl Stumpf, who engendered the theory of phenomenology, which utilizes the first-person examination of phenomena to reveal consciousness and its structures. Gestalt psychology employed the phenomenological method to gain an understanding of aesthetic perception and cognition.[9] Phenomenology was built from the theories of Johann Wolfgang Goethe. Goethe's methodolgy reacted to the reductionist, atomic approach to nature, and he based his research on the emphasis on intimate first-person encounters with stimuli.[10] Science, in the reductionist philosophy, was dominated by the certainty of terrestrial mechanics to construct a clockwork universe according to a Newtonian or Cartesian blueprint. The conventional science tended by its nature toward separating and isolating the levels of being commencing with the subject and object. Through intuitive perception, Goethe went in the opposite direction to unite subject and object, concept and percept.[11] Goethe could not accept that a glowing evening sunset was nothing more than waves that strike our eyes and have no more meaning to humans.[12] He strove to transform science and widen its scope to reach deeper and higher.[13] Rudolf Steiner, the architect and philosopher, borrowed the term *indwelling* from Michael Polanyi as the process through which one comes to know an object from the inside out, as actors come to know the characters they are portraying. Through indwelling, the dualism of the subject and object is vanquished.[14]

Goethe's work is related to the form of reasoning known as *induction*, whereby principles are formulated based on observations of reoccurring phenomenal patterns. It is reasoned that all ice is cold because every time I have touched ice, it was cold. He was not concerned with "objective truths" but with the subjective, holistic experience of phenomena.[15] Analytical understanding cannot proceed unless there is dissolution of the object into parts, by which the experience of the phenomenon is destroyed.[16] It is with the observation and exploration of phenomena that their deeper, broader patterns, structures, and meaning is derived.[17] He believed his method was grounded in *delicate empiricism*, which is the process of understanding an object's meaning through prolonged empathetic observation grounded in direct experience.[18] Human cognition is constructed from experience, with sensory experience being the basis from which much of cognition grows.[19]

Goethe's research helped to define the relationship between idea and external reality and between thinking and experience.[20]

Phenomenological knowledge forms the basis for expression in art. Certain colors, such as red, have cognitive properties, such as warm, as opposed to blue being cool. Red is associated with advancing, spatially endowing it with the sensation of movement and spatial experience, as well as with being a loud or shouting color, bestowing it with an auditory expression.[21] The analysis of red based on how the hues interact with the pupil and cortex does nothing to address these properties, which can only come about from observation and experience. Red cannot be adequately defined conceptually; rather, one has to experience what red is. Similarly, stretching your hands in front of you gives you a feeling that you are carrying something. From this experience, gestures were engendered, from which lines and shapes sprung forth onto media.[22]

One of Goethe's contributions to scientific inquiry is his unique way of science in which the first step is the harmonious interaction of observation and thinking. As this process builds, thinking interweaves with the observed phenomenon in an active beholding, and the essence of the phenomenon comes alive in thinking.[23] Initially, one perceives the sensory stimuli received from the object. Feelings are generated based on the perceptual processing of the stimuli from which meaning is derived. Each level replaces the previous level. A sensory stimulus replaces mental chatter. Feelings replace sensory observation, and the experience of meaning replaces feeling.[24]

Goethe's phenomenological study was broken down into four stages, the first being the study of the phenomenon after the "first impression." This stage corresponds to the period between *empirical phenomenon*, where we experience the world on a preconceptual level directly and immediately in all of the senses, and *scientific phenomenon*. In the second stage, one penetrates more deeply into the scientific phenomenon and the relationship between oneself and the phenomenon. Opening oneself to the dynamic relational character of the phenomenon causes one to apprehend how one quality relates to another, how one part relates to others, and how these relationships change over time in a metamorphosis of the phenomenon. In the third stage, there is a further distillation of the phenomenon to study the phenomenon's *gestures*, which are actions by which a definite meaning expresses itself and can be characterized as the phenomenon's *formative life principles.* Rudolf Steiner noted that the blossom of the common buttercup found in fields and meadows calls forth a spontaneous response that prompts humans to cultivate them and plant them in gardens. We sense an inner expressiveness in the culminating phase of the plants' unfolding that reveals its innermost nature.[25] The gesture of the buttercup's leaves is to reach out and open up to the surrounding world, which can be expressed as radiance.[26] In the analysis of humans, this is known as a physiognomic approach and can be most readily illustrated by our perception of people based on their facial expressions. As we read people in this manner, we read other phenomena as outer manifestations of their inner qualities.[27] The fourth stage corresponds to Goethe's *pure phenomenon*, which is the archetype or theory of the organism or phenomenon. Through "intuitive perception," we comprehend the "creative potency" or the *archetypal phenomenon* of the organism. The act of intuitive perception invokes thinking from the whole to the parts and the self-generated potency of the formative power of the whole.[28]

Goethe considered archetypal phenomena or pure phenomena to be the highest level of experience attainable. An archetypal phenomenon is the base principle from which all else is derived. Goethe's scientific method strove to see nature's multiplicity in the singular archetypal phenomenon. Its clarity is not readily apparent in the ordinary phenomena that we see, but employing methods similar to Goethe's "delicate empiricism," we can approach the archetypal phenomenon. In nature, when you examine its multiplicity of forms, you note a consistency in its form characteristics such as self-similarity at levels of scale and the part-to-whole-to-part relationship. As you delve deeper, integrating your spectrum of observations, the structure of fractal geometry emerges as an archetypal phenomenon of nature.

Goethe held that we grasp organic nature through intuitive perception, where the concept and the percept are identical.[29] When I initially look at a phenomenon, I have no idea what it is, and only after I have penetrated it and understand its essence does it become clear. Through a multitude of systematic experiments, an underlying lawfulness is presented in a multitude of variations by the experimental subjects. The researcher intuits this underlying idea or *Urphanomen,* the higher-order experience within experience. Nature presents itself as an expression of its hidden lawfulness that is revealed to us through our own active inner participation.[30]

Goethe's morphological research established the theoretical basis and methodology for studying organic nature.[31] He studied the life cycle of plants and their successive formations as a continual process of transformation or metamorphosis. He utilized his holistic methodology to enter into the dynamic process of nature.[32] The meaning and elicitation of knowledge from phenomena such as plants attain a singular elegance.[33] This sublimity stems from our kinship with nature's hidden lawfulness. As stated by Rudolf Steiner, there is no greater satisfaction for humans as to discern nature's archetypes and contemplate the creative principles at work in nature, as we are inextricably connected.[34]

EARLY CONCEPTS OF GESTALT PSYCHOLOGY

Wertheimer built on the foundation of Goethe's phenomenologically based research to author pioneering research. While teaching at the Psychological Institute in Frankfurt, Wertheimer published a paper, "Experimental Studies in the Perception of Movement," which is also known as the "dot paper" by his students because of the extensive use of dots to illustrate his concepts. In the article, various concepts constituting the foundation of Gestalt psychology were presented:

- The idea of group structures, which emphasized that although numbers are easily transposable, it is the transposition of the specific structure that is critical. One can easily identify a rectangle without counting the four corners or even being conscious of them. The arrangement of the parts to each other and to the whole as well as the consequential inherent relations is what is essential.

- The relative structure of numbers giving birth to concepts such as "a pinch of salt," which derives its meaning relative to other amounts. Certain concepts that are not numerically precise, for instance, "a bunch of radishes," are not deficient because of their lack of numerical precision. The structure of the task that involves these concepts does not require any more accuracy. Certain distinct numerical ideas like "baker's dozen" generate the universal idea of a group of thirteen items. These comprehensive sets of numerical structures used throughout the world reflect a rich variety of natural concepts, groups, and arrangements rather than utilizing a rigid system of counting in integers. The system of numerically counting is abstracted from reality, while other systems permit a plethora of distinct ideas of groups and quantities that are truer to reality.

- Certain entities by virtue of their form having predetermined methodologies of division from innate lines of cleavage relating to the preservation of their unitary identity. This quality is characteristic of natural structures. A related concept is demonstrated by the division of an eight-ring chain and the rings that make up that chain. The numerically based concept divides the chain into two halves of a chain with four rings each, or into four quarters of a chain made up of two rings each, or into eight eighths of a chain consisting of one ring each. The natural conception of entities recognizes the inherent structural changes whereby the first division produces a half chain and the second a quarter chain, if you can conceptualize two rings as a chain. The last division creates a discontinuity, as a single ring is not a chain. The deficiency of the numerically based concept is made clear when you continue the example to include the rings of the chain themselves, where you can half a ring, quarter a ring, and so on. In the natural concept of entities, a half or quarter of a ring is no longer a ring. Similarly, a melody cannot be broken down into notes as notes only exist as singular parts of a meaningful whole.
- Focus on natural, spatial, or logical quantities rather than arithmetical counting. The genesis of numbers is not in the process of counting but in natural groupings and articulated qualities whose structure is analogous to concepts or articulate wholes.[35]

GESTALT AND PHYSIOLOGICAL RESPONSES

Gestalt theory proposed a physiological-psychological isomorphism for relating perception to neural and cortical processes. When humans perceive stimuli, the nervous system is affected in involuntary and automated ways. There is a relationship between the experience of the stimuli and the underlying neural processes. Wertheimer postulated through the Phi phenomenon that these processes are the same for real and apparent movement. Kohler hypothesized that these brain processes could be thought of as fields of force organizing perception. The field interacts with its constituent parts in a dynamic manner whereby changes in one area affect the entire field. Stimuli entering these fields of force are organized by them. The brain transforms the incoming stimuli, and then humans experience the transformed sensations.

In *The Secret of Plants*, Steven Harrod Buhner discussed the physiological reactions in the processing of stimuli. The hippocampus extracts patterns encoded within environmental stimuli and ascribes meaning to the decoded patterns. As meaning is determined, it is transmitted to other parts of the brain to be encoded as memory. The stronger the emotional values associated with the meaning, the stronger the meaning is encoded as memory.[36] Cognition can be understood as involving a deeper, more holistic, intuitive perspective that holds that the act of cognition utilizes other parts of the body in addition to the brain.[37] Certain reactions to stimuli produce physiological changes, such as the slowing of the heart, producing a transformational cascade that affects physiological and cognitive functioning.[38] This sensation is dependent on the complexity, potency, and nature of the stimulus with the more consequential phenomenon causing a higher psychological state associated with these physiological changes.[39] This experience can be most readily demonstrated by the idea of opening your eyes and the gasp associated with beholding the Grand Canyon, the Alps, or the clear night sky in the country away from city lights (Figure 5.1).[40] The shift in cognitive function and concomitant physiological conditions are associated with a state of coherence. As coherence, the harmonious cooperation of integrated subsystems of a larger system that promotes the emergence of more complex functions escalates the hormonal cascade of the body's reactions. Hippocampal activity increases, and a new mode of perception and cognition is fostered that is inherently holistic, intuitive, and deep.[41] As its foundation, these physical reactions signify the potency that a phenomenologically based approach to perception has.

5.1a

Figure 5.1. a, The Grand Canyon.

5.1b

Figure 5.1. b, The Alps.

5.1c

Figure 5.1. c, A starry sky.

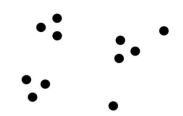

5.2

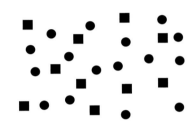

5.3

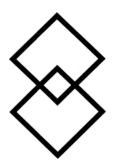

5.4

Figure 5.2. Proximity.
Figure 5.3. Similarity.
Figure 5.4. Symmetry.

PRINCIPLES OF GESTALT PSYCHOLOGY

While on the faculty of the Psychological Institute at the University of Berlin, Wertheimer wrote his seminal paper "Investigations in Gestalt Theory: II." Wertheimer contended that human perception is inherently organized into meaningful gestalten configurations so integrated through certain properties as to constitute a functional unit with attributes not derivable from the summation of its parts. This perceptual mechanism is influenced by experience and context through the views of cognition operating through memory and physiological change.[42] Form perception is based on the *law of Pragnanz*, a dynamic process of organization of our experience that tends to be regular, orderly, symmetrical, and simple. The principles of gestalt perceptual grouping are as follows:

- *Proximity.* Objects that are located in close proximity to each other spatially or temporally are perceived to be a group (Figure 5.2).
- *Similarity.* Objects that are similar in respect to some feature such as color, size, texture, and, in particular, shape are perceived to be grouped together as gestalten (Figure 5.3).
- *Symmetry.* Objects exhibiting similar types of symmetry are seen as being related (Figure 5.4).
- *Good continuation.* If objects are ordered in a pattern, whether visual, auditory, or kinetic, supplementary objects that are perceived as natural successors in the series are seen belonging to that series (Figure 5.5).
- *Common fate.* Objects that undergo the same motion or change are perceived as being grouped (Figure 5.6).
- *Closure.* Whole images are perceptually completed from partial visual data to complete a regular figure and attain maximum stability, balance, or symmetry in the entire configuration (Figure 5.7).[43]

Similarity is a dominant factor in perceptual organization. Confirming one of the oldest concepts of associative theory, objects that are similar are perceptually tied together visually. While this provides a strong impetus for grouping, the strength of the integration is dependent on the structure of the pattern and whether it reinforces the relationship between elements.[44] This relationship can be characterized as a constellation, uniting the object's elements, and compared to other objects of a similar visual structure.[45] Perceptual patterns that are organized and distinct from the surrounding stimuli have a higher

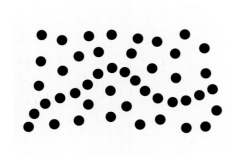

5.5

5.6

5.7

Figure 5.5. Good continuation.
Figure 5.6. Common fate.
Figure 5.7. Closure.

chance of recognition and being infused with meaning. The perception of shape involves the grasping of the layers of generic structural relationships.[46]

FRACTALS AND GESTALT

Fractal forms, by virtue of their inherent generative nature, possess strong gestalt qualities. A fractal form is derived by taking a simple typically geometric shape, a good base from which to achieve Pragnanz, as the seed shape and replicating it a number of times, with each instance of reproduction of the seed shape performing one or more affine transformations of translation, rotation, mirroring, or skewing. The synthesis of those copies composes the new seed shape from iteration 1. The new seed shape, which undergoes the same set of replications and affine transformations as in iteration 1, produces a new seed shape from iteration 2. This process goes on for as long as necessary to achieve the desired form. In analyzing forms composed in this manner, the preceding enumerated gestalt principles are exhibited.

- *Proximity.* The objects are typically located in close proximity to each other. In relation to the application of other gestalt principles, this is of a secondary nature reinforcing the other gestalt qualities.
- *Similarity.* An object generated by fractal geometric theory is inherently self-similar as it uses copies of itself to regenerate during each iteration of the fractal process. This quality goes beyond simple self-similarity to the essence of Gestalt theory in that the structure of the fractal process is directly concordant with the Gestalt paradigm. It is the intrinsic structure of the relationships produced by the nature of the fractal generation process that produces a part-to-whole-to-part structural relationship. All the parts are linked together in this manner under the umbrella of self-similarity.
- *Symmetry.* Fractal objects are inherently symmetrical about a scaling vector manifesting itself as a cascade of detail. Many times, fractal objects are designed so that the translations, rotations, and mirror transformations produce objects with geometrically symmetrical properties other than scale. Once that set of affine transformations is configured, each iteration exponentially reinforces that symmetrical property.

- *Good continuation.* Fractal forms "blossom" as they iterate, infusing themselves with their own set of inherent fractal structural relationships. This process, which is responsible for the cascade of self-similarity, is equivalent to the gestalt principle of good continuation. The fractal form is composed of a series of subwholes that manifest the good continuation of the fractal process.
- *Common fate.* Forms configured according to fractal geometric principles are composed of a group of objects that, after the initial set of affine transformations contained in iteration 1, are imbued with the structure of the whole. This characteristic unites all the form's elements in a common fate as they all are transformed by the same process. As the number of iterations increases, this property becomes stronger.
- *Closure.* Fractal forms typically are perceived as closed entities exuding the properties of stability, balance, and symmetry over the entire configuration.

EXAMPLE OF FRACTAL GESTALT

These gestalt properties inherent in fractal forms can best be demonstrated by example. In Figure 5.8, the seed shape of the fractal form is a rectangular prism orientated in a vertical position. Utilizing the collage method of fractal composition, the first iteration, denoted by I_1, is visualized and color coded in Figure 5.9 to articulate the various components. It consists of ten copies and corresponding affine transformations.

- The first copy, colored in blue and denoted by B_1, is scaled vertically and slightly in depth.
- The second copy of the seed shape, indicated in red and denoted by R_1, is scaled in both the horizontal and vertical directions and translated up. Note that R_1 by its relationship with the overall composition interpenetrates the lower element, the group of green elements, and any element that sits directly on top of the other elements.
- Copies 3 through 10 are scaled in both the horizontal and vertical directions. They are then rotated either clockwise or counterclockwise and are translated up and either to the left or the right so that they are evenly distributed along the lower portion of the second copy. These copies are colored in green and denoted by $G_{1.1-1.10}$.

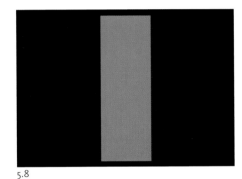

5.8

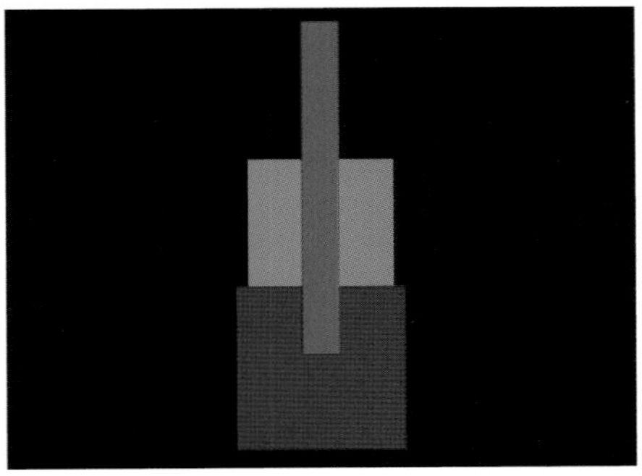

5.9

Figure 5.8. Gestalt seed shape.
Figure 5.9. Gestalt iteration 1.

133

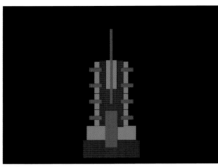

5.10

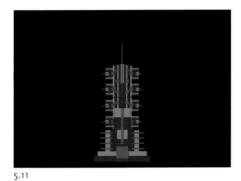

5.11

At this level of iteration, these copies overlap each other vertically and appear as two objects.

- The second iteration is indicated in Figure 5.10. Each of the ten objects is replaced by a group of the ten elements of the first iteration.

- The initial blue copy of iteration 1, B_1, is clearly replaced by a vertically scaled down copy of iteration 1 and is denoted as B_2.

- The initial red copy of iteration 1, R_1, is visible, although the vertical red element of the initial blue copy intersects it, and it is bordered by the rotated blue bases of the initial copies of green elements 3 through 10, $G_{2.1–2.10}$, which overlap each other to form two vertical blue elements on either side of the initial red copy.

- Each of the initial green copies of iteration 1, $G_{2.1–2.10}$, is articulated by the separation of the elements and the expression of the red elements of iteration 1 on each of the green copies, which articulates the 90 degree reorientation of these elements.

The third iteration is depicted in Figure 5.11, and as with the second iteration, each of the ten elements of iteration 1 is replaced by the synthesized structure of iteration 2. At this level of formation, it provides a higher level of articulated structure that enhances the gestalt of the form.

- Figure 5.12, which is a magnified section of the base of the third iteration of element 1, B_3, clearly shows the reduced copy of iteration 2, and at this level of development, particularly with the articulation of the horizontal red elements on each of its green components, the similarity with the other elements is reinforced.

- Figure 5.13 is a blowup of the top of the third iteration to highlight the red and green elements with the second element, R_3, in the middle and the third through the tenth elements, $G_{3.1–3.2}$, distributed symmetrically on either side of element 2. The focus should be on element R_3 only. Within this segment, the vertical red element of B_3 runs into the B_2 element of R_3. As with R_2, the blue elements of $G_{3.1–3.10}$ within this constituent partly overlap and form continuous vertical blue components that flank the center element, R_2. The red element on each of elements $G_{3.1–3.10}$. reinforces the horizontal orientation of these elements.

- Figure 5.14 shows one of the components of elements 3 through 10, $G_{3.1–3.10}$, which clearly shows a similarity with B_3, illustrated in

Figure 5.10. Gestalt iteration 2.
Figure 5.11. Gestalt iteration 3.
Figure 5.12. Magnified section of the base of the third iteration of element 1.
Figure 5.13. Blowup of the top of the third iteration.
Figure 5.14. One of the components of elements 3 through 10.

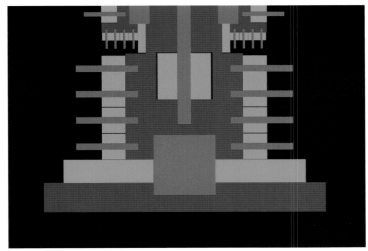

5.12

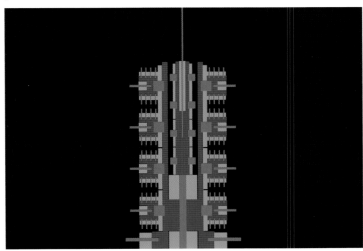

5.13

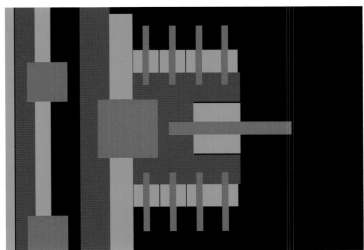

5.14

Figure 5.12; the notable exception is that it is rotated 90 degrees. As with B_3, the eight copies of the first iteration of the overall form that line the sides of each element structure a relationship with the other portions of this overall element and with the whole.

This composition conveys a gestalt that is derived from the nature of its formation by fractal geometry. This gestalt springs from the relationships between the whole and the various elements, the elements and the subelements, and the subelements and the whole. The integrated structure of these relationships bestows on the form gestalt properties to provide it innate appeal to human perception. These properties are as follows:

- *Proximity.* All the elements are proximate to each other to the point that many of them are either touching or intersecting. This property, while in and of itself providing a segregation from other environmental stimuli, is secondary to other gestalt properties.
- *Similarity.* Self-similarity is a hallmark property of fractal form as well as between the elements themselves. Elements $G_{3.1-3.10}$ are observably similar, differentiated by translation and rotational transformations. The most obvious similarity is between each of the elements $G_{3.1-3.10}$ being similar to B_3, the difference being scale and rotation transformations. R_3 is similar to other elements but in a slightly more nuanced way, which creates an additional layer of interest.
- *Symmetry.* In this form, there are two strong sources of symmetrical properties. The initial placement of the green elements in a symmetrical configuration about the red element establishes a strong symmetry that is reinforced by the second source of symmetry. The entire form is related by a symmetry of scale that connects the entities by the repetition of form at decreasing levels of scale. These two sources of symmetry provide a strong presence of form or gestalt.
- *Good continuation.* The symmetrical property of scale is integral to the property of good continuation. As you examine the various elements at decreasing levels of scale, you are presented with a cascade of detail that has the same structural relationships as the overall form, its elements and subelements. As you go from the overall form to element G_3, you note the similarity between the

two, and again when you go from G_3 to one of G_3's elements on its side. If we were to continue the iterations, this level of detail would continue as well.

- *Common fate.* The continuity and strength of the presence of the other gestalt properties in overall form and each of the elements strongly provides a perception of a common fate between all the elements and the whole. The structure of the overall relationship of elements is carried through each element, bonding the entire composition inextricably to relate together.
- *Closure.* The form is generated by a simple three-dimensional structure, and results of iteration 1 produce a regular, stable, balanced symmetrical figure. With each iteration, this form, which has a high degree of closure, is enfolded onto itself, producing a new form similar to the previous generation but with stronger properties of closure as a result of its generative process.

Figures 5.15 and 5.16 illustrate the same final form after iteration 3 but without the color coding. Figure 5.15 is a similar frontal view, while Figure 5.16 is a perspective from the front left corner. The result of eliminating the color coding is a form that reveals its gestalt in a more subtle but stronger manner.

5.15

Figure 5.15. Final form after iteration 3, but
without the color coding: frontal view.

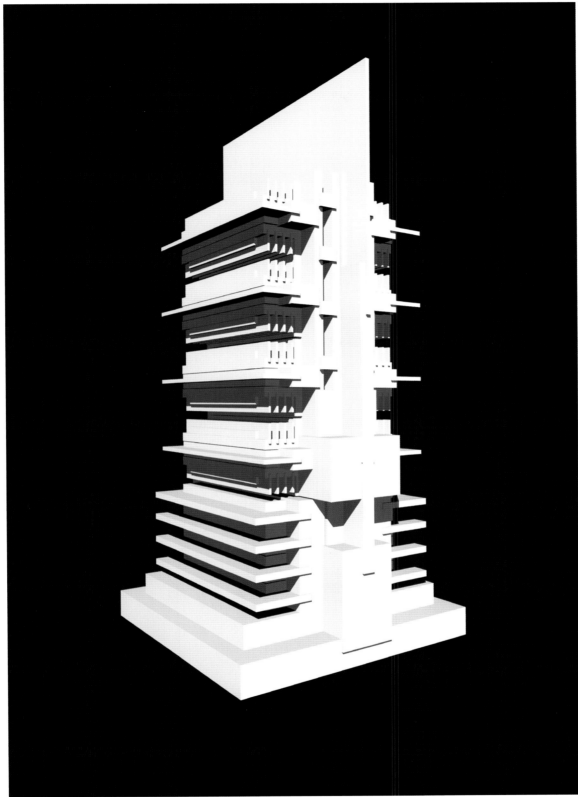

5.16

Figure 5.16. Final form after iteration 3, but
without the color coding: front left corner.

TRANSPOSITION

The importance of shape is evident in the consideration of the phenomenon of transposition. In the gestalt *law of transposition*, humans transmit the percepts from one experience to another experience because of the similarity in structural relationships. This concept is tied into the gestalt idea of invariance. Invariance is the property of perception where geometrical objects are recognized despite differences in rotation, translation, scale, deformations, different lighting, and so on. Enhrenfels stressed the invariance of shape and form as an important gestalt property. The crucial factor in transposition is that relations among the stimuli must remain approximately the same when the stimuli itself changes. While Wolfgang Kohler was stationed on the Canary Islands during World War I, he experimented with chicks who he trained to peck at the lighter of two colored sheets of paper. He then replaced the darker of the two sheets with a sheet that was even lighter than the one they had been pecking at. The chicks abandoned the sheet they were pecking at and began pecking at the sheet that was the lighter of the two before them. When the process was reversed and the chicks were trained to peck on the darker of the two sheets, the same results occurred. The chicks like humans transposed the relationship to the new set of circumstances, proving that the relation was the critical factor, rather than the absolute of the color of the paper at which they were pecking. The principles of gestalt perception in and of themselves provide extremely powerful affirmation of the innate affinity humans have for forms structured by fractal principles. The law of transposition amplifies that attraction by acting as the bridge to another fundamentally strong human cognitive and emotional value: nature. Much of nature is structured either perceptibly or subtly by the principles of fractal geometry. This structure is consciously or unconsciously embedded in our cognitive and emotional makeup as a highly valued concept. These values are transposed to man-made forms that are configured according to fractal geometry.

Pure sensory data are a mere mosaic, a simple additive agglomeration of sensory facts. The data exist as objects when the sensory information becomes thoroughly instilled with meaning generated from the innate perceptual organizational process.[47] Knowledge comes about when the individual actively imposes organization on the sensory data.

HOLISTIC CHARACTER

The hallmark of Wertheimer's later work was identifying the internal laws that governed the form's structure that produces gestalt qualities. He analyzed the forms in terms of the inherent structure of the whole, the specific, identifiable laws that generated its internal organization, its evocative structure.[48] The structure present in nature that produces its poignant gestalt is fundamentally different than the structure that characterizes man-made artifacts. In general, natural structure is complex and intricate, evoking the grand plan of a deity infinitely more intelligent than man, and comparatively, man-made artifacts are simple, frequently reflecting the narrow purpose for which they were conceived.[49] In his *Nature of Order* series, Christopher Alexander articulates that architecture can achieve a similar intricate gestalt as nature through the creation of living structure by the implementation of a structure of centers. A *center*, or focus of perceived organization, is an entity that is defined by its relationship to other visual nuclei whose strength either increases or decreases the vitality of that entity. This recursive relationship and its inherent circularity is the key to understanding Alexander's concept of wholeness.[50] This system of centers unfolds in a "morphogenetic" sequence of structure-preserving transformations creating a coherent whole. This produces a configuration of nested centers that coalesce to form subwholes that act as centers that combine to form wholes. Each of these configurations of "low-level" centers emits a quality of wholeness for that region. This wholeness, or gestalt, emanates from that region up through the structure above it and down through the elements that compose it.[51] "Living structure" is a recursive hierarchical configuration of layered relationships of integrated wholes, subwholes, and sub-subwholes. The level of living structure, wholeness, and "life" is inextricably linked to the gestalt of the form and is derived from the internal cohesion of the form's structural relationships.

Wherever we are in the world, we are enveloped in some degree of wholeness from the overall environment and from each of its component parts embroidered in an overlapping spatial field. Each of these occurrences of wholeness is composed of centers ranked according to their degree of coherence.[52] This coherence is derived by the presence of discernible structure responsible for the wholeness. For Alexander, wholeness goes beyond focusing on the gestalt of an object but rather focuses on the form's structure, which is the essence of the form. This structure is what we intuitively perceive as the overall gestalt of the object, the broad gestural sweep of a configuration, an overall composition of nested centers of relative intensities comprising a single structure. The relative harmony of "life" of a form emanates from the internal cohesion of this structure.[53] Alexander has adopted the gestalt concept of *Pragnanz* to create saliency of forms through the strength of their centers and segregate them as wholes. This wholeness is defined through the strength of its coherence relative to its environment.[54]

Fractal geometry is nature's "living structure," and forms composed by it exhibit nature's structure and gestalt qualities.[55] Wertheimer focused on the methodology of grasping this structure as well as the inherent structure of forms with high gestalt attributes. The process of penetration to the essential structure and inner essence of the phenomenon was essential.[56]

The inherent holistic quality of forms with high gestalt values is a trademark of organic compositions. By focusing on this quality, the difference between mechanical form and organic form is made clear. Mechanical forms are based on a unity that is derived of additions and subtractions in a sequential system that can be coordinated but is not integrated. It is fractionable and can be subdivided into independent subsystems. Because it is functionally localized, parts can be interchanged or replaced without invalidating its raison d'être.[57] The specialization of function causes just a few simple relations between the elements held together in a simple unity. It is a decentralized assemblage of parts that is only realized when all of its parts have been amassed.[58] The essential quality of organic form is its wholeness, in which the coherence of all the parts present in a single indivisible whole is so strong that the form appears complete. Wholeness has been desired throughout human history and was evidenced by Aristotle's definition as "the parts which constitute it must be inwardly connected, arranged in a certain order structurally related and combined into a system." The system's innerconnectedness is discernible in an external order based on a structural hierarchy of levels between the part and the whole. Each of these levels is made up of smaller parts in the same manner as the level relates to the whole. At each stage of the metamorphosis of an organic form, wholeness is present to a greater or lesser extent.[59] Any attempt at fractionalizing the form by removing a part alters the whole.[60] Organic forms are distinguished by a complexity of shape owing to a diffusion of function within the parts.[61]

The quality of holistic form is derived by the interaction of structure and recursion resulting in an unfolding of a holistic paradigm. Structure is the set of relationships between the parts that form the whole and between the whole and the parts. Certain relationships promote a mechanistic fractionable set of relationships that constitute the whole. Other sets of relationships are established on interrelations of all the parts such that the impact of a stimulus on one part reverberates throughout the whole. These relationships are recurrently mathematically based and provoke a geometric order as their expression. This geometric order is complex as it has variation through scale within the overall order to produce a certain character.[62] Christopher Alexander proposes that wholeness in the spatial domain is drawn from the structure present there. This structure is what we intuitively perceive as gestalt and is the source of coherence. It is parallel to a hierarchically layered vector field with the different centers pointing to the other components with which they have a relationship. This organized field of force structures space and in doing so induces coherence and arouses a sense of wholeness. The set of relationships among the elements acts as the glue that holds the structure of the space together. Structure becomes intricate, interwoven, and complex when these relationships are nested and overlap each other. Each local area of wholeness has been characterized as a center by Christopher Alexander and is composed of the organization and interplay of other centers. Each center can be understood and described only in terms of other centers and the inherent interconnected relationships. This circular structure is constructed by utilizing recursive generative mechanisms to produce the composition. In a recursive generation of form, a set of relationships is developed between a set of elements. The evolution of the entity can only occur in terms of these relationships and can be thought of as the unfolding of the form.

The morphogenesis of organic form has been increasingly correlated to the process that creates it. The initial generation of the structure has a relatively elemental, indistinct set of relationships. The next step in the evolution or unfolding is the regeneration of the various elements in terms of the relationships created in the previous stage of evolution. Each of the regenerated elements exhibits the initial set of relationships, creating an interconnection within the entire set of elements. The structure of the form begins to unfold. As successive iterations continue, the generative relationships become increasingly embedded into the form, analogous to the unfolding of a flower. The structure of the form unfolds and spreads deeper and deeper, reinforcing the singular essence of the generative concept. A change to any one of the initial set of relationships spreads throughout the structure in the same manner. This relationship is the essence of holism and a fundamental characteristic of fractal geometry.

INHERENT HOLISTIC QUALITY OF FRACTALS

The unique holistic aspect of fractally generated form is best illustrated by examining the effect of incremental changes. Figure 5.17 shows a rectangular prism as a seed shape, and Figure 5.18 illustrates the generative set of fractal relationships color coded to highlight them.

- The seed shape is copied, scaled down to 25 percent of the width of the seed shape, translated to the left edge of the seed shape and colored in red. This element is labeled R_1.
- The seed shape is scaled down to 25 percent of the width and height of the seed shape, translated just to the left of center of the seed shape and colored in green. This is repeated three more times, with each successive copy translated upward so it rests on top of the previous green element. These elements are labeled G_{1-4}.
- The seed shape is scaled down to 50 percent of the width and height of the seed shape, translated just to the right of center of the seed shape and colored in blue. This is repeated again with the next copy translated up so it rests on top of the first blue element. These elements are labeled B_{1-2}.

The composite form of this iteration forms the new seed shape. Figure 5.19 illustrates the next three fractal iterations utilizing this new seed shape. In examining the area that was the red element of the new seed shape, R_1, you see that it has been replaced with a copy of a new seed shape scaled down to 25 percent of that new seed shape's width. You see within it the red element to the left, the four green elements next to it, and the two blue elements next to that. When you examine G_{1-4} and B_{1-2}, you see a similar regeneration of these elements. Owing to the nature of the relationships determined in iteration 1, the next two iterations of the form the have an inherent vertically linear character that gets more and more pronounced as you continue the unfolding of the form through successive iterations.

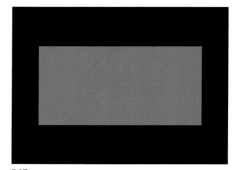

5.17

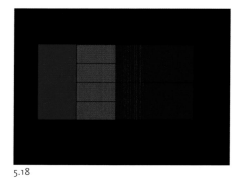

5.18

Figure 5.17. Rectangular prism as a seed shape.
Figure 5.18. Generative set of fractal relationships.
Figure 5.19. Iterations 2, 3, and 4.

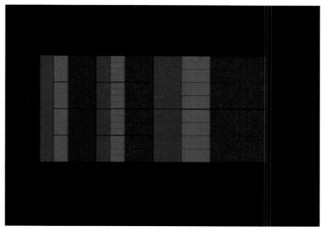

5.19a

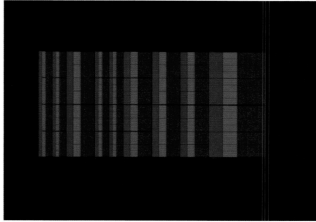

5.19b

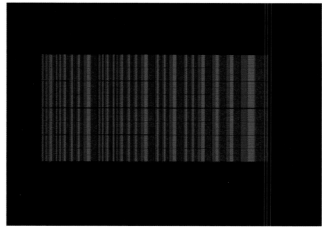

5.19c

In Figure 5.20, a revised fractal form is represented so that with the first iteration, it is virtually impossible to see the change in the relationships. All the relationships are the same with the exception of B_2, which, instead of being scaled down 50 percent of the width and height of the seed shape, is scaled down 25 percent in width, rotated 90 degrees counterclockwise and then translated up. Figure 5.21a illustrates the second iteration, which, when compared to iteration 2 of the previous form, clearly indicates the new horizontal relationship of element B_2. Figure 5.21b and Figure 5.21c show iterations 3 and 4, respectively. In analyzing these images, you can ascertain that the embedment of the new seed shape within each element produces the unfolding of the revised intrinsic relationships that constitute the form. The change in the relationship of B_1 affects every element of the form, which is the fundamental characteristic of holistic form. As you proceed from iteration 3 to iteration 4, the impact of the revised blue element, B_1, bursts across the image as the structural relationships unfold throughout the form.

Figure 5.22 demonstrates the equivalent process revised only to change the relationship of B_1 so that it has the same scaling and rotational transformations as B_2. As with the previous model, the new relationship integrally embeds itself within the structure of the form. As you increasingly iterate the form, this embedment spreads through the structure of the form or unfolds the new gestalt of the form.

Gestalt psychology and the overarching concept of holistic design is embedded in the generative process of fractally generated form. A composition composed through the use of fractal geometry inherently embodies the gestalt properties that cause the viewer to perceive an object that they cognitively conclude is a whole integrated form. As the examples that were presented demonstrate, this perception of a holistic quality is not unfounded. As you revise one element of the configuration, that change increasingly permeates through the composition as the iterations increase.

Figure 5.20. Revised fractal form.
Figure 5.21. Iterations 2, 3, and 4.
Figure 5.22. Equivalent process revised only to change the relationship of B_1.
Figure 5.23. Iterations 2, 3, and 4.

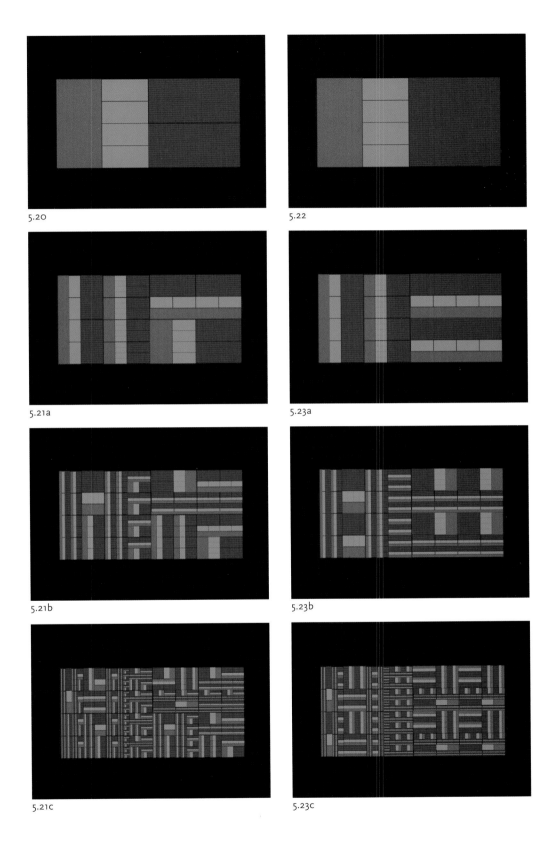

5.20

5.22

5.21a

5.23a

5.21b

5.23b

5.21c

5.23c

GESTALT LEGACY

With the advent of World War II, Max Wertheimer, Kurt Koffka, and Wolfgang Kohler emigrated to the United States and introduced Gestalt psychology there. In the United States, they reunited with Rudolf Arnheim, who had assimilated the concepts of Gestalt psychology and applied them to art and architecture. As did Wertheimer, Arnheim viewed the principles of Gestalt psychology as present throughout nature and uniquely applicable to the arts.[63] The principles of Gestalt psychology flourished and spread throughout cognitive research. Jean Piaget, a noted developmental theorist, formulated a theory of cognitive development in children that consisted of general stages in which each stage concludes with a rapid coalescing of knowledge into a gestalt. As children develop into adults, they form mental structures to classify objects and think in logical ways. The psychological properties of these structures are wholeness, relationships between parts, and homeostatic adjustments based on new experiences.[64]

The gestalt principles outline the way in which parts are seen, how grouping occurs and subwholes emerge, and the process in which the characteristics of the whole play a determining role.[65] Perception is a transformational process that proceeds from top to bottom or from the whole to the parts.[66] The content in the visual field is circumscribed into entities that belong together as a group and are segregated from their surroundings. Each element, while always an integrated part of the whole, has its own sovereign properties integral to its existence as an entity. The whole-to-part interaction and interdependence structuring the whole are in dynamic equilibrium with its constitutive elements as autonomous objects.[67] A given group can be segregated and belong to a larger group as a subwhole. Perceptual data are perceived in organized or configurational terms, where patterns take precedence over elements and have properties not in the elements themselves.[68] When these factors coalesce into a segregated gestalt, a "figure" is articulated separate and distinct from the loose "ground" of the environment around it.[69] If you try to form groups with other elements of the visual environment that are not presenting themselves as perceptual wholes, the results are frequently so strange as to reinforce the quality of the obvious wholes or the result is complete failure. The concept of wholes provides a connection between the experience of space and the experience of time. The temporal objects form temporal groups in the same simultaneous method as spatial objects form groups in

5.24

space. Proximity in time is analogous to the principle of proximity in spatial grouping.

As humans, we are connected to the natural order through this innate perceptual system that organizes sensory stimuli into wholes. This inherently holistic perceptual system guides humans as they progress through the sensory field of nature to instill meaning, integrate their experience, and actualize themselves in harmony with the environment.[70] Nature is a highly ordered system of systems. We understand and connect to this ordered system through the conscious and unconscious functioning of our perceptual system. We make sense of the natural world by a continuous and automatic processing of sensory data into meaning.[71] The organization of the sensory stimuli of natural forms into segregated wholes is an essential opening to the process of establishing meaning.[72]

SUMMARY

For researchers such as Max Wertheimer, Gestalt psychology presented itself as a new way of understanding nature. The core of what became an all-encompassing religion for him is that much of the world is organized not as individual atomized components but into meaningful parts forming a comprehensible whole. Natural forms possess their own inherent structure, and although a complete understanding of the natural world is elusive, humans can ascertain these structures. The analysis of these structures must be premised on the internal rules and principles of that phenomenon.[73] We must derive the essence of the inner organic processes and the formation of the organic gestalt that is manifested from them.[74]

Figure 5.24. Gestalt dog.

CHAPTER **6** **Perception and Cognition of Natural Form**

The ability of an individual to function in this world is highly dependent on the human abilities of perception and cognition. Although to an extent they occur serially, they are highly interdependent and integrated. To understand how architecture generated by fractal geometry appeals to people as organic, we need to assess the process of perception and cognition. In this review we will see that these processes function as detectors, filters, assimilators, and categorizers to give meaning to the sensory data. Objects structured by fractal geometry pass through these filters and are placed in cognitive categories similar to those of natural objects. This process is responsible for the positive attributes people associate with fractally generated architecture.

PERCEPTION

The Physiology of Perception
The first step in the cognitive process that transforms environmental stimuli into behavioral control mechanisms is perception. Perception is the process by which we receive and interpret the sensory data to which we are exposed in the environment. We receive this information through our sensory organs of eyes, ears, nose, mouth, and our tactile outer skin. These organs receive information pertinent to their function, such as the nose for smell, as part of an overall sensory system that transmits information to the brain. The physical energy received by these sensory organs establishes the foundation of humans'

perceptual experience.[1] As we are focusing on forms that exhibit fractal structure we will concentrate our scope on visual perception, which is initiated when images are focused through the lens of the eye onto the membrane known as the retina. The retina is the initial element of the brain's architecture utilized to transform the energy received from the environment in the form of images into the electrical energy the brain utilizes—neural signals—through the process of transduction.[2] On detecting the photons of light, it responds by generating neural impulses.

The brain is composed of a very large number of interconnected cells, called *neurons,* which send out electrical signals and communicate with each other. Neurons are composed of cell bodies that have dendrites extending from them, which receive from and transmit signals to other neurons through a nerve fiber called the *axon.* The communication between neurons occurs in the space between axons, called the *synapse.* The transmission from the axon of one neuron triggers a chemical process whereby the synaptic vesicles release neurotransmitters onto the next neuron. This process passes the information from one neuron on to the other in either an excitation mode or an inhibition mode. The release of an excitatory neurotransmitter increases the chances that the next neuron will fire, and conversely, the release of an inhibitory neurotransmitter will decrease the likelihood that the subsequent neuron will fire. The rate and pattern of neural firing forms a group of interconnected neurons or a neural circuit that causes neural processing of the sensory data.[3]

From the nerve cells in the eye to the architecture of the brain, research has shown that neurons exhibit specialization. Certain neurons respond to particular stimuli and not to others; in the perceptual architecture, these are termed *feature detectors* and are clustered in certain areas of the brain.[4] A fly's vision system is simple, but it provides the fly with the information it needs for its requisite speed and precision.[5] A frog's retinal neurons and its subsequent reactions are selectively stimulated to perform their function as a bug detector. A frog's perceptual system has five classes of specialized cells optimized to serve its particular needs. A more complicated creature has a higher number of these neural categories, or *trigger features,* which are used to detect patterns that are important to the particular organism's survival.[6] Similarly, the human perceptual-cognitive system has evolved to structure its neural reactions to optimize its survival and ability to

6.1

function in the world. This would include feature detectors optimized for natural forms.

The Perceptual Process

The process of visual perception commences as soon as we are born. Visual perception is utilized as an educational facility early in life as babies are exposed to brightly colored, geometrically shaped mobiles, blocks, and toys (Figure 6.1). In kindergarten, children augment their own cognitive development through perceptual creativity by experimenting with drawing, painting, and forming objects out of clay.[7]

This prioritization of the development of perceptual faculties taps into the innate importance of perception produced through genetic evolution. The sensory organs and the perceptual process for interpreting their data evolved as a biological capacity required for survival. Man needed to identify and focus on environmental elements that either enhanced or impeded life. The evolved perceptual process is purposive and selective.[8] As mechanisms are integrated into a species through heredity, they apply to the entire genus within a narrow range. The species at the apex of the biological ladder, such as humans, have more control over the choice of stimuli and reactions to them.[9]

The perception of sensory information is an essential element of the human condition. Experiments on sensory deprivation involving the visual, auditory, tactile, and kinesthetic senses that reduce

Figure 6.1. Baby looking at a mobile.

153

environmental stimulation to a steady buzz and just diffuse light significantly and detrimentally affect the subject. Subjects are unable to think and replace that lack of sensory stimuli by reminiscing and generating imagery that can develop into true hallucination. When a person is forced to stare at a given figure, he or she will eventually resort to mentally varying the image by reorganizing it to avoid the inherent monotony. The mind urgently works to replace the missing stimulation, indicating that perception is not merely a faculty for receiving environmental information but an integral element for cognitive functioning. The continual perceptual processing of sensory data is the foundation for the functioning of the nervous system.[10] In the absence of this information, it reacts to restore or replace the missing stimuli to continue functioning normally.

We are immersed in a continual stream of massive amounts of sensory data. The procedure used to manage this data is an active process that progressively provides an entity's identification and signification, sometimes quickly, sometimes slowly, and is subject to confirmation, change, correction, and reappraisal.[11] The perceptual process reduces the data into smaller, more manageable portions of information through the extraction of relevant "summaries" of the data.[12] These summaries are developed by ignoring those aspects of the environmental information that are not relevant for the task at hand and by focusing on the regularities present in the data. Not every element of the data is required, and the occurrence of regularities permits the replacement of literal depiction with shorter descriptions involving procedures for reproducing the data.[13]

This process of active selectivity is a basic trait of visual perception utilized to note changes in the environment.[14] The nervous system causes a selective reaction to certain features of the visual field. These responses are part of the human genetic composition that has evolved. It has been increasingly acknowledged that a significant amount of perception occurs below the threshold of awareness.[15] The rapid speed that can characterizes humans' and animals' reactions to movement highlights the short-cut neural connectivity controlled at the retinal level that distinguishes mobility from stationarity.[16]

The human visual system is composed of nerve cells that respond hierarchically to certain specific features of visual images. This includes data that match the requirements exactly but also data that match the requirements to some degree. The perception of shape involves comprehension found in the sensory data and consists of correlating stimulus data with templates of elementary shapes also known as visual concepts or form categories. These visual concepts are utilized because of their simplicity and generality, which permit the rapid processing of information.[17] The degree of sophistication of the visual concept is relative and can be an intricate shape if that is the simplest attainable configuration from the distillation of the visual information. The critical factor is that an object can be perceived to the extent it is fitted to some organized shape.[18]

The innate ability to select a perceptual target occurs at the retinal level and protects the mind from being overwhelmed by more data than it can or needs to process.[19] The signals that cause this type of response have two requisite qualities. They are clearly identifiable by their color, shape, or structure and are distinct from the rest of the environment. The degree of effort required to identify an object's critical qualities within its environmental context is significant.[20] The perceptual modus operandi is to quickly look for the relevant elements of the visual image hiding in the constantly changing environmental phenomena.[21] The varying nature of the context affects the size, shape, location, color, brightness, and movement of an object. Perception separates these nonessential factors in the identification of an entity from its essential properties.[22] In essence, the perceptual system acts as a filter to prioritize and extract certain specific features and to resolve the organizational issues inherent in processing the multitude of data.[23] Perception can be thought of as a continuous and rapid problem-solving process.[24]

Between the human eye and the objects in the environment exist the light waves that are the medium of visual communication. The stimulus that is received by the optic organs is not organized. The organization of these stimuli into specific units occurs in the neural functions. Sensory organization has a fundamental biological value in its reconstruction of the critical aspects of the environment that are scrambled in the mosaic of sensory data.[25] This segmentation of the visual fields into distinct entities that we regard as objects or "things" is one of the most basic functions of our perceptual systems.[26] One facet of this perceptual organization is the discernment of relationships that invoke a unity. These relationships are within the percept and between the percept and the context in which an object is viewed.

155

Theories of Perception: Top Down and Bottom Up

A number of theories of visual perception have emerged. These hypotheses include inferring meaning from incomplete data, the concept of codons, and the competing concepts of top-down and bottom-up processing of visual data. They represent various ways to examine human perception and the applicability to the perception of architectural form.

Hermann von Helmholtz theorized that perception is a form of unconscious inference stemming from the assumption that the eye is optically inferior. Visual perception occurs by deriving a probable interpretation of the incomplete data to some extent based on previous experiences.[27] This theory of visual perception based on probable inference was advanced by Bayesian studies. These studies appear to confirm that humans analyze sensory data by performing an optimization of the observed parameters. The person's internal model of the world, his or her generative model, serves as the basis for inferring meaning from the sensory data. The generative model is a synthesis of genetic predispositions and meaning from previous experience.[28] This theory of perception reinforces the logic that forms generated by fractal geometry tap into the human predisposition for natural structures. Natural forms that exhibit fractal characteristics and structure are a significant element of the human generative model. The observation of similar attributes guides the cognitive process toward similar intellectual and emotional reactions.

David Marr advanced a theory based his research on the interaction between neurons and how the functional group of neurons within the hippocampus and neocortex interact, store, process, and transmit information. His work is based on the theory that the brain's central functions are "statistical" pattern recognition and association. The basic building block is a *codon*, or subset of features, with which there may be associated a neural cell, wired as to fire in the presence of that particular codon. His theory conceptualizes three main symbolic representations of the visual world that are created, maintained, and interpreted by the process of visual perception.[29] A representation for an object's shape is a formal system for describing aspects of the shape together with rules that specify the application of that system to the shape, in the same way a musical score represents a symphony.[30] One of the critical aspects of a visual representation is the organization that the representation imposes on the information in its description.[31] First is a primal sketch representation concerned with intensity changes, geometrical distribution, and organizaton.[32] It is a fundamental entity constructed from symbolic primitives such as edges, contours, and blobs analogous to an artist's pencil sketch. It looks for spatial organization at different scales, utilizing virtual lines to connect areas of similarity and derive orientations.[33] The next representation is a two-and-a-half-dimensional sketch focused on relative distances, contours, and orientations of surfaces similar to the artist adding shading and highlights to a sketch. Through processes of stereopis, shading, and motion, an internal representation of the sensory information is created.[34] Last, a three-dimensional representation or model of the object is composed that possesses the organizational hierarchy and geometry of the form in an object-centered coordinate frame.[35] This representation is linked to a stored catalog of three-dimensional model descriptions through indexes according to specificity of the information, the relative relations of the components, and the application of a recognized component to the whole of the form. Through the interaction of the sensory data, its representations, and these indexes, a homology is constructed between the three-dimensional model and the image, providing it with recognition.[36]

In this model of perception, the fractal structure is the codon that causes the same neural activity that occurs when perceiving natural forms. Similarly, Marr's primal sketch and two-and-a-half-dimensional sketch of fractal forms originate from the same perceivable source as natural compositions. Key elements in each stage of Marr's process are the perception of similarities within the image and an organizational structure. These perceptual priorities give rise to the hypothesis that the neural activity generated from perception of fractal forms is similar to the neural activity that occurs when viewing natural forms because of the presence in each of a fractal organizational structure and a degree of self-similarity.

Two different theories of perception have emerged distinguished by the extent to which perception is directly influenced by the information present in the stimulus material. Richard Gregory has advocated an indirect constructivist premise also known as "top-down" processing. James Gibson believes that perception is a more direct process characterized as "bottom-up" processing.[37] These processes have also been characterized as organic/intuitive versus mechanical/intellectual.[38]

In top-down processing, contextual data are utilized to drive patterns. Perception attempts to make conjectures from the sensory data and develops a cognitive hypothesis. Elements of the visual field

157

engender recall of experiences associated with those elements. With visual perception, in a significant amount of instances, recall is triggered by a segregated entity with a specific shape that is associated with the experience in memory. If the organization constituting the specific shape were absent, recall would only be able to rely on aspects such as color and brightness of "sensations" and would not suffice for recall. A mosaic of "sensations" is unable to provide recall with sufficient information for a clear association. Recall is enabled by the specific attributes engendered by organization within the sensory world. In visual perception, the invariance of shape despite varying color, size, and location is a dominant factor.[39] Our perceptual physiological composition appears to be structured to extract certain high-level features such as three-dimensional topology to characterize the sensory data held in perception. Cognitive capabilities for generalization, analogy, and intuition provide a bridge to retrieve data based on the perception of similarity.[40]

Prior knowledge and experience can be critical factors in this process as they are the cognitive well from which we draw our deduction. The mind functions with a vast range of imagery available in memory, organizing the lifetime of experiences into a system of sensory concepts. The cognitive activity by which the mind directs these concepts takes place in direct perception and in the interaction between direct perception and memory.[41] Although the influence of memory, such as that of a shape, on a perception is powerful, it is necessary for the percept under consideration to possess that quality, in this case a shape, itself. The mind cannot identify a perception unless the percept has an identity of its own.[42] In natural forms, a significant identifying visual characteristic is a form's self-similarity because of its fractal organization.

An interesting theoretical dilemma for this theory is how this process is initiated in newborns as they have no prior experiences on which to draw. Research has determined that neonates are born with or extremely rapidly develop propensities toward shape constancy and preferences for normal features to scrambled features.

Rudolf Arnheim characterizes this perceptual model as intuitive and occurring in a perceptual field of freely interacting forces. Visual processing occurs at the physiological level of the nervous system, which functions as a field. The perceptual field allows free interaction among the visual forces inherent within its elements and generated by the interaction of those elements. The stimulus data organize themselves according to the basic overall pattern compliant to their forces. This process is an understanding of the structural features of the visual field and is a fundamental prerequisite of perception.[43] In scanning a painting, a person perceives the various elements of the composition: their shapes, their colors, and the relations among them. These components exert their perceptual influence on each other to compose a total accumulation of visual forces as an image to the observer. The interaction of visual forces is a complex field process that typically does not draw from the well of previous experience but rather from innate perceptual mechanisms. It is the ultimate accumulation of visual forces, or the percept of the painting in consciousness, organized according to the structure of the painting and consisting of shapes and colors characterized by their place and purpose within the whole.[44]

James Gibson's theory of bottom-up processing is data driven beginning with the stimulus itself. Interpretation of sensory material is not required as the information received—size, shape, color, distance, and so on—provides sufficient data for humans to interact directly with the environment. Perceptual processing is one directional from the retina to the visual cortex, with successive stages of the visual system carrying out increasingly complex analysis of the sensory data. A key component of Gibson's theory is the role of invariants in the environment as providing consistent information. An example of an invariant would be perspective, which provides consistent information about the relative distances of objects in the visual field. Arnheim has distinguished this perceptual paradigm as intellectual. In observing a painting, this perceptual process identifies the various elements and relations that constitute the work. A perceptual listing is prepared consisting of a description of shapes, an identification of each color, and an examination of the relations of individual elements. On the conclusion of this perceptual analysis, the data are used to reconstruct the whole. Each element of the whole and its relation to other elements is isolated to establish the nature of each. Stable and independent concepts are gradually built up until the mind acquires a stable and whole entity.[45]

In *The Dynamics of Architectural Form*, Rudolf Arnheim discusses the inherent bottom-up processing of architectural form owing to the typical lack of opportunity to view the building as a whole, which can only be done at significant distances, such as from a plane, and then only if the structure has a high degree of symmetry. The more typical experience is that because of the geometric breadth of human vision, a building can only be experienced in pieces by the eyes and head roving back and forth over the edifice and by transversing around it.[46] That is perhaps why classic architects such as Alberti endorsed organic architecture, whereas in a fractal philosophy, a section of the building reflected the whole composition.[47]

Fractal geometry is harmonious with perceptual processing models, top-down or bottom-up. In top-down processing, the sensory data are assimilated and a conjecture about them is developed. As the observer perceives the fractal object and its nested structure, the conjecture is either reinforced or adjusted. Continuing observation reinforces the supposition as the self-similar field of dynamic, integrated perceptual forces draws from an inherent perceptual predisposition for organic forms. The rapid perceptual analysis of a fractal form starts at the whole of the organic percept and exponentially reinforces itself by perceiving the nested series of self-similar elements. In a bottom-up perception of a fractal form, the elements are processed distinctly. A series of self-similar relations is discerned that achieves a higher level of potency as it is realized that the relations form the basis for the next level of nested self-similar relationships. This dynamic process builds to a crescendo of perception concluding in the organic nature of the object.

The dynamic process of awareness through the integration of top-down with bottom-up perception is exemplified by the work of musicians such as a pianist. If the pianist focuses on his or her hands, bottom-up, he or she falls out of the flow of the music; however, if the pianist concentrates on the whole of the melody, top-down, he or she may not play it correctly. The pianist shifts or integrates the two kinds of awareness in a from-to thinking in which the subsidiary details are expressions of the whole and reinforce it. In this type of perception, one seesaws back and forth between the investigation of lower-level clues and the understanding of the whole that is revealed through those clues. In doing so, one obtains an increasingly clear understanding of the phenomenon.[48] The perceptual interplay of the pianist is similar to that of an observer of an object generated by fractal geometry. They go back and forth between the relationship of the whole to the self-similar parts and from the parts to the whole.

Ulrich Neisser has developed a perceptual model, the "perceptual cycle," that synthesizes the top-down and bottom-up theories. In this theory, a set of cognitive schemata, either innate or developed through experience, directs the perceptual process that "samples" the environment. The sensory data obtained influence and modify the schemata, establishing a cyclic feedback mechanism. The schema, modified by the sensory information, directs the perceptual process for additional information. An observed fractal configuration correlates to innate evolutionized schemata that have high positive cognitive values. This inherent cognitive association directs the perceptual system toward the elements of organic structure in the sensory field, reinforcing the positive association and drawing the observer toward the organic entity.

Perception and Order

The perception of organization implies the perception of some type of order. Order is a fundamental tendency in inorganic and organic nature. It permeates every level of complexity with the more complex structures having a greater need for order. The complete lack of order can be identified intuitively as it goes against our innate effort to organize our environment.[49]

Humans are immersed in a sea of sensory data, and between the receipt of stimuli and the response are processes of organization. The physical entity and its environment are unified in the sensory image and are segregated during perception to the extent the entity is an organized whole rather than an agglomeration of pieces. In this process, if the percept is simply organized and visibly differs from its context, it has a high degree of recognizability. Perception abstracts objects from their environment because it comprehends the shape as an organized structure rather than a montage of unrelated elements.[50] When a person views the collection of four slightly uneven lines connected at angles that may be slightly off ninety degrees, the percept derived is still a rectangle (Figure 6.2). The person is referencing the pure geometrical ideal to convey the instantaneous perception of an organized whole.[51] The feat of extracting the organizational structure of a phenomenon is a substantiation of the integral perceptual mechanism that enables cognitive thinking.[52] Environmental psychologists have concluded that refining our environmental data influences our cognitive process as well as our intellectual development. The presence of a perceived order in the human environment engenders positive emotional responses.[53]

An object can be recognized as a segregated entity but still be associated to another structure as a subordinate part. Principles of perceptual organization pertain to this hierarchical integration similarly to those used to obtain a segregated entity.[54] It is common for objects

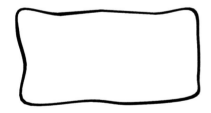

6.2

Figure 6.2. A hand-drawn rectangle.

to possess this twofold nature, one as a unit and the other as part of a pattern. That pattern can exist as a unit of a larger pattern and can have a dual nature as segregated entity and subordinated part.[55]

In the man-made world, a mechanistic type of order is prevalent. This order of the machine has an atomized structure that is clear but not necessarily integrated. In a mechanistic order a part can be removed without affecting the rest of the order. The perception of mechanistic order or rhythm of the machine is characterized by modularity. The use of modules has permeated the design process in part to create order and in part to be economical. Its aesthetic is one of units and series and relies on the effect of repeating forms. Another type of order prevalent in the world is organic order, which is derived from structures found in nature. The structure of these forms is reflective of the processes used to create them. They are characterized by a high degree of integration, where the addition or elimination of components has an effect that permeates throughout the organism. The rhythm of the organism has an overall unifying pattern, but within it there are fairly constant variations. The whole does not lose the essential unit of the pattern, and their organic rhythms are derived from a balanced relationship between pattern and variation.[56]

Order and Symmetry

One characteristic that demonstrates order to the visual perceptual system is geometric transformational symmetry. The presence of reflective, glide reflective, rotational, translational, or group symmetry is a universal marker of well-ordered perceptual wholes. Symmetry is a notable case of perceptual recognition because of the mutual completion derived from correlating objects that create organized wholes. A pair of objects is not just a quantity of items but a structured relationship that is diminished when the quantity is decreased and submerged when it is increased. Rudolf Arnheim employs the classic religious symmetrical configuration of two saints flanking the Madonna as a perceptually hierarchical structure that ingrains the work with intended meaning. The elimination or addition of another saint would not be a case of a segregated addition but would fundamentally alter the instilled meaning.

A local symmetrical structure, such the bilateral reflective symmetry of a flower petal, can be embedded within a higher-order symmetry, in this case, the radial symmetry of the petals around the stem. The presence of local symmetries in structures that exhibit tendencies of asymmetry facilitates the compositional goal of hitting the "sweet spot" of the order and surprise.[57]

Order and Pattern

The next level of perceptual recognition after segregated wholes is the detection of patterns. Behavioral patterns are ingrained into the human condition as the pattern of night and day, workweek and weekend, and seasonal as well as typical day patterns, that is, breakfast, lunch, and dinner at certain times. As a result of their generative self-organizing mandate, natural organisms and phenomena generate patterns in space and time. Visual patterns, denoted by regularity in some dimension inclusive of the scale dimension, are recommended to be utilized in child development, building on the human innate neurological structure.[58] The mind endeavors to organize information or even construct data when faced with random unknown visual information. When information becomes repetitive, the mind filters it and shifts to anticipating patterns. There are cognitive impulses for continuity and closure that suggest the preference for pattern, unity, or coherence in a configuration despite circumstances where these characteristics do not present themselves.[59] It is proposed that the human neurological infrastructure is configured to respond to particular local patterns existing in the sensory data formed on the retina. Neuropsychological experiments indicate that cells in the visual cortex respond to a variety of specific kinds of patterns.[60] The ability to create and detect patterns results from the influence of the environment on the evolution of our neural development. The neurological propensity toward pattern formation and generation mimics patterns found in nature. It is theorized that the evolution of the neurological and cognitive development resulted in an innate ability and need for pattern. This behavioral tendency is thought to be the externalization of connective structures developed in the mind during cognitive activity.[61]

In complex patterns, such as those found in fractals, information is revealed through different scales with interconnections between those levels of scale.[62] Discerning the order and interrelationships within the pattern appeals to our inherent perceptual propensity. The elements of a complex pattern can be diverse, with different sizes, shapes, orientations, and colors all existing in the same composition and held together by the order structuring the pattern (Figure 6.3).

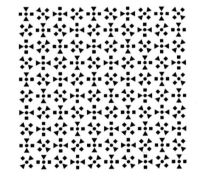

6.3

Figure 6.3. A pattern.

The whole is structured by this group of dependant parts to produce a pattern whose visual dynamics are more complex than shapes composing its parts.[63] Humans derive pleasure from perceiving patterns with increased complexity within the structure of the pattern which augments the initial gratification on perceiving order.[64]

Order and Nesting

Another order that is present in the natural environment is that arising from recursive growth processes. This order is characterized by self-similar symmetrically scaled forms and is associated with organic forms. These forms are structured so that the whole is nested within the initial stratum of structure. That level of structure is embedded in the next layer of structure and so on. This is a highly formulated field of elements that is readily perceived as an organized whole. The preponderance of this structure in the natural world significantly contributes to the perception of these structures as segregated entities.

The natural form of a tree, such as a pine tree (Figure 6.4), frequently has an overall perception of being symmetrical about the vertical axis. This perception is a general perception of the structure and epitomizes the concept of one type of symmetry, in which symmetry of scale or nested self-similarity is embedded in the overall percept of bilateral symmetry. These nested natural self-similar structures are not carbon copies of the exact angles and scaling factors. The variables for scaling and angles of growth typically fit within a relatively tight range inherent in the genetics of the natural forms DNA. These variables can be influenced by environmental variables to go outside these ranges, but left to themselves, they tend to stay within these ranges, which contributes to the character of each species. The natural structures are characterized by an order that percolates throughout the structure, achieving the perceptual and cognitive goal of organization and variation.

Perception and Relationships

The various levels of visual perception's organizational strata have a common thread of relationship running through them. Visual objects come about as configurations of perceivable forces. These relationships are not normally consciously perceived but affect and structure our awareness.[65] A dot with dimension is essentially perceived as a sphere that is a configuration of forces radiating out from and drawn toward a

6.4

Figure 6.4. A pine tree.

gravitational center, also known as *local symmetry*. This local symmetry is an aggregation of visual force relationships within the sphere. When another dot of equal dimension is placed close by, a new group of relationships is formed, the local symmetry of the second dot and the force vector that is established between the two dots linking them in a relationship such as that indicated in Figure 6.5. The strength of the relationship between the two element dots in this case is a function of the nature of the elements of the relationship, the nature of the structure of the relationship, their degree of similarity in topology, and the spatial distance of the elements:

6.5

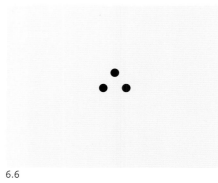

6.6

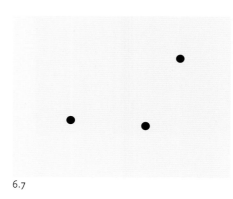

6.7

Figure 6.5. Two dots.
Figure 6.6. Three dots in a triangle.
Figure 6.7. Three haphazard dots.

- If the elements that comprise the relationship are strong, independent elements, they radiate visual energy more forcefully. The degree of visual force radiating from the elements affects the strength of the relationship between them.
- If the structure of the relationship is clearly perceivable—in this case, a clear horizontal link—the relationship is strong. If we add another dot between the two and displace vertically, as indicated in Figure 6.6, the triangular structure of the relationship is clearly perceived, resulting in a strong overall relationship. If we add another dot haphazardly, as in Figure 6.7, the relationship between the entities is diminished.
- As articulated in Gestalt theory, shape similarity is a strong variable in establishing relationship strength. In Figure 6.8 we have a pair of dots and a square. The relationship between the dots is stronger than the relationship between the dots and the square owing to similarity.
- The amount of space between the objects in a relationship affects the amount of independence or interdependence of the elements in a relationship. The relationship of the dots in the upper part of Figure 6.9 is a strong bond fitting in a subordinating relationship, while the relationship of the dots in the lower half is weaker as a mere affiliation.

Equilibrium is achieved when the constellation of forces in a dynamic interplay counterbalance each other. This constellation of forces can act as a complex hierarchy of weights related through coordination, integration and subordination. The perception of this composition and conclusion as to its state of equilibrium is intuitive.[66] The discernment of the nature of the visual relationships that is the understanding of the visual structure is the precursor for cognitive activity.[67] Through this comprehension we grasp the raison d'être of the inner structure.

The Nature of Order and Life

In addition to considering the methods of perception, we contemplate the perceptual mechanisms that produce emotional responses. In his *Nature of Order* series, Christopher Alexander asserts that there is a quality he terms *life* that we experience to some degree in all things living and inert. It exists in both natural and man-made environments and is the feeling that arises, according to Alexander, when

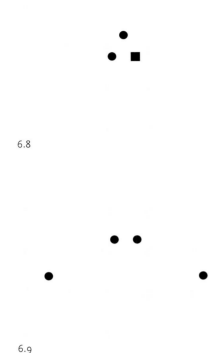

6.8

6.9

we are "drunk with God," blithe and unfettered. Free of imposed concepts, ideas, and mores, we respond to the enriching condition we perceive.[68] This type of perception is intuitive rather than analytical per se, connecting with innate ideals and related emotional reactions. It is more instinctive for children and more so-called primitive cultures but less intuitive for atomized societies. In these cultures, which function in a more bottom-up methodology, this level of perceptual awareness resides in a more unconscious state. As members of these societies retreat from the onrush of daily activity to the comfort of nature, this mode of perception advances to the forefront, bringing, then, positive effects to the perceiver.[69] Alexander analogizes the effect of entities that exhibit life to that of the effect of trace elements in humans. They are a low percentage of the body's intake, but they enable the construction of critical enzymes that then cause crucial processes of protein synthesis. The trace elements play a catalytic role in physiological processes. Similarly, entities that exhibit life, such as a beautiful arrangement of flowers (Figure 6.10), are the root of the intellectual, emotional, and physical benefits discussed earlier.[70]

This experience is a result of immersing oneself in the "huge ocean" of the connective human consciousness that distinguishes humans from a simple, sophisticated computational mechanism through the geyser of meaning.[71] The experiences that engender appreciation or "liking" are linked to the degree of life inherent in the objects viewed. They project qualities that innately connect to humans and make them increasingly "whole" and increase the quality of "life" within them. This causes a recursive cycle between the experience and the observer, augmenting the perception of life from outside and the feeling of life within.[72]

Alexander provides a number of examples that immediately link the reader with a connection to this intuitive experience. A grouping of flowers in a vase, a birthday cake in the middle of a table, and a collection of violinists practicing their craft all radiate life, whether it be through their inherent geometry, their color, their organizational arrangement, or their movement. They all animate the space around them. He also uses comparative examples such as two sets of windows, one a typical builder's double-hung window (Figure 6.11) and one an articulated stained glass window (Figure 6.12). Across cultures, people perceive the stained glass window to possess more life and appreciate it more than the builder's double-hung window.

Figure 6.8. Two dots and a square.
Figure 6.9. Two pairs of dots.

6.10

Figure 6.10. Flower arrangement.

6.11

6.12

Nesting and Living Structure

Christopher Alexander has premised his *Nature of Order* series on the concept of living structure and the subsequent perception of wholeness and life. The concept of nested configuration is fundamental to the concept of living structure. Living structure can be envisioned as a vector field with vectors emanating from and going toward points known as centers. Centers are defined by their appearance as areas of organization within a larger field. Because of their structure, their internal coherence, they are focused entities that radiate force vectors but at the same time exist as centers because of their relationship to other elements within the field of forces.[73] These centers are products of fields of other centers that are created in a recursive process that reinforces the level of centers at the preceding hierarchical level. The process that provides living structure consists of structure-preserving transformations. The relationship between levels both up and down is reciprocal, with each level reinforcing the other. The strength and intensity of centers is a global property as opposed to a local attribute of the center itself. The system of nested centers created through recursion and the consequential field of visual forces constitute living structure. Alexander terms this generative algorithmic process *unfolding structure* and produces the geometric character of living structure. The perception of living structure gives rise to the cognitive and emotional

Figure 6.11. Builder's double-hung window.
Figure 6.12. Articulated stained glass window.

169

experience of wholeness, which leads to the perception of life within the object being viewed.

The concept of living structure and centers is equivalent to fractal structures. They are both created through recursion, with the concept of centers corresponding to the fractal concept of points of attraction. The structure of relationships within a fractal form that both cascades from the whole and springs up through the parts epitomizes living structure. Fractal structure has been cited as a fundamental structure of nature that, for humans, exudes life. It can be reasonably concluded, either through Alexander's analysis or the general correlation of fractals with nature, that the perception of a fractal structure denotes life. Humans are continually exposed to natural fractal configurations present in everyday life and have an unconscious recognition and affiliation embedded in their perceptual system. The structure of the nervous system is configured to identify forms that exhibit fractal characteristics as significant, organized wholes.

COGNITION

Introduction to Cognition

The perceptual image is a significant but incomplete whole of the object. To make sense of the data derived from the process of perception, humans derive meaning and understanding through the process of cognition. This process is continuous and automatic and, as discussed for perception, can be thought of as data compression or optimization. The human brain is able to distinguish complex objects, such as a pine tree (Figure 6.13) from a maple tree (Figure 6.14), within a second. The analysis of a tree's structure through classical geometry is very difficult as compared to the analysis of the structure on a fractal basis. As will be indicated in chapter 10, on the convergence of nature and computation, the elemental fractal code for these trees can be compressed into a compact schema for extremely efficient encoding for the brain.[74] Encoding refers to the process of acquiring information and transferring it to memory.[75] It is proposed that the methodology by which natural forms are encoded is substantially based on the characteristics of their fractal structure, and other structures composed similarly provide analogous retrieval cues because of the presence of fractal geometry.

Cognitive ability confers competitive advantage and is linked to

6.13

6.14

the ability to function in social and human organizational situations. Michael Polyani has defied the perceptual-cognitive relationship as perception finds clues, locates parts, and discovers other subsidiary elements, and cognition connects them to a focally apprehended, comprehensive entity.[76] It is the indispensable unification of a precept to a concept, each of which cannot exist without the other. This link between perception and cognition occurs through abstraction.[77]

Humans can be viewed as information processing systems. The cognitive operations of active exploration, selection, grasping of essentials, simplification, abstraction, analysis and synthesis, completion, correction, comparison, combining, separating, and putting into context are the methodologies by which the human mind processes material throughout its various levels, inclusive of perception. These operations are initiated by field processes in the brain that organize the sensory data according to the simplest pattern compatible with them. The percepts are referential to the conceptual type of pattern their organization or structure accords with in memory or as ingrained through evolution within the neural circuitry.[78] The process can be characterized as visual input to a receptor of sensory data which is then outputted as a corresponding array of symbols stored in memory and a recording of qualitative and quantitative attributes.[79] The effectiveness of this process involves the meaningful encoding of the sensory data. Graphic representations are particularly effective in facilitating encoding and storage of information in memory.[80]

Figure 6.13. A pine tree.
Figure 6.14. A maple tree.

Cognitive Neuroscience

Cognitive neuroscience focuses on the biological substrate underlying cognition, in particular, the neural circuitry of cognitive processes. In neural processing, the synaptic firing due to the release of excitatory or inhibitory neurotransmitters has shown that certain neurons are specialized to react to certain stimuli. These cells react not only to pictures of things or people but to different depictions of them, suggesting that these cells were responding to the abstract concept of the thing stored in memory.[81] The information contained in the network of neural firing is the neural code of image, concept, or idea. This has also been termed *distributed coding* as the process is the result of distributed cooperation between many neurons.[82]

In research cosponsored by the University of California, Los Angeles and Tel Aviv University, brain cells were recorded in the act of summoning a spontaneous memory. Relative to the neural pathways of the brain, it appears that remembering is very similar to experiencing the event. The memories were located in some of the same neurons that fired with the most intensity when the event occurred. The researchers recorded the neural firing activity of approximately one hundred neurons per person concentrated in and around the hippocampus, a sliver of the brain known to be crucial in forming memories. The subjects were exposed to five- to ten-second clips of television shows and imagery such as animals or famous landmarks. After switching the attention of the subjects, the researchers asked them to think about the clips and tell them what came to mind. In recalling specific videos, such as one with Homer Simpson, the same cells that were activated during the viewing of that clip were reignited. These cells were not acting on their own but rather were part of a neural circuit pathway responding to the videos.[83] It is theorized that a similar phenomenon occurs when humans are exposed to objects structured according to fractal geometry. The neural circuitry that is fired is similar to that which is fired when experiencing natural objects. The perception of the scaled self-similar structure in each object causes similar neural pathways to be used, which cause analogous physical, cognitive, and emotional effects.

Cognition, Understanding, and Meaning

The psychological process whereby concepts are related to the neural data derived from retinal activity is termed *understanding*. It is the methodology of resolving the manifold of sensory information through apperception and tendencies hardwired through evolution. The process of understanding creates a conceptual unity from the multiplicity of sensory information. By understanding a visual object, we comprehend its nature and character through its organization of relationships. Understanding can be conceived of as an act of interpretation. Interpretation is actively receptive rather than projective and can be illustrated through the reading of text. This interpretation does not force the text into the mold of the reader's personality or his or her previous knowledge. The understanding of the text "passes through" and consists of the whole text. The whole text is not the same as the totality of the text. The totality of the text is not necessarily required to understand it and derive its meaning. That is accomplished through the progressive discernment of the text by which at some point its meaning is understood.[84] Closely linked to understanding and emanating from it is meaning. Meaning is manifested when the mosaic of sensations through emergent behavior coalesce into a coordinated whole in an act of self-organization. In this process, percepts are associated with concepts radiating awareness. We exist in a world of meaning rather than sensory objects. This assemblage of meaning is inherent in the objects and phenomena populating the environment.[85] As the sensory information emanating from a fractal form is processed from perception, the observer interprets the perceived relationships and understands their nature as organic. This meaning is a direct result of the relationships embedded in the sensory data.

Cognitive Information Processing

Cognitive psychology focuses on the storage and retrieval of cognitive information more generally known as memory. A prevalent theory of memory is labeled *stage theory*, developed from the work of Richard Atkinson and Richard Shriffin. The stage theory model proposes that the information is processed and stored in three stages: sensory memory, short-term memory, and long-term memory. In the initial stage of sensory memory, the information in sensory data is changed from the various forms of sensory energy into another, electrical energy that the brain can understand. This process is called *transduction*, and through this procedure a very short memory is created. This information is more likely to be transferred to the next stage of memory if it is of interest and if the stimulus activates a known pattern. The information is then passed on to short-term memory, which is also called *working memory*, and relates to what we are thinking at the moment. Information retention in short-term memory is influenced by repetition and organization and is transmitted to long-term memory. Within long-term memory, information is organized according to one or more of the structures of declarative memory, procedural memory (how to drive a car), and imagery. Declarative memory is bifurcated into episodic memory, consisting of unique personal experiences, and semantic memory, made up of facts and generalized information. Semantic memory is structured by schemata (data structures or networks of connected ideas or relationships for organizing the parts of experience into a meaningful system), propositions (interconnected set of concepts and relationships), scripts (declarative knowledge structure that captures general information regarding routine or recurrent activities), frame (complex conceptual organization that provides a reference within which stimuli and actions are judged), scheme (organization of concepts and principles that define a perspective and provide specific action patterns to follow), program (set of rules governing actions in particular situations), paradigm (basic way of perceiving and thinking associated with a particular vision of reality), and model (based on a paradigm, a set of propositions or equations that describe in a simplified form an aspect of experience).[86]

Long-term memory can be envisioned as being built by linking new images and concepts to ones previously stored in memory. Similar to a coral reef, it builds by adding new branches and cross ties to the edges of portions already established and anchored as the central portion settles and coalesces. This view is similar to the node-link model of learning in which nodes are concepts such as *dog, red, bark, above ground, running,* and *teeth.* Each node is linked to certain other nodes so that the activation of certain nodes will pull together the relevant group of nodes. New sensory data cause a widening circle of nodes and links in search for similarities until they find the best categories or analogies previously stored in long-term memory.[87]

Cognition and Recall

Information from memory is accessed through recall and association. In *association,* a bond is formed between phenomena that enables us to recall the first phenomenon when the second is experienced.[88] The properties, structure, and organization of visually segregated entities, through association, bring forth "facts" from memory.[89] If I hear a tone and then a few seconds later hear a second tone with the same pitch but sufficiently louder, I experience it as a specific reference to something in the past, not as a separate event. The trace of the first tone is not similar in all respects, but what is left in memory of the first tone must be sufficiently similar to bring forth the association.[90] The traces of the organizational processes are themselves organized entities that are subject to recall. Recall about organization is more persistent than retention of individual facts. Humans are able to recall the general structure of things even though they cannot recall the particulars about the object.[91] Recall is restricted to instances in which there is congruence between a portion of the properties of the entity considered and a portion of the properties of the original event. There is a correspondence or similarity between the present entity and at least a natural part or subwhole of the original configuration. If you draw a line down the profile of a face from the apex of the nose to the top of the chin, the line does not correspond to a complete subwhole of a face; however, because the line is visually similar to the whole profile, the process of cognition associated with that line corresponds to the process that underlies the cognition of the profile as a complete visual shape stimulating recall.[92] Because of their self-similar organizational structure, objects created through fractal geometry cause a recall of other objects organized in a similar manner. These objects are the many natural forms that display a fractal structure either obviously or subtly.

Identification occurs when there is an insistent reinforcement of the signifier and referent, also known as *strong penetration* and typified by religious symbols (Figure 6.15). Trademarks also demonstrate this phenomenon. An effective trademark, by the identification of relevant structural properties, interprets the character of the wearer by associating it with the distinctive defined pattern of visual forces. Any design has dynamic qualities that contribute to the characterization of the object. The dynamics inherent in an Impressionist landscape that invoke certain emotions, however, are quite different than those associated with the depiction of a swastika.[93] This association relies on the similarity of the inherent pattern and relation of the visual forces in which the organizational processes leave traces. The strength of association is dependent on the strength of the organization of these forces. It is regarded as a bond between two entities that causes the recall of the first when presented with the second. When these two objects become associated, they are not experienced as two totally independent things but as members or types of a group or category. The unitary experience demonstrates that a functional unit is formed in the neurological physiology in which the objects are relatively segregated

6.15

subunits.[94] The association of natural forms whose structure has been found to be fractal in nature and man-made artifacts structured by fractal geometry is cognitively considered as an isomorphism. In an isomorphism, there is a mapping of elements of a set—in this case, natural forms—to another set such as structures generated by fractal geometry. The similarity of form and the underlying structural governing principles invoke a correspondence or association, triggering similar physiological reactions.

Cognition and Category/Type

A significant structure of memory is based on the concepts of category and type. A category is a general or comprehensive division or class in which a group of things exhibits common characteristics. It is a structural or ontological distinction of general concepts resulting in a grouping of entities discrete from other entities based on their attributes and properties. The idea of family resemblance, where things in a category resemble one another in a number of critical ways, has been used to illustrate the concept of categories.[95] Entities that possess

Figure 6.15. Religious cross.

176

6.16a

6.16b

6.16c

6.16d

Figure 6.16. Archetypal cars; a. Mustang; b. Thunderbird; c. Volkswagon; d. Rolls Royce.

these attributes, properties, and characteristics of a class or category are called *types* of that category. Within a category, many variations can occur. Categorization is based on comparing the attributes of an object to standard representations of the category through the prototypical approach or the exemplar methodology. In the prototypical approach, the category members we have encountered in the past are averaged together to form a prototype. The exemplar approach compares the object to an object experienced in the past that exemplifies the attributes of the members of that category.[96]

Under the category of "people" are countless different forms of people who nonetheless have a commonality of attributes that puts them in that class or category. The word *car* stimulates memory to organize the complex network of relations within that category to bring forward into working memory the many types of cars or, for that person, the archetype of cars (Figure 6.16).[97] Natural forms are characterized by certain attributes such as their fractal structure, which is perceived instantly and subconsciously. This mode of perception provides an intuitive sense of structures that are appropriate or not appropriate to a given situation. When we see a square tree, we instantly know that something is wrong. Our sense of what is right and wrong depends on the subtle and detailed awareness of the kinds of structure that are appropriate and natural in a given situation.[98] Natural structures are a category characterized by their organic form developed through the principles of fractal geometry. On observing other forms with the same characteristic geometry, such as structures generated by fractal geometry, there is a conscious or unconscious association of that form to the category of natural structures.

SUMMARY

Humans receive sensory images emanating from natural objects, filtering them according to innate and learned criteria and consolidating the information for rapid and simple processing. In visual perception, shape is a conclusive determinant of how data are processed. The geometry of natural objects has a distinct shape derived from its unique geometrical structure that is equally discernible from top-down or bottom-up processing. The geometry of natural forms has unique qualities, such as symmetry and nesting patterns that provide a distinct order. The nature of the interdependent relationships in nature's diverse structures associates a cognitive quality of "life" with them. As sensory data from natural forms are transformed into electromagnetic impulses, they travel pathways to regions of the brain that are controlled by cognitive activities of recall and association of similar categories or types. Compositions other than nature's forms that display the same geometrical structure are processed in a similar manner as the sensory data received from natural objects. A person perceives an architectural form generated by fractal geometry and, although there are significant differences stemming from its obvious man-made quality, processes the data in a similar manner because of the overriding quality of their shape. As the form is to some degree placed in the same category as natural objects, it receives the same positive values as objects associated with nature.

CHAPTER **7**   **The Universal Quality of Fractal Expression**

The intrinsic power of nature as an influential factor in people's lives comes from its embodiment as one of the few clearly discernible manifestations of universals. Man has sought universal truths as a connection to the world beyond his comprehension. By their nature, universals are abstract entities, and fractal architecture extends the trajectory that starts with natural forms, traveling through abstraction to universal truths to go back through abstraction to manifest in the fractal structure.

UNIVERSALS

The concept of *universals* was first proposed in early Greek civilization by Plato in his theory of forms. For Plato, there were two kinds of forms: the *outward form*, which is the appearance of an object, and the idea or *Form* of the object. The forms we see are shadows of and mimic the idea of the Form or archetype of the many types we see around us. Form is the essence of an object without which the object would not be the kind of object it is. It is the true basis of reality beyond space and time and the most pure of all things. True knowledge is achieved by understanding the world of Forms: objective blueprints of perfection. A square drawn on a piece of paper may be imperfect, but the intelligibility of the Form square lets us understand the form as a square (Figure 7.1). Aristotle believed that the Form or universal existed within each object, affirming the existence of the universal. He conceived of universals as types, properties, and relations common

7.1

Figure 7.1. A hand-drawn square.

179

to the various instances of it. They exist only when they are initiated and subsist within the object. For Aristotle, a universal is engendered when we abstract a property from a family of instances.

The empirical reality that we experience through the senses is part of an integrated dual entity. It consists of the particular, individual physical instance and the ideal, universal nature that it represents.[1] The universal and the particular are reciprocally determinative as to some degree they both appear within and through each other. The universal appears through the particular, from which it is inseparable as a symbol.[2] In a moment of intuitive perception, the universal is seen within the particular, and in doing so, the particular instance is grasped as a living instance of the universal, a symbol of the universal. In a fractal sense, the whole is represented in the part. The whole, the universal, cannot appear until the part, the instance, is apprehended, but the part cannot be understood without the whole.[3]

A concept becomes a universal when it is thought to be standing for a population of instances.[4] It is abstracted when it is viewed as a distillate derived from the nature of an object or objects. This distillate can be the abstract pattern of forms or forces constituting the object. Owing to its abstract nature, the pattern becomes a generality representing the nature of the object.[5] The correlation between abstraction and generalization is related to the process of induction, whereby principles and concepts are determined through the observation and synthesis of a number of instances.[6] In this process, an attribute is perceived as constituting the essence of the object.

Christopher Alexander has proposed a set of fifteen transformations that produce living structure by which wholeness and life are perceived. The fifteen transformations are instances or forms of the Form wholeness. He considers that these transformations constitute the basis of a universal form language that, when continually iterated, will recursively embed itself in the geometry of the form.[7] This generative process produces an emergent structure through which "the light of the universe shines."[8]

The quality of being universal is closely tied to the concept of an archetype. As autonomous structures within Carl Jung's universal unconscious, they embody the universal qualities of an idea in a conceptual form. Goethe based a significant portion of his work on the archetypal concept of *Urpflanze,* which is the singular ultimate plant form from which all other plant forms are derived (Figure 7.2). The sense of a plant's holistic unity points toward its archetype.[9]

Goethe strove for the complex formative principles that organize the plant, what makes it what it is, the principle by which a natural form evokes in us the idea that this is a plant.[10] He saw a genetic connection between these forms, sensing the same fundamental code continually transforming itself from plant to plant.[11] This principle or set of principles is what constitutes the archetypal plant. This genetic basis functioned as the general blueprint of plants and provides the source for the inherent unity among the diversity of plant forms.[12] Conceptually, this supports the notion of nature's order, which can be intuited by humans as a universal.

The individual modifications of the diversity of plants are expressions of the archetypal organism taking on the form most suitable for its fitness in the environment. The external conditions of the environment are the only influences for the inner formative forces to develop in a particular way. These forces are the constitutive principle of the plant.[13] Their varied manifestations of the plant's generative principle caused by the environment and climate are manifold expressions of the plant's formative potential.[14] The outward form may change in infinite ways, but the formative principle remains the same.[15] The concept of Plant exists in an endless variety of plants of different colors, shapes, sizes, and gestures. It is inherent in each plant, but it is not identical with any one specimen.[16] The essence of an archetypal essentiality must, by virtue of its inherent inner necessity, develop content out of itself, which then manifests itself in the empirical environment as a form.[17] As the self-structuring tenet at the foundation of every phenomenon, one prioritizes its recognition in studying the phenomenon.[18]

Fractal geometry is closely affiliated with natural forms on a conscious or unconscious level. As the basis for the structure of natural forms, fractal geometry can be considered as the *Urpflanze* of natural forms. Its generative algorithm is the basis from which many natural forms are constituted. Its geometric structure is the archetypal configuration for natural form. Forms composed utilizing it embed this archetypal quality within them in the same manner as Alexander's transformations create living structure. The cognitive association of this archetypal structure is the perceptual trigger that causes humans to perceive universal values associated with nature.

The inherent character of nature and its fundamental value to humans makes the derivation of the essence of its underlying creative principles and attributes intrinsically significant. In his influential book *A New Kind of Science*, Stephen Wolfram suggested that there

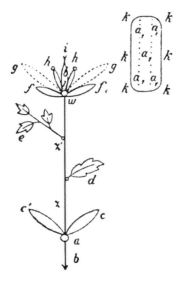

7.2

Figure 7.2. Goethe's *Urpflanze*, an archetypal plant form from which all other plant forms come.

are universal processes that occur throughout nature. He observes an expected tendency to assume that these are a result of an underlying mechanism that is itself complex. His research, however, concludes that simple functions can and do produce complexity and that capability is the basis for universality. In his study of natural systems, he noted that even when they have different underlying physical, biological, or other essential determining components, the overall pattern of the system's behavior is often quite similar.

This view was spawned from his fluency with computers, where universal systems with fixed underlying rules can be formulated to perform a vast range of computations. From this experience, he has proposed that the phenomenon of universality was immensely more pervasive in abstract systems and in nature.[19] Given the analogous behavior between computational systems and natural systems, Wolfram proposed that each system's behavior can be studied and analyzed. It does not matter whether the components are real molecules or the conceptual black-and-white squares of cellular automatica as the overall behavior should show the same universal features. The mechanisms that are responsible for the phenomena in nature correspond to phenomena in simple programs.[20]

Wolfram notes that a significant majority of the complex morphological structures in nature derive their form from the arrangement of a very limited number of types of cells and elements. The morphological principle whereby structures evolve according to rules that maximize their fitness is the determining factor for their development. This correlates to the belief that any significant property of an organism exists to maximize the fitness of it. Wolfram asserts that the complexity we see in nature originated in randomly chosen simple programs that gave rise to complex behavior.[21] The nature of the generative laws is responsible for the ubiquitous property of the nature's emergent behavior. Wolfram puts forward the theory of computational equivalence, which is applicable to any process, natural or artificial, to establish universality. A universal system has a fixed underlying construction but can perform a variety of tasks by being programmed in different ways.[22] With a universal system, a suitable encoding of the initial conditions, the behavior of other systems can be emulated.[23] A system exhibits the quality of universality if its exhibited behavior is computationally irreducible, which holds that a system cannot be shortcutted or its behavior described in a simpler way. Purely repetitive or nested systems can be described or analyzed as simpler structures, and hence their generative laws cannot be universal. Systems that exhibit behavior that appears to be computationally irreducible display what appears to be a blend of random compositions within which localized structures are present, straddling the line between order and disorder.

According to the definition of computational irreducibility, fractal geometry is a universal system. It has a fixed structure that can be encoded in numerous ways to produce an abundance of diverse forms. Its computational structure cannot be described in any simpler way. Structures generated with fractal geometry can be perceptibly simple and described in simpler terms. That caveat should not preclude fractal geometry from being considered as a universal system as complex and perceptibly irreducible structures can be generated. Forms based on fractal geometry involving various scaling, rotational, and skewing transformations perceptually display the universal characteristic of striding the line between order and disorder. The vast universe of natural forms that can be generated by fractal geometry is a testament to its validation as a universal computational system. Wolfram's thesis is in large part based on the universality of systems that create structures and systems found in nature. It should be no surprise that the geometry used to describe nature's behavior should be considered universal.

UNIVERSALS AND ABSTRACTION

The visualization of universals is frequently performed through abstraction. Rudolf Arnheim, a noted perceptual psychologist, provides in his book *Visual Thinking* a number of readily understandable examples of abstraction that are utilized in our daily lives:

- Owing to the diverse nature of mankind, no one man can serve as an abstraction of the human race. Humanity can be abstracted through the presentation of a number of people who embody the nature of all or many groups of people in significant respects. The nature of a significant portion of the U.S. government is based on this concept. The members of Congress are not intended to be a sample of the American people but an abstraction of it. They are considered to possess the capacity to enact laws that are representative of the views of the population they represent. Their actions are an abstraction of the wishes of their constituency.[24]
- Nagasaki was the second city in Japan to be hit with an atomic bomb in World War II. On a hill at the bomb site, there is a display

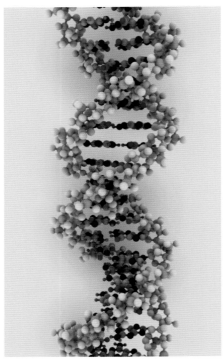

7.3

of old-fashioned mangled clocks and watches. This collection, all of which stopped at the time of the explosion at 11:02 A.M., serves as an abstraction to transmit the enormity of a concerted end of time and death of a large population of human beings. As it is an essential element of the event, it conveys a clear understanding of its significance. An essential aspect of the event elicits the significance of the event.[25]

- When you describe a person as a cold person, it evokes an inclusive representation of the kind of behavior you can expect from that person. The generative power of abstraction is demonstrated, as from this one "universal" attribute, a spectrum of behavior is spawned. This generative power is acquired because the attribute is a central one. Productive abstraction is concerned with description of structural or elemental properties rather than traits or peripheral qualities. The coldness of a stove is self-contained while the coldness of a person is an expansive overall quality that permeates throughout a person's behavior.[26]

- Newton's discovery of gravity by observing the fall of an apple was a distinct intellectual accomplishment. Newton was able to abstract the gravitational pull on the apple as a universal enduring value and applied it in a similar context to the bodies in the solar system gravitating to their common centers. In extracting the similarities from the dissimilar, abstraction incorporates the contextual factors from which the similarities were drawn.[27]

ABSTRACTION AND NATURE

Artists have used various methodologies for abstracting natural forms. Wind and water are abstracted by their movement expressed as curved and waved form lines. Energy forms and magnetic fields have been depicted by a series of spinning waves that represent radiation patterns. The spiral has been elemental in the expression of organic forms such as shells, and when extended in third dimension, it forms a helix that represents the very basis of life: the DNA structure (see Figure 7.3). It also represents the distribution of plant leaves and tree branches. Bare winter trees exhibit distinct types of branching structures that can be abstracted to convey the general type of tree. A related device integrating two curved arms drawn inward to a mutual center in which both arms turn represents a diverse group of natural phenomena such as hurricanes, ocean currents, sunflower seed patterns, and the spiral form of galaxies. Again, when expanded in the third dimension,

Figure 7.3. The double helix of DNA.
Figure 7.4. Vortex pattern in morning-glory growth.

7.4

a vortex form is generated that occurs in diverse natural phenomena such as water forms, tornados, and plant forms such as the morning glory (see Figure 7.4).[28]

Abstracting nature was a major component of Frank Lloyd Wright's architectural identity. Wright stated in one of his lectures that "design is the abstraction of nature's elements in purely geometric terms." On the basis of the abstraction of nature, his buildings grew similarly to a plant's morphogenesis, resulting in an internal harmony from the whole to the details of his ornamentation.[29]

The key to understanding the conceptual space between the structure of the forms we see in the natural environment and its use in generating architectural forms that provoke strong positive emotions similar to those experienced with natural forms lies in the concept of abstraction. Friedrich Schiller analyzed Goethe's archetypal plant and its essential nature and further abstracted it to the concept of an idea. In this analysis, the student detects the connections and relationships, such as the part-to-whole-to-part relationship, among the perceptual qualities of the environment's sensory mosaic. The phenomena that are caused by these relationships necessary for their existence are characterized as archetypal phenomena.[30] A spiritual unity is sensed at the foundation of archetypal phenomena that is the source of the relationship between the various facets of the phenomena.[31]

An archetypal phenomenon is manifested when the act of one sensory perception inevitably forms the source of another sensory perception. This relationship is the basis for natural law. The perception of heat and the causal effect of expansion forms a relationship identified as an archetypal phenomenon and expressed as natural law. The experience of drawing a magnet toward metal forms an indelible identity relationship between the two. Archetypal phenomena express the most universal relationships in nature.[32] Goethe searched for the universal principles that spawn the diversity of forming granite before it becomes granite or as another potentiality in slate before it becomes slate. It is a central archetypal phenomenon that manifests itself in the sensory world and accounts for the diversity of forms that spring from this principle.[33]

The concept of *Urphanomen* signifies the perceiving and cognizing being forming a binding unity with objects of cognition. In perceiving the archetypal phenomenon, the crucial nexus of factors that are required for the phenomenon to take place are made apparent. The event can be derived from the essential conditions that constitute the archetypal phenomenon and cannot occur if one of those factors is removed. It is a Goethian "pregnant point," a point where cognition is metaphysically alive, where understanding is brought forth out of itself much like the blossom is brought forth from the branch.[34] As one perceives a structure organized according to fractal geometry, *Ur-phanomen* is achieved by connecting the form to the universal concept of nature. The configuration of fractal forms embeds the archetypal structure of natural entities.

ENTELECHY

Living things develop by entelechy, which is a dynamic purpose and organizing field encoded within living things themselves. Its development is the act of becoming itself, having its essential potential fully actualized. It is the entelechy of a seed to be a plant, of a caterpillar to be a butterfly, and of a baby to be an adult. The idea of an organism works dynamically within the organism as its entelechy integrated by the paramount characteristic of unity.[35] The successive stages of becoming are all emergent from this unity. The entelechial principle unfolds its generative function according to a common formative principle. This common formative principle, what makes a plant a plant, is active in each of the parts as it is active in the whole.[36] Goethe's participatory scientific approach integrated the identification of the entity, which represented the entelechy of the organism, and traced it through its unfolding and the subsequent manifestations. In participating in the organism's process, he learned of its hidden laws, "nature's open secrets," and grasped the unifying idea that is present in all of its manifestations.[37] The understanding of this unifying principle manifested from the whole to the parts and from the parts to the whole is the discernment of the structural principles of the organism's entelechy. Universal entelechial principles are manifested in the sensory world by the archetypal phenomenon. The source of archetypal phenomena is the entelechy of the organism or phenomenon.

The entelechial principle within an organism or phenomenon is its essence. It is the lawfulness inherent within an organism that makes it what it is, the life that unfolds from itself in a diverse range of forms that are unified by the underlying principle.[38] To truly understand the organism, we have to grasp the underlying principle or its essence. In understanding an organism's form, while the evident characteristics are inevitably influential, they should not be thought of as responsible for the form's creation. The inconstancy, the continual varying of the external characteristics, leads to the search for its fundamental principle or essence at a deeper level. Separating the changing and mutable characteristics of an organism from the constant and enduring element of an organism results in the form's essence.[39] Goethe searched for the essential nature of the plant itself, what makes a plant a plant, the oneness in the manifold of forms.[40]

The nature of the inquiry into the inherent unity subsisting within an organism or phenomenon is essentially an abstract analysis of its nature. Organisms and phenomena are revelations of an idea that is their essential nature. The epistemological search for the fundamental nature of something is inherently abstract. By definition, abstraction is the act of drawing the essentials of a phenomenon to understand its essential nature.[41] Environmental formalism maintains that aesthetic appreciation of nature should focus on those aspects that constitute the form of an object. These "formal" qualities are whether they are unified or disorganized, balanced or uneven, harmonious or discordant and are a result of the objects' shapes, patterns, and designs. The components of a natural environment are abstracted relative to their individual form and how they relate to one another.[42] Perceptual abstraction is a positive realization of precision owing to the explicit nature of the elements derived from source material.[43] Components of abstract representation include line, shape-form-mass, pattern, scale-proportion-space, lightness-darkness, and color.[44] A natural environment is judged aesthetically pleasing if the abstracted qualities are perceived, consciously or unconsciously, as being concordant, composed, and having an elusive unity in variety.[45]

Rudolf Arnheim noted that the outcome of an abstraction is a smaller quantity, the entity's essence, containing the power and virtue of a greater quantity. To extract the principle unequivocally, we must identify the relevant factors by isolating them from the context of the total organism or phenomenon and discern what these aspects contribute and why their contributions produce the form or behavior.[46] The process of drawing essentials to understand the essence of an object requires that object to be an organized whole whereby there is a structure and a hierarchy such that certain aspects are essential and others secondary. The drawing of essentials produces an enlightening in the beholder by revealing the essential nature of the object. This correlates with cognitive behavior that endeavors to define things by what is important about them.[47] In the unity of perception and cognition, the sensory image of an object enhances the perception of its essence if the relevant features can be interpreted visually, revealing the forces underlying their appearance and behavior.[48]

Natural forms are composed of elements derived by the interaction of forces within themselves. These forces produce a composition that has an essential characteristic of self-similarity in a part-to-whole-to-part relationship. This distinguishing elemental quality points toward the essence of natural forms. It is manifested in nature by forms structured by fractal geometry. Abstracting of natural forms reveals an essence that is fractal in nature.

The essential quality that makes abstract forms organic is self-similarity in a part-to-whole-to-part relationship. In this self-reflective attribute, there are transformed copies of the whole in the parts of the total entity.[49] This holistic quality is the unifying principle of a significant portion of natural organisms and phenomena. The consequence of the part is that it shows the way to the whole; throughout the form there are traces that signify a higher unity. A part is a part only inasmuch as it lets the whole emerge; otherwise it is superfluous. A whole cannot emerge without the parts that constitute it. The emergence of the whole is dependent on the parts coming forth, which need the whole to be significant. The recognition of the part is possible through the "coming to presence" of the emergent whole, which occurs through the integration and unification of the parts. The process is termed the *unfolding of the enfolding* and is where the whole imparts itself through the parts it fulfills.[50]

An analogous phenomenon is the process of comprehending a sentence. We understand the meaning of a sentence when at a certain moment the letters and words coalesce and the whole is reflected in the parts, the letters and words, so that together they disclose the meaning of the whole. In this expository cycle, meaning is encountered in the circle of the reciprocal relationship of the whole and the parts.[51] When we read a written text, it is an act of interpretation. The reader is actively receptive and does not attempt to mold their understanding into the requirements of previous knowledge. The meaning of the text passes through to impart real meaning, which comes from the whole text. It is discerned and disclosed with a progressive indwelling through the text. We see the whole through the progressive integration of the parts. The whole emerges neither before nor after the parts. The parts show us the way to the whole and reinforce that the way to the whole is through the parts.

This dual sequence of cognition is demonstrated in the experience

189

of reading, where we move through the parts to enter into the whole that exists within the parts. In the process of understanding, both sequences come together. When we do not understand, we just pass through the parts, reading the sentences without understanding. To understand the text, we have to enter into it, which is initiated when we experience the meaning of the sentences. The whole is an active absence as we are not actively attempting to be aware of the whole but rather let ourselves be moved to the understanding of the whole. Absence can be understood by the analogy of a play. The actors are not separated from their parts as if they were objects but rather enter them similar to the way in which they enter the play. The play as a whole emerges within the parts so that the actors encounter the play through their parts. The genesis of acting becomes the play, and they enter into the play in such a way that the play speaks through them.[52]

ABSTRACTION AND STRUCTURE

A key element of abstraction is the visualization of relationships between figures. An abstract relation is perceived by grasping the structural features of the relationship between elements rather than noting indiscriminate details.[53] Analogously to the morphological concept of natural form from forces inherent in the function of natural organisms, visual abstraction can be regarded as the pattern of visual forces. An essential quality of abstraction is the capacity to reduce a theme visually to a skeleton of essential dynamic aspects. The minimal information contained in lines, colors, and shapes can convey with great precision the pattern of visual forces. In concentrating on its essential features, the perception of the object is intensified. The reduction of a human figure to a few lines configured appropriately can express through a gesture an emotional complexity.[54] The structure of the form's relationships provides the expression, movement, or gesture intended. A movement can be abstracted in a timeless image that crystallizes the nature of the complex action in one arresting configuration of forces. As the epitome of the deformations of the object, the abstraction represents a dynamic totality.[55]

The value of these simple, disembodied articulations of objects and phenomena is in the economy of their expression achieved by focusing on their underlying structure rather than material embellishments.[56] Visual images are presented in varying degrees of abstractness, but even the most abstract representation must be structurally similar or isomorphic to the pertinent features of the object or phenomenon it represents.[57] Perception is concerned with the grasping of consequential form, which is the perceptual bearer of meaning. The abstract discernment of the form's structural features is the fundamental nature of perception and the onset of cognition.[58] It is an essential function of cognitive logic to find unity in the multiplicity and create structures of elements and relations. When the abstraction, through the emulation of the phenomenon's structure, is accurate, new insight into the phenomenon is exposed by eliminating the unessential.[59] This relationship is closely related to the Gestalt concept of *Pragnanzstufen*, which holds that perceptual experiences are organized around phases of clear-cut structure. Concept formation is related to structural simplicity and the conservative power of visually economical shapes and relationships.[60] In the pattern of visual forces as a whole, an intuition emerges through an ordering phenomenon whereby a "phenomenon of a higher kind" is made transparent through its underlying structure.[61]

Natural morphology is controlled by a "natural law" or underlying determining agent responsible for the form's manifestation.[62] That natural form is an expression of a higher level of consciousness embodied in its organization and configuration. A Goethian axiom, "the beautiful is a manifestation of the hidden laws of nature,"[63] can be realized through the morphological structure of the natural form. The abstraction of natural objects utilizes the same essential concept of structural configuration as the generator of relevant meaning.[64] As a structure is a set of perceived relationships, the structure of natural forms is a set of perceived relationships inherent in nature. These relationships can be expressed as geometric structures such as the logarithmic spiral, radial symmetry, or fractal geometry.[65]

Fractal geometry has the unique ability to portray the relationships in nature over a broad range of phenomena. In understanding a natural form, an abstraction of its geometric structure is achieved whose signified meaning is transposed to other forms with a similar structure.[66] The conscious or subconscious awareness of the presence of fractal geometry in the natural environment and the emotional, physical, and cognitive affinity for it embeds an appreciation for forms structured according to the same principles. The presence of self-similarity in a part-to-whole-to-part integrated relationship is an inherent attraction for humans, whether it is in the structure of a tree or an abstract form composed of these nested relationships.

ABSTRACTION, PERCEPT, AND CONCEPT

Entities and phenomena exist in a dual reality, as a percept in its phenomenal form and as a concept that contains its essence. They exist as revelation of an idea revealed in a way particular to its circumstances. Ideal form is characterized by a spatial figure that can be perceived intuitively as an idea. When manifested in the sensory realm, the representative entity will correspond to some degree to the ideal form. The idea may not attain its full development. The closer the percept is to the concept, the closer it is to perfection.[67] The spectrum of ways in which a concept reveals itself in the sensory domain accounts for the differentiation in nature.

According to Rudolf Steiner, natural law, type, and concept are three varieties of an idea. Natural law is an abstraction that encompasses and unites the multiplicity and is separate from sensory reality. Type unites the idea and sensory reality. The concept is perceived in the percept and is characterized as organic nature. The concept is present in a form that is configured so that it can be perceived. Humans can perceive the idea within the natural form.[68]

When a concept is not abstracted from sensory data but develops out of itself and only out of itself, it is characterized as an intuitive concept, and its comprehension is through intuitive knowledge. Percepts of natural forms are understood through intuitive knowledge. The human intellect can understand the concept of an organic entity arising from the interaction and interrelation of its parts as an analytical generalization understood through abstract reasoning as an intuitive concept.[69] The quality of wholeness or organic unity cannot be pinpointed in the same manner that roundness is not perceptibly defined. When we say the ball is round, the mirror is round, or the moon is round, we are adducing the concept of roundness from a large set of previous percepts of roundness. This set of percepts exhibited in nature continually reorganizes the concept of organic unity abstracting the universal from the range of entities. The concept is not formulated strictly from the range of examples no more than "a magician really pulls a rabbit out of a hat. As the magician places the rabbit into the hat beforehand, the concept of wholeness is within the human cognitive library as an intuition."[70]

Imagine two points of light, *A* and *B*. Corresponding to unique human cognitive functions, a relationship is established between the two as we go from one point to the other, whether it be as juxtaposition, symmetry, and so on. Add two additional points of light, *C* and *D,* in

7.5a

7.5b

Figure 7.5. a. Two points of light, complemented by; b. four points of light.

a similar configuration. Not only do they form a similar relationship between each other but they form a relationship between *A* and *B* as well (Figure 7.5). The first set of relationships spatially relates two percepts in the concrete sensory world. In the second set of relationships, relationship is formed between relationships. The concrete percepts are eliminated, leaving the conceptual relationship, which is applied in other instances exhibiting similar structural relationships.[71] It is in this manner that the wholeness emerges from natural forms and transposes to other forms that reveal organic unity.

The abstraction of natural form is dependent on the perception of the pattern of forces or structure that is exhibited within it and manifested as a natural law in a large class of natural forms.[72] Abstract images represent objects at a lower level of abstractness than themselves through the comprehension and articulation of the essential quality of the object, whether it is shape, color, structure, or movement. This portrayal can be expressed at any level of abstraction, and its success is contingent on the articulation of this characteristic that represents its essence. When the mind encounters a percept, as in the case of abstraction of "incomplete" material, it "completes" the concept from the archive of stored experience. Abstraction is not incompleteness as a picture is a statement about relevant and essential visual qualities, and such a statement can be a complete representation of the essence of the object at any level of abstraction.[73]

Perception and cognition are indissolubly linked by their most common quality: abstraction.[74] The abstractive grasp of an object's structural features is the basis of perception and the beginning of cognition. Human cognition is a unitary process that continually relates the sensory data to generic theoretical concepts. In this process, distinguishing characteristics are identified to correlate the data in a process of generalization to concepts held in cognition.[75]

Throughout the human and animal domain, the nervous system has evolved a selective reaction toward particular features of the visual field. The stimuli that provoke these reactions possess two distinct prerequisites: they are identifiable by their pure color, elemental shape, or recognizable structure, and they are sufficiently distinct from the residue of the environment.[76] The two components of the image consisting of physical object and its surrounding context are separated through the recognition of the organization of the object's structure and the consequential recognition of the object as an organized whole rather than a mosaic of elements.[77] The process is hierarchical and

193

essentially abstract, attuning the receptor to the group of the essential features that correspond to a categorical type. The inbred process of abstraction is a property of the species.[78]

ASSOCIATION, ISOMORPHISM, AND TRANSPOSITION

Abstract concepts are applied to percepts of natural form and phenomena in a number of ways. In association, the common characteristics between two entities or processes act as a bond between them and as a means to recall the second object when the first is signified. Association is dependent on the characteristics of the two objects or processes being interrelated. If the association is contingent on the nature of the object's organization, it is also dependent on the strength and character of the organization. The traces of nature's organizational processes are themselves organized entities, and they leave their imprint on the objects they generate.[79] On the surface, a natural object, such as a bird, and a man-made artifact, such as an airplane, should not be associated (Figure 7.6). There are obvious and significant differences between the two, but they are functionally related, and a strong association is formed.[80] Similarly, natural forms, such as a tree, and artificial objects, such as a fractally generated building, are associated through the traces of their generative processes exhibited by the characteristic of self-similarity.

In an isomorphism, two objects are cognitively connected by a relationship that maps one onto the other. In mathematical theory, an isomorphism has a relatively strict definitive meaning with the relationship that associates A to B and B to A, termed the identity function or morphism. Isomorphic forms are structurally related, with each expressing the same configuration of relationships that constitute their form. Through the various transformations of scaling, rotation, skewing, and so on, a skeletal identity remains that can be perceived. Fractal geometry operates as the identity function between natural forms and man-made artifacts composed by fractal geometry. It serves as the bridge to cognitively assert that there is an equivalence between the two. In our mind, we conclude that in some way, the two objects "are essentially the same." The emotional and cognitive benefits from the exposure to natural forms are consciously or unconsciously mapped onto the fractally generated artificial form.

In *transposition*, significant elements of an object are changed; however, the new entity is recognized as relating or belonging to the

7.6

primary object. The most notable example is when a melody is played in a different key: the music is still recognized as belonging to the melody. Certain conditions relating to the form's organization must be kept constant for a transposition to take place. Relations between the stimuli involved must be kept constant when the stimuli are changed. The invariance of shape or form when the color, size, location, and so on are changed is a strong element for transposition to occur. The relationships within the form that are responsible for the shape's invariance or the structure of the object are a fundamental tenet for transposition.[81] The fractal structure of natural forms is a conscious or unconscious distinguishing characteristic of a natural object's fundamental structure which is transposed to other objects structured according to fractal geometry.

ABSTRACTION AND NONMIMETIC IMAGES

The use of analogy in abstracting the relations between forms in nature and man-made objects has been subverted by the use of conscious imitation. The inherent analogies between the two are beyond simplistic appearances and are focused on the generative forces that are similar between the two. The use of fractal geometry in generating architectural forms results in compositions that have an overarching organic quality. It is analogous to the challenges faced by abstraction, where the distillation of an object's essence into economical structured form proves a composition like the object being abstracted.[82]

Figure 7.6. An airplane and a bird.

195

Fractally generated forms exhibit a set of relationships analogous to those found in natural forms. This equivalence occurs on an abstract level regarding the fundamental relationships as opposed to a mere imitation of a natural form.

In his research, Rudolf Arnheim has determined that reasonably educated young adults readily understand the representation of abstract concepts through the use of nonmimetic drawings. The abstract portrayals reflect the essence of the concept that is being conveyed. These drawings are not offering evidence to define the concept but reflect the most refined structural forms emerging from that definition. The nonmimetic illustrations derive their meaning from the substance of the issues to which they refer. The primary reason why disembodied shapes are conducive in transmitting meaning is that they are concerned with structure as opposed to sheer matter.[83] These drawings are required to reflect the pertinent features of their referent. The images utilize more generic forms or "pure shapes."[84] In perceiving the complex forms of nature, man translates them into these more generic forms that are more responsive to the senses and comprehensible to the mind. The nonmimetic drawings are the physical equivalent of the nonmimetic abstract visualizations residing in cognition.[85]

Rudolf Arnheim has discussed how nonmimetic images can fulfill a function as a sign, picture, or symbol. When an image is representing content but does not reflect the characteristics of the content visually, it is acting as a sign. The sign displays visual characteristics that augments its use as a sign and fulfill the purpose intended. The visual content of the triangular shape of traffic warning signs is chosen to separate it from other signs in an easily identifiable shape. The visual characteristics are not arbitrary but rather are chosen to serve a function. When images serve as signs, their visual content only operates as a reference for the things for which they stand (cf. Figure 7.7).[86]

Images serve as pictures when they depict objects located at a lower level of abstractness than themselves. The abstraction is accomplished by focusing on and visualizing a distinctive characteristic of the object, whether its color, shape, or movement. The abstraction is a methodology where the picture interprets the object of its representation. In perception, the complete sensory array is recorded, and when a percept of incomplete material is sensed, the mind completes the sensory data with stored cognitive material. The level of abstraction can vary, but at any level, the picture's visual qualities provide a complete sensory depiction of the essential qualities of the object.[87]

7.7

While a picture is a higher level of abstraction than the object it represents, a symbol is a lower level of abstraction than the idea it represents.[88] In a symbol, an object is endowed with an intangible metaphysical force. Ideals, through the depiction of a constellation of forces in the symbol, give shape to its abstraction. An emotional state can be visualized by translating its dynamic properties into visual patterns.[89] Symbolism is a means of exteriorization of abstract ideals and concepts, frequently through the use of analogy and archetypes.[90]

DIAGRAMS AND VISUAL FIELDS OF FORCES

The concept of natural form as a diagram of forces was espoused by D. W. Thompson in his influential work *On Growth and Form*. This concept was transposed by Rudolf Arnheim in analyzing abstract visual images where the assembly of colored strokes on a surface presents the viewer with a pattern—or more accurately, a diagram—of visual forces. Through abstraction, the concept is distilled into a skeleton of dynamic elements that are not formally a part of the object. The various facets of the image through the relationship of their lines, shapes, and colors can accurately embody the forces to represent the concept.[91] The external shape of the object is not portrayed but rather the pure forces that represent it symbolically depict its inherent nature. In this type of abstraction, the image performs the cognitive task of fusing sensory appearances and conceptual nature in one visual statement. These aspects of the image are

Figure 7.7. An image acting as a sign.

197

in a continuous complementary relationship reflective of cognitive processes.[92]

Both Rudolf Arnheim and Christopher Alexander understand that visual objects come about as configurations of visual forces. Each object is a generator of a field of forces that spreads through the surrounding space. They act as visual vectors expressing the direction and strength of their forces.[93] Shapes are experienced as part of an integrated pattern of forces and are only relevant as part of that pattern.[94] The summation of these visual forces is for Arnheim a constellation of visual force and for Alexander living structure. Equilibrium, rather than static inertia, is achieved if the summation of the visual forces is balanced.

Christopher Alexander, in *Notes on the Synthesis of Form,* furthered this concept of form as a diagram of forces. When a pattern is abstracted from its physical manifestation and expresses the nature of the physical forces that shape the form, it is a *diagram.* The stroboscope image of the milk drop at the point of impact is a diagram of the forces that create the form of the surface and the drop of milk. A sphere acts as a diagram expressing the form that is created from the force requirement of enclosing the maximum space with minimum surface or as the commonality of the equidistance of a group from a point. Diagrams have either one of two characteristics or some degree of both. If a diagram epitomizes the physical aspects by presenting the constituent pattern of its organization and is principally an articulation of its formal characteristics, it is termed a *form diagram.* If a diagram is intended to summarize the functional properties and is principally a notation for the problem rather than the physical form, it is termed a *requirement diagram.*

A requirement diagram is useful if it contains some aspects of a form diagram, and a form diagram is useful if its function is projected as in a requirement diagram. A *constructive diagram* is a diagram that is at once both a form diagram and a requirement diagram and acts as a bridge between form and function. It reflects the duality of cognitive processes that unify what an object is and what an object does. An object can be described through a formal description of its physical characteristics or by what it does as a functional description. The unification of these two descriptions is the abstract equivalent of a constructive diagram, which, if it is sufficient, contributes to the understanding of the generative principle that calls the object into being. A form's basic organizational principles are indicated in a constructive diagram.[95] Nature's forms serve as this unifying constructive diagram as they are products of those forces that maximize its utility with the least amount of energy and that are concordant with its pattern or organization. Fractal forms inherently serve as diagrams of the generative forces that created them. They are visual representations of the relationships that created the form and are its essence.

NATURE, ABSTRACTION, AND THE NEOPLASTIC MOVEMENT IN ART

With Impressionism, aesthetic theory shifted its concept that the pictorial image is a concept of the mind rather than a direct correlation of a physical object. This understanding, that the percept differs from the physical object, laid the foundation for the abstraction of nature and the birth of modern art.[96] From Impressionism, the work of Fauvism took another step toward abstraction, as articulated by Maurice Vlaminck, "to liberate nature, to free it."[97] With Cubism, multiple viewpoints were integrated in one composition that utilized interpenetrating faceted planes in a relatively shallow, ambiguous pictorial space.

Perhaps one of the most noted turn-of-the-century abstract artists was Piet Mondrian, a Dutch-born member of the DeStijl movement, also known as Neoplasticism. Mondrian is best known for his genre of abstract compositions of rectilinear compositions of thin black lattices with panes of color such as *Composition in White, Blue and Yellow* (c. 1936), shown in Figure 7.8. He is acknowledged as an antecedent abstractionist whose work endures today. His work is not characteristically associated with nature, which is somewhat tragically incongruous with his intent. The basis for the belief that Mondrian's work was firmly entrenched in nature and a brief graphic overview of his work can best illustrate this. His early work *Geinrust Farm in Watery Landscape* (c. 1905–1906) (Figure 7.9) is clearly a naturalistic portrayal. Works such as *"Bosch" (Woods): Woods Near Oele* (1908) (Figure 7.10) are harbingers of the rectilinear series of perpendicular relationships and bold colors that were hallmarks of Mondrian's mature work. *Tableau No. 2/Composition No. VII* (1913) (Figure 7.11) exemplifies the connection between his naturalist work and his abstract compositions. With *Composition with Grid 9: Checkerboard Composition with Light Colors* (1919) (Figure 7.12) and finally *Composition in White, Blue and Yellow*, the abstract trajectory is complete. (See Figures 7.8–7.12 for examples of Mondrian's work.)

As with other Theosophical artists, such as Kandinsky and Steiner, Mondrian wanted to illuminate the universal truths that are inherent and relevant to human existence. Mondrian wrote a number of

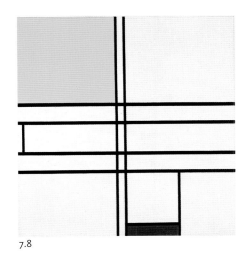

7.8

Figure 7.8. Mondrian, *Composition in White, Blue and Yellow* (c. 1936). © 2012 Mondrian/ Holtzman Trust, c/o HCR International Washington, D.C.

essays outlining the principles of Neoplasticism and its roots in nature. During 1919 and 1920, when trapped in Holland during World War I, Mondrian wrote "Natural Reality and Abstract Reality: A Trialogue (While Strolling from the Country to the City)." It is a conversation between X, a layman; Y, a naturalistic painter; and Z, an abstract painter (Mondrian) during seven scenes over the course of their walk. The purpose of the essay is "to show the direct connection between art and nature."[98]

In these conversations, Mondrian firmly establishes that the object and inspiration for his work is the phenomenon of nature. There is no difference in the essential nature between the naturalistic depiction of nature and the abstract depiction of nature. Each is concerned with the beauty of nature. Mondrian held that the universal truths inherent to nature were veiled and obscured by their manifestations in natural forms, despite their beauty. Mondrian termed the veiling of the universal truths as "the tragic." Man must not see beyond nature but see abstractly and universally through nature to the universal truths that lie within. By discussing the variability of the scenery because of its variable perception during different times of the day and under different conditions of sunlight, which changes the visual relationships, Mondrian cited the capriciousness of natural forms as an illustration of nature's veil. Deep within these mutable forms lies the immutable universal beauty.

The process of becoming one with the universal is what Mondrian terms the *plastic vision*. He believed that universal truths are perceived through the comprehension of visual relationships, and the more nature is abstracted, the more clearly these relationships are made apparent. The particularities of the universal apparent in natural forms must be annihilated and reconstruct the abstract universal through the relationship of visual forces. When freed from the attachment to the particular, our concept of beauty becomes freer and fuller. The expression of the relationships is determinate and depends on the placement of the parts. In a fractal philosophical orientation, Z, the abstract painter in the group, articulates that "all things are a part of the whole: each part obtains its visual value from the whole and the whole from its parts. Everything is expressed through relationship," and "everything is a complex must be seen as part of the complex: as part of a whole. Then we will always see relationships and always know one thing through the other."

At this point, we part company with Mondrian as he believes that

7.9

Figure 7.9. Mondrian, *Geinrust Farm in Watery Landscape* (c. 1905–1906). © 2012 Mondrian/ Holtzman Trust, c/o HCR International Washington, D.C.

7.10

Figure 7.10. Mondrian, *"Bosch" (Woods): Woods Near Oele* (1908). © 2012 Mondrian/Holtzman Trust, c/o HCR International Washington, D.C.

7.11

Figure 7.11. Mondrian, *Tableau No. 2/Composition
No. VII* (1913). © 2012 Mondrian/Holtzman
Trust, c/o HCR International Washington, D.C.

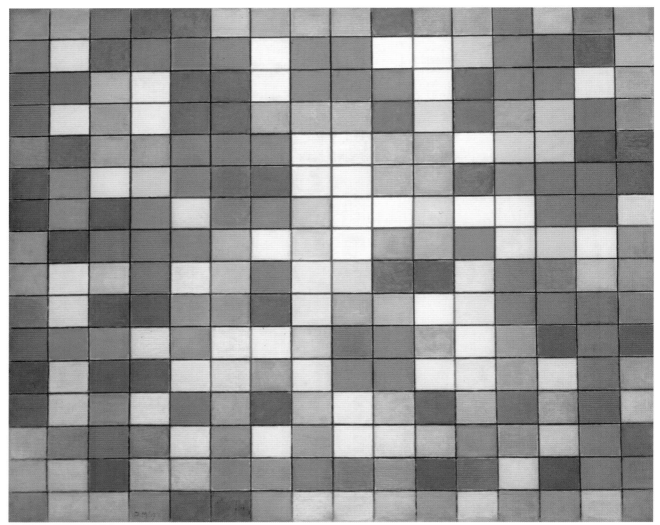

7.12

Figure 7.12. Mondrian, *Composition with Grid 9: Checkerboard Composition with Light Colors* (1919). © 2012 Mondrian/Holtzman Trust, c/o HCR International Washington, D.C.

the relationship that leads to achieving plastic vision is the juxtaposition of opposites, which he termed *equivalent duality*, whereas this volume holds that the relationship that leads to a natural universal truth is the relationship formed through fractal geometry. Mondrian, an avid jazz dancer, used the metaphor of dancing to illustrate his artistic philosophy. The relationship of dance to the music of the previous generation was to flow together, whereas in the new advanced dance paradigm, the music and the dance are in opposition. Through the duality of opposition, he believed that a greater harmony is achieved. As joy and suffering annihilate each other, Mondrian used expansion and limitation as the values held in an equivalence, destroying the particulars of both and resulting in repose.

Although the enduring value of Mondrian's work is a testament to the value of his artistic vision, I believe that a harmony that inherently resonates with humans is the harmony expressed in fractal relationships.

SUMMARY

The pursuit of the representation of universals in architecture has been desired since the ancient civilizations were creating their temples. Man has consistently seen understanding nature and embodying it within his artifacts as critical in his elusive pursuit of the collective consciousness of the universe. Nature is viewed as the key to the universal truths. Comprehension of its concepts can only be achieved through abstractive understanding. Owing to the human cognitive apparatus, the grasping of visual shape is of primary importance. The perception of a fractal structure connects the observer to the universal organizing principles of nature.

Coinciding with advances in scientific understanding, the pursuit of universals was reinvigorated in the early nineteenth century and continues today within the Modernism movement.

The Abstract Trajectory to the Fractal Modernist Form

Through the perceptual and cognitive capacities of humans, perceptual data are distilled into their fundamental characteristics to be processed. As the understanding of these processes became more widespread through scientific advances in concert with advances in construction technology, art and architecture evolved to reflect a more abstract orientation. The abstract expression reflects advances in the age-old search for universals. Within the grammar of abstraction, the utilization of fractal geometry produces compositions that overtly express an organic gestalt. Neither the high-tech materials nor the subsequent expression of those materials alter the nature of the composition, which is a result of the integrated relationship of its elements.

ORIGINS OF ABSTRACTION IN ART AND ARCHITECTURE

The seismic shift in art and architecture that commenced at the end of the nineteenth century and flourished at the beginning of the twentieth century merges a number of movements within a comprehensive category termed *Modernism*. Starting with the art movements of Impressionism through Cubism, Futurism, Constructivism, and Abstraction, reality was pictorially transformed from an attempt at realistic representation to an interpretation of the essence and message of nature itself. This revolution paralleled scientific breakthroughs that transformed and deepened the world's understanding of how the universe is constituted. Architecture during this period was also

8.1

transformed by advances in technological achievements as well as by a realignment of the perception of nature and the cosmos. As the evolution of the nature of architecture marked out a trajectory, world's fairs and expositions introduced the general public to these advances. Organized by Prince Albert and others, the Great Exhibition of the Works of the Industry of All Nations in 1851 featured a revolutionary structure, the Crystal Palace (Figure 8.1), designed by Joseph Paxton and Charles Fox. It was a beautiful structure of cast iron and glass that spanned approximately two thousand feet by five hundred feet and was over one hundred feet tall. It captured the public's conscious and became a symbol of modernity as it transformed architectural vocabulary from an aesthetic of heavy, bulky masonry structures to elegant compositions based on light and air.

Design philosophy began evolving toward a more structurally honest expression through the writings of architectural theorist Eugene Viollet-le-Duc. In his career as a restorer of medieval buildings, he was influenced by the structural implications of Gothic architecture. He envisioned the application of these principles to the new material derived from advances in technological achievements such as cast iron. He believed that new architectural forms would develop out of the synthesis of masonry with cast iron and be orientated toward structural expression. For Viollet-le-Duc, architecture should originate from structure, and the goal of architecture is to make its form and expression concordant with structure.[1] This architectural expression was based on function, from the flying buttresses to resist the building loads to the profiles of the moldings and the ornamental details to shed the rain.[2] His philosophical basis of architectural structure was that, as one can deduce the whole plant from seeing just its leaf, one

Figure 8.1. The Crystal Palace.

8.2

8.3

Figure 8.2. The Eiffel Tower.
Figure 8.3. Gallerie des Machines.

can understand an architectural structure from its cross section.[3] This philosophy emerged through what became known as the *engineer's aesthetic.* This transformation of architectural design orientation was put on display at the Exposition Universelle in Paris in 1889. The two principal structures, the Eiffel Tower (Figure 8.2) by Gustav Eiffel and the Galerie des Machines by Ferdinand Dutert and Victor Contamin (Figure 8.3), epitomized the new aesthetic. The form and expression were derived from the structural composition and materials of each structure.

Concurrent with the emergence of the engineer's aesthetic was a reconsideration of the influence of nature on architecture and the idea of organic design. John Ruskin, an influential English writer, criticized his contemporary artists in their depiction of nature as lacking its inherent truth. He wanted art to show a more profound understanding of nature through phemenonlogical observation of natural forms and phenomena. Art should communicate truth, and in the case of nature, that truth is an understanding of nature. The study of nature should be the common ground for artists and designers. Natural organisms, which developed their form through their internal laws of growth, epitomized beauty and were a direct revelation of the Divine. In architecture, this philosophy was represented by Gothic architecture, which for Ruskin was characterized by a naturalness achieved through close observation of natural form. As with natural forms, Gothic architecture developed its form through its structure, and for Ruskin the noblest buildings were those that invited the intelligent eye to discover the secrets of their structures.[4]

Toward the end of the nineteenth century, a design movement developed from the Arts and Craft movement. In general, this movement is known as Art Nouveau, but it is also known as Jugendstil and Secession, depending on the geographical location of the movement. Publications such as Owen Jones's *The Grammar of Ornament,* with illustrations by Christopher Dresser, on how to derive new ornament from plant forms and Ferdinand Moser's *Ornamental Plant Studies from the Sphere of Native Flora* contributed to Art Nouveau's organic foundation.[5] Art Nouveau is considered a "total style" that permeates a large spectrum of art, architecture, and decorative and applied arts to create an overall environment. It is noteworthy by its integration of organic forms and modern technologically driven materials. Art Nouveau–style architecture, such as Maison Atelier by Victor Horta (Figure 8.4) or the Paris Metro entrances by Hector Guimard, exhibits

8.4

8.5

8.6

the distinguishing use of natural archetypal forms as building elements. It is characterized by parabolic curves and stylized curvilinear forms. The use of curvilinear elements to create organic forms was epitomized by the work of Spanish architect Antonio Gaudi. His structures, such as the Casa Mila (Figure 8.5), Casa Battlo, and his masterpiece Sagrada Familia, exude an organic energy that is distinct from the surrounding architectural styles. Unlike the Arts and Crafts movement from which it sprung, Art Nouveau embraced the use of technologically driven machine-made material as well as abstraction in the expression of its architecture. The high point of Art Nouveau was in the Exposition Universelle of 1900 in Paris, where it was the prevalent style. The magnificent structures of the Gare D'Orsay, Grand Palais (Figure 8.6), and Petit Palais amazed their visitors with their beautiful use of iron and glass.

CUBISM, DESTIJL, AND THE BAUHAUS

At the beginning of the twentieth century, a number of art movements occurred either concurrently or with some overlap. Cubism reinterpreted reality with a fragmented, decentered composition within a shallow pictorial space. These compositions fused different views of the same object that occurred with the passage of time and repositioning within the object's viewing space. This effect was an example of the concept of *simultaneity* by Claude Bergson, which, with advances in scientific theory, captured the art world's attention.[6] Concurrently with Cubism, the concept of simultaneity was being interpreted by the

Figure 8.4. Victor Horta's Maison Atelier.
Figure 8.5. Antonio Gaudi's Casa Mila.
Figure 8.6. The Grand Palais.

211

8.7

8.8

Figure 8.7. Czech Cubism.
Figure 8.8. DeStijl architectural planes.
Figure 8.9. Gerrit Rietveld's Rietveld Schroeder House.
Figure 8.10. Reitveld's *Red/Blue Chair*.

Futurists through the depiction of movement in their work. Their work strove to achieve *universal dynamism* and expedited the transition from mimetic depiction to abstraction.[7] During this period, the Constructivist movement was flourishing in Russia. Compositions by artists such as Kasimir Malevich effectively broke with the creation of facsimiles of nature and embraced abstraction. These artists advocated the supremacy of pure feeling in creative art, with intuition as one's guide.[8]

Although these art movements had associated architectural manifestations, Cubist architecture in Prague (Figure 8.7), Sant'Elia's theoretical designs for a Futurist city in Italy, and Malevich's Architektons, architecture was fundamentally changed by the Bauhaus and DeStijl movements. DeStijl art was an attempt to achieve abstraction and universality through the conscious return to the basic principles of art: colors, shapes, planes, and lines.[9] The public face of DeStijl was represented by the work of Piet Mondrian, who endeavored through his art to strip away the chaotic outer layer of nature and represent the essence contained within. Mondrian's asymmetrical, decentered compositions spread all over from edge to edge and strove for a "dynamic rhythm of determinate mutual relations."[10] This concept of dynamic equilibrium governed the evolution of DeStijl architecture, where the orientation of architectural form transformed from a sculpting of mass to a decomposition of the enclosed volume into relationships of colored planes.[11] Ornament and readily perceivable symmetry were erased. The spaces were organized centrifugally, with walls and floors treated as boldly colored planes defining a space within a skeletal structure with non-load-bearing walls.[12] These principles were captured in a series of axonometric drawings by a leader of the DeStijl movement, Theo van Doeseberg, illustrated in Figure 8.8. The most distinct application of DeStijl architectural principles is seen in the Rietveld Schroeder House in the Netherlands by Gerrit Rietveld (Figure 8.9). This work can be seen as a clear antecedent to Reitveld's *Red/Blue Chair* (Figure 8.10). The structural framework was provided by planes that were painted white. Other elements were painted shades of gray, black, red, yellow, and white. Planes and lines were composed so that their colors and sizes were contrastive even when adjacent. Relationships are generated without the use of obvious symmetry (see Figure 8.8).[13]

The DeStijl movement was relatively brief, with its principles incorporated into a German school, the Bauhaus, that sought to unify art, craft, and technology. The legacy of the Bauhaus lasted for decades and is still present today, influencing the development of art,

8.9

8.10

architecture, typography, graphic design, and industrial design. The faculty and visiting speakers were a who's who of leading-edge artists and architects: Walter Gropius, Mies van der Rohe, Lyonel Feininger, Joseph Albers, Paul Klee, Wassily Kandinsky, Theo van Doesburg, El Lissizky, Laszlo Moholy-Nagy, and Marcel Breuer. Members of the Bauhaus drew on the Gestalt theory of psychology and visual perception. Bauhaus assimilated the Gestalt principle of understanding a form in its parts and in its totality, which is an essential element of fractal architecture. This affiliation helped lay the groundwork for the application of fractal geometry to architecture within a Modernist aesthetic. Gestalt theorists visited the Bauhaus school, and at times the two schools overlapped.[14] Paul Klee, Wassily Kandinsky, and Joseph Albers attended lecturers by Gestalt researchers and explicitly drew on Gestalt theory in their work.[15] This influence can be seen in their work through the incorporation of simultaneous contrasts and dynamic figure–ground relationships. Klee went on to cite Gestalt principles in his lectures and in his seminal book *The Thinking Eye*.[16] The architectural language of the Bauhaus was free of historical reference and focused on precise and unsentimental development of form with meticulous attention to details. The intrinsic nature of materials was respected, and there was an affinity for transparency and light in defiance of gravity.[17]

LE CORBUSIER

During this period, a single architect, Le Corbusier, was as influential on Modernism as the Bauhaus school. It is difficult to overstate Le Corbusier's importance to the development and dissemination of the Modernist aesthetic.[18] Early in his career, Le Corbusier collaborated with Cubist painter Amedee Ozenfant in pushing Cubism into a new phase called Purism. Purism, inspired by modern machinery, employed the golden ratio to generate paintings based on geometric structure and forms expressed in pure color, best exemplified by the work of Le Corbusier's friend and fellow artist Ferdinand Leger. Purism was grounded in the belief of universal aesthetic values expressed through a transmittable universal language that evoked intuitive primary sensations. It strove to achieve the highest form of aesthetic expression by the clear perception of a "great general law" achieved through mathematical lyricism. In architecture, Le Corbusier sought to create a machine-age structure that provided new freedom in arranging the elements of plan and façade.[19] The machine aesthetic had its foundation in the idea that nature's forms were based on the most efficient function to utilize the least amount of energy in achieving its purpose. This philosophy appreciated the beauty in the form derived from the fitness for its use, with each of its component parts subservient to and contributing to the greater purpose of the whole.[20] It viewed natural organisms as complex mechanisms to which man could look as a basis for creating their machines for human use.[21]

As with Mondrian, Le Corbusier's work does not evidently associate itself with organic architecture, but an examination of his writings and the theoretical underpinnings of his work reveals organic intentions. In *Towards a New Architecture*, he states that engineers produce architecture through the use of mathematical calculations that are derived from natural law to produce a composition that evokes a feeling of harmony.[22] Architecture is generated from harmonies that are obtained from universal laws that we recognize, respect, and obey.[23] Man creates his own universe by submitting to these laws of nature and producing creations in the image of nature.[24] The result of utilizing calculations derived from universal law is the creation of a living organism that is in unison with universal order.[25] Le Corbusier's intent places him squarely within the domain of fractal geometry. Fractal geometry was not known at that time, so Le Corbusier turned to the golden section, revered from the time of Renaissance architects as a symbol of cosmic perfection, and the related Fibonacci series, which is associated with the progression in plant growth.[26] Le Corbusier developed a system of proportions called *Le Modular* based on these geometric systems and utilized it as the controlling mechanism for his work. He considered the golden section and the Fibonacci series as the universal law on which to base his architecture to invoke a sense of natural harmony. Through *Le Modular*, Le Corbusier achieved a methodology of relating parts to the whole that comes closer to the character and purposeful unity that is a hallmark of living nature.[27] Although it is a step in the right direction, these geometrical ordering devices cannot provide the essential character of nature, the part-to-whole-to-part association that is present in fractal geometry.

INTERNATIONAL STYLE

The modernist movements of DeStijl, Bauhaus, and Le Corbusier were enveloped by the International Style. This term was derived from a book by Henry-Russell Hitchcock and Philip Johnson of the same title, as an account of the International Exhibition held at the Museum of Modern Art in 1932. In that exhibition, works by Bauhaus architects

8.11

8.12

Figure 8.11. The Trylon, Perisphere, and Helicline.
Figure 8.12. Mies's Barcelona Pavilion.

Walter Gropius and Mies Van Der Rohe as well as Le Corbusier and a number of other notable architects such as Erich Mendelsohn, Alvar Aalto, and Jacobus Oud were displayed. The book, *International Style*, identified three architectural traits: the volume of the building is articulated by surfaces rather than mass; formal regularity is achieved from proportional control and orderly structure; and there is an avoidance of applied ornament.[28] This style did not hesitate to break away from symmetrical form and embrace asymmetry. These characteristics led to the development of an abstract architectural style without reference to history or location. During the initial stages of the International Style, architecture was produced that had a striking, innovative character that captured the public's consciousness. This culminated with the 1939 World's Fair, whose symbols of Modernism, the structures of the Trylon, Perisphere, and Helicline (Figure 8.11), remain a symbol of the culmination of the Modernist aesthetic. Throughout this World's Fair, there were buildings that reflected the Modern style, including the United States Steel Subsidiaries Building, the Ford Motor Pavilion, the Beech-Nut Packing Company Building, the Schaefer Center, and the Borden Company Building.

The mature phase of the International Style was characterized by sleek geometrical structures that were embodied in the work of Mies Van Der Rohe and Skidmore Owings and Merrill. Mies Van Der Rohe, famous for the expressions "less is more" and "God is in the details," went on from his work at the Bauhaus to create elegantly refined prototypes of the International Style. In his career Mies was guided by the idea of nature as an ensemble governed by precise and perfectly balanced laws. His work is distinguished by the expression of a minimal structural framework overlaid by a tight, detailed curtain wall and the use of rich materials. His buildings employ metal, glass, and stone in simple rectilinear and planar forms, resulting in clean, crisp lines. Within this structure, space flowed freely, which is best exemplified by his Barcelona Pavilion (Figure 8.12). The form and interior space are defined by horizontal and vertical planes. With a minimal number of elements, he was able to create a structure of poetically flowing space that guides you through the pavilion with an intuitive sense of correctness. In the vernacular of skyscrapers, Mies's theoretical designs for all glass skyscrapers in the early 1920s remain the aspiration for graceful expression of the skyscraper form (Figure 8.13). This standard of excellence was realized in his Seagram Building in New York City (Figure 8.14). The exterior wall of the Seagram

8.13

8.14

Figure 8.13. Mies's theoretical skyscraper form.
Figure 8.14. The Seagram Building, New York.

Building is elegantly proportioned with structure metaphorically expressed through the use of I beam mullions. Mies's objective was to create a composition that had a defined structure and construction that expressed a universal rather than individual character.[29] He succeeded by creating the archetypal skyscraper form for the International Style.

Skidmore Owings and Merrill was formed in the late 1930s in Chicago and became renowned as the standard for glass box corporate architecture. In the early 1950s, they designed an icon of International Style architecture, the Lever House in New York City (Figure 8.15). The structure clearly epitomized the characteristics that represented International Style architecture. An elegant stainless steel and glass curtain wall sheathed an asymmetrical form composed of two rectilinear prisms. These two forms are oriented 90 degrees to each other with a recessed element separating them. The entire composition is lifted off the ground by a grid of columns and provides for gardens at its base. The appeal of the Lever House as a icon of the International Style rests in its abstract composition of form presented in the graceful skin of the movement.[30]

THE SWING AWAY FROM AND BACK TO ABSTRACTION

The tragedy of the International Style was that its spare abstract characteristics were hijacked by commercial interests to bastardize a refined architectural aesthetic into a architectural cloak to produce banal cookie-cutter money machines for real estate interests. Although one can find many notable masterpieces of the International Style and Modernist aesthetic, such as 333 Wacker Drive and Lake Point Tower in Chicago, the MOMA condominium tower (Figure 8.16) and Citicorp Building in New York, and the First Interstate Bank tower in Dallas, they were overwhelmed by the sea of cheap commercial imposters that repelled the public's aesthetic sensibilities. In a reaction to this wave of boring glass boxes, a new style of architecture emerged that was termed Post-Modern. The advent of Post-Modernism was a decisive movement away from abstraction and toward familiar ornament and images. The most striking characteristic of Post-Modern architecture was the return to previous periods of architecture to borrow elements of their respective styles and reformulate them according to current circumstances. The practitioners of Post-Modern architecture were represented by Philip Johnson and Michael Graves. Philip Johnson's AT&T project in New York City epitomized the return

217

8.15

8.16

Figure 8.15. Lever House, New York.
Figure 8.16. MOMA condominium tower.

to classic style. The thirty-seven-story granite tower built in the early 1980s borrowed Renaissance elements of a broken pediment at its crown and arches at its base. Although it possesses a compositional coherence, references to its similarity to a Chippendale highboy belies its importance as a counterpoint toward Modernism and abstraction. On the other side of the continent, Michael Graves designed the Portland Public Services Building, with its cubic form adorned with polychromatic classical elements that evoke styles from historical periods.

Despite this pause in the evolution of architectural form toward abstraction, the close of the twentieth century, with the advent of the integration of computer technology into the design process, brought a renewed genius to Modernism, springing forth like a fountain. The spectrum of this innovative class of Modernism was expansive and ingenious. The legacy of Modernism's most influential architects and artists was perpetuated and advanced by the evolution of the Modernist aesthetic. The stunning work of Richard Meier and Gwathmey and Siegel clearly carries the torch from Le Corbusier, while Frank Gehry has taken inspiration from Boccioni's sculptures to create flowing titanium edifices. Santiago Calatrava has synthesized the principles of structural articulation revealed in Gothic architecture with lyrical Modernist expression to create inspirational structures. Peter Eisenman has utilized metaphorical devices to abstract the essential content of the forces that influence the development of his form. Modernist designers such as Zia Hadid and Gregg Lynn have extended the tradition of the Futurist manifesto by abstracting movement as a vehicle for generating form. Norman Foster and Renzo Piano have taken Louis Sullivan's idiom that "form follows function" to its conclusion and have created architecture that turns its insides out. The most public expression of the new Modern aesthetic has been the strain of architecture known as Deconstructivism, which broke onto the public's consciousness through the Museum of Modern Art's 1988 exhibit "Deconstructivist Architecture," organized by Philip Johnson. Building from the theories of Russian Constructivists and the philosophical theories of Jacques Derrida, the effect from the Constructivist juxtaposition of forms was recalibrated to the destabilization or deconstruction of form emanating from within form. The resulting work by architects such as Rem Koolhaas, Coop Himmelblau, and Daniel Libeskind recalls the faceted, fragmented compositions of a period in Cubism translated into three-dimensional structures.

THE MODERN MOVEMENT
AND FRACTAL GEOMETRY

The Modern movement has undoubtedly arched toward abstraction and a reduction of ornament. This trend has been correlated with a movement away from organic architecture. Benoit Mandelbrot, the father of fractals, has in fact expressed a preference for Beaux Art architecture, such as the Paris Opera House, as exhibiting fractal qualities from its succeeding levels of detail as the scale of perception changes, as opposed to the Modernist work of Mies Van Der Rohe. The fractal dimension of various types of architectural expression has been presented as proof that Modernist architecture fails the test of organic architecture. The fractal dimension can be calculated using the box-counting method, in which a series of diminishing grids are placed over a line drawing elevation of a building. Each box that has a line of the drawing intersecting it is noted. From these data, a logarithmic calculation produces the fractal dimension for that elevation. The more the object has hits in an increasing diminishing grid of boxes, the higher its fractal dimension is. From this methodology, the proponents make the argument that certain architecture, such as a decorative Beaux Art structure, which has a higher calculated fractal dimension by the box-counting methodology, is more organic or fractal than Modernist buildings.[31] This damning assertion is incorrect. Though detail is a fundamental aspect of great architecture—as Mies Van Der Rohe said, "God is in the details"—the simple presence of it does not constitute fractal architecture. A structure based on brick masonry and windows with divided lites is not necessarily given the distinction of being organic, even though it has a fractal dimension from a high box-counting score due to the use of many small components. The critical aspect of forms that evoke emotional and cognitive responses similar to those experienced when perceiving natural forms is the presence of a unifying aspect based on the part-to-whole to part association. This attribute can be present in any part of the spectrum of architectural styles inclusive of the Modernist movement.

The perception of the part-to-whole-to-part quality of organic forms resides in the structure of the relationships of the constituent elements. In the Modernist aesthetic, abstraction facilitates the unambiguous perception of properties with precision. As discussed earlier, the grasping of the structural features of a form is the basis for perception and the initiating of cognition.[32] Concept formulation is assisted by the presence of structural simplicity that presents the relationships of the entity in a clear and explicit manner.[33] The mind searches for and comprehends man-made structures of elements and relations.[34] Structural features are those that contain the central attributes of the entity as opposed to peripheral ones. The perceptual capabilities embedded in them by virtue of their size, shape, orientation, or other integral features convey a visual force that, when organized correctly, can impart compelling meaning. To accurately convey their intended meaning, abstract images must be isomorphic to the entity to which they refer. There has to be a correspondence between elements of each such isomorphism such that they exhibit the same structural properties.[35] If these structural forces are composed so that the relationships foster a part-to-whole-to-part interdependence throughout the range of scales within the form, the meaning that is conveyed is indistinguishable from that of natural structures. This organic relationship is the isomorphism that relates abstract forms to natural structures.

MID-RISE MODERNIST FRACTAL ARCHITECTURAL FORM EXAMPLE

The use of fractal geometry to generate organic form within a Modernist aesthetic is demonstrated by generating a mid-rise structure. Utilizing the collage technique, a seed shape is created that approximates the final mass of the building and then is copied a number of times, with each copy modified by scaling, rotation, shearing, and translation transformations. The accumulation of copies is synthesized into one new seed shape that replaces the original seed shape. This new seed shape is encoded with the array of relationships of iteration 1, and by creating a duplicate array of copies, you produce a group of elements each encoded with the relationships that constituted not only each part of iteration 1 but the whole that represents the summation of these interrelationships. By applying the same group of rules that constituted iteration 1 each to this new array of elements and synthesizing them into a new seed shape, you enfold an exponentially increased set of generative instructions that give rise to a greater unfolding of the wholeness that is created.

- In Figure 8.17a, the major horizontal element is shown in black. It consists of two elements that constitute the top and bottom of the structure, both of which are copies of the seed shape reduced by 5 percent in depth and 98.5 percent in height. One is translated to the top of the seed shape, whereas the other is positioned at

8.17a

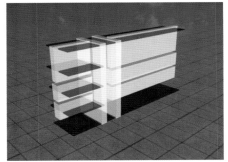

8.17b

8.17c

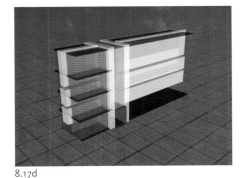

8.17d

Figure 8.17. Modern building form, iteration 1.

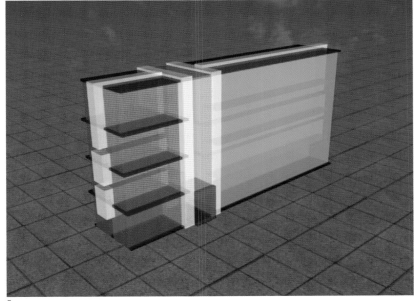

8.17e

the bottom. An additional series of three components that provide horizontal articulation are positioned along the left side. Each element is a copy that is scaled down by 87 percent in length, 5 percent in depth, and 98.5 percent in height and translated both horizontally and vertically.

- Figure 8.17b shows the major vertical elements in white. They consist of two elements spanning the depth of the form adjacent to the group of black horizontal elements and a group of six components scaled down and extending from the first two vertical elements to just beyond the edge of the seed shape. The first two elements are copies of the seed shape scaled down by 96 percent in width and scaled up by 3 percent in height. These transformed copies are translated horizontally so that one is adjacent to the black horizontal elements on the left side and the other is placed closer to the middle so that they form a strong vertical expression. The bottom two vertical elements on both sides are scaled down 75 percent in depth and 80 percent in height and length; the left side elements are reduced by 67 percent in width; and the right side elements are reduced by 32.5 percent in width. Each group of three elements is then translated horizontally and vertically to be placed on either side of the vertical elements that transverse the depth of the structure.

- In Figures 8.17c, the elements that fill in the black horizontal integrants are shown in red. Each of these copies of the seed shape is transformed by reducing 88 percent in length, 62.5 percent in depth, and 75 percent in height and then is translated horizontally and vertically to fit within the space between the black horizontal elements and on either side of the white vertical elements that span from the pair of middle white elements to just outside the edge of the seed shape.

- Figure 8.17d shows two elements, one in gray and the other in blue, that fill in the space between the two white vertical elements that form the upward expression of the front elevation. The gray component is a copy of the seed shape scaled down by 82 percent in length and 23 percent in height, while the blue element is scaled down 82 percent in length and 75 percent in height. These two components are translated horizontally to fit between the two white vertical elements with the gray part translated vertically so that it is on top of the blue element. The blue element protrudes from the face of the form.

- In Figure 8.17e, green elements that are similar to the red elements are shown filling in the space adjacent to the white vertical elements. Each of these copies of the seed shape is scaled down by 88 percent in length and 62.5 percent in depth and is scaled up by 33 percent in height. These copies are then rotated 90 degrees counterclockwise and translated horizontally to be to the right of the white vertical elements and distributed on either side of the vertical components that span from the pair of middle white elements to just outside the edge of the seed shape.

All these elements are fused together, each embedded with the generative rules of the whole composition to form the new seed shape. With the new seed shape, iteration 2 is initiated. You should note that elements, such as the blue element, that either protrude or recede from the other elements distinguish the form and provide reference that assists in perceiving the part-to-whole-to-part relationships.

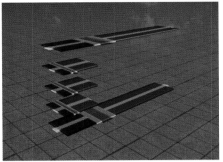

8.18a

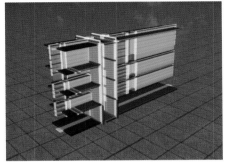

8.18b

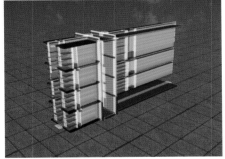

8.18c

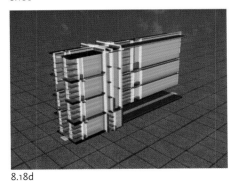

8.18d

Figure 8.18. Modern building form, iteration 2.

8.18e

- In Figure 8.18a, the elements that constituted the black horizontal elements are shown in their iteration 2 state. You can see the imprint of iteration 1 on each element. The portions representing the upper horizontal element on the right side have a blend of the black of the horizontal elements and the yellow of the four stacked elements that constitute the right side of the composition.

- Figure 8.18b shows the components that constitute the vertical white elements from iteration 1. These parts illustrate the imprint of iteration 1 more clearly.

- Figure 8.18c illustrates the four red elements that fill the area between the horizontal elements along the left side. A copy of the fused first iteration is inserted at each location, providing a concentration of elements, each bearing the blueprint of the first iteration.

- In Figure 8.18d, the transformed copies of the new seed shape are placed for the gray and blue elements. Because these elements are significantly contracted in length, the effect is to emphasize the verticality of the central element.

- Figure 8.18e shows the four elements that constitute the yellow section of iteration 1. As these parts are considerably contradicted in length and then rotated 90 degrees counterclockwise, the effect is to accent the horizontality in general through their red and gray subcomponents. A vertical accent is created by the stacking of their integrated blue subcomponents.

223

This iteration exhibits verticality principally from the major element that is just left of center. This group of components has subcomponents (the blue and gray elements in iteration 1) that reinforce its verticality. In both the compact lower element (blue element in iteration 1) and the larger element above it (gray element in iteration 1), the red elements of iteration 1 give an added vertical rhythm to both components. The vertical expression is also emphasized by the four elements (red parts of iteration 1) that are stacked vertically. As they are further articulated, the vertical rhythm is strengthened, as evidenced by each group of red subcomponents within each part. Each of the stacked elements on the left side also has a significant horizontal element that is its integrated portion of the black horizontal element of iteration 1. The four yellow elements of iteration 1 provide some verticality from their stacked nature, but because of their overall horizontal shape and the fact that each is rotated 90 degrees, each of their subcomponents that work toward verticality in the overall composition work horizontally within each of these elements. With each of these components, the blue, red, and gray components work to emphasize a horizontal expression.

As with the previous iterations, these elements are synthesized to form the new seed shape of iteration 3. Each element embodying the generative diagram is further ingrained into each component.

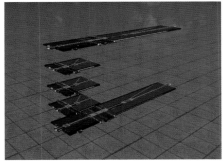

8.19a

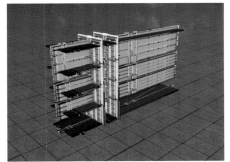

8.19b

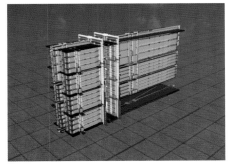

8.19c

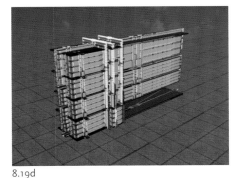

8.19d

Figure 8.19. Modern building form, iteration 3.

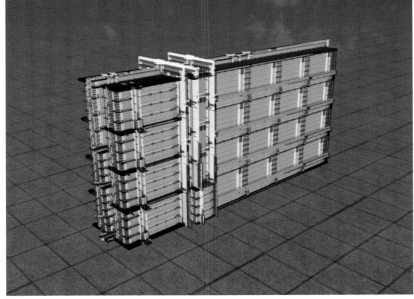

8.19e

- Figure 8.19a illustrates the horizontal black planes that, when compared to the previous iteration, have the generative structure more intricately embedded. You can note the blue elements protruding horizontally and the white vertical elements extending above the top as well as from the two sides.
- Figure 8.19b shows the vertical white components that are clearly articulated with the generative structure of iteration 2. Although most of this will be embedded in the overall form, these elements will be visible at the ends and top of the structure as well as being expressed in the main vertical elements in the front and back façades.
- In Figure 8.19c, the red components are added, providing a dynamic aspect in which the horizontal emphasis present within each component is balanced by the vertical stacking as well as the central vertical element within each component, which is articulated by their protruding blue subcomponents at the base.
- In Figure 8.19d, the central vertical elements, gray and blue components of iteration 1, are inserted, reinforcing the vertical emphasis in most of the elements, but at the base, the horizontality is emphasized.
- Figure 8.19e displays, the final form as the yellow elements of iteration 1 are added. As indicated in iteration 2, these elements have a strong horizontal orientation because their transformations include

8.20a

Figure 8.20a. Modern building, final form, corner
perspective.

8.20b

Figure 8.20b. Modern building, final form,
ground perspective.

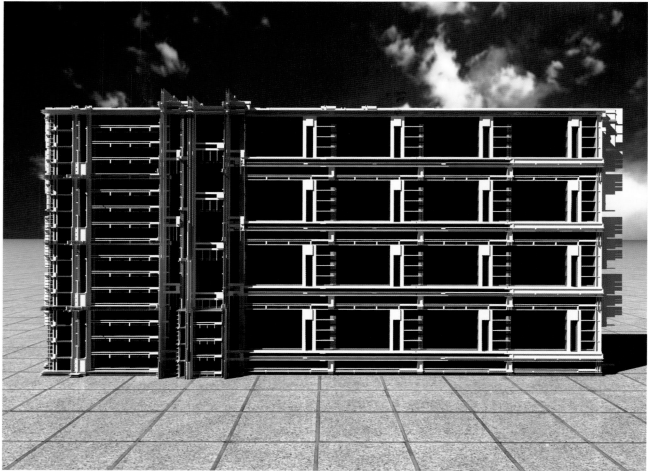

8.20c

Figure 8.20c. Modern building, final form, front
perspective.

8.21a

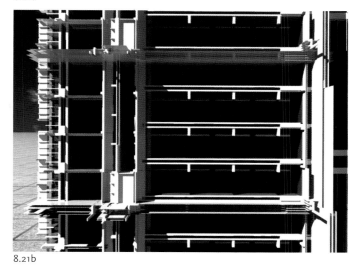

8.21b

8.21c

Figure 8.21. Front elevation left side levels of scale.

8.22a

8.22b

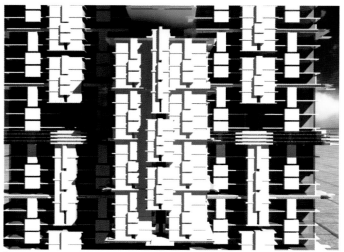

8.22c

Figure 8.22. Side elevation levels of scale.

8.23a

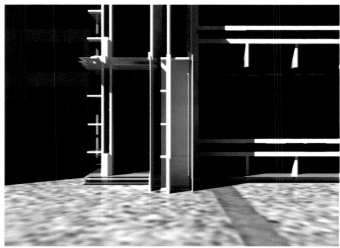

8.23b

8.23c

Figure 8.23. Front elevation middle levels of scale.

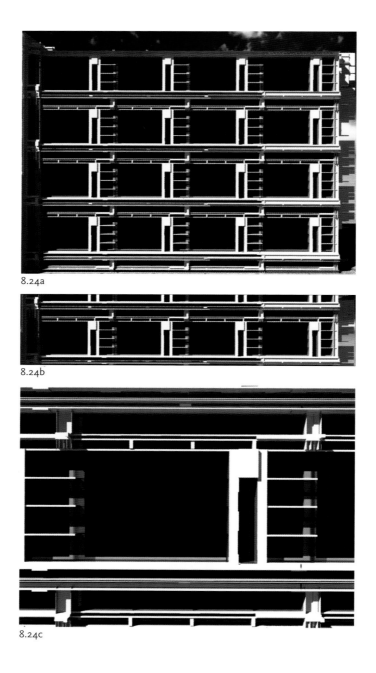

8.24a

8.24b

8.24c

Figure 8.24. Front elevation right side levels of scale.

a 90 degree rotation. At this level of iteration, a counterbalancing vertical emphasis appears as the gray, blue, and red elements appear within the main body of the component. These have been in effect rotated twice so that they are now inverted vertically.

Figure 8.20 shows the final form: in iteration 1, the red, green, and gray components are composed in glass, while the other elements are created in a white metal material. Figure 8.20a depicts the building from a corner perspective, Figure 8.20b from a frontal ground perspective, and Figure 8.20c a frontal elevation. These renderings demonstrate the part-to-whole-to-part relationship as you examine a potion of the structure and note its relationship to other parts and to the whole. This examination pierces the different levels of scale, as illustrated by Figures 8.21–8.24. Figure 8.21 concentrates on the red elements on the left side of the front elevation. At the first level, you see the third iteration of the element, and within that you observe the second iteration of the part, and within that you see the first iteration of the segment. The structure of each level of study of the element reveals the structure of the whole. Figure 8.22 examines the side elevation, which is predominately the white elements with either the red or green elements, depending on which side elevation you are viewing. Figure 8.23 shows the center element composed of the blue and gray parts, and Figure 8.24 illustrates the green elements. In each of the component's progression of detail, you observe the same phenomena.

SUMMARY

The composition created in this chapter is quite different than anything that is commonly held as organic as it is rooted in Modernist expression. The grammar of metal and glass first introduced in the Crystal Palace produces a fundamentally different expression than that of masonry and stone. This expression reinforces its man-made quality and resulting abstract character. Despite its abstract expression, the architectural form possesses the organic structure that triggers perceptual and cognitive linkages to the emotional and intellectual responses of natural forms. The Modernist appearance clearly presents the fractal part-to-whole-to-part relationship of the elements of organic entities. Owing to the relationships embedded within the structure, humans infuse the structure with positive associations because of an unconscious familiarity with the form's structure.

PART III

Architecture from Nature

CHAPTER **9** Nature's Generative Character

Though fractal geometry was born from advancements in the study of nature, the development of computer technology is integral not only to its flourishing but also to its application to architecture. Science and nature converge to reveal commonalities never before realized. This connectivity gives insight into physical phenomena that exist in the natural world that are exhibited in the behavior of fractal geometry. By tracing the evolution of computational systems, we can see not only the development of fractal architecture but an additional connection with natural systems.

FORERUNNERS OF FRACTAL ALGORITHMS
From the invention of the abacus in ancient Asia and the concept of algorithms first formed in ninth-century Persia, the use of computational devices and the development of computer technology have taken a few quantum leaps. The technology has evolved from the era of tapes, cards, and the cavernous mainframe to comprehensive computational power sitting literally on one's laptop. The amazing technological advancement has made possible the scientific exploration of areas previously impossible because of budgetary and technological constraints. This new avenue of exploration has affected not only the opening of new areas of research but the nature of thought itself. Investigations delving into the area of computational thought have evolved from detached abstract possibilities into intuition that spans scientific study to philosophical inquiry.

The contribution of Alan Turing was very instrumental not only in the advancement of computer technology but also in the development of the algorithmic processes that were the precursors of fractal geometry. He was an English mathematician, code breaker, and logician who pioneered the synthesis of algorithms with computational technology. He integrated the ideas of Bertrand Russell, Kurt Godel, and David Hilbert regarding the concept of *decidability*, whereby a mathematical proposition, through the discovery of an appropriate algorithm, could be proven true or false.[1] In 1936 Turing introduced an abstract machine, a Turing machine, that manipulated symbols from one state into another according to a precise set of rules. It was premised on the idea that if you could devise a set of rules, the machine could faithfully carry out the calculation according to those rules. Conceptually, Turing viewed his Turing machine as revising the human computer's normal method of recording computations on a sheet of paper into a continuous one-dimensional string or series of cells. Each cell was observed by the "mind" of the machine. The universe of operations performed by the machine was refined to an elementary set that could not be divided any further. It consisted of an input-output tape, the machine itself, and the set of rules. The tape was a scroll running between rollers such that it could be wound forward and backward. It was divided into cells that contained the input and output symbols, which would change frequently as the machine was running. The machine was the algorithm theoretically sitting in the black box above the tape reading the symbols one at a time from the read-write head. The rule list determined the machine's behavior at any particular point. In its operation, a Turing machine reads a symbol from the input-output tape, consults the list of rules, modifies its internal state accordingly, and writes a symbol on the tape and/or moves the head either to the right or left.[2] Despite their obvious simplicity, a Turing machine can be adapted to simulate the logic of any computer that can be constructed. The concept of a Turing machine, which had to be reprogrammed for every computational problem sought, was expanded into the concept of a universal Turing machine, whereby the universe of rule lists is set in the same "memory" as the input data. By encoding the rule lists of other possible Turing machines within itself, the unit becomes a universal Turing machine and the paradigm for modern computer architecture. Alan Turing collaborated with Alonzo Church to formulate the Church-Turing thesis, a fundamental concept in calculable functions and the basis for computer architecture. The

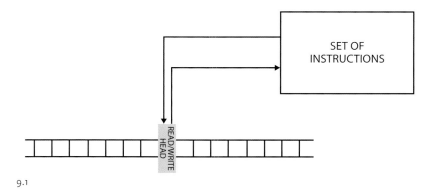

9.1

theory relates to recursion and Turing machines and states that for every algorithm, there is a corresponding Turing machine.

The concept of a universal Turing machine (Figure 9.1) has been metaphysically transposed by Karl Chu to proliferate a synthesis of architectural, biological, and organic forms. In his thesis, the universal Turing machine becomes a conceptual mechanism perpetually inducing an internal generational principle that is continually modified to arrive at a more comprehensive version of the idealized form. He sees the universal Turing machine as a machine-like idea of a perpetual computing machine endowed with a latent capacity to self-organize its internal state into all possible states of a conceptual entity. As the most general type of computing system, the internal principle can accommodate a generative algorithm that could evolve through self-modification and optimization of its internal state. This principle could be extended to self-replication and mutation, which encode new rules into its internal state, expanding the universal Turing machine.[3] For Chu, these new axioms, with their inherent ability to self-organize and manifest themselves in a physical state, epitomize Leibniz's monad. The universe is composed of an infinite number of monads, which are simple elemental substances that cannot be further divided or distilled. In metaphysics, they are analogous to atoms of the physical world. Monads operate according to a preprogrammed set of instructions, reflecting the essence of the universe in a preestablished harmony.[4]

Fractal geometry is essentially a universal Turing machine as within its "memory," the instruction set can generate a diverse set of outputs. From fractal geometry, an instruction set exists that can create a diverse set of natural forms in a manner that is innately commensurable with the principles of the universal Turing machine. Metaphysically considered, this universal fractal geometric Turing machine is a monad

Figure 9.1. Turing machine.

239

as it is an irreducible set of instructions that guides its manifestation in physical form. This physical expression is generated and reflects the preestablished harmony of the universe as manifested in nature.

COMPUTATIONAL SYSTEMS AND NATURE

Stephen Wolfram, in his book *A New Kind of Science*, performs a systematic study of computational systems, or simple programs, and their applicability to the other areas of study. He proposes that the substance of computing can be studied similar to other fields of study and in particular its relevance to nature. The underlying premise is that much of the study of computing can be reduced to simple abstract rules or, in effect, simple computer programs. The behavior produced by the iterations of these simple programs can be as complex as anything experienced. This extends to the complexity that nature produces as part of its inherent character. Wolfram notes that in examining nature, there is a correlation of the overall pattern of behavior between various systems that have significant underlying physical, biological, or other inherent differences. His research has detected a similar phenomenon in the area of computing, where programs that have different underlying rules converge toward a similarity of behavior. Wolfram contends that there is a plateau of universality that extends not only across the stratum of programs that is independent of the underlying rules but also to systems in nature. He postulates that it doesn't matter whether the components of a system are the black-and-white cells of cellular automata or the molecules of an organism as the overall behavior has the same universal attributes.

The fundamental mechanisms responsible for the behavior we see in nature are in some way similarly responsible for the behavior of simple programs. The operational mechanism of systems in nature is similar to those in the elemental computational systems to which Wolfram contends the vast majority of complex behavior can be distilled.[5] By studying the nature of simple programs, we can obtain insight into the behavior of systems in nature and understand what mechanism in nature causes the complex forms in vegetation, animals, and phenomena.[6] Wolfram's central point to his thesis is that processes that occur in nature can be viewed as a computation.[7] Nature's rules of growth can be viewed as a program and the resulting behavior as a computation.[8] This relationship exemplifies the alternating relationship between nature and mathematics of divergence and convergence. The relationship between math and nature for the last century has been one of divergence, but it seems to have reached its nadir and is now coming back to convergence.[9] Wolfram proposes that the similarity he has found between natural phenomena and mathematics must have a deeper origin.[10]

Wolfram cites a number of growth processes exhibited in nature that support the theory that natural entities and phenomena are derived from simple rules:

- Plant structures, where at the tip of the stem, new stems form and branch off. In many cases, these new stems are in essence reduced copies of the principal stem with the same innate mechanism for growth and the same innate rules for branching. This type of growth for Wolfram is characterized as a neighbor-independent substitution system in which each tip of a stem is replaced by a collection of smaller stems in a configuration whose variables for rotation and orientation are within some relatively small range. It is proposed that the distance between the appearance of new stem configurations is determined by the rates of production and diffusion of plant hormones. These rates are derived from the thickness and structure of the stem and the biochemical properties of the plant. At the point of formation of the new stem or stem set, the level of chemical composition within the ring of the stem has reached a level or tipping point to cause the formation of new stems, which causes the chemical level to recede to an equilibrium level. The growth process within the stem reiterates in the original stem as well as initiating in the new stem, causing the responsible hormonal level to creep up again until it again reaches the tipping point. When analyzing a mature structure based on this type of system, the composition appears complex despite the great simplicity of the underlying rules for growth. This system of growth extends beyond the branching structure and into the composition of the leaf. In examining the veining structure in leaves, a similar configuration emerges. Wolfram concludes that there is an overriding process responsible for the structure of the leaf, the branching system, and the overall form of the plant.[11] The generation of this natural structure is in accordance with the self-organizational process of fractal geometry.
- Horn structures grow by adding material at their base. If the rate at which the material is added is consistent, the horn will grow in a straight manner. If the material is added at differing rates across

9.2

the area, the growth will be inconsistent, with the portion receiving more material growing at an accelerated rate relative to the other areas receiving less material. Coiling typically occurs when there is a progressive diminution of material from one edge of the perimeter to the other. If this process occurs inconsistently, whereby the high concentration of material is not directly across from the low concentration of material, the coiling will occur in three dimensions (Figure 9.2). It is thought that an organism that lives at the open end of the shell secretes chemicals in a consistently inconsistent manner, which causes the shell to grow in a spiral configuration. The rates of secretion are presumably determined by the biochemical DNA of the organism. Small changes in the rate of secretion can have dramatic effects on the resulting form. This class of natural forms is a simple consequence of the application of three-dimensional geometry to simple underlying rules of growth.[12]

- The patterns of mollusk shells have a remarkable similarity to patterns generated by cellular automata (Figure 9.3). The growth of a mollusk shell, like the growth of cellular automata, in effect occurs one line at a time, similarly to the coiled structures. In this case, the material secreted to form the geometrical structure interacts with the previous line of growth material in the same manner as cellular automata determine the color of the cell based on the

Figure 9.2. A spiral shell.

9.3a

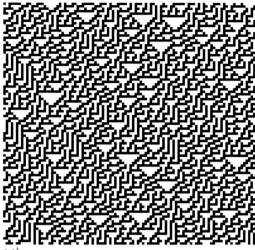

9.3b

Figure 9.3. a. A mollusk shell; b. Cellular automata.

condition of the previous cell and that of its neighbors. Wolfram believes that the rules that control the secretions that generate these patterns are chosen at random from a collection of the simplest possibilities. Another explanation is that the rules have a connection to either the fitness of the organism or the principle of expending the least amount of energy.[13]

• Crystals start from some sort of seed element to which they aggregate additional mass. This system behavior can be viewed as similar to the process of growth exhibited in cellular automata.

Wolfram has continually observed that highly complex structures emerge from generative systems that are based on simple rules and simple starting conditions and that this phenomenon is responsible for a great deal of the complexity we experience in nature.[14] One of the fundamental points *A New Kind of Science* makes is that (1) after a certain point, adding complexity to either the initial conditions or the rules of the generating program does not result in added complexity in the system's behavior, and (2) the threshold of that point of dramatically decreased returns of complexity is very low. On the basis of these findings, Wolfram believes that the vast majority of natural phenomena can be analyzed and understood by simple programs. The fundamental categories of repetition, nesting, and randomness with localized structures appear to represent the dominant behavior in many natural systems.[15] The consequence of his observation is a profound shift in the study of computational systems and nature that suggests there is

243

no immediate reason to go beyond the study of simple systems.[16] One of the important factors that underpin this concept is the idea of *iteration*, a fundamental aspect of fractal geometry. In Wolfram's studies of the various systems, such as cellular automata, the presentation of complexity frequently occurs from a significant amount of iterations of the system. Similarly, fractal geometry produces forms of significant complexity from iterating the set of generative rules; however fractal structures, in particular fractal architecture, can produce this complexity after a considerably smaller number of iterations.

COMPUTATIONAL UNIVERSALITY

A contemporary of Alan Turing, Konrad Zuse, pioneered the idea that the universe is structured as a computational system such as cellular automata or a universal Turing machine. He referred to this concept as *Rechnender Raum*, or "computing cosmos."[17] Other researchers have advanced the theory to be compatible with quantum physics, resulting in quantum versions of digital physics. Wolfram has advanced this concept by postulating that a simple program iterating an incomprehensibly large amount of cycles could produce the universe.[18] There may not be one underlying rule or generational principle but an infinite sequence of rules, with each level possessing an elegant simplicity that becomes increasingly independent of the levels below it.[19] Wolfram hypothesizes the structure of a computational universe as a loose series of casually connected nodes, and within the pattern of its connectivity is encoded our visible universe. The properties of the universe's casual network relate to our notions of space and time, with successive slices through the casual network corresponding to states at successive moments in time.[20]

Wolfram reorients this concept of the universe toward instances of universality. On the basis of his observations of systems in nature and computational systems where various underlying conditions nonetheless produce a commonality of behavior, he concludes that there is a universality that exists. As an example, he cites the similarity in subsets of biological systems that exhibit patterns and structures that appear in ion physics. In biological systems in particular, he notes a correlation in behavior with simple programs.[21] This universality underpins his thesis that systems in nature can be understood through the study of simple programs. A universal system is a system whose underlying structure is fixed but that can perform different tasks through programming. A system is universal if it can support universal computation

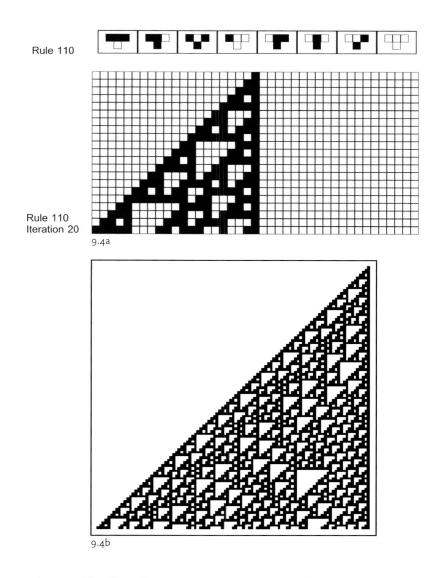

Rule 110

Rule 110
Iteration 20

9.4a

9.4b

and is capable of emulating other systems and producing an equivalent level of complexity. Universality is more common than conventional thought and is associated with the majority of instances of complex behavior. Wolfram divides system behavior into four classifications, with class 1 exhibiting simple repetition and class 4 exhibiting overall random behavior, with locally organized structures emerging sporadically. Substitution systems to which fractal geometry is analogous fall technically into class 3 behavior but, when sufficiently structured, visually exhibit class 4 behavior. Wolfram contends that the quality universality is associated with some class 3 and most class 4 systems.[22] In particular, he cites rule 110 of cellular automata, illustrated in Figure 9.4 as epitomizing universality.

Figure 9.4. Wolfram's rule 110.

The concept of universality is connected to universal Turing machines, and similarly fractal geometry meets the technical standards of universality as well as its philosophical foundation. Fractal geometry is a fixed system that can be programmed to emulate a number of structures or growth systems in nature from geological structures to plants and trees to clouds and to cosmological systems such as the archetypal structure of a galaxy. As anyone can attest, all these natural systems, despite being structured by a set of rules that operate within tight ranges, exhibit the characteristics of universality through localized structures within apparent randomness. When not influenced by environmental forces, the apparent randomness is not really randomness but the complexity of the structure that can only be discerned by careful study. Universality is a characteristic that has been desired by various intellectual disciplines inclusive of architecture. Architects from ancient Greece through the Bauhaus and the International Style period have sought to base their architecture on the concept of universality. Architecture derived from fractal geometry may be a path to achieving universality in architecture.

SELF-ORGANIZATION AND EMERGENCE

A universal phenomenon that appears to occur in physics and biology is the tendency for self-organization and the production of generated structure or phenomena. This concept was initiated by Descartes, who held that the ordinary laws of nature tend to produce organization. It was continued by D'Arcy Wentworth Thompson, who promoted the understanding that there are universal laws that govern growth and form in biological systems. Antonio Lima-de-Faria has developed the theory of *autoevolution*, which is the transformational phenomenon inherent to the construction of matter and energy. From this foundation came the emergence of forms and functions. Life has no beginning as it is a process inherent to the structure of the universe. Seemingly coincidental patterns arise in living organisms because they are based on the same atoms and symmetries of minerals transferred intact to the cell level.[23] With the increased integration of computer technology into scientific research, this phenomenon is being explored to a higher degree and understood more deeply.

This tendency for self-organization has manifested itself in physics through phase transition, crystallization, crystal growth, superconductivity, and percolation; in chemistry by molecular self-assembly; in biology by homeostasis, embryonic development, morphogenesis, and spontaneous folding of proteins; in mathematics through cellular automata; and in culture through herd behavior, the behavior of a market economy, and other aspects of societal behavior.

It is not uncommon to see natural systems whose initial states are disordered and featureless spontaneously organizing themselves via feedback loops to produce a discernible structure and order.[24] As the organism continues in the self-organizational process, the complexity of the system increases. The lowest level of the system generates emergent properties that form the building blocks of the next level of development. This level generates its own set of emergent properties that form the basis for a subsequent level of complexity.[25] The evolving system encoded within the genetic structure causes the organism to coalesce according to its own internal ordering principles. This set of instructions for self-organization is encoded as a generative program into the genome of the organism and specifies how the system evolves from step to step.[26] The act of self-organization denotes the idea of a system that has a capacity for order without the intervention of an outside force. The process of self-organization causes the potential organism's constituent elements to configure themselves and interrelate with other components to form an integrated whole.[27]

The state precedent to self-organization has been termed *chaos*. In this state, there is no proportionality between cause and effect, and the variables that establish the behavior of the system are not clearly determinable. At the edge of chaos or the point of criticality, the system moves from a state of complexity without order toward a state of complexity with order. At this point in the process of self-organization, certain systems, such as fractals, exhibit a tendency to move toward certain positions called *attractors*. A system that moves toward a fixed structure can be said to be drawn to an attractor.[28] The nature of a fractal structure is based on attractors that are developed within the generative instruction set. Each iteration of the fractal self-organizational program articulates the move toward the attractor.

Associated with self-organization is the concept of emergence. *Emergence* is the ascension of innovative and coherent structures, patterns, and properties during the process of self-organization. It comes when an observer recognizes a pattern or unprecedented property coming from the interaction of the component parts. Relatively simple agents follow simple rules in a bottom-up mode to produce a complexity that arises from deep simplicity. Emergent phenomena develop from the pattern of interactions between elements of the system over time. An emergent property or behavior is shown when a number of agents form more complex behavior as a collective.[29] The property is a result of "deep structure" emanating from the interrelationships within the synergistic system. As with fractal structures, emergence can occur across various dimensions or scales, forming causal relationships across the various levels of scale. The nature of the emergent qualities is influenced by the character and amount of interconnectivity within the system. In strong emergence, the emergent property is generally unpredictable from a lower-level description or behavior and is irreducible to the system's constituent parts. Similarly with fractals, the whole of emergence is greater than the parts. Some illustrative examples follow:

- A car is composed of between fifteen thousand and twenty thousand parts. If these separate parts were put into one heap, they would be ordered relative to their proximity as opposed to being randomly distributed across the world. Although they are "ordered," they do not constitute a car. They become organized, emergent phenomena when they are assembled in a purposeful way to form a car. As a disorganized heap, they are nothing more than a sum of parts, but when properly organized, a synergistic entity emerges: the car.[30]
- The substances of hydrogen and oxygen are separate, extremely light gases at room temperature. In combination as water, they form a heavy liquid. Liquidity is one of the emergent properties of their combination. The properties of liquidity, wetness, hydraulic dynamics, and so on, cannot be predicted from examining the properties of either substance.[31]
- Termites build their nests to house their colonies, and when they rise above the concealing ground, they become mounds (Figure 9.5). These mounds are orientated according to thermoregulatory factors, and the resulting architectural form exudes an emergent property of a Gaudiesque cathedral.
- The World Wide Web is an example of a decentralized system that has emergent properties of knowledge and communication. Billions of users coalesce to form a society whose spontaneous behavior causes cultural shifts.
- The stock market has no central controlling entity, but as a whole it regulates the relative security prices of companies across the world.

9.5

In compositions generated by fractal geometry, as with natural forms, the essential property that emerges is an organic quality. The separate elements by themselves do not possess this quality, but in the process of self-organization, they relate to other entities in an integrated manner and form a unit at the next level of organization that inter-relates with other units on that level in a similar manner, forming an integrated unit on that level. This process continues up through the levels of organization until an organic whole emerges which is more than the sum of the elements. As discussed in previous chapters, this emergent property has strong positive emotional and consequently intellectual and physiological connotations for humans. The process of self-organization that generates this emergent property is analogous to the process that produces the quality of wholeness that Christopher Alexander has outlined in his *Nature of Order* series. Wholeness is created by the presence of living structure. A fundamental property of living structure is that it is generated by a "living process" in which, through transformational sequences, the structure is unfolded in the same manner as "a developing embryo unfolds in nature."[32]

COMPUTATIONAL GENERATIVE DESIGN

With the increased integration of computer technology into science research and design processes, a confluence of these disciplines has spawned design processes that integrate self-organizational processes of biology and other life sciences. These processes are frequently based on the use of an *algorithm*, which is a sequence of instructions for completing a task or computation. It is related to Turing machines, and an algorithm is considered a computational process defined by a Turing machine. Starting with an initial state, the instruction set causes a defined series of successive states eventually ending in the final or end state. A recursive algorithm is one that references itself until a specified state is reached and is integrated into the instruction set. Iterative algorithms utilize repetitive constructs such as loops, which are sets of instructions that are repeated a distinct number of times. Algorithms utilized for generating fractal forms utilize a computational procedure that integrates both recursive and iterative algorithms. Al-gorithms are utilized in the design process by providing a framework for articulating and defining both the input data and procedures. This procedure supports the structure and coherency of the process as well as the transparency of the input data.[33] They are especially useful in the speed by which they evaluate alternatives. The algorithmically

Figure 9.5. Termite nest.

249

based generative schema can be interfaced with concepts developed in evolutionary computation and artificial life–based processes to explore new avenues of organic growth models based on biology.[34]

As with other periods in history when science and design merged, the present fusing of these disciplines has produced a new design paradigm that utilizes the generative principles inherent within natural processes and the evolutionary course of nature as the generating mechanism of architectural form. Algorithms are formulated according to the generative processes in nature such as the fractal growth model. Then a prototype or a series of prototypes is generated from this algorithm and evaluated according to either an objective set of criteria, a set of performance-based standards, subjective evaluation, or a combination of these evaluation benchmarks. The prototype or prototypes are kept if satisfactory or the variables and/or the generative structure is revised. It is an interactive iterative process whereby, through generative design, algorithms, and programmatic intervention, forms evolve through successive refinements. Generative form evolves through many iterations of both parametric modifications and generative structure revisions, producing a network structure representing the investigatory paths and decision points. It is not unusual for the evolution of form to produce dead ends where you have backtrack through the decision points until you reach the critical point in the network where you advance the design inquiry in another direction through a revision to the generative structure.

An early application of this generative model was the development of the algorithmic basis of Lindenmayer systems (L-systems), which have been widely used to model plant growth. Similar to the fractal growth process, the algorithm consists of an initial seed, a set of production rules, and a rewrite process whereby the production rules are repeatedly applied to the seed and its successive states. Algorithmically based systems for modeling organic forms have been developed such as Xfrog. Xfrog utilizes various arithmetical procedural components, such as algorithms, to simulate the various mathematical structures found in nature such as realistic trees, plants, and flowers.[35]

Stephen Todd and William Latham have explored the use of algorithms to generate biomorphic forms in their book *Evolutionary Art and Computers*. Utilizing the underlying geometric principles observed in nature and the algorithmic processes of iteration and recursion, they developed biological forms that range from organisms found in nature to any biomorphic form imagined.[36] Central to their process is visual observation of the generated form and interventive editing of either the parametric variables or the generative structure of the algorithm.[37] They utilized three complementary systems to formulate an evolutionary artificial life process: Form Grow to generate a life-form according to a geometrically based system of instructions; Mutator to select forms from the population of forms produced by Form Grow and combine their parametric values and/or their generative instruction sets; and Life Cycle, which can run the form through the life cycle of birth, growth, and decay.[38]

A research pioneer in the integration of computation and architectural design is John Frazer, an English architect and researcher. In his book *An Evolutionary Architecture* and subsequent publications, he formulates methodologies to integrate the fundamental form-generating process in architecture with the concepts of morphogenesis in the natural world. He endeavors to incorporate the biological concepts of symbiosis and coevolution with architectural form, generated through the development of an integrated algorithm.[39] Frazer conceptualizes two different types of design systems that utilize growth processes that replicate natural strategies: generative design systems and evolutionary design systems. In the generative design system, large numbers of solutions emerge, with significant differences between them. The system encodes growth processes to transform the seed form into a complex structure. Minor adjustments are made to either the process structure or seed to produce alternate designs. In evolutionary design systems, there is a cyclic manipulation of design parameters in response to environmental considerations, causing the population of design solutions to evolve gradually.[40]

Within these systems, three models are employed: the concept seeding model, the generative evolutionary model, and the combined model. The concept seeding model codifies in generic form the components of architectural style, such as those elements of Gaudi, Wright, or Le Corbusier, into a set of standard details and methodologies. A set of generation rules is classified according to the components of the designer's style. A concept seed is then developed to capture key elements of the architectural concept, and then designs are generated in response to the environment. The concept seed model is not cyclic but generates a single design solution with minor modifications made to either the concept seed or the generative rules to produce design alternatives.[41]

The generative evolutionary model is based on the natural evolutionary process to produce architectural form. Architectural form is

251

composed within the parameters of artificial life and morphogenesis. A series of generative instruction sets is compiled that produce forms that are evaluated within environmental criteria. Unlike the concept seeding model, the generative rules tend to be general and do not reflect particular architectural concepts or styles. For each instruction set, design solutions are generated, producing a matrix of forms reflecting solutions within each instruction set as well as an array of the various instruction sets. Each form is then evaluated and the most successful are selected. From this total population of successful forms, parameters and generative instruction sets are cross-mapped to produce a new array of instruction sets and a corresponding population of forms or design solutions. The process continues until a form or group of forms is obtained that satisfies the objective and/or subjective criteria.[42]

The combined model synthesizes the generation of forms according to conceptual or stylistic rules and according to the concept seeding model with the evolutionary process of the generative-evolutionary model. The population of design solutions is generated according to the conceptual parameters of a design solution, the most successful of which is selected and utilized to develop the next group of instruction sets and corresponding population of forms. This combined process can produce a variety of forms that can be perceived as either diverse, where the population has differences between parameters but coherence of organization and configuration, or disparity, where there are fundamental differences in organization and composition of elements.[43]

FORM LANGUAGE

The advent of the confluence of computational methodology and architectural design has produced a new design paradigm derived from the concept of form language. *Form language* is the combinatory system that systematizes the compositional rules that produce structure with certain desired qualities. One of the earliest conceptualizations of architecture as language was by Leon Battista Alberti. His concept of beauty was espoused in the idea of *concinnitas*, which is the composition of elements that by nature are quite separate, in a manner of innate relationships, form an organic whole. Architecture was analogous to a spoken language to be used as a means of expressing human thought. The rules of the orders used in the Renaissance and subsequent vocabularies were considered the grammar or syntax of the order.

In *Logic of Architecture*, William Mitchell has developed a language structure that is derived regressively by describing structures in words and then formulating the description by using first-order predicate calculus. This process leads to a vital language for categorizing qualities of buildings that can be used in constructing forms utilizing a graphic token that can be manipulated according to "grammatical" rules. The design process becomes a computation with the objective of satisfying predicates of form and function within the form language. The process consists of three components: the first is understanding design criticism as truth-functional semantics, the second is specifying design according to a formal grammar, and the third is that the rules of this grammar encode the capacity to generate functional buildings.[44] Robert Williams designates the universe of discourse as the referential set of objects and a function as a particular kind of relationship among the objects in the universe of discourse. The set of functions or relationships for the universe of discourse is termed the functional basis set. From this grammatical configuration, a conceptualization is established consisting of the universe of discourse and the functional basis set. Through this language structure, the design process is treated as a computation with the goal of satisfying predicates of form and function.[45]

Robert Williams, in *The Geometrical Foundation of Natural Structure*, outlines the basis for form language. He submits that a language can be considered as a set of entities with rules for their combinations and, when properly combined, can transmit ideas and information. This communicative structure consists of four elements: a grammatical component, a syntactical component, a semantic component, and a symbolic component. Rules of combinations constitute the grammatical component describing how the entities are constituted for both speaker and listener. Meaning is associated with the organization of the entities in the syntactical component, and any change in the organization of the entities will produce a change of meaning. Meaning is transferred from the transmitter to the receiver, and the semantic component interprets and analyzes the communicated meaning. The symbolic component is activated when the transferred meanings go beyond the entity itself and invoke unconscious and collective meanings. For some languages, it is inherent that all the components are operating. In form language, there is a set of entities with rules for their combination, the result of which transfers a concept in the form of a physical object. The object communicates meaning, tying the designer and receiver together. Form language is analogous to music where meaning is not associated with individual notes but is evoked by the combination of notes by the composer.[46]

A form language embodies a perceivable order or style utilizing geometric components. It functions as schemata from which architectural form can be generated. The structure of the form language leaves an indelible imprint on the morphological qualities of the generated form. The form language for natural structures provides the methodology for articulating the qualities that respond to perceptual and cognitive ideas of organic form. It is developed by utilizing the geometric schemata that are present in natural phenomena and forms. It is a grammar that incorporates transformations, iteration, and recursion.

For Christopher Alexander, form language is transformational grammar that produces structure-preserving transformations that reinforce living structure. Each of the transformations builds on the living structure substrate and through its form language transforms it according to rules that "unfold" the living structure through the form-reinforcing process. The transformation rules are based on the differentiating processes found in nature that correspond to Alexander's fifteen natural properties, including levels of scale, centers as fields, local symmetries, echoes, simplicity and inner calm, and good shape (described in chapter 2).

Fractal geometry has been called a new language, and as Barnsley noted, "once you can communicate through it you can describe the shape of a cloud as you describe the shape of a house."[47] It is a language that describes the structural forms that are left in the wake of chaotic behavior, giving visible order to chaos. Fractal geometry can be considered the first and foremost language to describe the complex forms in nature. Its form language consists of a large library of algorithms that produce compositions that reflect the diversity and complexity found in nature.[48] By noting in nature that the seemingly exceptional was more like the rule, the father of fractals, Benoit Mandelbrot, developed a systematic language into which characters could be embedded. Fractal geometry should be considered a new language in mathematics. As a language can be broken down into letters or characters, fractal geometry provides the means to break down the patterns and form of nature into primitive geometric elements that can be composed into "words" and "sentences" to describe natural forms. In this dialect, the elements are primitive transformations and words are primitive algorithms.[49]

GENERATIVE FORM AND SCRIPTS

The concepts of computing, algorithms, self-organization, generative growth models, and form language are crystallized through the use of scripts. A scripting language is an extension of a computer programming language that controls a software application. It is embedded in but distinct from the actual program and is accessible to the user and enables the user to manage the behavior of the software to fit his or her objectives. The concept of scripting originated from the written scripts used in performing arts, where dialogue is written down to be recited by actors to convey a concept or emotion. Scripts are incorporated into CAD modelers to provide the ability for the user to customize the methodology for modeling, permit precise placement of elements or processes that are controlled by a mathematical formula, and permit instantaneous processing of the instruction set. Instead of laboriously copying, scaling, rotating, translating, and combining the different elements of a fractal model at each level and then repeating the process for the number of iterations desired, a script can be developed that completes the task instantaneously. Each scripting language has its own syntax rules, which are necessary for the program to read and execute the script. They can be very idiosyncratic, and unless you have a working knowledge of them, they can bedevil any attempt at developing a script.

One of the most common modelers utilized by architects is 3DMax, a powerful modeling, rendering, and animation program developed by Autodesk Media and Entertainment. Within this package is a scripting language, MAXScript, which utilizes the base program to visualize the forms resulting from its scripts. Each scripting language has its own distinct syntax or grammar for communicating within the language. The language is a type of shorthand English that incorporates algebraic functionality. The sequence of operations you want the "program" to perform is written down in text form. Some characteristics of scripts are the following:

- The layout of the script utilizes indents to segment areas to assist in providing a comprehensible structure or hierarchy that enables understanding of the script.

- Typically, notes are added that can assist in your understanding of the structure of the script. They are annotated so that they are not confused as part of the script. In MAXScript, the annotation consists of a couple of dashes at the start of the note.

- Script structuring uses block statements, where parentheses are used to separate a group of instructions from the body of the script and are typically used in sequence control statements.

- Variables are frequently utilized, and a variable assignment can be thought of as a cell in a spreadsheet and assignment as putting a value in that cell. In MAXScript, variable assignments utilize the equals sign to assign the value to the variable; it is not congruous with the algebraic definition of the symbol. For instance, $X = X + 2$ is nonsense in algebra, but in MAXScript, $X = X + 2$ means "replace the value of X with the value $X + 2$."

- Object properties can be specified through the dot notation syntax, where after the subject object, you insert a dot, the property, an equal sign, and the value or keyword parameter settings. An example would be box.color=red.

- Objects are created using a constructor that consists of a class or type of object, such as a box, and creation parameters such as width, length, height, and position. A box would be created by the command Box=(10,20,30) pos(5,5,5).

- Actions, such as "move" or "copy," are termed *functions*, and the entire command is called a *function call*. The function is specified by a list of things, called *parameters*, that it requires to perform its task, which is called an *operand* or *function argument*. They define the object, called the *positional parameter*, subject to the action and a set of keyword parameters such as a movement vector in terms of the standard Cartesian x, y, and z axes. The box created earlier would be moved by the command Move Box (10,10,10).

- Functions can be created by naming the function, the parameters, and then a code block to define the operations to be performed on the parameters.

- Expressions can be constructed to execute various mathematical and logic operations such as $z = 2 + 2$ or midpoint=(obj1.pos + obj2.pos)/2.

- MAXScript runs the script's sequence of operations in the order it is written, unless a sequence control mechanism or constructor is utilized. Some of the sequence control mechanisms are conditional structures and loop structures.

- Your script may entail making decisions within the script and using different options depending on the circumstances.
  - One sequence control mechanism for this situation is the conditional if statement, where if a test function or condition is true, then a certain action is performed, and if it is not true, then another action is performed. The terminology used is "if . . . then . . . else." The decision operation may not be restricted to one condition. For more than one condition to be evaluated to decide what action to perform, a Boolean construct is utilized where the "if . . . then . . . else" is modified to "if . . . and . . . then . . . else." The if statement can also be written in the form "if . . . do," where if a condition exists, the program performs this action, and if it does not exist, the program simply moves through the rest of the script. Another sequence control mechanism is the while loop or "while . . . do" construct, where while a condition exists, the instruction is to do an action; this is useful if the condition is in the form of a true-false condition.
  - To step through and evaluate a group of elements, another sequence control construct is used: the for loop. The source portion of the for loop specifies the class of objects we want to loop through and the loop variable that temporarily holds the test object as the script tests each one of the objects. The for loop can also loop through a series of numbers or a range specification with a loop variable, performing a task for each step. Loop structures can be embedded in other sequence control structures and in another loop control.

FRACTAL SKYSCRAPER FORM SCRIPT EXAMPLE

In chapter 4, I described how fractal geometry was utilized in generating an architectural form that embodied the characteristics of a classic skyscraper design. That form was derived using the collage method of fractal composition, where a seed shape was created that approximated the scale of the desired form, and elements were created by copying the seed shape and transforming those copies at various scales, positions, and orientations to compose the structural relationships between elements. The original seed shape is deleted, and the group of copies are synthesized to form the new seed shape. The procedure was repeated for a number of iterations until the design met the intended aesthetic criteria. The following is a general script flow that does not use any particular program syntax.

The first step was the creation of a rectangular prism seed shape (variable values are in inches) that creates a basis for a fifty-story building; it is named Box01:

Box01= box length:2100 width:2100 height:7200

The initial element of a counter is set up to control the loop construct that is used for the purpose of iterating the process as many times as desired. The first part of that process is to set the counter variable to zero:

i=0

Next we set up a "while . . . do" construct that instructs the program to run the loop process as long as the counter is 3 or less:

while i<3 do

The initial part of the loop process is to copy and scale down the seed object to half its width and length dimensions and a quarter of its height four times to form four elements at the base that are translated so that each element occupies one quarter of the footprint of the prism. The first element is used as the base component to which each of these parts is attached:

    copy Box01 scale:[.5,.5,.25] pos:[1000,1000,0] name:"Element01"
    copy Box01 scale:[.5,.5,.25] pos:[−1000,−1000,0] name:"Element02"
    attach Element01 Element02
    copy Box01 scale:[.5,.5,.25] pos:[−1000,1000,0] name:"Element03"
    attach Element01 Element03
    copy Box01 scale:[.5,.5,.25] pos:[1000,−1000,0] name:"Element04"
    attach Element01 Element04

The next part of the loop process is to create the shaft of the composition by creating two elements. One is created by copying and slightly scaling down in the z dimension the seed object to form the basic central shaft of the building. A copy of the seed shape is then scaled down by 10 percent in its width and length dimensions and

2 percent in height and is rotated about the *z* axis by 45 degrees and integrated with the copy of the central shaft:

```
copy Box01 scale:[.98,.98,.85] pos:[0,0,0] name:"Elemento5"
attach Elemento1 Elemento5
copy Box01 scale:[.9,.9,.98] pos:[0,0,0] name:"Elemento6"
rotate Elemento6 Z axis 45 degrees
attach Elemento1 Elemento6
```

The crown of the building is created by five elements. Four copies of the seed shape that are scaled down in the width and length dimensions to 21 percent of the seed shape and 10 percent in height are added to the position of the top corners of the shaft element. After iteration 3, they protrude through the rotated element of the shaft, which decreases in height with each iteration. The last part of the crown of the building is a copy of the seed shape that is scaled down to 55 percent in width and length and 27 percent in height and then translated up so that it is placed on top of the rotated prism:

```
copy Box01 scale:[.21,.21,.1] pos:[625,625,5250] name:"Elemento7"
attach Elemento1 Elemento7
copy Box01 scale:[.21,.21,.1] pos:[−625,−625,5250] name:"Elemento8"
attach Elemento1 Elemento8
copy Box01 scale:[.21,.21,.1] pos:[−625,625,5250] name:"Elemento9"
attach Elemento1 Elemento9
copy Box01 scale:[.21,.21,.1] pos:[625,−625,5250] name:"Element10"
attach Elemento1 Element10
copy Box01 scale:[.55,.55,.27] pos:[0,0,5200] name:"Element11"
attach Elemento1 Element11
```

The last set of eight elements is the vertical ribs, which bisect the halves of the unrotated portion of the shaft. Each of these is a copy of the seed shape reduced by 97.5 percent in length, 95 percent in depth, and 60 percent in height. Each is then translated to a position in the middle of the side of the unrotated shaft created by the integration of the rotated portion of the shaft:

```
copy Box01 scale:[.025,.05,.60] pos:[679,−1050,1600]
name:"Element12"
attach Elemento1 Element12
```

```
copy Box01 scale:[.025,.05,.60] pos:[−679,−1050,1600]
name:"Element13"
attach Element01 Element13
copy Box01 scale:[.025,.05,.60] pos:[679,1050,1600]
name:"Element14"
attach Element01 Element14
copy Box01 scale:[.025,.05,.60] pos:[−679,1050,1600]
name:"Element15"
attach Element01 Element15
copy Box01 scale:[.025,.05,.60] pos:[1050,679,1600]
name:"Element16"
attach Element01 Element16
copy Box01 scale:[.05,.025,.60] pos:[−1050,679,1600]
name:"Element17"
attach Element01 Element17
copy Box01 scale:[.05,.025,.60] pos:[1050,−679,1600]
name:"Element18"
attach Element01 Element18
copy Box01 scale:[.05,.025,.60] pos:[−1050,−679,1600]
name:"Element19"
attach Element01 Element19
```

The existing seed shape is then deleted, and the aggregation of elements which is Element01, with all the other elements attached to it, is renamed Box01:

```
delete Box01
Rename Element01 Box01
```

An important step is to reset the pivot point of the new seed shape, Box01, to the same pivot point of the original rectangular prism (0,0,0) which was the original seed shape. As each element was added to Element01, the pivot point of the composite entity moved. All affine transformations are made relative to the pivot point, and if it is not reset to its original location, most if not all of the subsequent transformations will not be accurate:

```
Reset Box01 Pivot Point (0,0,0)
```

Last, the counter is increased by 1:

i=i+1

Because the loop control states that the process continues until the counter reaches 3, the process repeats two more times. The entire script reads as follows:

```
Box01=box length:2100 width:2100 height:7200
i=0
while i<3 do
copy Box01 scale:[1,1,.9] pos:[0,0,0] name:"Element01"
copy Box01 scale:[.5,.5,.25] pos:[1000,1000,0] name:"Element02"
attach Element01 Element02
copy Box01 scale:[.5,.5,.25] pos:[–1000,–1000,0] name:"Element03"
attach Element01 Element03
copy Box01 scale:[.5,.5,.25] pos:[–1000,1000,0] name:"Element04"
attach Element01 Element04
copy Box01 scale:[.5,.5,.25] pos:[1000,–1000,0] name:"Element05"
attach Element01 Element05
copy Box01 scale:[.9,.9,.96] pos:[0,0,0] name:"Element06"
rotate Element06 Z axis 45 degrees
attach Element01 Element06
copy Box01 scale:[.23,.23,.125] pos:[625,625,5250] name:"Element07"
attach Element01 Element07
copy Box01 scale:[.23,.23,.125] pos:[–625,–625,5250] name:"Element08"
attach Element01 Element08
copy Box01 scale:[.23,.23,.125] pos:[–625,625,5250] name:"Element09"
attach Element01 Element09
copy Box01 scale:[.23,.23,.125] pos:[625,–625,5250] name:"Element10"
attach Element01 Element10
copy Box01 scale:[.55,.55,.27] pos:[0,0,5200] name:"Element11"
attach Element01 Element11
delete Box01
Rename Element01 Box01
Reset Box01 Pivot Point (0,0,0)
i=i+1
```

It is useful when first developing a fractally structured form to iterate a level at a time to understand the relationships and their effect on the fractally desired aesthetic properties of the form. If you set the number of iterations to the final level, you anticipate that you can generate an undesirable form and not understand the set of structured relationships that produced it. By generating a fractal iteration by iteration, you can understand the nature and consequence of the various relationships that constitute the composition. Through this understanding, the designer can make the modifications necessary to achieve the design objectives.

IMPLEMENTATION OF GENETIC METHODOLOGIES

Throughout history, nature has served as an inspiration for architecture. This trajectory spanned the initial employment of natural motifs as appliqués to the current investigations into biomimicry and utilization of natural generative processes to create architectural form. The confluence of computer technology, science, and design has given rise to the application of genetics and genetic methodologies to the design process. The set of instructions that are utilized as the grammar in form language and compiled in scripting language serve as the genetic constitution of the architectural form. This genetic template encodes the design characteristics in DNA-like code scripts that function in an evolutionary process.[50] Pioneers in this field of research have grasped the idea of utilizing natural processes as the source for architectural form. The applicable evolutionary template for this purpose is Darwinian natural selection and utilizes genetic operators such as crossover, mutation, and inversion.

Living organisms are composed of cells, with each cell containing the same set of chromosomes, strings of DNA, that serves as the blueprint for the organism. Chromosomes can be conceptually divided into genes or functional blocks of DNA with each one encoding a particular protein. Genes can be thought of as encoding a trait, such as hair color, and the different settings for the trait, such as blond, brunette, or redhead for hair color, termed *alleles*. The collection of the chromosomes or genetic material is called the organism's *genome*, and the set of genes contained in the genome is termed the *genotype*. During sexual reproduction, crossover occurs where each parent contributes genes from which portions are encoded into a composite set of chromosomes. In addition, during the process, the composition of the parent chromosome changes or mutates because of inaccuracies in the copying process, producing changes between parent and child.[51] The configuration of the chromosomes can be conceptualized as the genetic structure that operates as a key to unlock the potential of the genes to create form.[52]

The use of genetic algorithms in the design process has been described by Karl Chu in his proposition of the universal Turing machine for the information age. The genetic algorithmic process consists of three possible operators:

- It is initiated by a population of possible architectural forms, each with its own unique algorithm either by its structure or the variables utilized. From this population, the most suitable forms are selected and others deleted.
- From this population, parents are selected, and the designer chooses a locus within the string of genetic code and exchanges the genetic code between the two parents about the locus point. This process can be expanded to include more than one locus.
- From the population, certain forms are selected, and the designer mutates the chromosome by randomly changing the values in some of the genes. Genetic researchers such as John Holland believe that mutation preserves diversity.

Each iteration of the process is called a *generation*, and the entire set of generations is termed a *run*.[53] The run of a genetic algorithm for form generation comprises the universe of genotypes with their configurations of chromosomes and genes. The universe of forms from a run of a genetic algorithm can be considered the family for that algorithm.

The component parts of genetic algorithms are constituent of the idea of schemata or building blocks.[54] The schemata are analogous to the genetic structure of the genotype, which is manifested in the form of the phenotype.

When you use fractal geometry to model a natural structure such as a mountain or tree, you are trying to decode the essential formative forces at work. The decoding of nature's secret code has been a goal of artists, scientists, and philosophers since the dawn of recorded time. This code governs the formation and direction of growth and articulation of the organic form. Natural forms possess a uniqueness

263

among their genetic families owing to mutation and environmental influences. The fractal algorithm condenses the essence of a complex form into a simple code.[55] In the algorithms utilized to generate fractal forms, the set instructions for the geometric transformations are the chromosomes of the fractal organism, and the individual portions that constitute the traits of the individual transformations are the genes, with each setting being the alleles.

The following is a script for a fractally generated architectural form whose three iterations are illustrated in Figure 9.6:

```
I=0
While 1<1 do (
copy Box01 scale:[.33,.9,.3] pos:[9,0,25} name:"Element01"
rotate Element01 Y−90
copy Box01 scale:[.33,.9,.3] pos:[−9,0,25} name:"Element02"
rotate Element02 Y90
attach Element01 Element02
copy Box01 scale:[.75,.75,.9] pos:[0,0,0} name:"Element03"
attach Element01 Element03
copy Box01 scale:[.35,.35,.8] pos:[−50,0,0} name:"Element04"
rotate Element04 Z90
attach Element01 Element04
copy Box01 scale:[.35,.35,.8] pos:[50,0,0} name:"Element05"
rotate Element05 Z−90
attach Element01 Element05
copy Box01 scale:[.15,1.15,.15] pos:[0,0,207} name:"Element06"
rotate Element06 Z−90
attach Element01 Element06
copy Box01 scale:[.75,.75 ,.5] pos:[0,0,0} name:"Element07"
attach Element01 Element07
copy Box01 scale:[.05,.87,.81] pos:[0,0,32} name:"Element08"
attach Element01 Element08
copy Box01 scale:[.95,.85,.4] pos:[0,0,0} name:"Element09"
attach Element01 Element09
delete Box01
Rename Element01
Box01
Reset Box01 Pivot Point (0,0,0)
I=i+1)
```

9.6a

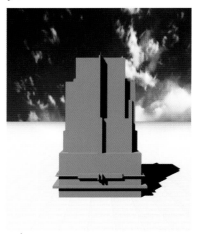

9.6b

9.6c

Figure 9.6. Fractally generated architectural form; a. Iteration 1; b. Iteration 2; c. Iteration 3.

This script can be restated in terms of genetic nomenclature, where each line is a chromosome, each parameter a gene, and each setting an allele (see Table 9.1, next page).

In Karl Chu's universal Turing machine, a generation of genetic solutions are developed to produce a set of architectural forms. Forms meeting aesthetic or other criteria are selected and either mutated or paired with another selected form and mated through crossover. This process produces another generation of forms, and the process repeats itself. Stephen Todd and William Latham have analogized the role of the designer in the process as a type of gardener who weeds out the unsatisfactory solution and steers the evolution of architectural form, presiding not over the survival of the fittest but over the survival of the most aesthetic.[56]

I utilize this process in an analogous manner, evolving not a generation of forms but one form in a guided mutation. A single proposed solution is generated and evaluated, with visual feedback being essential. Given the inherent holistic nature of the fractal design process, it can be difficult to foresee the effect of any proposed change. That is why it is recommended at times during the fractal design process to walk the generation of an architectural form one iteration at a time to see the unfolding of the interrelationships that constitute the fundamental basis of fractal design. By doing this, you can understand the nature of the relationships and why the form is evolving in the manner that it is. After evaluating the design generated by the initial set of fractal genetics, revisions could be made to any of the genes or to the structure of the genome through the addition or deletion of chromosomes (see Table 9.2).

After evaluating the architectural form, changes were made to both the structure of the genome and the genes themselves, which are highlighted in boldface (see Table 9.3). The revised architectural form is rendered in Figure 9.7.

Not only were a number of the alleles revised but a chromosome was deleted and another was added. The deleted chromosome that was one of the rotated elements is sitting on the shoulders flanking the large central element. The other element was made larger in width, making the model more efficient. The chromosome that was added was a square central element that is positioned at the base of the shaft and mediates the transition between the base and the shaft. This example truncated the process to two steps, but the processing

Chromosome Number	Scale			Position			Rotation		
	X	Y	Z	X	Y	Z	X	Y	Z
1	033	090	030	009	000	025	000	−090	000
2	033	090	030	−009	000	025	000	090	000
3	075	075	090	000	000	000	000	000	000
4	035	035	080	−050	000	000	000	000	090
5	035	035	080	050	000	000	000	000	−090
6	015	1.015	015	000	000	207	000	000	−090
7	075	075	050	000	000	000	000	000	000
8	005	087	081	000	000	032	000	000	000
9	095	085	040	000	000	000	000	000	000

Table 9.1

Chromosome Number	Scale			Position			Rotation		
	X	Y	Z	X	Y	Z	X	Y	Z
1	005	100	030	009	000	040	000	−090	000
2	005	100	030	−009	000	040	000	090	000
3	075	075	090	000	000	000	000	000	000
4	035	035	050	−050	000	000	000	000	000
5	035	035	050	050	000	000	000	000	000
6	025	025	015	−040	000	130	000	000	−090
7	025	025	015	040	000	130	000	000	000
8	075	075	050	000	000	000	000	000	000
9	050	090	091	000	000	000	000	000	000

Table 9.2

Chromosome Number	Scale			Position			Rotation		
	X	Y	Z	X	Y	Z	X	Y	Z
1	**033**	**090**	030	009	000	**025**	000	−090	000
2	**033**	**090**	030	−009	000	**025**	000	090	000
3	075	075	090	000	000	000	000	000	000
4	035	035	**080**	−050	000	000	000	000	090
5	035	035	**080**	050	000	000	000	000	−090
6									
7	025	**110**	015	**000**	000	**200**	000	000	−090
8	075	075	050	000	000	000	000	000	000
9	**005**	**086**	091	000	000	000	000	000	000
10	**095**	**085**	**040**	**000**	**000**	**000**	**000**	**000**	**000**

Table 9.3

typically takes a larger number of steps between initial form solution and final architectural form.

SUMMARY

As science is propelled to a greater understanding of natural processes through the utilization of the new broad range of technically driven tools, the possible answers to the dreams and philosophical queries in understanding nature are manifesting themselves. The application of this understanding to architectural design can produce forms that are innately gratifying to human cognition, perhaps because of the thread of nature that runs through them. One such application, fractally based architectural form generation, utilizes scripting tools available in state-of-the-art modelers. The correlation between the input variables that lend themselves to a code structure and similar structures in DNA code is at worst an interesting coincidence and at best an affirmation of this direction in architectural design methodologies.

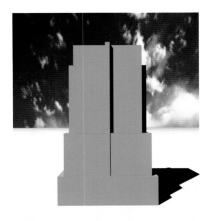

9.7a

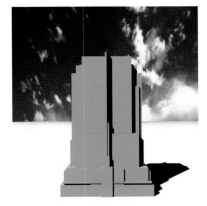

9.7b

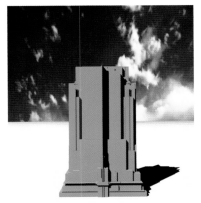

9.7c

Figure 9.7. Revised fractally generated architectural form; a. Iteration 1; b. Iteration 2; c. Iteration 3.

CHAPTER **10** **Elements of Fractal Form**

The greater part of this proposal on the applicability of fractal geometry as a means to generate architectural configurations has centered on the overall form of the building. It argues that nature has a fundamental significance to humans that affects them emotionally, cognitively, and physically. The presence of and exposure to nature provide positive nourishment to these fundamental human attributes, and conversely, the absence of nature's phenomena and natural form is essentially detrimental to the human experience. The recognition of nature's value has been embodied in architectural design throughout the ages. Ancient cultures based their most important structures, temples, on their philosophical relationship with nature and its extension, the cosmos. The integration of this philosophy through the use of the acanthus leaf motif as a metaphor for man's connection with the cosmos paralleled the incorporation of natural forms in an appliqué manner that continues to this day. The emulation of nature within architectural design was augmented by the use of mathematical constructs, such as the Fibonacci series, that appeared to emulate the factors that controlled the growth of natural plant forms. Eventually, design utilized the structural basis of nature's forms as the source of its design, epitomized in the architecture of Gothic cathedrals. As the architectural trajectory extended, the desire to espouse the ideals of organic form, where there is a part-to-whole-to-part relationship, increased. Architecture continued to incorporate natural structure as its basis through the work of Art Nouveau, while concurrently, architects such as Frank Lloyd Wright sought the elusive basis of organic form. As the architectural pendulum swung toward abstraction, Mies Van Der Rohe, Le Corbusier, and others still sought to grasp the principles of organic design within their abstract vernacular. Through recent advances in building technology, architects are able to extend the utilization of natural structure as a basis for architecture, incorporating its geometry and new materials never before possible into a biomorphic renaissance. The spectrum of natural configurations that can be used as the source of organic form has expanded from floral structures used in Art Nouveau to microscopic life-forms and cosmogenic structures. The use of biomorphic structures illustrates the swing back from pure abstraction to a renewed interest in capturing the organic quality of natural forms. Research into the use of biomimicry, or the replication of natural processes to produce form, hopes to generate structures that by virtue of their formative principles produce an organic quality that would resonate with humans. Fractal geometry can be considered as being under the umbrella of biomimicry. It produces geometric structure that results from the morphogenic processes inherent to a vast array of natural forms. By replicating the structuring principles that control the development of natural form, the structure that is produced by utilizing fractal geometry is inherently organic, displaying the hallmark part-to-whole-to-part characteristic.

The brain processes perceptual information according to certain innate functions that strive to produce a gestalt or organized, unified whole possessing a character that is more than the mere summation of its parts. Strongly organized stimuli with a substantial gestalt character produce a positive association with the stimuli. In the case of structures generated by fractal geometry, these forms are processed by the neurological architecture of human comprehension in the same manner as that for natural form. In both cases, the gestalt comprehended by the mind is associated with natural form. As with the perception of natural phenomena, fractal structures produce similar emotional, cognitive, and physical reactions as those experienced with natural forms. Whether consciously or subconsciously, forms generated according to fractal geometric principles are inherently appealing to humans.

FRACTAL ARCHITECTURE AND VARIED ITERATIONS

In this discussion of the applicability of fractal geometry and architecture, the fractal algorithm has been applied evenly throughout the elements that constitute the architectural form. In many if not most instances, the algorithm is applied three times to produce a form that exhibits the organic ideal of an inherent part-to-whole-to-part characteristic. Frequently, iterating less does not permit the relationships between the parts and whole to achieve a depth that exudes the historically desired organic quality, and iterating more may cause the organic characteristics to overwhelm the nature of the form's architectural identity. The typically blanket use of a consistent level of iteration throughout the form's constituent parts is not necessarily required. Different parts can be iterated a different number of times within the same composition. By applying this concept, the composition is characterized by a heightened sense of order and surprise. The elements are held together by the inherent set of relationships constituting the order of the form which is counterbalanced by the surprise found in observing the varying degree to which these relationships are embedded in the various constituent parts. The heightened tension between order and surprise can produce a perceptibly more interesting form.

In the example illustrated in Figure 10.1, the various elements were compiled after the fractal algorithm had completed the maximum number of iterations of any one element that was to be included in the final composition. Components were selected from the various levels of iteration and assembled to constitute a cohesive form consisting of parts with varying degrees of embedment of the fractal algorithm. An alternate methodology would be to take a component or components of a higher iteration and substitute them within a lower iteration of the form and then continue the iterative process of that lower form. As an example, if a fractal algorithm consists of ten components, four different iterations of the fractal algorithm can be completed. One group is composed of iteration 1, the next iteration 2, and so on, forming groups of substitution elements of varying levels of complexity. The fractal algorithm is run again on the original seed shape, and at any iteration the designer can replace a component or components from one of the four substitution groups into the fractal form being composed. This substitution is embedded further and further with each iteration throughout each of the elements, providing a highlight that further links each of the elements.

Figure 10.1 displays the first iteration of a fractal algorithm that will compose a high-rise structure utilizing a simple substitution of elements of different levels of iteration. From a rectangular prism seed shape 150 feet wide, 65 feet deep, and 300 feet high, fourteen elements are created to form a fractal composition using the collage technique.

- The first group of three parts is generated by copying the seed shape and scaling it down by 33 percent in width and 82 percent in height. This produces an element that in the front elevation is square and extends the full depth of the structure. The three elements are distributed along the base to produce the front elevation, whose base consists of a group of three squares.

- Above these three components are two pairs of elements. The first pair is a copy of the seed shape reduced by 67 percent in width, 30 percent in depth, and 35 percent in height. It is then rotated 180 degrees about its y axis so that in the front and rear elevation, it is inverted. The pair is translated to a position directly above the left component of the group of three elements that compose the base. One of the pair is translated to the front edge of the form, and the other is translated to the back edge. As the reduction factor of the depth of each part is 30 percent, there is a gap between the pair that is 40 percent of the depth of the seed shape. The second of this pair of elements is a copy of the seed shape scaled down by 33 percent in width, 30 percent in depth, and 18 percent in height. It is then rotated 180 degrees about its y axis and placed adjacent to the other rotated part and just above the two rightmost cubes that compose the base. As with the other pair of this subgroup, each part is translated either to the front or back edge of the seed shape, leaving a gap between the two of about 40 percent of the depth of the seed shape.

- An additional pair of elements is generated that is similar to the three parts that constitute the base. Like those parts, these two elements are produced by scaling down two copies of the whole by 33 percent in width and 82 percent in height. Unlike the three base components, they do not extend the full depth of the seed shape but are scaled down in depth to 30 percent of the seed shape, similar to the other pair of elements. These two elements are translated to the upper left corner, with one placed at the front edge of the seed shape and the other at the rear.

- Two components are generated to form the vertical accent that runs up the sides of the form. The first is a copy of the seed shape

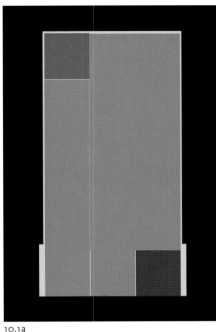

10.1a

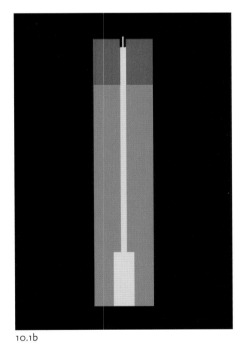

10.1b

Figure 10.1. Fractal high-rise structure, iteration 1; a. Front façade; b. Side façade.

reduced by 10 percent in width, 90 percent in depth, and 3 percent in height. The second element is scaled up by 2 percent in width and 1 percent in height and is scaled down by 98 percent in depth. Both these elements are not translated and occupy the void running across the elements above the three base components.

- Two elements are created by copies of the seed shape that are scaled down by 85 percent in width and 80 percent in both depth and height. Both components are rotated by 90 degrees about their z axis, one clockwise and the other counterclockwise. They were then translated to either side of the base along the center line of the seed shape.

As seen in Figure 10.1a, the rightmost element of the group of three elements that compose the base is colored blue, and the pair of elements at the top left corner of the façade are rendered in red. Figure 10.1b illustrates the side façade, which shows the pair of red parts at the top. The two elements that span the width of the middle of the form and the two elements on either side of the base are rendered in white. The remainder of elements of the form are rendered in a neutral gray. Each color is a placeholder for the materiality to be applied. The blue elements are flat white metal façade panels, the red elements are white metal shadow boxes, the white elements are white metal three-dimensional elements, and the gray material is glass curtain wall.

Figure 10.2a shows the front façade of iteration 2 with the fractal blueprint, the red element in the upper left corner, and the blue element in the lower right corner, clearly evident in the three parts of the base and the upper left element. The diagonal relationship is reversed in the other two elements as they are rotated 180 degrees about their y axes. In the element between the two parts on the left side of the façade and the component above the middle and right parts of the base, the positions of their blue and red subcomponents are reversed. The gestalt of the fractal algorithm begins to assert itself as two areas of spiraling groups of subelements, one across the base and the other at the upper left of the façade. Figure 10.2b depicts the side façade of iteration 2, which shows a predominately balanced composition, with the red and blue elements turning the corner to initiate the upward spiraling that takes place on the front and rear façades. Recalling the 180 degree rotation about the y axis of the tall element on either side

273

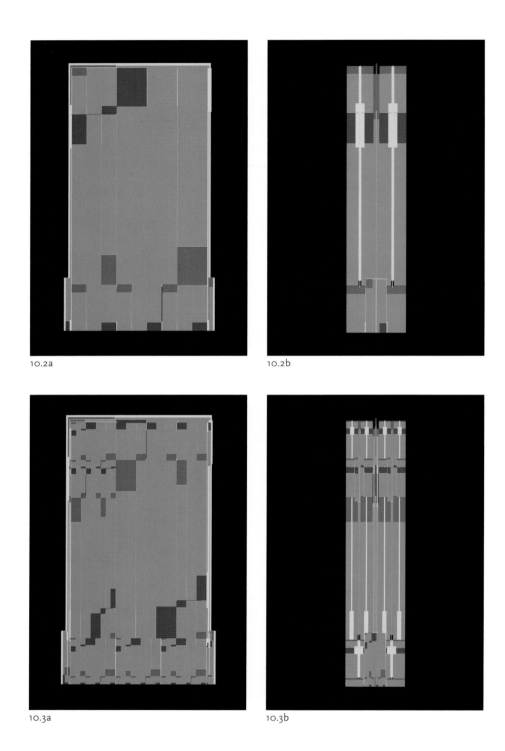

10.2a

10.2b

10.3a

10.3b

Figure 10.2. Iteration 2; a. Front façade; b. Side
façade.
Figure 10.3. Iteration 3; a. Front façade; b. Side
façade.

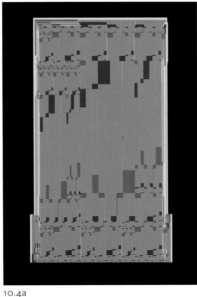
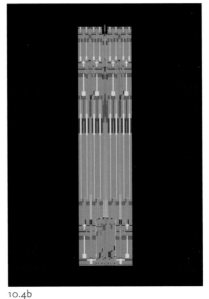

10.4a   10.4b

Figure 10.4. Iteration 4; a. Front façade; b. Side façade.

of the central accent component, you note that its white side subelement is adjacent to the white side subelements of the two elements above it.

Figure 10.3a renders iteration 3's front façade. In addition to the augmentation of the spiraling that emerges at the lower portion and upper right area, a strong horizontal visual force has emerged along the base and top of the façade. At the base, this arises from the repetition stemming from its composition of three equal elements. At the top, the horizontal force arises from the inversion of the largest element on the façade, which extends from the top of the middle and right components of the base to the top of the form. Owing to its 180 degree rotation, the three strong subcomponents that constitute its "base" are aligned across most of the top of the overall form. The same strong visual force that ran across the base of iteration 2 occurs along most of the "top" of this component. Figure 10.3b shows the side elevation of iteration 3. With each iteration, this façade increases the articulation of the horizontal visual forces, which dilate as they turn onto the front and rear façades in a spiraling visual force. The fractal algorithm programs the elements that are positioned at the sides of the base of the composition, which start as white boxes to rotate 90 degrees. This causes their façade, which faces the side elevation, to bear the front façade of the previous iteration. For each iteration of the side façade that shows the white box subelement, the subsequent

275

iteration will replace that with the front façade of the previous iteration. A comparison between the two iterations will confirm this as well as the emergence of new white boxes as sub-subelements.

Figure 10.4 shows the front and side elevations of iteration 4. These show a finer and deeper embedment of the visual forces that emerged in earlier iterations. The front elevation further integrates the spiraling and horizontal elements, while the side elevation refines the weave of the horizontal forces with the vertical white central subelements, sub-subelements, and sub-sub-subelements.

When viewing the various elevations, the designer may prefer the look of a particular component at a certain iteration and other elements of different iterations. The various elements of discrete iterations can be synthesized and still preserve the organic quality of the overall form and its constituent parts. This is possible because the same visual manifestation of the fractal algorithm runs through all the elements but at different levels of embedment. This provides the same fractal part-to-whole-to-part characteristic but applied with variation that in the natural world is brought about by environmental forces. Figure 10.5 shows the front and side elevations of iterations 3 and 4 on either side of a composite form that integrates elements of both. The composite form is composed by substituting the three base elements and the two small cubes positioned at the upper left corner of the front elevation to straddle the center vertical elements of the side elevation of iteration 3 for the corresponding components of iteration 4. In the front composite elevation, you can see the three base elements and one of the elements at the top left of the façade of iteration 3 integrated with the two large components that are positioned just above the three base elements, the side base elements, and the center vertical elements of iteration 4.

Figure 10.6 renders the front and side elevations as well as a corner perspective of the composite form. As discussed earlier, the various colors serve as placeholders for the application of gray glass, white metal panels, and white metal shadow boxes. As the shadow boxes are behind the gray glass, they have a gray tinge to them.

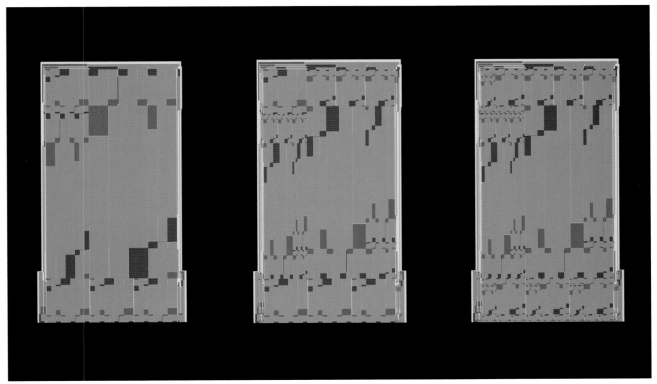

10.5a

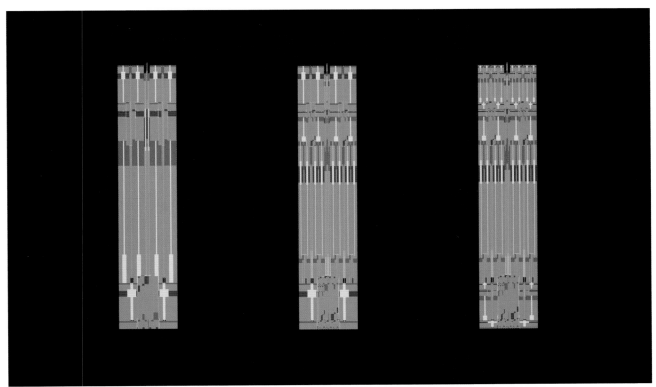

10.5b

Figure 10.5. Elevations of iterations 3 and 4 on either side of a composite form; a. Front elevation; b. Side elevation.

10.6a

Figure 10.6. Rendered composite elevations;
a. Front elevation; b. Side elevation; c. Corner
perspective.

10.6b

10.6c

FRACTAL DISTRIBUTION OF POSITIVE AND NEGATIVE ELEMENTS

As indicated earlier, one can employ the fractal algorithm in ways other than the typical methodology that generates fractal form. In the preceding example, fractal geometry is utilized to generate a pattern of components from different iterations that are placeholders designated to receive discrete material treatments, in this case, metal panels, metal shadow boxes, and dark glass. In the next example, fractal geometry is used to generate a pattern of elements that designate areas of positive or negative treatment to the plane of the façade. The elements that are designated as positive project from the face of the façade, and the elements that are assigned as negative components create negative spaces within the plane of the façade. It is inherent to the fractal generational algorithm that positive and negative elements are embedded within each of these components whether primarily designated positive or negative. Each iteration of the negative or positive elements is applied to the façade, generating a sequence of positive and negative spaces in the plane of the façade.

In Figure 10.7, the first iteration is shown along with the seed shape that represents the plane of the façade. The seed shape, rendered in white, is a rectangular prism 8 feet in depth, 150 feet in width, and 300 feet in height. The relationships that form the first iteration are defined by the fractal algorithm that consists of four elements.

- The three negative components are copies of the seed shape reduced by 67 percent in length, 50 percent in depth, and 84 percent in height. These parts, depicted in red, are rotated 90 degrees about the y axis and are translated vertically so that they are evenly distributed at third points. They are then shifted to the right side of the façade.
- The final element, which represents the positive component of the façade, is created by reducing the seed shape by 20 percent in length and 90 percent in height. This part, shown in green, is then translated vertically approximately one third up the height of the façade and shifted out and to the left.

These parts are merged together to create a composition that has a strong vertical and horizontal emphasis. The vertical component consists of three strongly organized wholes of perceivable squares whose off-center alignment contributes to their independent strength. The

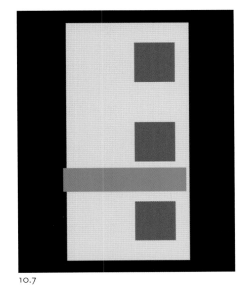

10.7

Figure 10.7. Fractal distribution of positive and negative elements, iteration 1.

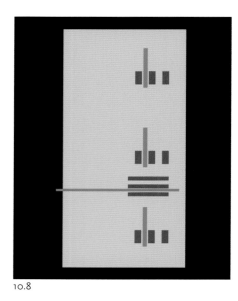

10.8

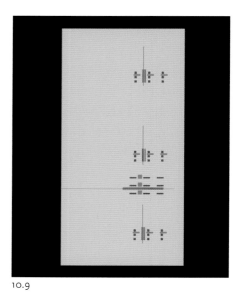

10.9

horizontal element is also a strong organized whole whose geometry and position relative to the elements that compose the vertically oriented group enhance its prominence as an independent element. With each iteration, the rotation of the red elements about their y axes will shift the emphasis of the summation of visual forces within each element or subelement. At one iteration, the emphasis will be either horizontal or vertical, and with the next iteration, the emphasis will shift 90 degrees.

Figure 10.8 shows iteration 2, which is the set of copies of the new seed shape composed of the red and green elements of iteration 1 fused together. The white seed shape is kept as a point of reference. Although not apparent in iteration 1, the effect of the rotation of the red "negative" elements is to reinforce their vertical orientation, while their red subcomponents provide a counterbalancing horizontal thrust. Their green "positive" subcomponent, in particular, contributes to this vertical visual force vector. The green element by its very nature retains its visual strength, and the alignment of its red negative subcomponents with the vertical red elements provides an elegant integration of the two opposing visual forces. Figure 10.9 renders iteration 3, which exhibits a further integration of the vertical and horizontal forces within each element. The effect is to distill the nature of the relationships created in iteration 1 to the point of an elegant refinement of their inherent visual forces. With an additional iteration, the red negative elements are again rotated 90 degrees about their y axes. Owing to this rotation, the three red negative elements have their individual verticality emphasized by their red negative sub-subcomponents, which in the previous iteration provided a horizontal visual emphasis. Their vertical emphasis is also reinforced by their large green subcomponent. This vertical emphasis is counterbalanced by their green sub-subcomponents' horizontal orientation. The green positive element refines its horizontal emphasis through its red subcomponents. These are counterbalanced by a vertical force of green subcomponents. The green and red elements are integrated by the similar alignment of their respective red subcomponents and the alignment of the green element's green subcomponents with the red element's vertical green subcomponent.

Figure 10.10 renders these diagrammatic elements integrated into a typical commercial curtain wall façade.

Figure 10.8. Fractal distribution of positive and negative elements, iteration 2.
Figure 10.9. Fractal distribution of positive and negative elements, iteration 3.

10.10a

Figure 10.10. Elements integrated into a typical
commercial curtain wall façade; a. Front
perspective; b. Façade detail; c. Top perspective;
d. Ground perspective.

10.10b

10.10C

10.10d

FRACTAL GENERATION OF ELEMENTS OF ARCHITECTURAL FORM

The use of fractal geometry in architecture is not confined to the creation of overall form or the generation of a pattern of placeholder visual forces that constitute the form. It can be utilized to compose the discrete components of the overall form and produce similar cognitive reactions. Fractal geometry can be used to generate façades, individual façade panels, and ornament. Although as you reduce the scope where fractal geometry is utilized from form to façade to façade panel and then to ornament, the cognitive effect is transformed depending on its context, and the forms that incorporate the elements of fractal geometry still retain their inherent appeal.

- The pedestrian perception of an urban façade where it is the only perceivable portion of the architectural form, as the other three sides are hidden by adjacent buildings, is essentially as strong as the oblique perception of a three-dimensional form. The inherent human gestalt perceptual mechanisms compositionally complete the rest of the architectural form with the same organic quality that exists of the façade that is able to be seen. The design of an architectural façade can be utilized as a wrap that is applied to a simple geometric form that dominates commercial architecture. While the form is devoid of organic characteristics, the façade still imbues the overall composition with organic characteristics.
- The use of modulized façade panels generated through fractal geometry combines the organic gestalt inherent within one panel with the gestalt operation of repetition to produce a form that strides the line between disorder of the individual panel, with its own integral fractal form, and the order of the façade created by repetition. The organic individuality of the façade panel provides the cognitive spark that resonates throughout the façade via repetition of the panel for each module.
- The development of ornament according to fractal geometry creates a composition that possesses the same strong perceptual qualities as other fractal forms. It can be utilized within the composition to provide a perceptual highlight of fractal form that resonates with humans.

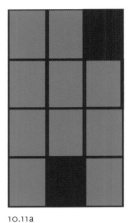

10.11a

Figure 10.11. a. Overlapping elements, iteration 1;
b. Exploded view.

Fractal Architectural Façade Example 1: Overlapping Elements

The first example of a façade generated through fractal geometry utilizes the collage technique, which is based on a seed shape that, like many fractal designs, approximates the overall size of the façade. In this instance, the collage methodology overlaps elements to produce a composition with a discernible but somewhat obscured gestalt. It creates an increased level of interest through a more complex analysis of the façade but is still rooted in the fractal stratum that resonates in people. In most of the prior examples, the seed shape was a simple geometric shape; in this example, it is a thin rectilinear metal tube with a glass panel at its center.

- The first iteration is pictured in Figure 10.11a and consists of twelve obvious copies of the seed shape, each of which is scaled down by 66 percent in width and 75 percent in height and then distributed across the façade so that the façade consists of a four by three grid of copies of the seed shape. Two of the copies have the glass panels within them changed from transparent glass to opaque metal panel.

- What is not obvious from Figure 10.11a is that there are three additional copies overlaid on a portion of the grid of twelve copies. Shown in Figure 10.11b, which is an exploded view of iteration 1, they consist of one copy of the seed shape reduced by 66 percent in width and 25 percent in height, which is then translated horizontally and vertically so that it is positioned at the upper right corner and covers the top three copies of the right column.

- The next element is created by reducing a copy of the seed shape by 66 percent in width and 50 percent in height. As with the previous element, it is positioned at the upper right corner, covering the upper two components of the right column of the grid.

- The last component is produced by copying the seed shape and reducing it by 33 percent in width and 75 percent in height. It is translated so that it is located to cover the two rightmost elements of the second row of parts from the top. As with most of the other components, the middle plane of glass remains transparent with these three overlay elements.

The original seed shape is deleted, and all these elements, including the three overlay elements, are merged to form the new seed shape. The same set of fifteen generative rules, those forming the grid of

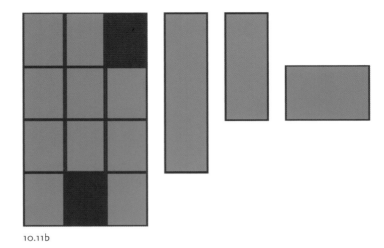

10.11b

elements and those constituting the overlay elements, are applied to the new seed shape. The result of iteration 2 is shown in Figure 10.12a. The effect of the integration of the two opaque panels is apparent through most of the façade, providing it with a horizontal rhythm. As you move toward the upper right corner, it is masked within the effect of the overlay panels. Figure 10.12b explodes iteration 2 to separate the overlay panels. By going back and forth between Figure 10.12a and Figure 10.12b, you can observe the effect of the overlay panels on the composite form. You can observe that these panels add a primarily vertical emphasis of opaque panels with a secondary horizontal visual force. As all these panels are combined to form the new seed shape, each of the elements in iteration 3 is expected to contain these two additional lines of visual force within them, in addition to the horizontal cadence that is due to the two opaque panels of iteration 1. Figure 10.13a shows the effect of iteration 3. The refinement of horizontal emphasis that is provided by the additional integration of the effects of the two opaque panels is evident. The integration of iteration 2's overlay elements bestows a primary vertical and secondary horizontal emphasis that is also clearly observable. Again, as you move toward the upper right section of the façade, there is an increasing opaqueness to the façade provided by the three overlay panels. In Figure 10.13b, iteration 3 is exploded, showing the effect of each of the overlay elements. Each

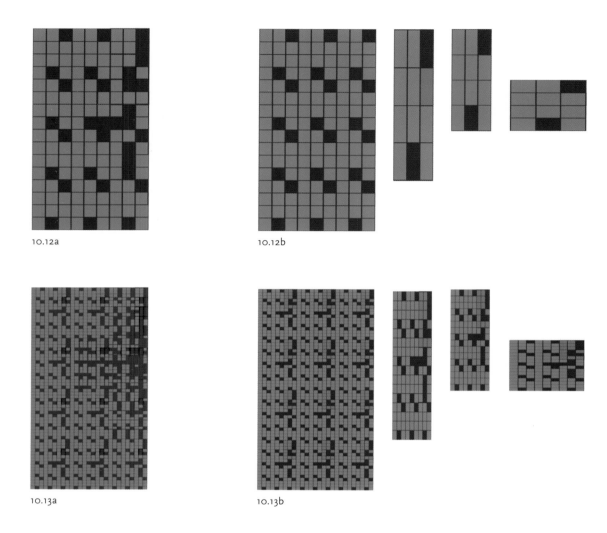

10.12a

10.12b

10.13a

10.13b

Figure 10.12. a. Overlapping elements, iteration 2;
b. Exploded view.
Figure 10.13. a. Overlapping elements, iteration 3;
b. Exploded view.
Figure 10.14. Overlapping elements rendered
façade.

of those elements has the characteristic horizontal rhythms from the opaque panels and the vertical and horizontal lines of visual force from the previous iterations of the overlay panels.

Figure 10.14 shows the façade applied to the curved surface that constitutes two sides of the façade of a proposed building. The use of the overlay elements provides a characteristic of vitality to what would be an interestingly syncopated but more regular façade. It does so within the vernacular of the grammar of the façade's design. This is inherent in the use of fractal geometry to generate the façade. Fractal geometry utilizes the nature of the relationships within the façade to regenerate itself at a deeper layer of meaning onto itself. Resulting is a form that exhibits the characteristic of organic design.

10.14

Fractal Architectural Façade Example 2:
Distribution of Façade Elements

Traditional building façades frequently have compositional elements placed within the façade to create an aesthetically pleasing configuration of visual parts. Frequently, these configurations involve the relationships between horizontal and vertical elements and their corresponding visual forces. An analysis of a group of traditional urban façades can reveal the configuration of their visual forces. Figure 10.15 depicts typical façades in New York City, in this case, along Park Avenue on the Upper East Side.

- In Figure 10.15a, the façade is divided vertically into approximate thirds. Against a masonry base plane with a regular distribution of punched openings for windows, various horizontal limestone string courses are distributed mainly at the lower and upper thirds of the façade. At the base, there is a strong horizontal limestone section at the ground level with a major vertical configuration of elements at the center of the base denoting the entrance. The top of this vertical grouping connects to a horizontal configuration of two limestone string courses within which are interspersed groups of small, vertically oriented posts, with the center group pulled forward from the façade to form a balcony. The balcony acts to integrate this horizontally oriented group of components with the vertically orientated elements at the base. A similar horizontal group of elements is repeated at the base of the top third of the façade but without the protruding balcony. From this horizontal group of elements springs a group of four two-story arches, each with two center limestone spandrel panels. In the middle of this group is a center configuration of three groups of two floors of windows each, separated by a limestone spandrel similar to the other limestone panels. At the top of this group is an articulated cornice element that acts similar to the protruding balcony below. It integrates the horizontal band of arches to the vertical line of visual force emanating from the base. Above these parts of the façade is a heavy horizontal limestone string course and a horizontal limestone cornice.
- Figure 10.15b illustrates a façade that is dominated by horizontally orientated sections that act to divide the façade roughly into thirds. The underlying substrate is again a masonry plane with a regular distribution of punched openings. The bottom third of the façade

10.15a

10.15b

10.15c

10.15d

Figure 10.15. a. Façade divided vertically into approximate thirds; b. A façade dominated by horizontally orientated sections; c. Elevation consisting of a masonry plane perforated by an array of openings for windows that is divided vertically into five similarly sized sections; d. A façade with a decorative terra cotta base and a terra cotta string course.

consists of a major horizontal limestone band at its base, within which the entrance is set. Above that is a horizontal group of punched openings, each of which is cased in a limestone frame. Two stories above that is a series of limestone string courses with a group of limestone frames between each window of a horizontal group of fenestration to form a frieze of windows and limestone frames. Above this group of string courses, the group of limestone cased windows is repeated with another limestone string course, but this string course is articulated with a protruding element at each window. Two floors above this, the configuration of limestone string courses, a window-limestone frieze, and an articulated limestone string course is repeated. At the top of the uppermost third of the façade, the limestone frame and window frieze is repeated with additional limestone string courses.

10.15e

- Figure 10.15c shows a building elevation consisting of a masonry plane perforated by an array of openings for windows that is divided vertically into five similarly sized sections. The bottom section comprises a dominant limestone section and a horizontal line of windows cased in limestone frames. Above the windows is a strong horizontal element consisting of two similar lines of horizontal limestone friezes at different scales and a limestone string course. The punched openings on either side of the middle three divisions of the elevation have double windows, whereas the center portion has a series of four individual windows. This configuration is the same on all of the floors of the façade, establishing a centrally oriented verticality. The middle three sections are identical, each with a series of four thin limestone arches each encasing two windows one on top of the other. These groups of arches, which span about 75 percent of the vertical dimension of each section, reinforce the verticality established by the configuration of punched openings. The top section reverses the location of the limestone elements from the middle to the flanking sections. Each pair of double window punched openings, one above the other, is framed by limestone articulation. At the top of this section is a strong cornice component.

- Figure 10.15d displays a façade with a decorative terra cotta base and a terra cotta string course that defines the base. In addition to the nature of the façade's overall orientation, the composition establishes its verticality by placing a substantial element, a bay window, on either side of the façade. In the center of the façade, two windows are placed. The group of four windows repeats itself on each floor. Looking closely, you can see that each of the bay windows has a decorative masonry spandrel that reinforces the strength of the bay window group's verticality. The top of the overall composition is reinforced by terra cotta column cover elements, and the entire façade is capped by a strong terra cotta cornice.

- Figure 10.15e shows a façade that is compositionally similar to that shown in Figure 10.15a. It is divided into five relatively similar sized sections; the center group of windows articulated with limestone ornamentation and the window groups on either side are composed as double window units, whereas the center group of windows consists of two groups of three segregated windows. The bottom section is dominated by a two-story limestone section separated from the next floor by a limestone string course. Each of the

Figure 10.15. e. A façade compositionally similar to that shown in Figure 10.15a.

window openings on this floor is framed by a decorative limestone surround, and the entire lower section is capped by a decorative limestone frieze and string course. As with Figure 10.14a, the next three sections are similar, with a set of three windows on either side of a strong central masonry element. Each of the windows of the center group has a decorative limestone spandrel, and at the top of each section, the center group of windows has a decorative limestone crown that covers the entire horizontal expanse of that section. The middle portion of the top section keeps and expands the limestone decorative component so that it covers the entire expanse of that area, which does not have a window opening. The side window openings in this section are similarly united by a decorative limestone frame. At the top of this section is a strong limestone cornice.

In reviewing these façades, you can see that their appeal is related to the nature and strength of the inherent or structural relationships of the façade's elements. The term *structural* does not refer to the expression of structure on the façade but rather to an overall configuration, or subset thereof, of visual forces without which the nature of the perceivable gestalt would change, diminish, or cease to exist. By utilizing fractal geometry as the generator of this configuration, the elevation possesses an inherent organic quality through the part-to-whole-to-part relationships embedded throughout. Figure 10.16 shows iteration 1 of a façade created by employing fractal geometry applied to a rectilinear prism seed shape.

- The white element at the center of the base is a copy of the seed shape scaled down by 80 percent in width and 75 percent in height.
- On either side of this element are two parts that are duplications of the seed shape reduced by 60 percent in width and 85 percent in height. Each part, rendered in black, is rotated 180 degrees and then translated to either side of the white element.
- Above the white and black parts are two additional copies of the seed shape, rendered in gray, reduced by 60 percent in width and 90 percent in height. These parts are translated to a position on either side of the white element and on top of the black components.
- On top of this group of elements that form the base of the façade is a strong horizontal component composed of two copies of the seed shape, shown in red, reduced in height by 99.5 percent and separated by a group of five components, rendered in green, each a copy of the seed shape scaled down by 80 percent in width and 88 percent in height. The green components are placed side to side, and the two red elements are positioned one on top of the green components and the other just below them. This entire group is placed on top of the group of five elements that constitute the base.
- Last, two copies of the seed shape reduced by 50 percent in width and 28 percent in height are created. Each of these parts is rotated 180 degrees about the y axis and placed side by side on top of the green and red group.

As with other examples in this section, this use of fractal geometry is a significant departure from the previous chapter's fractally generated architecture in that these elements are not literal components of the final architecture. They serve only as placeholders for different types of elements, each receiving a different material treatment. All the gray-colored elements receive one type of treatment, such as running bond masonry, while the white components may be clad in a limestone material. As with all fractally generated forms, the components of iteration 1 are fused together to form the new seed shape.

In Figure 10.17, iteration 2 is depicted with the fractal structure clearly evident in the center component of the base or iteration 1's white element. The two large, gray components that constitute 75 percent of the façade illustrate the fractal structure of iteration 1 turned upside down because of their rotational transformation of 180 degrees as their white and black subcomponents are at the very

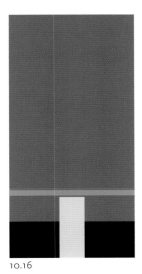

10.16

10.17

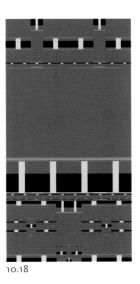

10.18

Figure 10.16. A façade created employing fractal geometry applied to a rectilinear prism seed shape, iteration 1.
Figure 10.17. A façade created employing fractal geometry applied to a rectilinear prism seed shape, iteration 2.
Figure 10.18. A façade created employing fractal geometry applied to a rectilinear prism seed shape, iteration 3.

top of the elevation. The two sets of elements from iteration 1, one black and one gray, on either side of iteration 1's white component appear to be fused together because of a rotation of 180 degrees about the *y* axis of the black components. The black-and-white subcomponent of the two gray parts visually fuses with the black-and-white subcomponent of the black elements. This visual merging of these elements is intensified by each part's red and green subcomponents, which work to further frame this section as a unified segment. The segregation of the five components that make up the horizontal element at the top of the base start to emerge through their white subcomponents.

In Figure 10.18, iteration 3 is rendered to show the play between the horizontal and vertical elements. The most prevalent subcomponent is the central element of the base, which is the vertical white element of iteration 1. It is embedded in horizontal bands of the subcomponents of the black and gray elements of iteration 1, which are compositionally fused together through the rotation of the black elements. As the white central base component with its vertical emphasis is framed by strong horizontal elements, it is capped by a strong horizontal force emanating from the fractally articulated red and green components of iteration 1. As with all fractally generated forms, as you increase the number of iterations, you exponentially embed the structure of form created through the relationships of the visual elements. By consecutively comparing the iterations, this can be readily seen to result in a richer play of horizontal and vertical forces.

Figure 10.19 illustrates iteration 3 with windows integrated into the façade structure and materials applied to the various components. Each of the subcomponents receives the same treatment, that is, all of the white components receive the same material. In addition, some subcomponents are either partially raised or recessed from the plane of the façade. The white, red, and green elements are all clad in limestone and are extruded from the base plane to varying degrees based on their color, with red projecting the most, then green, and then white. This could have also been accomplished within the definition of the fractal code. The gray subcomponent receives a running bond masonry material, and the black subcomponent receives a running bond material but with two rows of brick recessed for every one row of masonry in the same plane as the base façade. The choice of materials as well as the configuration of windows is flexible and up to the discretion of the designer. For instance, instead of plain limestone panels, they may be articulated decorative limestone reliefs, as in the building in Figure 10.15e. The panels with raised brick could be exchanged with masonry panels with decorative patterns, as in the spandrel panels in Figure 10.15d. The key point is that the material is applied consistently to subcomponents of the same designation, in this case by color. By doing so, the inherent strength of the structural relationships of the visual forces remains.

Figure 10.19. Iteration 3 with windows integrated into the façade structure and materials applied to the various components.

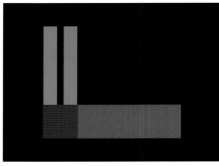

10.20

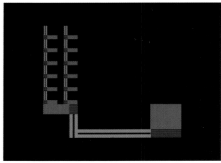

10.21

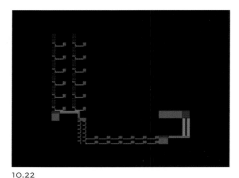

10.22

Figure 10.20. Façade panel 1, iteration 1.
Figure 10.21. Façade panel 1, iteration 2.
Figure 10.22. Façade panel 1, iteration 3.

Fractal Façade Panels Example 1

In this façade panel design, the elements consist of two significant elements that are rotated to varying degrees and a group of twelve elements that provide a strong component through a relationship of translation. Using a seed shape approximates the module of a typical residential exterior wall module in New York, a twelve foot wide by ten foot high by eight inch thick rectangular prism. The group of relationships generates a façade unit that is used throughout the façade through translation of the panel.

- For the first rotated part, the seed shape is copied and reduced by 75 percent in width and 70 percent in height, rotated 180 degrees, and then translated over four feet, six inches and down three feet. This series of transformations places an element, shown in blue in Figure 10.20, at the bottom left-hand corner of the seed shape, which rotates the content of the seed shape downward.
- The next element of the façade, depicted in red in Figure 10.20, is the spandrel panel that covers the structural slab and typically the mechanical unit that provides heating and cooling. This unit is constructed by copying the seed shape and scaling it down 75 percent in width, 50 percent in depth, and 10 percent in height and rotating it 90 degrees counterclockwise. It is then translated to the right six feet and down one foot six inches so that it is next to and even with the corner element.
- The remaining twelve parts are all copies of the seed shape scaled down by 90 percent in width, 25 percent in depth, and 88 percent in height. They are then arranged in two columns above the corner element by translating either by 3 feet, 7.5 inches or 5 feet, 4.5 inches to the left and from 3 feet to 8 feet, 10 inches vertically. These are shown in green in Figure 10.20, but since they are adjacent to each other, they appear as two upstanding rectangles.

The group of red, blue, and green components are merged to form the new seed shape. In this new seed shape, the blue element protrudes the most, with the group of twelve green elements receding a little behind that and the red component scaled down in depth a little more than the green elements.

The second iteration of façade panel 1 is shown in Figure 10.21. The twelve elements that constitute the green components are clearly perceivable reduced copies of the new seed element arranged in two columns along the left side. Underneath it is the corner blue element, which is a reduced copy of the seed shape rotated 180 degrees so that it is an inverted copy of the relationships within the seed shape. The red component is shown next to the blue element and illustrates its identity transformation as a 90 degree rotation of the seed shape with its green subcomponent touching the green component of the blue element. The various subcomponents of blue, red, and green represent various levels of depth being distributed throughout the design of the panel. As with the first iteration, these parts are fused to form the new seed shape, which is then transformed by the same transformational rules that generated the previous iterations.

The third iteration of façade panel 1 is shown in Figure 10.22. Each of the green elements is highly articulated, forming a group of dynamic structures that are related to the other components through their inherent set of organizational relationships. The blue component with its inverted orientation provides an interesting counterpoint to this group, in particular, with its sub-subgroup of green elements. The red element exhibits a significant horizontal visual through its 90 degree orientation and the nature of the relationship of the green sub-subcomponents. Its red and blue subcomponent provides a significant element at the right side of the façade panel.

The group of components of iteration 3 is set onto an L-shaped panel that conceals the structural and mechanical parts of the building to form, with the glass window, the exterior wall panel illustrated in Figure 10.23. This composite panel is translated horizontally by the dimension of a composite panel to form a floor or a portion of a floor. This group is then translated vertically to form the full façade or portion of the façade. In Figure 10.24, a portion of such a full façade is shown, with strong vertical elements composed of the articulated green components offset by their more understated horizontal red subelement. The intersection of the vertical and horizontal is punctuated by the blue element, which interacts with the right side of the red element to produce an accent that is repeated across the face of the façade. The organic nature of the integral ornament is similar to that used by Frank Lloyd Wright in some of his most notable buildings. In Figure 10.25, a façade within an inner courtyard of Wright's Hollyhock House in California shows a similar geometrically based structural ornamentation to produce an organic composition. Both the composition of the Hollyhock House columns and the organization of façade panel 1 exude the characteristics that make it an organized whole whose gestalt manifests organic qualities through the use of self-similarity.

301

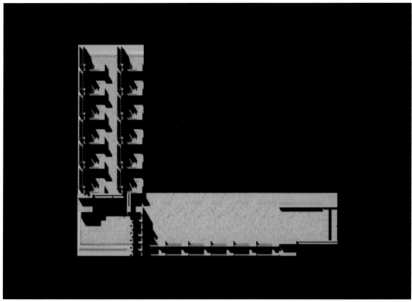

10.23

Fractal Façade Panels Example 2

While façade panel 1 was composed in the vernacular of Modernist architecture, façade panel 2 is organized within the language of more historical architecture. As with façade panel 1, its seed shape consists of a standard building module, in this case, ten feet by ten feet.

- A significant vertical group which organizes the whole panel is created by first copying the seed shape and reducing it by 80 percent in width and then translating it back six inches. This element, shown in gray in Figure 10.26, provides a distinct vertical axis that organizes the elements at the top and bottom of the panel.
- Within the gray element are two parts, shown in white, that are copies of the seed shape scaled down by 90 percent in width and 30 percent in height. They are translated back six inches, up two feet, and then each one is offset by three inches to either side of the center of the gray element. These three pieces compose a vertical spine that becomes increasingly articulated with each iteration to ultimately be visually similar to a ribbed column in a Gothic cathedral.
- The two elements to either side of the central vertical group's base are made by copying the seed shape and scaling it down by 50 percent in both its width and depth and by 80 percent in height. These two components, shown in red in Figure 10.26, are

Figure 10.23. Iteration 3: exterior wall panel.

10.24

10.25

Figure 10.24. Iteration 3: portion of a full façade.
Figure 10.25. Façade within the inner courtyard of
Hollyhock House.

translated to the left and right by two feet six inches and back by
two inches.

- Six elements at the top of the panel are created by taking six copies
  of the seed shape and reducing them by 90 percent in both their
  width and height. These parts, shown in green in Figure 10.25,
  are then translated nine feet vertically, four inches back in depth,
  and either one foot, six inches, three feet, or four feet, six inches
  horizontally to either side of the gray vertical component. Along
  with the two red elements at the bottom of the panel, they work
  to provide a strong horizontal visual force within the panel, counterbalancing the major vertical axis composed of the gray and
  white elements.

- At the upper intersection of these visual forces, an element is
  placed as illustrated in blue in Figure 10.26. It is a copy of the seed

303

shape reduced by 80 percent in both the width and height and then translated one foot, two inches back in depth and nine feet in height. This part provides a crown for the vertical component and an accent point for the panel, which will act, at a certain level of scale, as a unifying element with copies of the panel that are offset by translation across the façade.

As with all fractally based designs, these parts are joined to form the new seed shape, to which the same set of generative rules is applied to produce iteration 2. Figure 10.27 depicts the increased assimilation of façade panel 2's fractal structure in iteration 2. This structure, represented by the relationships generated in iteration 1, is clearly visible in iteration 1's red and green elements that are positioned along the top and bottom of the panel. These elements provide a horizontal rhythm, with the green elements at the top primarily by the perception of their overall organization of the six green elements. Their subelements, green, red, blue, and gray, reinforce this established rhythm. In the red elements, the rhythm is established principally by the perception of their subelements, in particular, the green subelements. The gray component becomes more refined, and its intersection with the blue element works to articulate the center accent element, principally through the green subelements of both the gray and blue components. The white parts are submerged within the gray component, but their presence can be seen as their red subcomponents are seen resting on top of the gray element's red subcomponent.

Iteration 3 is shown in Figure 10.28, with each of the elements illustrating the further embedment of the innate fractal structure formed by the relationships generated in iteration 1. The red components are articulated to form a rhythm along the base, while retaining their own organizational identity. As with all the elements of façade panel 2, the strength of their organizational identity relates to their bilateral symmetry as well as to the perceived set of organizational relationships which reflect that of the whole. The green elements along the top trade off the strength of the individual elements for a higher degree of refinement. They continue their potency as a horizontal rhythm, but in a more elegant manner. The gray and white elements are distilled to produce a vertically articulated centerpiece with a significant base and crown subelement. The strength of the base and crown of this portion of the structure arises from the triangulation of those subelements of the white and gray components. The two white bases sit directly on

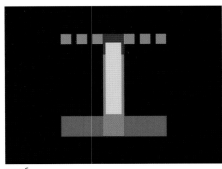

10.26

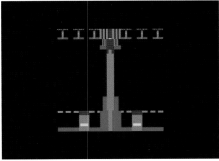

10.27

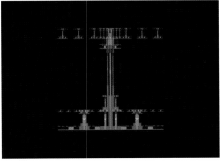

10.28

top of the gray base, causing the perceptual grouping of like elements reinforced by proximity. A similar perceptual condition occurs at the crown portion of these parts. In addition, the blue element works with the gray and white elements to form a densely articulated accent component. In interacting with the green components, it visually functions as a vortex from which the green elements emanate.

Façade panel 2's fractal structure is backed by flat spandrel panels and a window to compose a full façade panel, which is then translated horizontally across the floor to some degree. Similarly, that portion of floor is then translated vertically to form the entire façade section. As depicted in Figure 10.29, the design balances the clear horizontal cadence with strong vertical elements and a plane of accent points. The compositional effect of the use of this façade panel design is to produce an articulated façade that has a Gothic character to it. This trait arises from the high degree and elegant nature of its articulation. This character can be traced back to the nature of the relationships created in iteration 1, which are then exponentially embedded within the design with each iteration. If the structural relationships devised point toward a characteristic, that quality will be amplified with each ensuing iteration.

Figure 10.26. Façade panel 2, iteration 1.
Figure 10.27. Façade panel 2, iteration 2.
Figure 10.28. Façade panel 2, iteration 3.

305

10.29a

Figure 10.29. Façade composed of façade panel 2.

10.29b

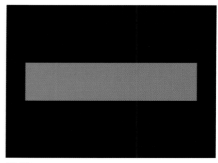

10.30

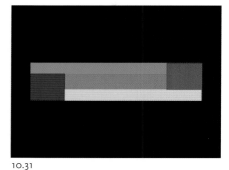

10.31

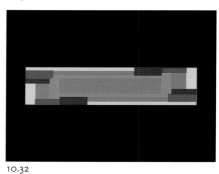

10.32

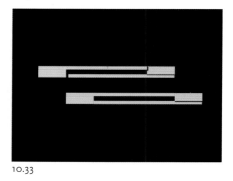

10.33

Figure 10.30. Façade panel 3, seed shape.
Figure 10.31. Façade panel 3, iteration 1.
Figure 10.32. Façade panel 3, iteration 2.
Figure 10.33. Disturbance of fractal structure as the two compact elements are eliminated and the remaining components are shifted slightly.

Fractal Façade Panels Example 3

Façade panels 1 and 2 consisted of the creation of a complete panel that was combined with a window and translated across and up the façade to cover it in a relatively rectilinear manner. Façade panel 3 is created by developing a spandrel panel design, disassembling it, and taking a portion of the elements to form a new panel through the reproduction and rotation of these elements. Figure 10.30 shows the seed shape, which is a rectangular slab that is eight feet deep, nine feet long, and two feet, ten inches high. The first iteration is illustrated in Figure 10.31 and is composed of five elements.

- The first is a copy of the seed shape, shown in green, which is reduced by 20 percent in length, 40 percent in depth, and 70 percent in height. It is rotated 180 degrees and then translated up and to the left so that it is the upper left corner of the seed shape's edge.
- The second component consists of a reproduced seed shape that is scaled down by 84 percent in length, 30 percent in depth, and 10 percent in height and rotated 90 degrees. It is then translated to the left so that it is at the bottom left corner of the seed shape.
- The next part, rendered in white, is created by reducing the copy of the seed shape by 20 percent in length and depth and 70 percent in height but is translated to the lower right until it occupies the lower right corner of the seed shape.
- The next element is a copy of the seed shape scaled down by 84 percent in length and 10 percent in depth and height. Shown in red in Figure 10.30, it is then rotated 270 degrees clockwise and translated to the upper right corner. The last part, shown in gray, is a simple reduction of the seed shape by 95 percent in depth and then translated back so that it is just behind the other parts.

An important constituent of the design that is embedded within the configuration of relationships is that as you travel from the first element and move around the various parts that constitute the outside ring—the green, red, white, and blue units—each component increases in depth from the scaling down of the seed shape in depth by 40 percent, 30 percent, 20 percent, and 10 percent and is incrementally rotated 90 degrees clockwise. Thus a hierarchical rotation is integral to the nature of this fractal structure. This is evident when viewing iteration 2, shown in Figure 10.32. In each of the parts, the ring of

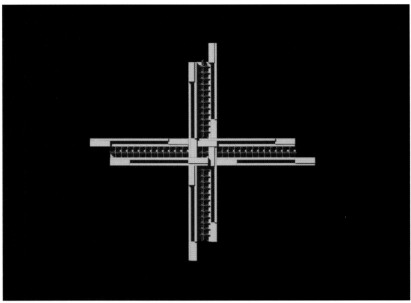

10.34

elements of the first iteration is manifested. By locating a specific color in each, such as the white part, you can easily see the rotational nature of the fractal structure. Starting with the top element, it is at the top left portion. Looking at the next element in a clockwise rotation, the white part is located at the upper right corner. Going on to the next element, the white subelement is at the bottom right position. Going to the last component, the white portion is at the bottom left position. Not only does each of these elements progress in depth as you progress clockwise but contained in each of them is this same depth hierarchy rotating within them but also oriented according to the element's rotation. The resultant effect is to embed similar rotations within the overall rotational structure.

The next few steps are different than most of the fractal designs discussed so far. The fractal structure is disturbed as the two compact elements at the upper left and right corners, the red and blue parts, are eliminated and the remaining green, white, and gray components are shifted slightly, as illustrated in Figure 10.33. Similar to the fractal structure schema, this entity is copied and rotated clockwise every 90 degrees, with each copy increasing in depth. This new group of components becomes the new seed shape, which is then copied, reduced in scale, and translated to positions at the center of the new seed shape, and a group of thirteen is positioned in the middle of each arm. Figure 10.34 renders the structure composed of this new group

Figure 10.34. Reconstituted façade panel 3.

309

of relationships, some fractal in nature and others the result of symmetry operations. Despite the deviation from the strict application of fractal geometry, the image emits an organic character.

The previous façade panels were distributed across the façade in a two-step translation process, one by horizontal translation and a subsequent one by vertical translation of a group of façade panels. In this panel's design, the central element is a composite of the four panels around it. To achieve this, the base panel has to be distributed in a diamond network, which is achieved by translating it horizontally by a unit twice the width of the panel so that there is a gap between the horizontal legs of every panel. After it is distributed horizontally across the façade, a copy of that floor is translated down one floor and over one panel unit. The vertical legs fill in the gap between the horizontal legs of the group of panels on the floor above. In the middle of these intersections, a backer flat panel and a reduced copy of the panel design are incorporated as they exist in the other panels. In this methodology, at one end of the floor, a panel is offset from the face of the façade, while the other end is missing a panel. The offset panel is translated over to fill in the missing panel. To complete the façade, a window unit is designed and positioned in the gap between each fractal façade panel. The final façade design is shown in Figure 10.35.

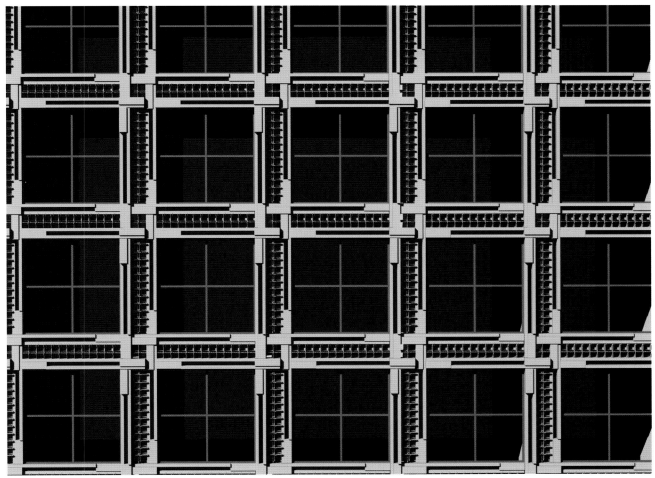

10.35

Figure 10.35. Front elevation of a façade
composed of façade panel 3.

Façade 3 is important in that it is an example of utilizing a portion of a fractally generated form and employing it in a different methodology. Although it is not a formal fractal per se, the fractal qualities inherent in the elements that are utilized shine through and imbue the form with an organic gestalt to some degree. Figure 10.36 is another view of the façade that exhibits a dynamic rhythm at different levels of scale, a hallmark of fractal and organic design.

SUMMARY

This chapter demonstrated that utilizing fractal geometry to generate three-dimensional architectural form is only one aspect of the array of possible uses that span the range of architectural grammars. It can be used to generate façades or elements of façades such as modular panels or ornament that reflects the overall composition of the building. The extent to which these various uses evoke the organic quality that manifests itself in compositions structured by fractal geometry is dependent on the degree and context of the application. Within these different uses of fractal geometry, various techniques, such as overlapping of elements, fractal distribution of placeholder elements, and the incorporation of different iterations within the same composition, were introduced to show some of the many compositional techniques that are possible. These applications and techniques are only a few of the possibilities for the utilization of fractal geometry in architectural design.

10.36

Figure 10.36. Perspective view of the façade panel 3.

CHAPTER **11** **The Fractal Confluence
of Science and Art**

Philosophers and scientists from Pythagoras, Plato, St. Augustine, and
St. Thomas Aquinas through Kant, Darwin, and Freud have explored
the "nature" of nature.[1] The dance that science, nature, and art have
performed since the beginning of recorded time took a remarkable turn
in the early twentieth century. Breakthroughs in physics epitomized by
Albert Einstein's theory of relativity led to a reevaluation of the essence
of nature and the composition of the universe, which substantially influenced the direction of art. This dance has been analyzed by Leonard
Shlain in his book *Art and Physics: Parallel Visions in Space, Time, and
Light*. Even before Plato's quest for the ideal forms hidden in nature,
art and philosophy sought to strip away the outer veil of appearances
to determine the ideal form that lay beneath.[2] *Physis* in Greek means
"nature," and from this point of departure, the scientist has tradition-
ally sought to analyze nature by breaking it down to its component
parts and examining the relationship of those parts in a reductionist
methodology. Conversely, an artist juxtaposes different attributes of
reality and synthesizes them to produce a whole work that is greater
than the sum of its parts.[3] An analysis of the art of this period reveals
parallels to the concepts that underlie fractal design.

EINSTEIN, RELATIVITY, AND THE INFLUENCE
ON ART AND ARCHITECTURE

Up through the late 1800s, the notion of space and time were thought
to be distinct from each other. With Einstein's theories of relativity

315

published in the Annus Mirabilis Papers, this distinction radically changed to the point that space and time were considered interchangeable. His theories of relativity, energy, and matter formed the basis for the concept of the space-time continuum, where the three dimensions of space and the one dimensionality of time are integrated into one construct. As culture was influenced by advances into the scientific inquiry of the nature of the universe, nonmimetic art developed, whose conceptualization represented the force or energy by which laws of nature and the universe exist. Art was no longer a copy of nature, but by adopting the creative forces of nature and the forces that shaped it, objects were created that embodied these principles.[4]

In *Art and Physics*, Leonard Shlain explains the space-time theory Einstein espoused in Annus Mirabilis within the context of a lunchtime trip aboard a train. Young Einstein boards a train leaving the Berlin station precisely at 12:00 P.M., according to the tower clock that is in plain view. If the train moves at a leisurely pace of five miles an hour, after a minute of travel, Einstein can look back and observe the clock at 12:01. At this speed, space and time appear absolute, and light seems to travel across these two coordinates instantly. Light from the sun strikes the clock, imprints the image of the timepiece and the setting of its hands, and reflects off the clock and into our eyes, carrying the image of the clock. The interval of time from when light hits the face of the clock to the point at which it strikes our pupils, although measurable, is extremely short. What we are seeing is the state of the clock a moment before. Light continually carries the frozen moment of an image's creation. If instead of traveling at a mere five miles an hour, the train immediately travels at the speed of light, or 186,000 miles per hour, then the image of the clock at 12:00 would always be traveling with the train, and no subsequent image would reach Einstein's pupils. For Einstein and any other passenger looking at the clock, it would appear that time stood still. If, however, Einstein looked down at his watch, he would see it behaving normally, with the arms moving according to the normal concept of time. If the train was traveling at half the speed of light, or 93,000 miles per hour, time would still move on the clock but at half the time on his wristwatch. From this conceptualization, Einstein concluded that time was not absolute but relative to how fast the observer is moving away from the image source.

Although when traveling at speeds approaching the speed of light, the past and future appear to come together, what is really happening is that the present is expanding to encompass the past and future. As you approach the speed of light, physical forms change their appearance. At one half the speed of light, objects off to the side of the train appear elongated, and as the speed increases, their tops begin to curve away from the perpendicular, and right angles are replaced by arcs. The objects themselves change shape because of the plastic deformation of the space in which they reside. Space is interactive with the volume, shape, and size of the objects residing in it.

Relative to its effect on art, one of the critical concepts emanating from this relativistic aspect of Einstein's theory is the simultaneous perception of more than one side of an object when seen from the windows of the train. As the train accelerates toward the speed of light, the space along the train's axis of direction shortens until at the speed of light it contracts into an infinitely thin layer. If the chair Einstein is sitting on in this train can swivel, when he swivels to look forward as the speed approaches half the speed of light, the scenery distorts as its depth flattens, and the background moves closer to the foreground. Figures become flattened, looking like playing cards. The present moment outside the train, or what Monet has termed *instantaneity*, is expanding to include more of the past and the future, which is causing the objects and events from the past and future to become closer to the present and hence lose their depth. At the speed of light, the terms *ahead* and *behind* lose meaning as the past and future come in contact. The person looking out of the front of the train sees the rear of the train. Front, back, and sides are all squeezed into an infinitely flat, two-dimensional plane vertically oriented. Outside the train, the three durations of time merge, but on the train, everything is "normal." Space and time are intimately intertwined. As time dilates, space contracts, and as time contracts, space dilates.

The linkage between Einstein's theory of relativity and the revolutionary art movements at that time has been debated. I think it is safe to say that Einstein's theory exemplifies the reevaluation of the nature of the universe that occurred during this period. This general scientific discourse undoubtedly affected the direction of artistic thinking, as exemplified by the art movements of Cubism, Futurism, and Constructivism.

11.1

11.2

Figure 11.1. Picasso.
Figure 11.2. Braque.
Figure 11.3. Juan Gris.

CUBISM

It would appear that Cubism was directly related to this reevaluation of the nature of the universe. Cubism was a decisive break with the mimetic convention of Western art and can be considered the start of Modern art.[5] The importance of Cubism is in its revolutionary concepts of space and time, which stimulated an artistic reconsideration of the nature of reality.[6] In a Cubist composition, objects are fractured into visual fragments so that the viewer does not have to move through space within a certain time period to view them in sequence. Elements of the front, top, sides, back, and bottom of an object are presented to the viewer simultaneously. In Cubist theory, the world did not have to be processed sequentially. At the speed of light, there is no sequence because there is no time. Time comes to a halt, and therefore there can be no movement. All events are superimposed on each other and are seen simultaneously. Perceiving all aspects of an object at once was seeing all of space here in the everlasting present. The only place in the universe that correlated to a Cubist image was that of a viewer riding astride a beam of light.[7]

Cubism was influenced by primitive art and Cezanne, who applied several different viewpoints in his pictures.[8] It can also be traced to aspects of early medieval art, which repeated the main figure many times in a composition. This was done to represent the range of possible relationships to the figure through the depiction of various actions. The different actions and representations depicted on one canvas converge simultaneously, splintering time as well as space.[9] Cubism was characterized by decentered, entirely fragmented compositions that emphasized different planes and facets derived by the breakup of the image into its various views being considered all at once. The notable artists of the Cubist period were Picasso (Figure 11.1), Braque (Figure 11.2), Juan Gris (Figure 11.3), and Jean Metzinger (Figure 11.4). Cubism's transition to architecture only occurred in Prague, Czechoslovakia, where Joseph Chochol (Figure 11.5), Josef Gocar (Figure 11.6), and Otakar Novotny (Figure 11.7) constructed a number of low and mid-rise Cubist buildings. These structures emphasized the faceted and crystallized aspects of the Cubist style but did not touch on the central characteristic of viewing other aspects of the composition within one view.

Fractal architecture, because of its iterative nature, can incorporate the fundamental aspect of simultaneity in architectural form. This can be achieved by taking a seed shape, such as a rectilinear prism;

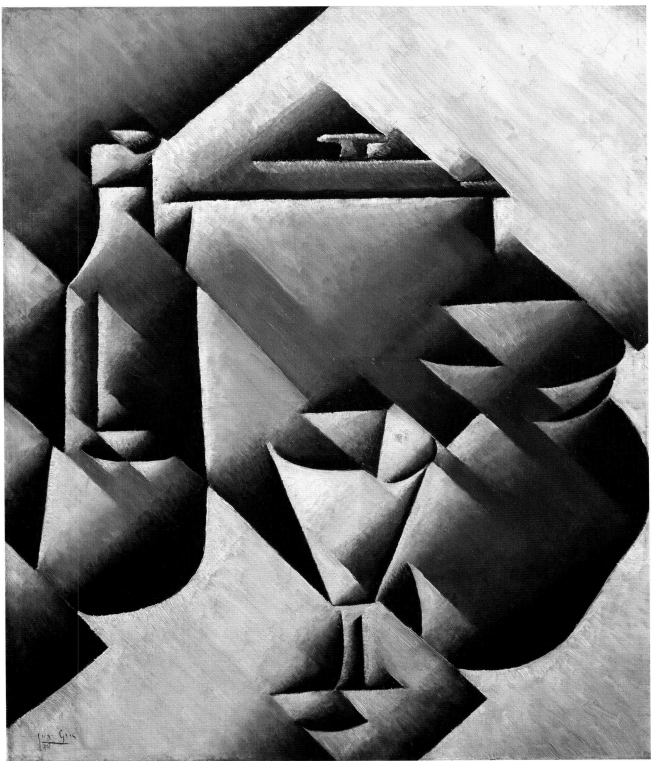

11.4

11.5

11.6

11.7

copying it at least six times; and rotating and translating each copy so that on every façade of the architectural form, a copy of each of the four façades as well as the top and bottom is present. As you iterate the fractal model, within each elevation, the elements of the other façades that you are observing are the state of that elevation—right, left, front, back, top, and bottom—at the previous iteration. This is not quite the view of a person riding a beam of light but of one riding a beam that is slightly slower than a beam of light. This is illustrated in Figure 11.8, showing the transformation of the structure through four iterations. In Figures 11.8a and 11.8f, the rectangular prism seed shape is shown with each side colored red (front), blue (left), green (back), white (top), black (bottom), or gray (right) to distinguish the sides in the subsequent iterations. Figures 11.8a–11.8e use an oblique view of the front, top, and left sides of the prism to show the transformation through four iterations. Figures 11.8f–11.8j depict an analogous transformation but at the opposite viewpoint, which shows the back, bottom, and right side of the rectangular prism.

While the transformations produce interesting images, it is difficult to discern the multiple façades that compose each elevation in part because each element has a similar transformation. If the transformations on each element were to vary, each façade would develop a uniqueness that would increase its chance of perception when embedded in an elevation of the building. Figure 11.9 shows the front top and left side of a revised design through four iterations, while Figure 11.10 illustrates the back, bottom, and right side. In general, some elements were changed in one or more of the height and length dimensions to form an asymmetrical composition in the front and back elevations. A vertical fin is added at the middle of the composition's sides, which will provide some framing of elements. The middle band of elements was skewed to give a more faceted appearance. Figure 11.11 shows the front elevation of the final composition through the three iterations. Figure 11.12 shows the iterations of this design rendered predominately in a blue glass, with certain elements rendered in a white metal.

Figure 11.4. Jean Metzinger.
Figure 11.5. Joseph Chochol.
Figure 11.6. Josef Gocar.
Figure 11.7. Otakar Novotny.

11.8a

11.8f

11.8b

11.8g

11.8c

11.8h

11.8d

11.8i

11.8e

11.8j

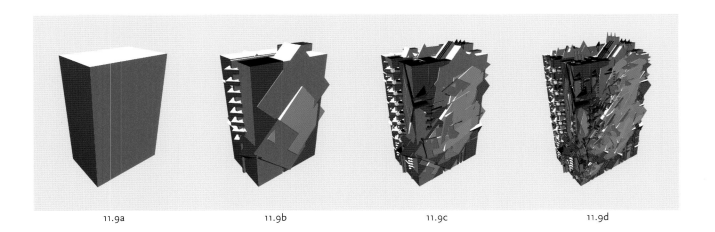

11.9a   11.9b   11.9c   11.9d

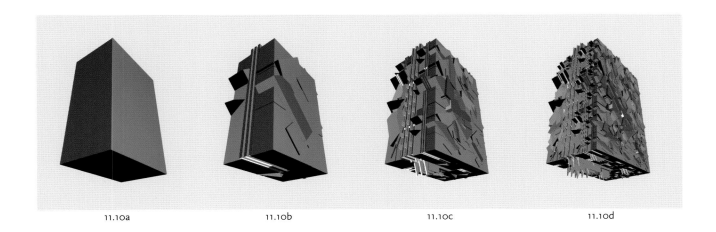

11.10a   11.10b   11.10c   11.10d

Figure 11.8. Transformation of a fractal structure
through four iterations.
Figure 11.9. Revised design through four
iterations: front, top, and left.
Figure 11.10. Revised design through four
iterations: back, bottom, and right.

11.11

Figure 11.11. Front elevation of the final
composition through three iterations.
Figure 11.12. Revised design rendered
predominately in a blue glass with certain
elements rendered in a white metal.

11.12

FUTURISM

At the same time as Cubism was flourishing in France, a movement was forming in Italy, championed by the poet Filippo Tommaso Martinetti. In 1909 Martinetti christened the movement Futurism and believed it reflected the speed and movement of modern society. The notable artists of the Futurism movement were Umberto Boccioni (Figure 11.13), Giacomo Balla (Figure 11.14), and Gino Severini (Figure 11.15). Although it used elements of Divisionism, where color was broken down into fields of dots and stripes, the Futurist movement shared the conceptual basis and compositional characteristics of Cubism. Central to the idea of Futurism was the depiction of the element of time and movement in one frozen moment. As discussed in Einstein's theory of relativity, this occurred as the viewer riding the beam of energy approached the speed of light where the past and future are merging into the present, and a moment of simultaneity composed itself within the shallow Cubist space. The Futurist concept of Dynamism dominated their philosophical foundation and is defined by Umberto Boccioni in one of the Futurist manifestos as "a general law of simultaneity and interpenetration dominating everything." For Futurists, Dynamism "signified the difference between participating in an evolving, expanding universe and withdrawal into an eddy of personal isolation."[10] One of the underlying fundamentals of Futurism is this connection to universal forces. Boccioni sought in the Futurist manifesto *Plastic Dynamism* "the key to making the object live in universal terms" and "the law of unity of universal motion."[11] Contact with the "universal rhythm" is the Futurist's moment of ecstasy.[12]

Rudolf Arnheim has noted that an abstraction of a movement or action in a timeless image that crystallized the nature of the complex event in one arresting pattern is not isolated from its surroundings but acts as its center produces a dynamic concept.[13] This observation by Arnheim essentially summarizes the fundamental characteristic of Futurist composition. They depicted simultaneity by the representation of an object through slices of time that act as the compositional vortex of the plastic pictorial space. This concept was extended to the third dimension by Umberto Boccioni in the Futurist manifesto *Plastic Dynamism*, in which he stated, "Instead Futurist sculpture will put the figure at the center of a plastic orientation of space."[14] The idea of motion influencing the surrounding space was for Futurism an influence from Cezanne, who put forth that no object, moving or still, can be seen in isolation but absorbs its surroundings just as it contributes to

Figure 11.13. Umberto Bocciononi.
Figure 11.14. Giacomo Balla.
Figure 11.15. Gino Severini.

11.13

11.14

11.15

them. It makes the action more influential by extending its influence to the very forms of the objects. This relationship extended between an object and its surroundings affects the forms of actual motion in space because our perception of movement changes our perception of an object. The Futurist artists looked on all objects, whether a static bottle or a racing horse, as embodying two kinds of motion: that which tends to move in on itself, suggesting in its centripetal force the internal mass of an object, and that which moves outward into space, mingling its rhythms with those of other objects and eventually merging with space itself. Boccioni's "line/force" was devised to express this shifting relationship between "objectivity" and constant change, depicting neither the object itself nor its motion but a synthesized image of both. They used the mind's own language, exploiting the mind's capacity for association and sequential observation to produce a new aesthetic satisfaction consistent with their modern consciousness.[15] The element of time can be encompassed with architectural forms by employing simultaneous systems overlaid in a single space.[16] The iterative mechanism utilized to generate fractal forms is essentially a process of the repeated performance of a creative event. It serves as an ordering process that produces visual patterns that suggest the presence of motion, change, or growth.[17] This generative model is modified to depict the various stages of motion or growth in one form, revealing the moment of simultaneity. As Boccioni stated in the manifesto *Plastic Dynamism*, "form in movement and the movement of form."

The Futurist movement, in particular Umberto Bocciononi and his concept of force-form, was influenced by the work of French philosopher Henri Bergson. In his work, Bergson introduced the concepts of fusion, simultaneities, and duration, which became staples of the new art movement's vocabulary.[18] Becoming is the original dynamism or animating energy of the universe, which is continually in a state of becoming again, producing new forms to emerge within this perpetual flow. Duration was the unified flow of time in which becoming occurred. Intuition, the key to understanding life and time, was a sympathetic experience in which you are moved into the inner being of an object to understand what is unique and indescribable about it. Bergson's philosophy was similar to that of a contemporary, Rudolf Steiner, who built his ideas from the work of Wolfgang Goethe. For Steiner, the manifestation of becoming was through metamorphosis, and understanding was based on phenomenological intuition. In metamorphosis, a being undergoes continual change but nevertheless remains the same essence. The German term *Bildung* describes morphologically the informing power of the organism that is placed within the context of becoming. It describes the goal of becoming and the process used for becoming as well. It is not the outward alteration of one form into another but the differing outward expressions of an inward idea. Each form cannot be separated from its before and after. The static representation is a representation of the organism caught in the process of becoming something else within the context of its unifying idea. Each manifestation is a fractal-like partial representation of the process and of the whole.[19] As El Lissitzky stated, "every form is the frozen instantaneous picture of a process, thus a work is a stopping place on the road to becoming and not the fixed goal."[20] The Futurist depiction of the microevent of an individual organism is emblematic of the macroevent of the universe. As theorized by physicist David Bohm, the universe enfolds an implicate order, the ultimate connected reality behind physical manifestations, and unfolds the explicate order we see.[21] The universe is not a noun but a verb, not a place but an event.[22]

Christopher Alexander has cited the process of unfolding within nature as the crucial aspect that exudes familiarity and reassurance for humans. The natural environment is a structure, a living structure, which consists of centers and symmetries that provide an environmental order. As the natural system moves forward in time, it evolves to preserve the previous point in time's centers and symmetries and build from them to create new centers and symmetries to form a nested structure of life. This structure of centers and symmetries has a gestalt of wholeness. From this wholeness the perception of life emanates from the organism.

The Futurist derivative of Steiner's morphological thesis is not simply to portray one instant of the process of becoming but a series of instances of the process, thereby injecting the representation with the dynamism of the process. The iterative process of fractal geometry is one that by definition reinforces the relationships created by the prescribed set of transformations. With each iteration, these transformations are further embedded, and a comparison of a number of iterations reveals a progression of internal structure manifesting itself, or as Bergson states, becoming. This internal structure is Boccioni's force-form, and understanding it signifies grasping the inherent nature of the forces creating the form. This understanding is within the context of a frozen snapshot of the process, revealing a number of the states of becoming

329

in one instant. Figure 11.16 shows the first iteration of a form utilizing fractal geometry within the context of Futurist compositional and philosophical influences. The seed shape is a rectangular prism that is copied ten times, all of which are skewed horizontally to contribute to the perception of movement from left to right.

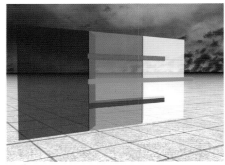

11.16

- The first element, colored in black, is a copy of the seed shape reduced to 33 percent in length and translated to the left edge.
- The next two parts, indicated in gray, are reduced clones of the seed shape 33 percent in length and 50 percent in height, with one of the copies translated vertically so that it is on top of the other gray copy.
- Components 4 through 7, shown in white, are duplicates of the seed shape reduced to 33 percent in length and 25 percent in height and translated so that all four are stacked vertically, and that assemblage is translated to the right edge of the seed shape.
- The last three elements are copies of the seed shape reduced to 5 percent in height and 50 percent in depth, and two copies, one indicated in red and the other in blue, are reduced to 50 percent in length, and the other, rendered in green, to 67 percent in length. These copies are translated to the left edge of the middle copy of the first three copies. These copies are moved out so that they protrude from the body of the composition and are translated vertically to third points, with the longer green copy placed between the two shorter copies.

11.17

11.18

Figure 11.17 shows the next iteration, which shows a vertical striping of the black, gray, and white elements within each of the black, gray, and white elements of iteration 1. As you progress from left to right, the horizontal red, green, and blue elements increase as the number of vertically stacked copies increases. Within each of the red, green, and blue horizontal elements, a compressed striation is developing. Figure 11.18 illustrates iteration 3 with all the relationships described in iterations 1 and 2 embedding themselves exponentially within the overall form. These sets of relationships were structured to cause the viewer to perceive movement from left to right. A comparison of the three renderings clearly indicates this phenomenon. Figure 11.19 shows iteration 3 rendered in a consistent material, and Figure 11.20 shows the same model with its front elevation rendered.

Figure 11.16. Futurist fractal form, iteration 1.
Figure 11.17. Futurist fractal form, iteration 2.
Figure 11.18. Futurist fractal form, iteration 3.
Figure 11.19. Futurist fractal form, iteration 3, rendered in a consistent material.

11.19

11.20

Figure 11.20. Futurist fractal form: front elevation
of iteration 3 rendered in a consistent material.

CONSTRUCTIVISM

The journey that was spurred on by the newly discovered forces of the universe, from mimetic representation of nature to nonobjective representation, spread through Western Europe with Cubism, Italy with Futurism, and Russia with the Constructivist and Suprematism movements from 1915 onward. Constructivism was an outgrowth of Futurism with an angular, industrial orientation of abstract geometric forms that connected it to Suprematism. Suprematism, founded by Kasimir Malevich, was an art movement focused on fundamental geometric forms to signify a new beginning by denying objective representation. Utilizing geometric patterns that were totally abstract, he sought to acknowledge "the supremacy of pure feeling." These movements were embodied in the umbrella category of the Russian avant-garde of the early twentieth century.

These movements, while not exhibiting an obvious connection to natural structures, sought to incorporate an organic unity. Tatlin was focused, through the medium of the mechanical and the machine, on the organic, and his work was described as Organic Constructivism. He studied structures in nature to discover the law that governed their organization and their creative potential. The Constructivists desired to weave the aesthetic of the machine with the organic laws of nature.[23] The defining expression of Constructivist architecture was Tatlin's Monument to the Third International (Figure 11.21). It was a tower that was to rise approximately four hundred meters over St. Petersburg, and its structural dynamism was to be in stark contrast to the analogous but static structure of the Eiffel Tower. The tower was the epitome of the Constructivist ethos of synthesizing the modern industrial technology, represented in the choice of materials of iron, glass, and steel, with aspects of organic form. The core of the structure consisted of four geometric forms—cube, pyramid, cylinder, and sphere—placed one on top of the other along an axis parallel to the earth's axis. Each of these vertically placed archetypal forms rotated at different intervals. Enveloping this series of primal forms was a double helix orientated along the central axis, which gave it an overriding organic connotation. This unbuilt tower was intended to synthesize organic principles with modern technological building materials in a dynamic archetypal structure intended to evoke primal transcendental associations.

Kasimir Malevich launched Suprematism at "0.10 The Last Futurist Exhibition" in Petrograd in December 1915 and was republished in expanded form as *From Cubism and Futurism to Suprematism: The New*

11.21

Figure 11.21. Tatlin's Monument to the Third International.

11.22

11.23

Realism in Painting (see Figures 11.22 and 11.23). In viewing his work, an immediate reaction might be to view it as a complete disassociation with nature, but as with Mondrian, Malevich embraces nature but not the theretofore depiction of nature through mimetic forms. In his initial manifesto *From Cubism and Futurism, to Suprematism: The New Realism in Painting*, he states, "The further his consciousness embraced nature, the more complicated his work became and the more his knowledge and ability increased. His consciousness developed only on one side, the side of nature's creation, and not on the side of new forms of art. Therefore his primitive pictures cannot be considered creative work."

In his writings, Malevich illustrates that Suprematism is interwoven with the ideals of organic form. He believed that the organism serves as not only a metaphoric construct but also as an end point for the creative task. The Constructivist goal was the generation of a form so perfectly refined that it attained living autonomy.[24] He believed in the Futurist deconstruction of form by the morphological transformation caused by the integration of movement. In this deconstruction of the wholeness of natural form, the hidden meaning or essence was revealed. The dynamic of plastic painting required the mass to emerge from the object and become an end to itself.[25] Malevich declared that the

Figure 11.22. Kasimir Malevich.
Figure 11.23. Another example of the work of Kasimir Malevich.

Suprematist machine is a new organic machine. In *Thirty-four Drawings*, basically a theoretical and visual textbook of Suprematism, Malevich stated that like any organism, the Suprematist work would the result of a "smooth harnessing of form to natural processes through some magnetic interrelations within a single form, which will comprise all the natural forces inherent in these interrelations."[26] This description of the basis of plastic design is consistent with the foundation of fractally based design where the process causes the form to emerge from and manifest the characteristics of the generating process.

In *The Structurist*, Patricia Railing noted that El Lissitzky declared in an article in the publication *Nasci* (Nature) that the machine had not separated humans from nature, but rather through it, they discovered a new nature never before deduced. Modern art like science has reduced form to its basic elements to reconstruct it according to the universal laws of nature.[27] Suprematism should be understood as an analogy to natural processes having similar structural laws, processes, and structure determined by projective geometry. According to El Lissitzky, a characteristic of Suprematist work is dematerialization, but within that characteristic they still must be something the human mind can grasp as an organized entity. The Suprematist utilized the concept of *construction* to denote the laws and systems that create natural forms and which art and architecture should use to generate their forms.[28]

Malevich's evolution led him to the generation of architectural forms that he termed Architektons (Figure 11.24). The surviving Architektons models exhibit four types of forms. The first is a long basilica format with an overriding symmetry, with one main axis crossed by smaller subsidiary axes forming cross forms that are Suprematist motifs. This format also incorporates horizontal planes that provide the dynamic perception of movement. The second, known as Beta, is similar to the basilica form, with a long axis and numerous crossings that develop their own symmetries, to which is added the stacking and crossing of blocks of intermediate scale. Within this format, he incorporates variations where he positions the elements on the top on one side and a similar group at the bottom overhanging an edge. These are counterbalanced by elements at the heart of the structure. The third Architekton form was termed Gota, comprised long structures that incorporated circular forms. The last form, Alpha, constituted vertically orientated forms. In this form category, Malevich incorporates a variety in the proportion system of the blocks so that the blocks interrelate. In this way he incorporates the quintessential fractal quality where the

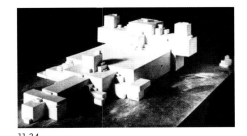

11.24

Figure 11.24. Malevich's Basilica Architekton.

part invokes the whole. The development of axis and subsidiary axis occurs in the same fractal methodology.[29] In viewing these models, the fractal characteristics are apparent and invite the formal exploration of a fractally generated Suprematist form.

The first iteration of a fractal Basilica Architekton is shown in Figure 11.25.

- In this composition, there is a major rectangular prism, shown in gray, which is a copy of the seed shape reduced in length by 25 percent, by 15 percent in width, and in height by 18 percent.
- To the left of the rectangular prism are five elements shown in red, green, and blue.
  - The two green elements, which are side by side, are copies reduced by 83 percent in length, 85 percent in width, and 70 percent in height. Each of these is rotated by 90 degrees, one clockwise and the other counterclockwise so that the tops of each component face outward.
  - At the left end of the green elements are two red parts that are copies reduced by 82 percent in length, 87 percent in width, and 60 percent in height. As with the green elements, they are rotated 90 degrees about the x axis so that the tops of each face outward.
  - The last component on the left side is colored in blue and is a copy reduced by 82 percent in length, 87 percent in width, and 65 percent in height. Unlike the green and red components, it is not rotated.

This group of green, red, and blue elements is translated horizontally to occupy the space adjacent to the gray element, which was reduced by 25 percent so that the total of the green, red, blue, and gray parts occupies the entire length of the seed shape.

- At the right side of the composition is a group of six elements all rendered in white.
  - The first two parts, which are lower than the other components, are two copies reduced by 70 percent in length, 75 percent in width, and 50 percent in height. Each of these parts is rotated 90 degrees about the z axis, one clockwise and the other counterclockwise, so that the front part of these elements is facing outward.

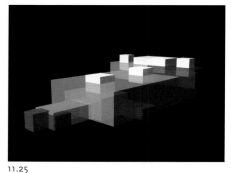

11.25

Figure 11.25. Basilica Architekton, iteration 1.

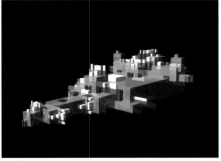

11.26

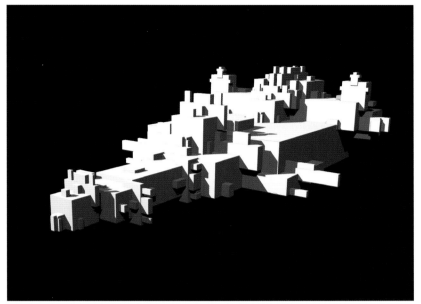

11.27

o   In the middle of this group of components are two sections that are copies of the seed shape reduced by 88 percent in length, 70 percent in width, and 60 percent in height that are also rotated 90 degrees by their *z* axes to face outward.

o   Just outboard of these two elements are two sections that are copies reduced by 90 percent in length, 85 percent in width, and 70 percent in height. Both are rotated by 90 degrees about the *y* axis so that the front section of each is pointing upward.

• Between these two sets of elements are three components centered in the width of the gray rectangular prism.

o   The first element adjacent to the group of six components on the right side, and rendered in white, is a copy reduced by 90 percent in length, 80 percent in width, and 60 percent in height.

o   Adjacent to the group of elements on the left side is two elements, one reduced by 84 percent in length and 50 percent in both width and height and rendered in green.

o   Above that section is a white copy of the seed shape reduced 90 percent in length, 80 percent in width, and 48 percent in height.

The assemblage of these elements forms a composition that has a distinctive end condition created by the group of components on

Figure 11.26. Basilica Architekton, iteration 2.
Figure 11.27. Composition in a light gray material.

11.28

11.29

Figure 11.28. Malevich's Alpha form.
Figure 11.29. Alpha form, iteration 1.

the left side. By rotating the various elements, this group develops an articulation of the entire composition that invokes the organic quality arising from part-to-whole-to-part relationships. As with all fractal forms, the group of elements constituting iteration 1 are fused together to form the new seed shape to which the transformations are again applied. Figure 11.26 shows iteration 2, in which a higher degree of complexity is apparent. In viewing this form, the color coding assists in deriving the nature of the structural relationships. Figure 11.27 renders the composition in a light gray material, revealing a set of structural relationships and forms similar to Malevich's Basilica Architekton.

Figure 11.28 shows an example of Malevich's fourth Architekton form, the Alpha form. The Alpha form, unlike the other three Architekton forms, has a vertical orientation that lends itself to its application as a skyscraper form. In surveying the Alpha form, there are evident efforts by Malevich to incorporate a sense of self-similarity, the most notable aspect of which is the inclusion of subforms mostly at the base of the intersection of rectangular prisms. Figure 11.29 depicts the set of structural relationships that form the basis for iteration 1 of a fractal Malevich Alpha form.

- The form consists of six elements or groups of elements, the first of which is the large central white element, which is a copy of the seed shape reduced by 10 percent in length and width and 5 percent in height.
- Within this element are two parts, indicated in black, that intersect each other in a cruciform configuration, one reduced by 25 percent in width and 20 percent in height and increased by 20 percent in length and the other decreased by 25 percent in length and 20 percent in height and increased by 20 percent in width.
- At the base, where the black elements penetrate through the white section, are four cubes shown in red, which are copies reduced by 45 percent in length and width and 75 percent in height.
- On top of each red element is a copy of the seed shape reduced by 35 percent in length, 30 percent in width, and 55 percent in height and rendered in gray material.
- At the base of the corners of the central white orthogonal prism which connect the red elements are four cubes shown in yellow. Each are copies of the seed shape reduced by 75 percent in both length and width and 83 percent in height.

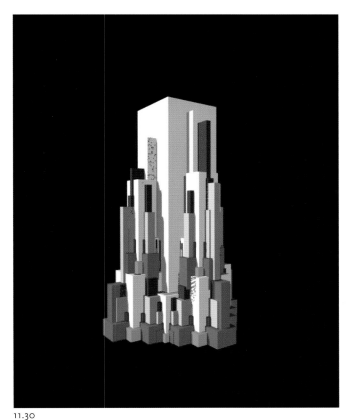

11.30

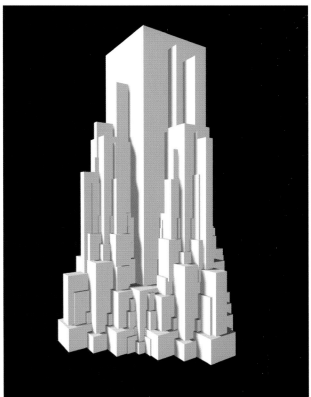

11.31

- At the intersection of the white, red, and gray components is a copy of the seed shape colored blue and reduced by 92 percent in length and width and 88 percent in height. These blue elements relate to the portions of the Malevich Alpha model that most readily trigger the perception of an organic unity through the use of self-similarity.

Figure 11.30 shows the second iteration of the fractal Alpha Architekton. As with other fractal models, the color coding highlights the self-similar relationships between parts and between the parts and the whole. Relative to the Malevich Alpha form, the blue elements provide the most perceptually obvious connection. Figure 11.31 renders iteration 2 completely in white to permit a direct comparison with the original Malevich Alpha form. As with other notable artists and architects, this comparison highlights the conscious or subconscious artistic goal of organic unity. The achievement of the desired organic unity is achieved through the appropriate use of fractal geometry.

Figure 11.30. Alpha form,– iteration 2.
Figure 11.31. Iteration 2 in white.

THE FOURTH DIMENSION

There has been consideration of the dimensions of matter beyond the three-dimensional world to which we are accustomed. The nature of the next dimension, the fourth dimension, beyond the three dimensions we know has been debated as being either temporal in nature, as explored by the Futurists, or spatial. The fourth dimension as a spatial entity has been a subject of scientific examination since the early nineteenth century, when August Mobius and later Louis Schlafi and Charles Hinton explored spatial possibilities beyond the third dimension.[30] In 1884 an English educator, Edward Abbot, published a book titled *Flatland: A Romance of Many Dimensions*. The setting for this book is a two-dimensional world in which women are straight lines, and men vary in social rank according to the number of sides they have, from the lowly square up to the priests, who are perfect circles. One day, Flatland is visited by a three-dimensional sphere that the people of Flatland are unaware of until it touches the plane of Flatland and creates a small, solid circle. The sphere is actually passing through the plane of Flatland, but the Flatlanders just see the solid circle getting larger and larger as the center of the sphere gets closer and closer to the plane of Flatland. After it passes the center, the solid circle gets smaller and smaller, until it becomes a dot and then disappears. It is conceptualized that the four-dimensional figures we construct, such as the four-dimensional cube or hypercube, are only shadows or slices of the fourth dimension as they project onto or pass through our three-dimensional world. Similarly to the two-dimensional world of Flatland, where the inhabitants cannot see three dimensions but only the shadow of the three-dimensional object on the surface of their two-dimensional world, we can only perceive a shadow of a fourth-dimensional object. The rotation of a backlit wire frame cube projects a warped image that turns in on itself. The analogous three-dimensional phenomenon occurs when the hypercube is rotated.

The new concepts regarding the nature of space propelled by Einstein's theories and other technological achievements of that era, such as X-rays and the discovery of atomic structure, inspired the examination of dimensions of space. The idea of a fourth dimension was an extension or push of a copy of a lower dimension's elements into the next dimension. The point of zero dimension is copied and extended by a vector into space to create a one-dimensional entity, the line, which consists of the initial point, the copy of the initial point, and an edge that connects the two points. The one-dimensional line is copied and extruded to create a two-dimensional plane that consists of four points and four edges. The two-dimensional plane is copied and extended into the third dimension, producing a cube that consists of eight points, twelve edges, and six planes. The three-dimensional cube is copied and in this case, for simplicity of illustration, is pushed into the next dimension by a vector oriented to the center of the original cube. This geometric entity consists of sixteen points, thirty-two edges, twenty-four planes, and eight cubes. Owing to our lack of ability to see in four dimensions, some of the cubes appear to be warped.

It has been noted by researcher Linda Henderson that in the early twentieth century, the fourth dimension was being explored by the general public as evidenced by a *Scientific American* essay contest in 1909 for "the best possible explanation of the Fourth Dimension." Maurice Princet, a mathematician, taught the principles of the fourth dimension to a number of Cubist artists at the time, including Jean Metzinger, Juan Gris, Marcel Duchamp, and Jacques Villon. In 1903 E. Jouffret published a treatise on the fourth dimension that included illustrations and is thought to have influenced contemporary artists. From her research, Linda Henderson concludes that the concept of the fourth dimension permeated many of the artistic movements at the time and thereafter included Cubists, Futurists, Suprematists, Constructivists, and the members of DeStijl.[31] As the forms generated by these movements have similarities to fractal compositions, it appears that there is a fractal connection to this underlying understanding of space.

The progression from one dimension to the next can be viewed as a fractal expansion as the seed entity of the lower dimension, such as the point, is copied and translated by a linear offset. The transformation from one dimension to two dimensions is more pronounced fractally as the initial seed shape is copied, rotated, and translated to produce a new seed shape of four points and four edges defining a plane. This seed shape is copied six times, rotated, and translated to generate the new seed shape of the three-dimensional cube. In the next iteration, this three-dimensional cubic seed shape is copied eight times, rotated, and translated to form the hypercube. In the fractal concept of space, the hypercube is again copied, rotated, and translated to form the next dimension of space.

SUMMARY

The depiction of nature has evolved through time from flat representation in the Middle Ages and the introduction of perspective in the Renaissance to the revolution that occurred at the beginning of the twentieth century. Concurrent with scientific theoretical advancements in the character of the universe, art reevaluated its representation of nature. The art movements of Cubism, Futurism, and Constructivism and the consideration of the fourth dimension fundamentally altered society's perception of our world. These movements have varied connections to fractal geometry. Cubism's characteristic of the simultaneous depiction of multiple viewpoints, Futurism's delineation of movement, Constructivism's Architekton constructions, and the unfolding of space resulting in the fourth dimension are inherently achievable with fractal geometry.

**The Spectrum of Architecture's
Relationship to Nature**

Architecture has sought a connection with nature since the dawn of civilization. This desire has manifested itself in the appliqué of nature's forms, the replication of biological designs, and the glorification of natural materials. Underlying this quest is the desire to know and embody in architecture the essence of nature and its forms. The spectrum of this relationship between the built environment and nature is exemplified by the seminal works of Frank Lloyd Wright and Le Corbusier, which define the terminus points of this continuum. These two architects provided the foundation of the Modernist revolution of architecture that still reverberates today. An examination of their histories and the values of significant aspects of their architectural philosophy reveal a convergence of influences affecting their relationship with nature, producing a unity in the importance of nature relative to the form of the built environment. From this common center, these two architects diverge, each traveling in opposite directions to form the boundaries of architecture's connection with nature.

The convergence of influences started with their childhood experiences, which left indelible marks on their relationship to nature, which formed the basis for their architectural philosophy. Both Le Corbusier and Wright had mentors who enhanced the connection they were striving to make between nature and architecture. Both architects referred to their mentors as "Master." These architectural icons were affected by the industrial revolution and had an infatuation with the "Machine." As both Wright's and Le Corbusier's architecture matured, it developed certain distinct characteristics. These characteristics included an abstract, mathematical basis for their work, utilizing pure forms to reflect their belief in universal values. They utilized the latest building technology, in particular, reinforced concrete, and relied on the structure of the work to embody their ideas of organic design and harmony. These varied factors influenced both men to affirm the importance of nature and the importance of reflecting this value in their work.

CONVERGENCE: FRANK LLOYD WRIGHT

Childhood Experience of Nature

Frank Lloyd Wright was born to Welsh parents whose family crest was an old Druid symbol signifying "Truth against the World."[1] The Unitarianism of his ancestors, the Lloyd-Jones, instilled in him the unity of all things and that life was a gift from the Divine Source.[2] His experience of growing up in Wisconsin and working on his grandparents' farm formulated the basis of his architectural philosophy. It was on these plains and in the surrounding woods that he developed a Goethian relationship with nature. He explored the woods and learned to understand nature from the trees, through the shrubs, and by the grass beneath his feet. For him this experience, *Nature-Experience,* was the only true understanding of basic universal questions.[3] He considered these elements of nature to be truth, a manifestation of the "very word of God."[4] In his autobiography, he stated that his farm experience was transformational as the intimate exposure to nature's beauty and cruelty stimulated his intellectual curiosity. The experience of the "interlocking interchanges of the universe" there initiated a lifelong quest to seek "Truth of Form from the inside out."[5] The farm topography and processes were ingrained in Wright, where the waving fields of the harvest produced a rhythmic, patterned order.[6] The horizontal expanse of the prairie terrain became one of the fundamental tenants of his design philosophy and his hope for a cultural transformation.

Wright was also influenced in his childhood by a gift from his mother: Froebel blocks. Friedrich Froebel theorized that kindergarten children should be exposed to objects, colors, textures, and cause and effect through interacting with sets of simple geometric blocks. Using these basic three-dimensional shapes, children were encouraged to use their imagination to explore by assembling and organizing the elements in various ways. These blocks developed Wright's ability for abstraction, which he utilized to channel his desire to incorporate the essence of nature's organizational structure into architectural forms and ornament.[7]

Influence of the Master

Frank Lloyd Wright left college and Wisconsin and traveled to Chicago, eventually to meet his *Leiber Meister*, Louis Sullivan. Sullivan was the only architect who Wright would acknowledge had an influence on him. According to Wright, "A good pencil I became in my Master's hand,"[8] and Wright was elevated to being his chief draftsman in charge of all residential commissions. Sullivan developed an integral sense of architecture that started with his creed "form follows function." Sullivan found that the forms in nature established their beauty in the integration of function and form.[9] Their aesthetic characteristics of this integral relationship of form and function revealed themselves in structure and invoked deep visceral reactions. For Sullivan, this response was a product of spirit uniting with matter.[10] He deemed that forms found in nature held a deeper meaning that could provide the basis for a new architectural presence in both architectural form and its expression through its ornamentation.[11] Sullivan published his methodology for creating ornament according to this aesthetic philosophy in his influential book *A System of Architectural Ornament*. Sullivan's method utilized matrices to develop sequential designs based on fundamental geometric shapes integrating curvilinear forms of nature.[12] Sullivan characterized his ornament as "plastic," which is distinguished by continuity of his ornament, eliminating background from the composition. This concept of plasticity was extended to the overall configuration of the building so that it was an integrated whole. He derived from nature the organization of natural entities embodying form and function and sought to apply it to architecture that he defined as organic.[13] Wright assimilated the foundation that Sullivan laid for ornamentation, plasticity, and organic architecture and took it to another level of abstraction and integration. Wright absorbed Sullivan's edification and reacted against the status quo of architecture he termed "classic." He objected to the separation of horizontal, the beam, and vertical, the post, as constituting the basis of architecture. The historical aesthetic of many separate interior spaces arranged according to axes divorced from the exterior through thick walls that served as protective layers was to fall away to a new aesthetic based on flowing space. Wright was inspired by Lao Tze, who declared that the reality of a building consisted not in the four walls and roof but in the space within.[14] Wright's space would be redefined through Sullivan's expanded concept of continuity and made possible through advances in building technology so that the walls, floors, and ceilings could flow together.[15] The new architecture threw off the dictates of style and taste and sought a new integrity in which a railroad station would look like a railroad station and not like an ancient temple or imperial palazzo.[16]

Development of Architectural Signature

Wright worked on some notable Adler and Sullivan buildings such as the Wainright Building, which Wright considered the "master key" to skyscraper design.[17] Wright and Sullivan eventually had a falling out, with Wright leaving Adler and Sullivan and going out on his own, working principally on residential commissions. It was during this time that Wright developed his Prairie Style residential archetype with flowing interior spaces, overhanging eaves, low-pitched roofs, and a distinct horizontal emphasis. Examples of this period of his work are the Willits House, the Dana House, and the Robie House. Also completed during this period was Unity Temple, which Wright considered his first conscious attempt to express his "new" idea of architecture.[18] Late during this period, Wright began to set the foundation for a new phase in his career that was characterized by an increased interest in abstraction and geometry. This commenced with his first trip to Japan, a country that made a dramatic impact on him. Wright observed that for the Japanese, the word *nature* signifies an inner harmony that penetrates the outward form and is its determining character and significance.[19] He believed Japan to be the most nature inspired country on earth and that the term *organic* inherently applied to Japanese art and architecture.[20] Wright noted that a characteristic of Japanese design that contributed to this character was the recognition of geometry and structure in nature. There was an ability to grasp the underlying structure and geometry of natural forms and thereby determine their essence.[21] This fundamental characteristic was effectuated through abstraction achieved by the elimination of the insignificant and reducing the fundamental conditions of form to simple geometry.[22]

Wright returned from Japan and continued working on Prairie Style projects, but owing to personal scandal, Wright left the United States

12.1

12.2

Figure 12.1. Midway Gardens.
Figure 12.2. Imperial Hotel.

for Europe. There Wright absorbed the work of some of the architects who inspired Le Corbusier such as August Perret and Peter Behrens. By the further development of his abstract vocabulary, it appears that he was influenced by the Vienna Secession and Hendrik Berlage, who shared the belief of a form's unity within diversity, which is characteristically found in natural forms.[23] They also shared a geometrization of form utilizing lattices, based both on rectilinear and triangular grids, to provide the substrate of geometric forms of circles, squares, and triangles transformed through addition, subtraction, multiplication, and transposition to create unified compositions that espoused their organic philosophy.[24] The gravitation to these basic geometric shapes was rooted in the belief in pure forms that reoccurred in history and were present in primitive cultures.[25] The process of dissection and resynthesis of geometric forms was to provide a unity that was based on natural processes. It was to serve as the foundation for a new design vocabulary on which modern architecture could be based.

Wright returned to the United States and Japan to create two projects that epitomized his renewed aesthetic: Midway Gardens in Chicago (Figure 12.1) and the Imperial Hotel in Tokyo (Figure 12.2). The Midway Gardens project was an indoor and outdoor entertainment complex where Wright transformed the Secessionist, two-dimensional vocabulary into a three-dimensional language that served as the unifying thread in the diversity of applications in the complex.[26] In the Imperial Hotel project, Wright increased the complexity of the vocabulary he employed at Midway Gardens with the inclusion of a principal diagonal orientation termed "Dancing Glass," an expansion of the geometric forms utilized, and an increased asymmetry.[27] In these projects, the use of geometric forms to unify the diversity of elements was intended to achieve a *Gesamtkunstwerk*, an integrated work of art.

For Wright, plasticity in both a spatial sense and in the sense of the nature of the enclosing elements was a prevailing quality of his designs. Wright's buildings freed themselves from the compartmentalization of functions to a sense of flowing space throughout the structure. Similarly, the enclosing elements—walls, floors, and ceilings—flowed together in a plastic continuity distinct from the previous discrete treatment of vertical and horizontal surfaces.[28] A Wright design reversed the relationship of inside and outside from an opaque protective shield to a more transparent minimally perceived separation uniting the interior and exterior.[29] He celebrated the nature of the materials he used, only using those that were appropriate and showed "each for itself and all as themselves."[30] A stone building would be designed based on that material and would not use the same aesthetic principles as a masonry or steel building. Wright revised the nature of ornament from a disparate appliqué of motifs on a substrate to an essential extension of the design that emerges from the nature of the structure and hence is naturally integral to it. The structure propagates a pattern from itself that crystallizes as its ornament.[31] His buildings were integrated into the earth as if they sprung forth similar to a plant opening itself to the sun. The overriding quality for which he strove in his diaphanous plastic designs based on material and ornamental integrity was for a sense of an organic unity between the whole and its elements.[32]

The Impact of the "Machine"

Most people do not relate Frank Lloyd Wright with any positive associations to the concept of the "Machine." To the contrary, Wright readily embraced the machine as a tool that freed designers to new possibilities as well as having a direct impact on architectural form and expression. He viewed the machine as a liberator of labor and was lauded by his friend Ashbee for his efforts to master the machine and use it. For Wright, "the machine provided the simplification required to do organic work."[33] By using the Machine, striking new economics were opened to architecture, creating "entirely new materials from entirely new methods."[34] The most significant example of this was the development of steel-reinforced concrete, which made cantilever construction possible. For Wright, the cantilever was the "most romantic, most free, of all principles of construction."[35] One of Wright's most notable speeches was titled "The Art and Craft of the Machine." In this lecture, he provided the metaphor of the Gutenberg printing press and its product, the book, to illustrate his philosophical position on the Machine. In that historical event, rather than the printing press, the book for Wright was the first machine and that great architecture was a granite book, a form of communication that draws humanity toward the "universal automatic fabric."[36] Wright believed that the Machine was a generator of architectural form and that architecture was to evolve toward a new aesthetic based on the Machine.[37]

Mathematical Basis of Design

Wright's design vocabulary was firmly entrenched in mathematics, in particular, geometry and pattern generation. He drew on his love for music and his personal connection to musical rhythm, mathematics, and universal truths.[38] For Wright, music's rhythmic quality was sublimated mathematics, and mathematics was the basis of coordinated form in architecture. In utilizing mathematics, he strove to visually transpose the universal principles in musical rhythms to architecture.[39] As he stated, "Design is the abstraction of nature's elements in purely geometric terms," and these mathematical tools served as the conduit between the beauty in nature and that which he strove to emulate in his architecture.[40] Anticipating the discovery of fractal geometry, Wright articulated in his book *Architecture and Modern Life* that geometry was the basis on which nature created her forms, resulting in their natural scaling and self-similar qualities.[41] Geometry was the grammar of form that provided a connection with human cognition and the resulting symbolic value. In the geometry of natural forms, such as a pine tree, there is a particular "pine" character of the tree or what Plato termed its *eternal idea*.[42] Wright based his architecture on the power he believed to be inherent to the utilization of geometry. Employing grids, primary geometric forms, and basic transformational operations of repetition, addition, and subtraction, he created compositions that exuded an energy that resonated with people.

Abstraction

Wright's journey into abstraction commenced when his mother provided him with the primary forms of the Froebel blocks.[43] These simple toys induced him to conceptualize in basic geometric forms and derive the essence of form relationships in an abstract representation. Even early in his career, Wright was not attracted to incorporating "realistic" aspects of nature but rather its abstracted forms.[44] This abstract propensity flourished after his trips to Japan and Europe. Wright was fascinated by the Japanese design theory that emphasized simplification through the elimination of the insignificant. In "The Japanese Print," he observed, "Beauty abstract in immaculate form; so concise in expression," highlighting his belief that this process did not diminish the subject but rather dramatized it.[45] He strove for *organic simplicity*, where the secret of simplicity was not within the object itself but was a clearly realized part of an organic whole.[46] The tendency toward simplification, the elimination of the insignificant, and the generation of abstract relationships manifested itself in "structure." For Wright, true form was a matter of structure.[47] The search for truth of integral form led Wright toward patterns of nature abstracted into structure such that the form and idea are synthesized, as they are in the relationship between the structure and conceptualization of a tree.[48] The structural relationships that constituted the architectural form cascaded down through its ornament, which poetically was the inherent melody of structure, a manifestation of the abstract pattern of the structure.[49] Building on his European experience with Franz Metzner, Hendrik Petrus Berlage, and the Secessionists, Wright developed a method of abstracting nature and termed it *conventionalization*, a process that produced a visual expression of its essential values.[50] One of the key differences between Wright and his contemporary abstractionists was that while most were generating two-dimensional elements, Wright transformed his geometric abstraction to the third dimension.[51] It was through this process that Wright was able to make a decisive break with the historical use of natural forms and conceive the basis of a new architecture. The grammar for this new architectural vernacular resided in the use of primary forms. These forms contained universal attributes that resonated with humans: the circle, infinity; the triangle, structural unity; the spire, aspiration; the spiral, organic progress; the square, integrity.[52] These elemental forms were found throughout history, spanning a variety of cultures, and therefore possessed a universal quality. These simple geometric forms possess a common symbolic visual language that touches the human collective consciousness, forming connections between people and between them and the cosmos.[53] Wright termed the connection between the geometrical qualities of these forms their *universal associations* and the consequential human cognitive response as *spell power*. The "Structure" was the grouping of primary forms in a set of abstracted geometrical relationships to generate an idea that was consistent with that experienced in the perception of natural forms. This structure, which generated spell power, was a product of the universal geometric shapes and the organic nature of their interdependent relationships.

Structure

Wright's architectural philosophy developed an emphasis on structure, a term with a varied but integrated set of meanings, that evolved from the time he left Wisconsin and traveled to Chicago. The Chicago architectural stratum was influenced by the German rationalism that had its roots in the theories of Karl Schisler and Viollet-le-Duc.[54] Its emphasis on the expression of structure was transposed to commercial building and emerged particularly in the new skyscraper form. Wright became immersed in this new architectural paradigm through his employment at Adler and Sullivan. The experience with Sullivan also opened his eyes to the expression of structure within the forms of nature and the possibility of integrating nature's principles of structure within an architectural form.[55] His sense of structure was expanded by his study of primitive cultures that embodied nature's principles in the development of its building structure and his experience with Japanese architecture. Wright derived from his exposure to Japanese culture and architecture that Japanese artists understand nature's forms from the geometry of their structure. The antecedent of structure is with its geometry. Structure is not only the framework that holds the form intact, but more important, it is an expression of the organization of the parts to form a larger entity.

The perception and cognitive processing of the stimuli emanating from this organization is the idea of the structure that the Japanese artists were proficient in extracting from natural forms and implementing within their art and architecture.[56] Wright believed that architecture based on the organizational structure of natural forms would serve as the foundation for the new archetype of modern architecture and what he termed the *architecture of Democracy*. This paradigm, termed *organic architecture*, would be an architecture for nature and of nature by being consistent with the laws of nature.[57] A characteristic of this architecture would be organic simplicity, which reveals the organic concept to the observer consistent with that exhibited by nature.[58] The revealed organic concept is the organizational structure where the "part to the whole is as the whole is to the part," all working to a purpose inherent to the organizational structure.[59] Similar to the growth of a plant, Wright's architectural design is a process from the inside, the idea to be manifested, to the outside, the physical form from the structure of its overall form through its integral ornament.[60] Wright stated that ideas exist by virtue of form and that form could not be detached from the idea.[61] By basing his architecture on the part-to-whole-to-part organizational structure, he synthesized the idea of natural form to his architectural designs and imbued them with the same natural or organic characteristics. He believed this organic integrity was the fundamental law of beauty.[62]

Nature

From his experience on his grandparents' farm, Frank Lloyd Wright established a visceral relationship with nature. It began his voyage of discovery of nature's inner mechanism and laws, understanding those

351

qualities that constitute its essence. He saw an organic simplicity as the agent that produced the "significant character in the harmonious order we call nature." The prairie was an enduring influence on Wright as in its organic nature he celebrated its flowers, its trees, and the sky.[63] He made a direct connection between God and nature, believing it to be the very essence of God.[64] During his career, Wright became infatuated with the desert, which brought to his mind Victor Hugo's quote that "the desert is where God is and Man is not."[65] Wright was so intuitively attracted to nature that he characterized a car trip through the desert to the site of San Marcos as riding while "Nature staged a show for us all the way."[66] For Wright, it was fundamental for an architect to know life, and to know life was to study nature.[67] He noted that "the wisest savants and noblest poets have therefore gone direct to Nature for the secret."[68] The intimate relationship with nature was encouraged at Taliesin, Wright's school or fellowship of architects, as illustrated by two of its stated tenets: "An eye to see nature and the courage to follow nature."[69]

Goethe was a meaningful influence on Wright, as illustrated by his reading of Goethe's "Hymn to Nature" at the funeral of Wright's infamous lover, Mamath Borthwick. He paralleled Goethe in his quest to understand the essence of nature's forms and to understand the force that causes a pine tree to be characterized as a pine tree, a willow tree as a willow tree, and transpose it to understand the qualities that make an organic design organic.[70] Nature was a comprehensive realization that manifested itself in various forms. The idea within and unique to each of nature's forms was a step in the continual evolution of the idea, manifesting with the concept that natural forms are always in a state of becoming. Wright understood nature as being in a "process of flowing in some continuous state of becoming" its essence. During this process, their geometrical and other sensuous qualities resonate within humans an empathetic chord. This consonance is generated by the perception of these qualities and the ensuing comprehension of them as life, and a sense of harmony is engendered.[71]

Wright believed that similar to the laws of physics, the laws of beauty preexist and are latent and inherent within people as a significant part of their nature.[72] He utilized geometry, which he believed to be similarly inherent within humans and therefore manifesting spell power or the same emotional response. By utilizing geometry within a plastic organic structure, his architecture resonated with key elements of human nature and exuded a sense of life.

CONVERGENCE: LE CORBUSIER

Childhood Experience of Nature

Charles Edouard Jeanneret, later known as Le Corbusier, was born approximately twenty years later than Wright in the Swiss town of Le Chaux-de-Fonds, within the mountainous area of Swiss Jura. His birthplace was internationally known for the design, fabrication, and decoration of watches.[73] Typical for the population of Le Chaux-de-Fonds, Le Corbusier's family was connected for generations with the manufacture of watches.[74] The mathematical precision and machine aesthetic that was to dominate a period of Le Corbusier's architectural forms and eventually become his signature had its roots in this environment of his formative years. This Swiss precision lived in harmony with a devotion to nature. Jeanneret's father was the president of the local Alpine Club and spent his leisure hours trekking and mountain climbing, frequently taking his son with him and encouraging him to study and understand nature.[75] Le Corbusier remembered in his book *Modulor 2* taking walks with his father "through the valleys and up the mountains, pointing out what he admired most; the diversity of contrasts, the staggering personality of objects, but also the unity of laws."[76] These childhood experiences engendered his lifelong quest for harmony within his architectural forms and their relationship to nature. As with Wright, Le Corbusier adopted a Goethian perspective on nature, striving to penetrate the cause behind natural appearances and capture the harmony that holds them together. Le Corbusier noted nature's vast array of purposeful forms, each with its proper place within the overall order, spurring Le Corbusier to think according to species and type.[77] Le Corbusier transformed the forms he observed in his treks with his father through abstraction into regionalist imagery with similarities to Art Nouveau.[78] He translated the Jurassic emblems he saw into abstract forms that he incorporated in his watchcase designs. His designs appear to be influenced by Eugene Grasset's *Methods de Composition Ornamenteale*, which espouses a system of ornament predicated in geometry and the simplification of natural forms. It utilized the combination and recombination of simple geometric shapes according to certain rules of repetition, scaling, and transformation.[79]

353

Influence of the Master

During his mid-teens, Le Corbusier enrolled in the local trade school to learn watch engraving. It was there that he became a student of Charles L'Eplattener. L'Eplattener bestowed on this provincial art school the philosophy whereby the students were challenged to enhance society through the translation of the principles obtained from the observation of nature into high-quality artifacts. Both L'Eplattener and Le Corbusier were influenced by Owen Jones's *Grammar of Ornament*, which held that the true basis for architectural forms and decorative motifs lay in the transformation of local, natural features. L'Eplattener believed the appropriate forms for the Jura area were to be derived from the rock strata and conifer trees, in particular, the form and structure of the fir and pine trees. His aesthetic philosophy was rooted in a true understanding of nature, not in shallow imitation but in its underlying structure or essence. From this understanding, the essential geometric features were abstracted to form symbolic patterns from elementary laws of combination.[80] Le Corbusier came to focus on the fundamental logic of life that causes the development of an embryo from roots to the stalk and leaves through to the flower. He transposed his understanding of the essence of natural forms into an aesthetic logic that would prevail throughout his architectural career.[81] Le Corbusier reminisced,

> My teacher, an excellent instructor, was an outdoor man, and he turned his students into outdoor men. I spent my childhood with my friends outdoors. . . . I knew what flowers look like, outside and inside . . . I understood how a tree grows and why it is able to stand upright, even in a storm. My teacher said, "Nature alone is truthful: it can inspire man made works. But do not treat nature as landscape painters do and show only its outward appearance. Search for the cause, the form, the animating spirit of things and synthesize this in the ornaments that you design."[82]

Development of Architectural Signature

Le Corbusier left Le Chaux-de-Fonds and traveled Europe and the Mediterranean, settling first in Vienna. He came to react against the teaching of the traditional architectural schools, such as the French Ecoles des Beaux Arts,[83] and repudiated ninetieth-century Revivalism. Recalling the teachings of his master, he rejected more florid aspects of Art Nouveau to search for a deeper, more enduring association with the universal values embodied in the essence of natural forms.[84] Architects Otto Wagner and Josef Hoffman influenced Jeanneret to move beyond the forms of Art Nouveau and develop an architectural vocabulary that represented modern life based on modern construction technology.[85] Le Corbusier eventually settled in Paris, where he was employed by August Perret, who displaced to a large extent L'Eplattener as his source of design support. Perret introduced Le Corbusier to the structural potentials of concrete through the Classical principles of composition. After Paris, he went to Berlin, where he joined Peter Behren's office, which also employed Mies Van der Rohe and Walter Gropius at various times. At Behren's office, and influenced by the Deutscher Werkbund, mathematical proportions and modulor systems were espoused to create forms utilizing modern production techniques while still approximating Platonic ideas.[86] Working within a classicist discipline, Behren's office produced a new design vocabulary through the design of industrial and utilitarian buildings.[87]

Le Corbusier left Berlin and traveled again, culminating in an auspicious visit to the Acropolis in Athens. The complex at the Acropolis transcended the clichés about Classicism and resonated a desire within Le Corbusier to achieve a universality that he first encountered in the natural forms in the Jura Mountains. The universality that he perceived was a product of mathematics that distilled certain ideals in a sculptural form.[88] That form established the perfect balance of architecture within a natural setting, which was to become a hallmark of Le Corbusier's work.

He eventually came back to Paris, where he became involved in the Cubist art movement and associated with the Cubist artists Delaunay, Duchamp, Metzinger, Gris, and Leger. This abstractive influence came at an historical period after World War I during which the Zeitgeist was to reflect the modern life transformed by the machine. Despite the veneer of the new artistic expression of the machine, the universality that composed its foundation was rooted in the essence found in nature. There was an underlying theme synthesizing universal ideals with mechanization that produced a fundamentally different artistic expression. It was at this time that Gris and Le Corbusier absorbed the ideals of the *Section d'Or* (Golden Section) group experiments into proportional systems that were to affect Jeanneret's design aesthetic for the rest of his career.[89] Le Corbusier, with his colleague Ozenfant, published a periodical, *L'Espirit Nouveau*, and in doing so established

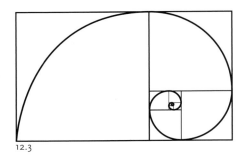
12.3

12.4a

12.4b

Figure 12.3. Golden Section.
Figure 12.4. Villa Stein.

their pseudonyms, Jeanneret's being an ancestral name Lecorbusier, which was transformed into Le Corbusier.[90] This marked the full transformation of Le Corbusier from the nature-centric adolescent to the young architect who transformed those concepts and ideals into "new reality" of a cubocentric machinistic expression. Despite the veneer of the new artistic expression of the machine, the universality that composed its foundation was rooted in the essence found in nature.

With an aesthetic and philosophical foundation built on natural forms that was transformed by the Zeitgeist of society resurrecting itself from World War I, Le Corbusier developed a signature vocabulary within a machinistic vernacular. The vocabulary consisted of five main elements: the use of piloti to raise the composition off the ground, enabling greenery to continue underneath; the free plan within the interior and the free façade on the exterior, both liberated by the lack of structural requirements of their elements; the strip window; and the rooftop garden.[91] This grammar was structured through the use of regulating lines and the Golden Section (Figure 12.3). Within the machinistic aesthetic, Le Corbusier and his Cubist associates based compositional essentials on the Golden Section and *regulating lines*. Early in his career, Le Corbusier employed regulating lines to provide a "tangible form of mathematics which gives reassuring perception of order." The choice of regulating lines fixes the fundamental geometry of the work, establishing one of the "fundamental characters" in Le Corbusier's representative projects of this period: Villa Stein at Garches (Figure 12.4) and Villa Savoy at Poissy (Figure 12.5).[92] For Le Corbusier, the Golden Section governed natural structure such as the subdivisions of a leaf, the organization of trees and shrubs, and the bone structure of animals. Le Corbusier viewed it as the organizational basis for most of the entities of the natural environment and utilized it extensively in the later period of his career.[93]

The Impact of the Machine

For Le Corbusier, the impact of the Machine was a result of a transposition of the significant impression the Acropolis made on him during his youth, his quest for universals, and finally, the Zeitgeist of society. The visit to the Acropolis was probably the most influential experience of Le Corbusier's life. It resonated within him as it was a precise expression of an idea within a sculptural form. He held that it was a result of "supreme mathematics," which therefore spoke of universality.[94] Le Corbusier, like many before him, was enthralled with the concept

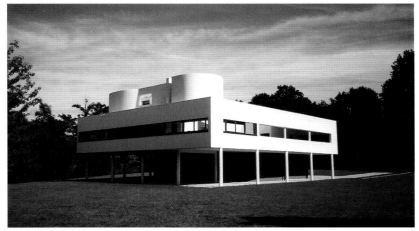

12.5

of universals toward which one should strive as one represents truth. Nature was one such universal held dear by Le Corbusier and endorsing a long-held belief that the universe operated according to precise laws governed by mathematics.[95] Against the background of the end of World War I, Le Corbusier's return to Paris, to the Zeitgeist of the age and exposure to the Cubist artists, transposed the honesty found in nature to an honesty that he believed to be inherent to the new age of machines. It was, to an extent, a reaction to the pseudo-naturalism of previous artistic periods and a desire to found a contemporary analogy to the efficiency found in natural forms championed by Darwin and D'Arcy Thompson.[96] In his influential book *Towards a New Architecture,* Le Corbusier stated, "The creations of mechanical technique are organisms tending to be pure functioning, and obey the same evolutionary laws as the objects in nature which excite our admiration."[97]

Mathematical Basis of Design

Le Corbusier was certainly influenced to appreciate mathematics from his childhood environment of Le Chaux-de-Fonds, whose principal industry was the design and manufacture of high-end timepieces. After leaving the Jura Mountains area of his youth, the time he spent with August Perret, who stated, "If I had time, I would study mathematics; it develops the mind," undoubtedly reinforced Jeanneret's youthful predilection toward mathematics.[98] His visit to the Parthenon was a critical point in his life, when his mathematical core realized its architectural manifestation. In his *Modulor* volumes, he discussed his belief that mathematics was a "majestic structure" created by man to

Figure 12.5. Villa Savoy.

357

comprehend the universe. The path to understanding the universe is obstructed by a wall that prevents understanding. Mathematics is a door through this wall that permits man to enter a realm where man can see the gods at play with numbers of which the universe is constituted.[99] In this realm, man is not the operative force but is bathed in the all-pervading light emerging from the universe's mathematical structure.[100] He believed that numbers made "a temple out of an ordinary dwelling" and that it was man's destiny to project forms in space animated by numbers.[101] Le Corbusier became a devotee of the ideas of Matila Ghyka on proportion and geometry in nature and its applications in art.[102] As outlined in his *Modulor* volumes, he believed that nature is ruled by mathematics and that the masterpieces of art are in consonance with nature—governed by natural laws—and express these mathematical laws of nature in their forms. He cited the elegant proportioning in trees from their trunks through their branches and leaves to their veins and believed that there was a mathematical link running through all its components and linking them. The artist must discern nature's structure and incorporate those principles in his work. The key to this task was in geometry.[103]

Abstraction

Le Corbusier grew up in an environment that held nature and its forms in high regard. From this environment, he began his architectural career by setting out on a series of trips throughout Europe and the Mediterranean in search of the application of the universals he came to know in nature to architecture. From his fascination with universal values, mathematics, and the transposition of beauty of natural structure to the machine aesthetic, Le Corbusier's work evolved to exhibit an abstract quality that resonates with an organic vitality. By employing mathematics, he transformed his aesthetic philosophy's foundation of nature's forms into the grammar of a machine aesthetic. This transformation was based on utilizing abstraction to convert the essence of natural structure into a machinistic expression. For Le Corbusier, the materialization of an idea was a consequence of architectural abstraction.[104] It was through geometrical abstraction that he emulated the "idea" of the mathematical harmony of natural order.[105] Using clearly perceivable primary forms, Le Corbusier sought to touch within humans the universal higher order that was perceived in nature. Le Corbusier appeared to intuitively comprehend the strong gestalt that primary forms possessed and utilized them in the creation

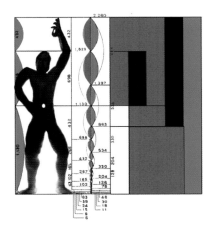

12.6

Figure 12.6. The Modulor.

of relationships that constituted his creations. This understanding is embodied in his famous quote that "architecture is the masterly, correct and magnificent play of masses brought together in light."[106] The "magnificent play" is the abstracted set of relationships he created among his architectural elements. These relationships were habitually created using the Modulor (Figure 12.6), which consisted of two series, one red and one blue. The Modulor was derived by utilizing the proportions of a man's naval, the top of his head, and the height of his outstretched arm above his head with the concept of a Fibonacci Series, in which a number is the product of the addition of the previous two numbers in the series.[107] The red series, with the measurement to a man's naval as the base unit, and the measurement to his head were associated through a Fibonacci relationship. The blue series used as its base measurement the distance to the man's vertically outstretched arm, which was double the red series's base measurement to the navel. The blue series is related to the red series as a double as well as through the common Fibonacci structure. From these two base measurements, a series of numbers were generated progressively and regressively, all related through the Fibonacci relationship. The space between each of the intervals can be broken down in a similar manner. Le Corbusier graphically depicted the Modular in a vertical placement of the intervals connected by curves alongside a silhouette of a man with his arm raised up.

Le Corbusier's travels exposed him to architectural phenomena of the antiquities, such as the Parthenon and Indian temples, that exhibited a central unity arising from their design being rooted in a coherent system of human elements of measurement such as the elbow, the foot, and so on.[108] He viewed the heretofore mathematically based foundations of architecture, such as the Renaissance's geometrical basis of generated star-shaped icosahedrons and dodecahedrons for design schemata, as static because of their lack of relationship with human perception and cognition. That medium cannot communicate the idea behind the design as nature can communicate its organic idea in the relationships that constitute natural form.[109] He believed that the use of the Modular system, whose foundation was the critical dimensions of a man's body transformed by nature's Fibonacci extrapolation, would produce a "sensation of organic unity" inherent to man.[110] He strove for his architecture to exhibit universality, which he believed was achieved by using the Modulor, his system of proportional measurement that guaranteed a form that expressed unity. This system of proportional measurement would produce this organic attribute in various applications, thus proving its universality.[111]

Structure

When Le Corbusier left Le Chaux-de-Fonds for Paris, it represented a decisive step in the development of his architectural career. In Le Chaux-de-Fonds, he cultivated a solid foundation in nature, its forms, and its structures. In Paris he worked in the office of August Perret, who, through his precept of honesty in structural expression, encouraged Le Corbusier's transition from the ornamental details of architecture and toward the structure of the underlying forms. Perret's influence can be seen in Le Corbusier's recollection of Perret exhorting him, "Grasp the skeleton and you grasp the art."[112] While under Perret's mentoring, as he pioneered innovations in concrete structure, Le Corbusier was studying Edouard Courroyer and Auguste Choisy, providing historical information on structure in architecture as well as Charles Henry's research on aesthetic theory and structure. The time he spent in Paris with Perret and the emphasis on structure enabled Le Corbusier to transpose his knowledge of natural forms and the nature of their organization into the structural aspects of an architectural aesthetic of the Machine. Through his evolution of design instruments, regulating lines, the Golden Section, and finally, the Modulor, Le Corbusier developed a grammar that would unite physical structure with his aspirations for universal and organic form.

The structure he created consisted of the reinforced concrete physical substance as well as the relationships that constituted the *Texturique*, or visual acoustics of its form. Le Corbusier would frequently use the metaphor of music to describe the configuration of relationships that resonated with humans.[113] He strove to create a unity through the rhythmic qualities in the group of relationships between his compositional elements all within the whole of the composition.[114] He termed this unity *Harmony* and believed it was generated through mathematical calculations derived from natural law. There is an axis of organization within man that is in perfect accord with nature and the universe. All natural phenomena and objects are organized according to this axis, and it signifies a unity of conduct in the universe and a singular will behind this universal law. When architecture is created according to this universal law, the axis within man resonates in the same manner as it does in the perception of natural form.[115] Le Corbusier believed that utilizing the Modulor, which was a system of proportional relationships based on natural form embodied in the Golden Section, would produce the requisite rhythmic scaling and the perception of Harmony.

Nature

Le Corbusier was exposed to the harmony of nature from earliest childhood through the hiking he did with his father and into adolescence by his mentor Charles L'Eplattener. As he began his travels, he was enthralled by the harmony he witnessed among people, their architecture, and nature. He was attracted to the fusion of their life with the rhythms of nature and the fundamental unity or universality of human nature. Influenced by the writings of John Ruskin and building on the foundation established by L'Eplattener, Le Corbusier followed Goethe's phenomenological approach to understanding nature. He strove to penetrate the physical manifestation of nature, to understand the inner law responsible for natural structure, and to abstract and transpose it through mathematics to architecture. He aspired through this process to link man to the universals present in nature and the cosmos. He advised architects to "go to the Museum of Natural History and study a class of shells to learn the infallible law of unity, variety and harmony. Nature whispers: look here." Le Corbusier wanted architects to develop their creative powers by "adventuring into the inexhaustible realm of natural riches" and "observe the harmonious creations and serene perfection present in natural forms." From these observations, he intended that architects would sketch a variety of natural forms in a manner that shows "the significance of a tree, the essential harmony of a sea shell and discover the different expressions of its inner force."[116] As he hoped, students of architecture would understand the inner force or law generating the natural form, and he believed that architecture should reveal the generative force responsible for its form.[117] The manifested generative force is a product of relationships created according to principles such as those in the Modulor that organize the architectural form according to universal laws. On such perception, the observer reaches what Gestalt terms the "AHA" point and what Le Corbusier characterizes as the fourth dimension, where the visual stimuli are understood in consonance with the generative idea in a "moment of boundless freedom."[118] The key to reaching this moment in the fourth dimension is comprehending the underlying geometric law that governs and determines the character of the composition at the moment when it enters the consciousness and unifies the parts in an organic harmony.[119] Le Corbusier made a distinction so that an engineer creates structures but an architect creates emotions. He sought to imbue his architecture with life, the experience of the fourth dimension, which he believed was achieved when man's perceptions denoted an organized phenomenon that resonated with the innate sounding board of harmony that resides within each person. The path to that sounding board was through the universal laws he believed were present throughout nature and the cosmos.

DIVERGENCE

Convergence and Divergence in the Philosophies of Wright and Le Corbusier on Nature and Architecture

The substrata from which Le Corbusier and Wright produced the most influential architecture of the modern era are interconnected in fundamental areas of their respective architectural geniuses. Both architects grew up in an environment that provided them with an intimate relationship with nature, which was augmented by the influence of an important mentor. The early development of their architectural dialect was a rejection of the status quo and an acknowledgment of the influence of industrialization in the form of the Machine. The wellspring of their creative brilliance was situated in mathematics, abstraction, and the embodiment of universals. These conceptual ideals were manifested in a structure of relationships that strove to embody the organic harmony they perceived in nature. From this common base sprung two fundamentally different relationships between architectural creation and the natural environment. To some extent, this is a result of the physical orientation of their work. Undoubtedly owing to his prairie upbringing in Wisconsin, Wright believed that the horizontal was an expression not only of nature but also of freedom that he sought to embody in his new Democratic architecture. He believed that the vertical orientation was antithetical to the human condition and provoked a emotional response of vertigo, whereas the horizontal orientation was "the life line of human kind" and harmonious with our natural condition.[120] The embedment of Le Corbusier's relationship with nature, propagated from his childhood hikes with his father, is reflected in his proclivity for a vertical orientation. He noted that the flower, the plant, and the mountain are all vertically orientated from their horizontal base.[121] He also made the connection between the fundamental upright nature of man's existence and therefore surmised that the natural orientation of the works to which man was to respond should be vertical.[122]

Frank Lloyd Wright's Relationship of Nature and Architecture

Frank Lloyd Wright's philosophy on how the built environment should relate to nature is at the opposite end of the spectrum from Le Corbusier's philosophy. He could not conceive of an abstract Corbusian form hovering above the landscape. Inspired by the structures of indigenous cultures that created their structures to be fitted within the natural environment in which they existed, he believed that architecture should be complementary with nature. He conceived of a building growing out of the soil into the light as does a plant. It is an independent structure but still maintains a connection to the earth as part of its nature.[123] The native conditions of the natural environment had a direct impact on the form and expression of what he termed *indigenous organic architecture*.[124] He believed that his structures should appear as part of the surrounding environment as its natural extension, reflecting the characteristics present there.[125] He wanted the perception of the observer to be that the building not only belonged there but enhanced its natural characteristics.[126] He endeavored to establish a connection between his work and the natural environment at a subliminal and conscious level based on a complementary blending of the two.

Any reading of Wright's writings would illuminate his inherent attraction to the use of fractal geometry to generate his architectural forms. His manuscripts were replete with references to organic form being the source of modern architecture. His constant references to natural structure as the source of form point toward using fractal geometry as it produces a structure with the same set of relationships as those that constitute natural form. The part-to-whole-to-part schema that is inherent to fractal geometry generates organic form. An architectural object composed with fractal geometry will exude this organic character, which will provide the exact relationship Wright was seeking between his structure and the surrounding natural environment. Wright desired his architecture to be complementary to the environment and appear as an outgrowth of the natural forms contiguous to it. Fractal geometry would provide a stronger link between the two than any of the other techniques he used such as using materials sympathetic to the natural setting. The perceptual link in the similarity of the structural relationships, those that create the essence or idea of the form, provides a strong bond between the two.

Frank Lloyd Wright House Example

Of all Frank Lloyd Wright's houses, Fallingwater (Figure 12.7) is the best known and probably the most integrated with the surrounding landscape. The house was a weekend retreat outside of Pittsburgh for Edward Kaufman, a successful businessman. Wright's visits to the site inspired him to interweave his house into the rock ledges and the stream that ran through the property. He wanted the house to be an "extension of the cliff beside a mountain stream . . . seemingly leaping out from the rock ledge behind." His structure makes use of one of Wright's favorite architectural elements, the cantilever, and exhibits his signature horizontal emphasis. The fractal model of Fallingwater creates the main horizontal and vertical elements of the building. The horizontal elements are organized in a pinwheel array, a preferred Wright compositional structure, anchored to the ground by the vertical elements. The fractal model starts with a seed shape that approximates the overall volume of the building. The main horizontal and vertical elements are transformed copies of this seed shape and are shown in Figure 12.8.

- The green element is a copy that is scaled down by 70 percent in length, 13 percent in width, and 85 percent in height, rotated 90 degrees about its z axis, and translated to the right by five feet, back by twenty-one feet, and up by nine feet.
- The blue element is a copy reduced by 40 percent in length, 23 percent in width, and 85 percent in height. It is then moved twelve feet to the right, eleven feet back, and eighteen feet up.
- The next horizontal plane, shown in red, is a copy of the seed shape that is condensed by 45 percent in length, 50 percent in width, and 85 percent in height. It is then rotated 180 degrees about its z axis and moved twenty-three feet to the left, seven feet back, and twenty-three feet up.
- The white horizontal plane above it is a copy of the seed shape shrunk by 20 percent in length, 60 percent in width, and 97 percent in height and translated eighteen feet to the right, six feet back, and thirty-one feet up.
- Figure 12.8e shows the vertical elements rendered in black with the element on the left a copy of the seed shape reduced by 83 percent in length and 35 percent in width, rotated 180 degrees about its z axis, and translated twenty-five feet to the left and thirteen feet forward.

Figure 12.7. Wright's Fallingwater.

12.7a

12.7b

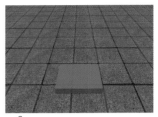

12.8a

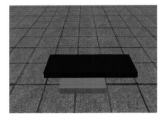

12.8b

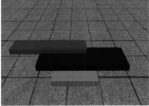

12.8c

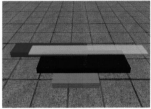

12.8d

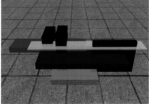

12.8e

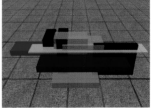

12.8e

Figure 12.8. Fractal Fallingwater, iteration 1.

- The middle vertical element is scaled similarly to the first vertical element, but its height dimension is increased by 8 percent, rotated 180 degrees about the z axis, and translated nine feet to the left and eight feet forward.
- The third vertical part is a copy of the seed shape scaled down by 70 percent in length, 90 percent in width, and 5 percent in height and then translated forty-six feet to the right and back eight feet.

Two elements shown in gray in Figure 12.8f form a central element at the top that provides the perception of central mass.

- One of these forms is a copy of the seed shape reduced 83 percent in length, 15 percent in width, and 85 percent in height, rotated 270 degrees about its z axis, and translated thirteen feet to the right, one foot forward, and thirty-two feet upward.
- The other gray element copies the seed shape, reduces it by 87 percent in length, 30 percent in width, and 70 percent in height, rotates it by 270 degrees about its z axis, and translates it one foot forward and thirty-two feet up.

All the elements are synthesized into one structure to form the new seed shape, to which the same set of transformations is applied. Figure 12.9 renders the elements of iteration 2 and shows the embedment of iteration 1's structure of relationships as modified by the transformations, such as rotation, characteristic to that part. The inherent swirling horizontal planes with vertical anchors now compose each element as well as maintaining the overall gestalt of the structure.

Iteration 2 is synthesized to form the new seed shape for iteration 3, which is shown in Figure 12.10. The complexity of the relationships is apparent in this iteration. As opposed to the Corbusian model, which has clearly discernible relationships, the appearance of the Fallingwater model manifests less apparent relationships and provides more of an overall organic gestalt. The Fallingwater model is regenerated applying a stucco finish to the horizontal planes, and a river stone material is employed on the vertical elements at iteration 1. After the third iteration, the model is modified to depress the area within the horizontal planes, and windows and minor stone in-fills are added where appropriate.

The final structure is rendered in Figure 12.11. Owing to the complex integrated relationships of the model, the fractal Fallingwater has

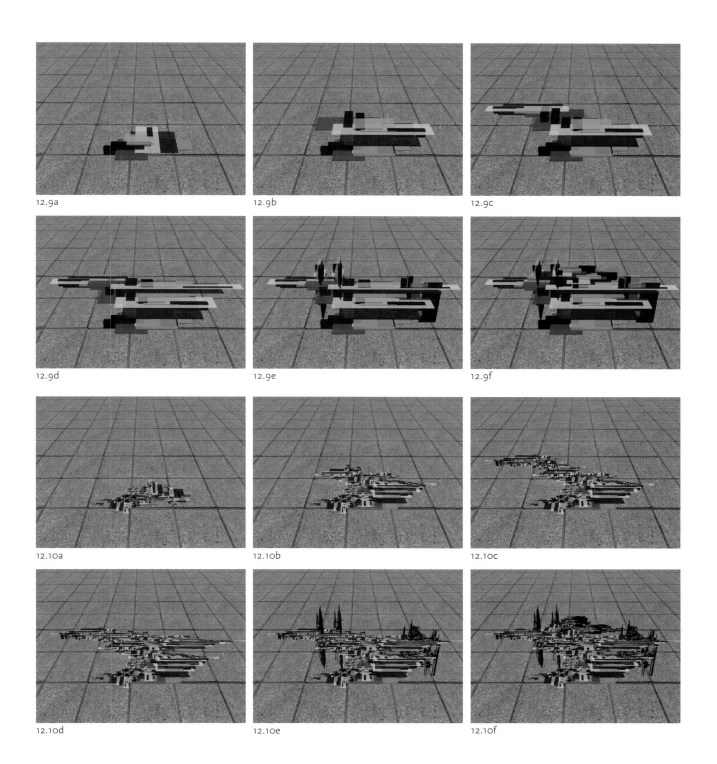

Figure 12.9. Fractal Fallingwater, iteration 2.
Figure 12.10. Fractal Fallingwater, iteration 3.

12.11a

Figure 12.11. Fractal Fallingwater, final.

12.11b

12.11C

more characteristics of the surrounding natural environment than the original building. The use of fractal geometry has embedded the inexplicable roughness and intertwining of nature's forms, as opposed to the more streamlined original, to provide a form congruent with the environment.

Le Corbusier's Relationship of Nature and Architecture

The fundamental relationship of the built environment to nature is the defining difference between these two architectural geniuses and establishes the ends of this architectural spectrum. Le Corbusier was drawn not only to the vertical, upright orientation of natural objects, such as the flower, the plant, and the mountain, but more important to the power and beauty paradoxically contained within their inner immutable forces but producing resonances within the surrounding environment. This relationship between the forces issuing from the natural object and the reaction of the surrounding environment should be thought of in mathematical terms as visual acoustics. Similarly, he believed that architecture exuding abstract mathematical purity should radiate lines of aesthetic force to the surrounding landscape that are affected and transformed by them. They in turn issue responding vectors of energy back toward the built structure, and this visual reverberation continues until equilibrium is established. Le Corbusier's visit to the Acropolis solidified this conceptual orientation that started with his childhood frolics in the mountains of Le Chaux-de-Fonds. The abstract visualization of what he perceived as universal truths situated within the mountainous Greek landscape established the prototype that he would follow the rest of his life. The placing of a pure abstract structure exuding universal truths within a beautiful natural setting produced for Le Corbusier a beautiful and appropriate resonance between the two. By lifting his compositions off the ground on pilotis and using materials and generative devices to produce a machinistic aesthetic embodying universal attributes, he undoubtedly created a composition in contrast with nature. It was in this contrast and the relating visual acoustics between it and the environment that Le Corbusier produced an architecture that was intertwined with its natural environment.

This intertwining of Le Corbusier's architecture and the natural setting in which it is placed and with which it interacts would be enhanced by the use of fractal geometry. His quest to establish a system of proportions related to human dimensions and those proportions found in natural structure, such as the Golden Section, resulted in the Modulor. Le Corbusier hoped that by utilizing the Modulor, a harmonious set of relationships would be generated, producing an inherently organic form with a machinistic vocabulary. Fractal geometry is the mathematical Holy Grail that he was seeking that embodies universal truths found in the organizational structure of nature's forms. By utilizing fractal geometry, Le Corbusier's goal of producing a resonance between the abstract machinistic architectural object and its surrounding natural environment would be made richer.

The distinction between Le Corbusier's building and the natural setting cannot and should not be overcome. The association between two opposites is a fundamental perceptual concept that is a compelling methodology for producing a dynamic union between the two. The overt distinction between the abstract structure embodying universal organic percepts and the surrounding environment composed of natural forms will not be overcome owing to easily perceived differences, but if, similar to the musical composition of a fugue, an underlying melody that is in *unison between the two* is established, the entire arrangement is made richer. If the architectural form is composed utilizing fractal geometry, it will embody the same set of relationships that is employed to compose the natural forms that surround it. While the overt distinction of opposition between the architectural object and its environment remains dominant, a countermelody of equivalence is established between the two entities. The resulting relationship produces a stronger, richer interlock between the two.

Le Corbusian House Example

Le Corbusier was one of the most influential architects whose legacy has been carried on by architects such as Richard Meier (Figure 12.12), whose houses are jewels of Corbusian grammar. Meier's architecture characteristically employs the use of white metal, which provides his compositions with an increased level of abstraction and universality than Le Corbusier's predominantly concrete forms. The fractal model of a similar residential structure starts with a seed shape that is a white tube with a glass panel within it, as depicted in Figure 12.13. The fractal model consists of four separate but integrated façades and a roof, as opposed to a three-dimensional form. Figure 12.14 shows the three iterations of the front façade, which consists of eight elements.

Figure 12.12. Richard Meier House (opposite).

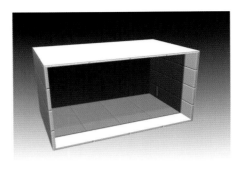

12.13

- In the first iteration, two copies of the seed shape, shown in black in Figure 12.14a, are generated, each scaled down 75 percent in length, 88 percent in depth, and 50 percent in height. They are then translated to the right edge with one placed on top of the other.
- Four additional copies of the seed shape are each reduced by 87 percent in length, 88 percent in depth, and 74 percent in height, rotated 90 degrees clockwise about the y axis, and translated to be adjacent to the black elements, placed one over the other. Three of the elements are rendered in gray and one is rendered in yellow.
- Two copies of the seed shape, shown in white, are reduced by 74 percent in length and 88 percent in depth and increased by 16 percent in height, rotated 90 degrees clockwise about the y axis, and then translated to the left side of the front façade, one on top of the other.

In iteration 2, shown in Figure 12.14b, the effect of the elements' rotation is evident, proving a significant overall horizontality counterbalanced by the vertical repetition of parts, in particular, the four parts just to the right of the façade's center. Figure 12.14c illustrates the third iteration, which arises from the 90 degree rotation of the majority of elements that turns the horizontal orientation of the previous iteration into an overall vertical emphasis. The stacking of parts exacerbates the vertical emphasis of this iteration.

The left side of the composition is composed of four parts whose iterations are depicted in Figure 12.15.

- The first two parts, shown in dark gray in Figure 12.15a, copy the seed shape, reducing each copy by 74 percent in length, 88 percent in depth, and 75 percent in height. They are then each rotated 90 degrees clockwise about their y axes and 90 degrees counterclockwise about their z axes. The copies are translated to the right side of the left façade with one element on top of the other. The effect of these transformations is to reflect, in each of these copies, the previous iteration of the front façade turned 90 degrees to the right.
- The next part of this façade, rendered in red, is a copy of the seed shape scaled down by 88 percent in length and 23 percent in depth and translated to be adjacent to the first two parts of the left façade.
- The last element of the left façade copies the seed shape and

Figure 12.13. The seed shape of a fractal Le Corbusier.

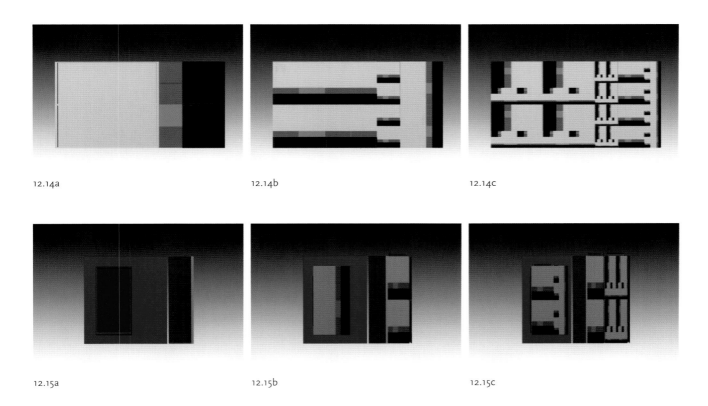

12.14a   12.14b   12.14c

12.15a   12.15b   12.15c

Figure 12.14. Three iterations of the front façade.
Figure 12.15. Three iterations of the left façade.

reduces it by 80 percent in length, 85 percent in depth, and 25 percent in height and rotated 90 degrees counterclockwise about its z axis. Shown in blue, it is translated so that it is protruding from the plane of the façade on the left side of the previous element centered vertically. By rotating it 90 degrees about its z axis, it reflects the previous iteration of the front façade, but unlike the other parts, which reflect the front façade, it is not rotated 90 degrees about its y axis.

Iteration 2, displayed in Figure 12.15b, clearly exhibits the structure of the front façade, with two copies that, because of their 90 degree rotation about their y axes, are horizontally oriented on the right side and with one element with a vertical emphasis on the left side. The red part of iteration 1 now has two dark gray subelements, which, in the next iteration, will be replaced with rotated copies of the front elevation. In iteration 3, shown in Figure 12.15b, the two right dark gray parts of the first iteration are replaced with rotated copies of iteration 2 of the front façade. The second iteration of the front façade has an overall horizontal emphasis, but because these elements are rotated,

375

they are reoriented vertically. The two dark gray parts of iteration 2 are replaced with rotated copies of the front façade and the red element recedes horizontally to frame the blue element, which displays the second iteration of the front façade.

The rear façade, shown in Figure 12.16, consists of four parts.

- The first part is a copy of the seed shape reduced by 88 percent in depth and rendered in red.
- The next two elements of the façade are two copies of the seed shape reduced by 55 percent in length, 82 percent in depth, and 80 percent in height. These two copies, shown in dark gray, are rotated 180 degrees about their z axes and placed to the right side of this façade, one above the other and each just off the centerline of the height of the first element. Each of these parts, by virtue of its 180 degree rotation about its z axis, reflects the previous iteration of the front façade.
- The last part of this façade, shown in blue, transforms a copy of the seed shape by reducing it by 87 percent in length and 88 percent in depth and translating it just to the left side of the façade. Similar to the element on the left façade, it protrudes from the plane of the façade.

The prominent feature of iteration 2 is the clear presence of the front façade structure in the two horizontal window elements. The blue element now has two dark gray subelements, which, similar to their respective counterparts in the overall façade, in the next iteration will be replaced by the structure of the front façade. Iteration 3 highlights the presence of the front façade structure within all of the window elements.

The right side of the model is rendered in Figure 12.17 and consists of seven parts.

- The first two parts, shown in gray, are copies of the seed shape reduced by 95 percent in length, 88 percent in depth, and 50 percent in height and then rotated 90 degrees about their z axes. These two copies, which reflect the previous iteration of the front façade, are placed one on top of the other and translated to the left side of the right façade.
- The next element, rendered in blue, reduces a copy of the seed shape by 88 percent in length and 13 percent in depth and translates it to be adjacent to the first two parts of the right façade.

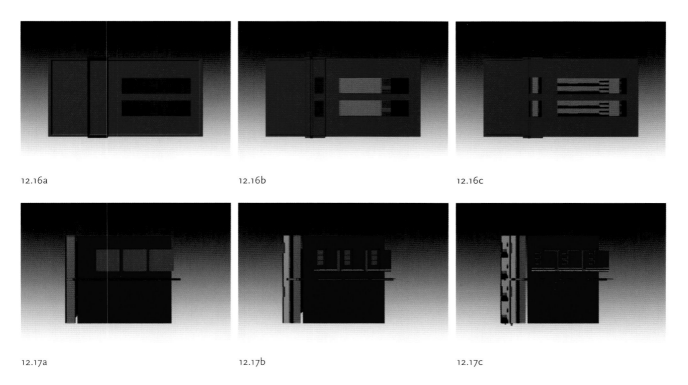

12.16a   12.16b   12.16c

12.17a   12.17b   12.17c

- The next three elements are copies of the seed shape reduced by 85 percent in length, 80 percent in depth, and 75 percent in height. Each of these, shown in red, is rotated 90 degrees about its x axis and is then translated to the upper right portion of the façade one after the other.
- The last element, rendered in dark gray, is a copy of the seed shape reduced by 25 percent in length, 1 percent in depth, and 88 percent in height. It is translated to the right and outward so that it forms a horizontal rib that starts at the two elements on the left and wraps around to the rear façade.

The next iteration illustrates the front façade within the two elements on the left side. Because of the rotation about their x axes, the three parts at the upper portion of the façade rotate their own characteristic subelements. As with the left façade, the left side of the blue element has two gray subelements, which, in the next iteration, will be replaced with the structure of the front façade. In iteration 3, the three upper elements are further developed, the two left gray parts show the next iteration of the front façade, and the element that forms the substrate of the majority of the façade incorporates a pair of window elements on the left.

Figure 12.16. Three iterations of the rear façade.
Figure 12.17. Three iterations of the right façade.

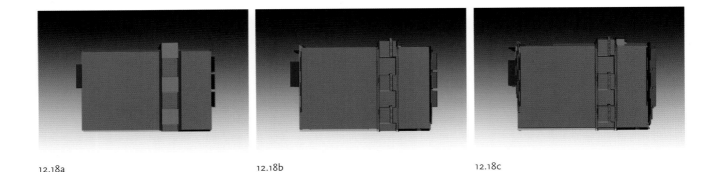

12.18a   12.18b   12.18c

Figure 12.18 shows the iterations of the roof of the house, which consists of its horizontal plane, two rails that travel the depth of the structure, and three elements that are placed between these rails.

- The roof plane is a simple copy of the seed shape reduced 85 percent in height and translated vertically to be on top of the four façades.
- The two rails are created by reducing two copies of the seed shape scaled down by 88 percent in length and 85 percent in height. Each is placed at roof level so that they unite the group of four elements colored in gray and yellow on the front façade with the protruding element on the rear façade rendered in blue.
- The last three elements of the roof, shown in yellow, are copies of the façade reduced by 88 percent in length, 21 percent in depth, and 80 percent in height. They are translated vertically to be on top of the roof plane and placed between the two rails so that one is on top of the protruding element of the rear façade and the other two are distributed going forward toward the front façade.

On the left façade, there is a protruding rear element, and there is a similar element on the rear façade as well as two horizontally oriented elements. At the conclusion of each iteration but prior to the iteration's synthesis procedure, a Boolean operation is performed on the back walls at each of these areas to create an opening. All the façades and the roof are combined to form the new seed shape to be transformed in iteration 2 according to the same generative rules. Figure 12.19 shows rendered versions of the model with the white tube and glass in-fill seed shape substituted for the color-coded elements.

Figure 12.18. Three iterations of the roof.

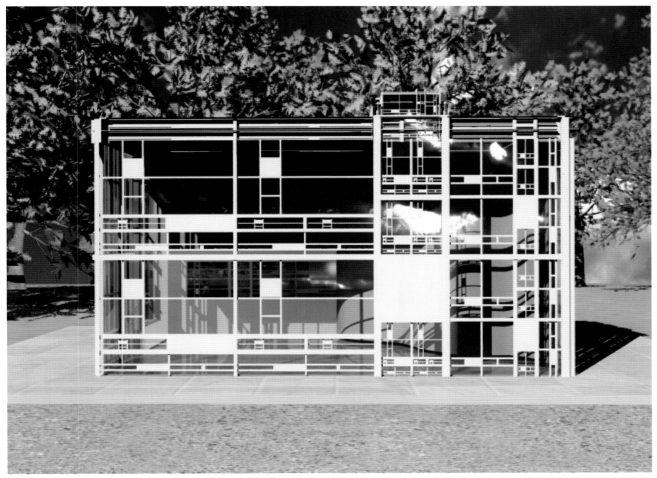

12.19a

Figure 12.19. Model with materials substituted
for colors; a. Front; b. Left; c. Upper front left;
and d. Nighttime.

12.19b

12.19c

12.19d

SUMMARY

The house, though the smallest of building typologies, can be the most complex. It is a fitting architectural form to embody the breadth of its relationship from the built environment. The icons of modern architectural design, Le Corbusier and Frank Lloyd Wright, illustrate the ends of this spectrum. Frank Lloyd Wright believed that structures should grow out of the environment surrounding them, whereas Le Corbusier evoked the magnetic theory of the attraction of opposites as the strongest bond between nature and architecture. Whether its expression is in direct contrast with or a concurring extension of nature, structuring architectural form by utilizing fractal geometry strengthens the link.

Notes

Introduction

1 Michael Barnsley, *Fractals Everywhere* (Boston: Academic Press, 1988), 1

1. The Journey from Mathematical Monsters to the Key to Nature's Structure

1 Dick Oliver, *Fractal Vision* (Boston: Sams, 1992), 5.
2 Ibid., 201.
3 Benoit Mandelbrot, *The Fractal Geometry of Nature* (New York: W. H. Freeman, 1983), 3, 4.
4 Heinz-Otto Peitgen, Hartmut Jurgens, and Dietmar Saupe, *Fractals for the Classroom* (New York: Springer, 1991), 75.
5 Oliver, *Fractal Vision*, 2.
6 Ibid., 36.
7 Mandelbrot, *Fractal Geometry of Nature*, 21.
8 Oliver, *Fractal Vision*, 54.
9 Peitgen et al., *Fractals for the Classroom*, viii.
10 Oliver, *Fractal Vision*, 76.
11 Michael Barnsley, *Fractals Everywhere* (Boston: Academic, 1998), 1.
12 Peitgen et al., *Fractals for the Classroom*, viii.
13 Ibid., 21, 22.
14 Ibid., 22–24.
15 Ibid., 28.
16 Ibid., 260.
17 Ibid., 157.
18 Oliver, *Fractal Vision*, 321.
19 Ibid., 251.
20 Ibid., 95.
21 Ibid., 100.
22 Peitgen et al., *Fractals for the Classroom*, 161.
23 Caroline Van Eck, "Goethe and Alberti: Organic Unity in Nature and Architecture," *The Structurist* 35/36 (1995): 22–24.
24 Peitgen et al., *Fractals for the Classroom*, 29, 30.
25 Robert Williams, *The Geometrical Foundation of Natural Structures* (New York: Dover, 1979), 20.
26 Christopher Alexander, *The Nature of Order: The Process of Creating Life* (Berkeley, CA: Center for Environmental Structure, 2003), 3.
27 Charles Jenks, *The Architecture of the Jumping Universe* (London: Academy, 1997), 73.
28 Alexander, *Nature of Order*, 440.
29 David Pearce, *New Organic Architecture (The Breaking Wave)* (Berkeley: University of California Press, 2001), 48.
30 Rudolf Steiner, *Nature's Open Secret* (Great Barrington, MA: Steiner Books, 2000), 249.
31 Steven Harrod Buhner, *The Secret Teachings of Plants* (Rochester, VT: Bear, 2004), 37.
32 Stephen Wolfram, *A New Kind of Science* (Champaign, IL: Wolfram Media, 2002), 28; Alexander, *Nature of Order*, 567.
33 Oliver, *Fractal Vision*, 79.
34 Gayla Chandler, "Fractals: An Introduction through Symmetry," http://local.wasp.uwa.edu.au/~pbourke/fractals/symmetry/.
35 Oliver, *Fractal Vision*, 77.
36 Mandelbrot, *Fractal Geometry of Nature*, 99.
37 Ibid., 88–90.
38 Ibid., 84, 85.
39 Oliver, *Fractal Vision*, 134.
40 Ibid., 132, 133.
41 Oliver, *Fractal Vision*, 157–59.
42 Leading Edge Research Group, "Fractal Evolution," http://www.fractal.org/Bewustzijns-Besturings-Model/Fractal-Evolution.htm.
43 "Fractal Evolution."
44 Oliver, *Fractal Vision*, 113.
45 "Fractal Evolution."
46 Oliver, *Fractal Vision*, 146–48.
47 Mandelbrot, *Fractal Geometry of Nature*, 113.
48 Oliver, *Fractal Vision*, 220.
49 David Seamon and Arthur Zajonc, eds., *Goethe's Way of Science* (Albany: State University of New York Press, 1998), 279.
50 Stephen Kellert and Edward Wilson, *The Biophilia Hypothesis* (Washington, D.C.: Island Press, 1995), 351–55.

2. The Human Desire for Nature

1 Susan Clayton and Susan Opotow, eds., *Identity and the Natural Environment: The Psychological Significance of Nature* (Cambridge, MA: MIT Press, 2003), 185.
2 Ibid., 61.
3 Ibid., 47.
4 Ibid., 119, 122.
5 Stephen Kellert, *Building for Life* (Washington, D.C.: Island Press, 2005), 2, 3.
6 Ibid., 160, 161.

7   Clayton and Opotow, *Identity and the Natural Environment*, 48.

8   Ibid., 48.

9   Kellert, *Building for Life*, 13, 14.

10 Ibid., 21.

11 Ibid., 22–25.

12 Ibid., 29–30.

13 Ibid., 30–46.

14 Clayton and Opotow, *Identity and the Natural Environment*, 92.

15 Ibid., 136.

16 Kellert, *Building for Life*, 14, 15.

17 Edward Wilson, *Biophilia* (Cambridge, MA: Harvard University Press, 1986), 85, 86.

18 Stephen Kellert and Edward Wilson, *The Biophilia Hypothesis* (Washington, D.C.: Island Press, 1995), 21.

19 Ibid., 451.

20 Ibid., 20.

21 Ibid., 229, 233.

22 Wilson, *Biophilia*, 85.

23 Kellert and Wilson, *Biophilia Hypothesis*, 20.

24 Ibid., 25, 26.

25 Ibid., 32.

26 Ibid., 79.

27 Clayton and Opotow, *Identity and the Natural Environment*, 41, 42, 60.

28 Kellert and Wilson, *Biophilia Hypothesis*, 32, 33.

29 Ibid., 42.

30 Wilson, *Biophilia*, 93, 94.

31 Ibid., 106, 109.

32 Ibid., 99, 100.

33 Kellert and Wilson, *Biophilia Hypothesis*, 449, 450.

34 Ibid., 138–40.

35 Ibid., 118.

36 Ibid., 89–91.

37 Wilson, *Biophilia*, 110.

38 Kellert, *Building for Life*, 50–57.

39 Kellert and Wilson, *Biophilia Hypothesis*, 96.

40 Ibid., 100–2.

41 Ibid., 113, 114.

42 Ibid., 133, 114.

43 Kellert, *Building for Life*, 92.

44 Ibid., 2, 3.

45 Clayton and Opotow, *Identity and the Natural Environment*, 47.

46 Ibid., 179.

47 Ibid., 227.

48 Ibid., 179.

49 Ibid., 179.

50 Ibid., 190–94.

51 Kellert, *Building for Life*, 12.

52 Clayton and Opotow, *Identity and the Natural Environment*, 194–98.

53 Ibid., 194, 198

54 Ibid., 5.

55 Ibid., 34–37.

56 Ibid., 36.

57 Ibid., 45.

58 Ibid., 83.

59 Ibid., 228.

60 Ibid., 6, 7, 227.

61 Ibid., 105, 229.

62 Ibid., 104, 105.

63 Ibid., 27.

64 Ibid., 103.

65 Wilson, *Biophilia*, 1.

66 Clayton and Opotow, *Identity and the Natural Environment*, 115, 116.

67 Ibid., 131.

68 Kellert, *Building for Life*, 61.

69 Clayton and Opotow, *Identity and the Natural Environment*, 57–59.

70 Ibid., 1.

71 Kellert and Wilson, *Biophilia Hypothesis*, 251–60.

72 Christopher Alexander, *The Nature of Order: The Process of Creating Life* (Berkeley, CA: Center for Environmental Structure, 2003), 567.

73 Ron Eglash, *African Fractals: Modern Computing and Indigenous Design* (Piscataway, NJ: Rutgers University Press, 1999), 22, 27, 30.

74 Malcolm Budd, *An Aesthetic Appreciation of Nature* (New York: Oxford University Press, 2002), 33, 34.

75 Ibid., 112.

76 Ibid., 117.

77 Ibid., 16, 47.

78 Ibid., 51–53.

79 Ibid., 54–57.

80 Ibid., 61.

81 Ibid., 139–45.

82 Ibid., 21

83 Ibid., 88.

84 Ibid. 22

85 Ibid., 67, 68.

86 Ibid., 70, 71.

87 Clayton and Opotow, *Identity and the Natural Environment*, 4.

88 Ibid., 62.

89 Ibid., 180, 182.

90 Rudolf Steiner, *Nature's Open Secret* (Great Barrington, MA: Steiner Books, 2000), 48.

91 Steven Harrod Buhner, *The Secret Teaching of Plants* (Rochester, VT: Bear, 2004), 265, 266.

92 Rudolf Steiner, *Architecture* (Vancouver, BC: Sophia Brooks, 2004), 134.

3. Nature's Order and Its Architectural Embodiment

1 "The Golden Mean," http://community.middlebury.edu/~harris/Humanities/TheGoldenMean.html.

2 Paolo M. Portoghesi, *Nature and Architecture* (Milan, Italy: Skira, 2000), 160, 161.

3 Christopher Alexander, *The Nature of Order: The Process of Creating Life* (Berkeley, CA: Center of Environmental Structure, 2003), 8.

4 Dick Oliver, *Fractal Vision* (Boston: Sams, 1992), 79.

5 Malcolm Budd, *An Aesthetic Appreciation of Nature* (New York: Oxford University Press, 2002), 111.

6 Portoghesi, *Nature and Architecture*, 34, 35.

7 Carl Bovill, *Fractal Geometry in Architecture and Design* (Basel, Switzerland: Birkhauser, 1996), 137.

8 Budd, *An Aesthetic Appreciation*, 99, 100.

9 Brigitte Williams and Shai Yeshayahu, "Systems in Nature: Connecting the Unconnected," http://www.choreographyofspace.org/Papers/Williams.doc.

10 Charles Jencks, *The Architecture of the Jumping Universe* (London; Academy, 1997), 75, 76.

11 Stephen Kellert, *Building for Life* (Washington, D.C.: Island Press, 2005), 147, 148.

12 John A. Gowan, "The Fractal Organization of Nature," http://people.cornell.edu/pages/jag8/sect3.html.

13 Jencks, *Architecture of the Jumping Universe*, 55.

14 Alexander, *The Nature of Order*, 28, 29.

15 Ibid., 32, 45, 77.

16 D'Arcy Thompson, *On Growth and Form* (New York: Cambridge University Press, 1961), 7–9.

17 Christopher Alexander, *Phenomenon of Life* (Berkeley, CA: Center for Environmental Studies, 2001), 300.

18 Ibid., 427, 428.

19 Ibid., 404.

20 David Seamon and Arthur Zajonc, eds., *Goethe's Way of Science* (Albany: State University of New York Press, 1998), 40, 41.

21 Alexander, *Process of Creating Life*, 568.

22 Ibid., 19, 567.

23 Alexander, *Phenomenon of Life*, 110.

24 Ibid., 106, 244, 245.

25 Ibid., 246.

26 Ibid., 246, 248.

27 Ibid., 251.

28 Ibid., 254, 256.

29 Ibid., 257–60.

30 Ibid., 261, 262.

31 Ibid., 264.

32 Ibid., 266, 269.

33 Ibid., 270.

34 Ibid., 272.

35 Ibid., 275.

36 Ibid., 278, 279.

37 Ibid., 281.

38 Ibid., 284.

39 Ibid., 287.

40 Ibid., 288.

41 Ibid., 309–12.

42 Nikos Salingaros, *A Theory of Architecture* (Solingen, Germany: Umbau, 2006), 47.

43 Ibid., 75.

44 Ibid., 110, 111.

45 Ibid., 126.

46 Rudolf Steiner, *Architecture as a Synthesis of the Arts* (London: Steiner Press, 1999), 59–61, 66.

47 Ibid., 99.

48 William Jackson, "Hindu Temple Fractals," http://liberalarts.iupui.edu/~wijackso/tempfrac/.

49 Caroline Van Eck, "Goethe and Alberti: Organic Unity in Nature and Architecture," *The Structurist* 35/36 (1995): 23, 26.

50 Budd, *An Aesthetic Appreciation*.

51 Van Eck, "Goethe and Alberti," 23, 26.

52 Rudolf Steiner, *Architecture* (Vancouver, BC: Sophia Brooks, 2004), 11.

53 Rudolf Steiner, *Nature's Open Secret* (Washington, D.C.: Steiner Books, 2000), 217.

54 Van Eck, "Goethe and Alberti," 23.

55 Richard Weston, *Modernism* (London: Phaidon Press, 1996), 53.

56 Portoghesi, *Nature and Architecture*, 16.

57 Ibid., 20, 21.

58 Ibid., 32, 33.

59 Ibid., 40, 41.

60 Ibid., 44.

61 Ibid., 54

62 Ibid., 56.

63 Ibid., 54, 55.

64 Ibid., 56.

65 Ibid., 60.

66 Ibid., 64, 65.

67 Kellert, *Building for Life*, 134.

68 Van Eck, "Goethe and Alberti," 23.

69 Kamon Jirapong and Robert Kraweczk, "Architectural Form by Abstracting Nature," http://www.iit.edu/~krawczyk/kjga02.pdf; Van Eck, "Goethe and Alberti," 100.

70 Kellert, *Building for Life*, 5, 96, 97.

71 Ibid., 127.

72 David Pearce, *New Organic Architecture (The Breaking Wave)* (Berkeley: University of California Press, 2001), 64.

73 Kellert, *Building for Life*, 147, 148.

74 Ibid.

75 Steiner, *Architecture as a Synthesis of the Arts*, 72.

76 Le Corbusier, *Towards a New Architecture* (New York: Dover, 1986), 72.

4. Skyscraper Form and Its Fractal Derivative

1 Columbia University, "The Architecture and Development of New York City," http://nycarchitecture.columbia.edu.

2 Ibid.

3 Louis Sullivan, *The Tall Office Building Artistically Considered*, http://academics.triton.edu/faculty/fheitzman/tallofficebuilding.html.

4 Patricia Bayer, *Art Deco Architecture* (New York: Harry N. Abrams, 1992), 10–12.

5 Ibid., 19.

6 Paul Laseau and James Tice, *Frank Lloyd Wright: Between Principle and Form* (New York: Van Nostrand Reinhold, 1992), 138.

7 http://www.nbm.org/exhibitions-collections/exhibitions/praierie-skyscraper.html.

8 Paul Laseau and James Tice, *Frank Lloyd Wright: Between Principle and Form* (New York: Van Nostrand Reinhold, 1992), 141.

9 Ibid.

10 Ibid., 147.

5. Gestalt and the Wholeness of Fractal Structure

1 Roy Behrens, "Art, Design and Gestalt Theory," http://leonard.info/iast/articles/behrens.html.

2 D. Brett King and Michael Wertheimer, *Max Wertheimer and Gestalt Theory* (Edison, NJ: Transaction, 2007), 41, 42.

3 Ibid., 42.

4 Ibid., 96.

5 Behrens, "Art, Design."

6 King and Wertheimer, *Max Wertheimer and Gestalt Theory*, 97.

7 Ibid., 99.

8 Ibid., 54.

9 Andrew Lyons, "Gestalt Approaches to Gesamtkunstwerk," http://oldsite.vislab.usvd.edu.au/ gallery/music/alvons/gestalt.html.

10 David Seamon and Arthur Zajonc, eds., *Goethe's Way of Science* (Albany: State University of New York Press, 1998), 2.

11 Rudolf Steiner, *Nature's Open Secret* (Great Barrington, MA: Steiner Books, 2000), 53.

12 Seamon and Zajonc, *Goethe's Way of Science*, 57.

13 Ibid., 15–18.

14 Steiner, *Nature's Open Secret*, 253.

15 Seamon and Zajonc, *Goethe's Way of Science*, 77.

16 Ibid., 71.

17 Ibid., 3.

18 Ibid., 49.

19 Ibid., 71.

20 Malcom Budd, *An Aesthetic Appreciation of Nature* (New York: Oxford University Press, 2003), 67.

21 Seamon and Zajonc, *Goethe's Way of Science*, 79.

22 Rudolf Steiner, *Architecture as a Synthesis of the Arts* (London: Rudolf Steiner Press, 1999), 58.

23 Seamon and Zajonc, *Goethe's Way of Science*, 258, 259.

24 Steven Harrod Buhner, *The Secret Teaching of Plants* (Rochester, VT: Bear, 2004), 185, 186.

25 Steiner, *Nature's Open Secret*, 260.

26 Ibid., 265, 266.

27 Ibid., 272, 273.

28 Seamon and Zajonc, *Goethe's Way of Science*, 131–35.

29 Ibid., 53.

30 Ibid., 223, 224.

31 Ibid., 42.

32 Ibid., 223–25.

33 Buhner, *Secret Teaching of Plants*, 165.

34 Steiner, *Nature's Open Secret*, 224.

35 King and Wertheimer, *Max Wertheimer and Gestalt Theory*, 88–96.

36 Buhner, *Secret Teaching of Plants*, 65.

37 Ibid., 71.

38 Ibid., 97.

39 Ibid., 98.

40 Ibid., 118–21.

41 Ibid., 99–104

42 D. Brett King, Michael Wertheimer, Heidi Keller, and Kevin Crochetiere, "The Legacy of Max Wertheimer and Gestalt Psychology—Sixtieth Anniversary, 1934–1994: The Legacy of Our Past," http://findarticles.com/p/articles/mi_m2267/is_n4_v61/ai_15955167/pg_3.

43 King and Wertheimer, *Max Wertheimer and Gestalt Theory*; Thomas Detrie, "Gestalt Principles and Dynamic Symmetry: Nature's Design Connections to Our Built Environment," http://ww.public.asu.edu/~detrie/msi.uc_daap/article.html.

44 Rudolf Arnheim, *Visual Thinking* (Berkeley: University of California Press, 2004), 55.

45 Ibid.

46 Ibid., 28, 29.

47 Wolfgang Kohler, *Gestalt Psychology* (New York: Liveright, 1992), 69.

48 King and Wertheimer, *Max Wertheimer and Gestalt Theory*, 77, 81.

49 Stephen Wolfram, *A New Kind of Science* (Champaign, IL: Wolfram Media, 2002), 828.

50 Christopher Alexander, *The Nature of Order: The Phenomenon of Life* (Berkeley: Center for Environmental Studies, 2001), 118.

51 Ibid., 96.

52 Ibid., 120.

53 Ibid., 110, 90.

54 Ibid., 364, 365.

55 Ibid., 124, 508.

56 King and Wertheimer, *Max Wertheimer and Gestalt Theory*, 106, 125.

57 Stephen Grabow, "Organic and Mechanical Form Principles," *The Structurist* 35/36 (1995): 5–6.

58 Eli Bornstein, "Notes on the Mechanical and Organic in Art and Nature," *The Structurist* 35/36 (1995): 45.

59 Ibid.

60 Grabow, "Organic and Mechanical Form Principles," 5–6.

61 Ibid., 6.

62 Ibid., 7, 9.

63 King and Wertheimer, *Max Wertheimer and Gestalt Theory*, 370.

64 "Psychological Patterns," http://www.gardenvisit.com/history_theory/library_online_ebooks/ architecture_city_as_landscape/psychological_patterns.

65 King and Wertheimer, *Max Wertheimer and Gestalt Theory*, 375.

66 Ibid., 154–56.

67 Ibid., 42.

68 Detrie, "Gestalt Principles."

69 Kohler, *Gestalt Psychology*, 202, 203.

70 Tim Boston, "Ecopsychology: An Earth–Psyche Bond," http://trumpeter.athabascau.ca/ index.php/trumpet/article/ view/Article/269/402.

71 Detrie, "Gestalt Principles."

72 Kohler, *Gestalt Psychology*, 139.

73 King and Wertheimer, *Max Wertheimer and Gestalt Theory*, 367, 368.

74 Werner Biaser, *Nature in Building: Rudolf Steiner in Dornach* (New York: Birkhauser, 2002), 6.

6. Perception and the Cognition of Natural Form

1 "Perception Theory," http://www.simplypsychology.pwp.blueyonder.co.uk/perception-theories.html.

2 Bruce Goldstein, *Cognitive Psychology: Connecting Mind, Research and Everyday Experience* (Florence, KY: Wadsworth CENGAGE Learning, 2008), 30, 31.

3 Ibid., 30–36.

4 Ibid., 39, 43.

5 David Marr, *Vision* (New York: W. H. Freeman, 1982), 34.

6 Ibid., 12.

7 Rudolf Arnheim, *Visual Thinking* (Berkeley: University of California Press, 2004), 12, 13.

8 Ibid., 19.

9 Ibid., 23.

10 Ibid., 18–21.

11 Ibid., 14, 15.

12 Stephen Wolfram, *A New Kind of Science* (Champaign, IL: Wolfram Media, 2002), 548.

13 Ibid., 549.

14 Arnheim, *Visual Thinking*, 20.

15 Ibid., 39.

16 Ibid., 22.

17 Ibid., 37.

18 Ibid., 27.

19 Ibid., 26.

20 Ibid., 67, 68.

21 Ibid., 455–57.

22 Ibid., 54.

23 Wolfram, *A New Kind of Science*, 623–27; Arnheim, *Visual Thinking*, 78.

24 Arnheim, *Visual Thinking*.

25 Wolfgang Kohler, *Gestalt Psychology* (New York: Liveright, 1992), 160.

26 William Mitchell, *The Logic of Architecture* (Cambridge, MA: MIT Press, 1990), 3.

27 "Hermann von Helmholtz," http://plato.stanford.edu/entries/hermann-helmholtz/.

28 Gergo Orbán, József Fiser, Richard N. Aslin, and Máté Lengyel, "Bayesian Model Learning in Human Visual Perception," http://books.nips.cc/papers/files/nips18/NIPS2005_0669.pdf.

29 Lucia M. Vaina, "Marr, David," http://www.bu.edu/bravi/publications/Vaina_2004.pdf.

30 Marr, *Vision*, 296.

31 Ibid., 298.

32 Ibid., 52.

33 Ibid., 82.

34 Ibid., 269.

35 Ibid., 302–7.

36 Ibid., 321, 322.

37 "Perception Theory."

38 D. Brett King and Michael Wertheimer, *Max Wertheimer and Gestalt Theory* (Edison NJ: Transaction, 2007), 326; Arnheim, *Visual Thinking*, 233, 234.

39 Kohler, *Gestalt Psychology*, 196, 197.

40 Wolfram, *A New Kind of Science*, 623–27.

41 Arnheim, *Visual Thinking*, 294.

42 Ibid., 80, 81.

43 Ibid.

44 Ibid., 233.

45 Ibid., 234.

46 Rudolf Arnheim, *The Dynamics of Architectural Form* (Berkeley: University of California Press, 1984), 125, 129.

47 Ibid., 131.

48 Rudolf Steiner, *Nature's Open Secret* (Washington, D.C.: Steiner Books, 2000), 255, 256.

49 Arnheim, *Dynamics of Architectural Form*, 164, 175–78.

50 Arnheim, *Visual Thinking*, 28, 41.

51 Ibid., 224.

52 Ibid., 79.

53 Nikos Salingaros, "Architecture, Patterns and Mathematics," *Nexus Network Journal* 1 (1999): 75–86.

54 Kohler, *Gestalt Psychology*, 168, 169.

55 Christopher Alexander, *Notes on the Synthesis of Form* (Cambridge, MA: Harvard University Press, 1964), 44.

56 Stephen Grabow, "Organic and Mechanical Form Principals," *The Structurist* No. 35/36 (1995): 8, 9.

57 Christopher Alexander, *The Nature of Order: The Process of Creating Life* (Berkeley, CA: Center for Environmental Studies, 2003), 472.

58 Salingaros, "Architecture, Patterns and Mathematics."

59 W. Popow, "A Report on Psychology and Architecture," http://sric-canada.org/Architecture.htm.

60 Wolfram, *A New Kind of Science*, 623–27.

61 Salingaros, "Architecture, Patterns and Mathematics."

62 Ibid.

63 Arnheim, *Dynamics of Architectural Form*, 178–80, 189.

64 Popow, "A Report on Psychology and Architecture."

65 Arnheim, *Dynamics of Architectural Form*, 45, 17.

66 Ibid., 74, 83, 181, 183.

67 Arnheim, *Visual Thinking*, 257.

68 Christopher Alexander, *The Nature of Order: The Phenomenon of Life* (Berkeley, CA: Center for Environmental Studies, 2001), 38.

69 Ibid., 315.

70 Ibid., 373.

71 Ibid., 309.

72 Ibid., 315.

73 Alexander, *Phenomenon of Life*, 84.

74 Heinz-Otto Peitgen, Hartmut Jurgens, and Dietmar Saupe, *Fractals for the Classroom* (New York: Springer, 1991), 279.

75 Goldstein, *Cognitive Psychology*, 229.

76 Steiner, *Nature's Open Secret*, 248.

77 Arnheim, *Visual Thinking*, 153.

78 Ibid., 13, 28.

79 Mitchell, *Logic of Architecture*, 2.

80 "Cognitive Theories of Learning," http://www.personal.psu.edu/users/w/x/wxh139/cognitive_1.htm.

81 Goldstein, *Cognitive Psychology*, 51.

82 Ibid., 41, 42.

83 Greg Miller, "Hippocampal Firing Patterns Linked to Memory Recall," *Science Magazine*, September 5, 2008.

84 David Seamon and Arthur Zajonc, eds., *Goethe's Way of Science* (Albany: State University of New York Press, 1998), 280, 281.

85 Steven Harrod Buhner, *The Secret Teaching of Plants* (Rochester, VT: Bear, 2004), 255.

86 W. Huitt, "The Information Processing Approach to Cognition," http://chiron.valdosta.edu/whuitt/col/cogsys/infoproc.html.

87 Edward Wilson, *Biophilia* (Cambridge, MA: Harvard University Press, 1986), 77.

88 Kohler, *Gestalt Psychology*, 256, 257.

89 Ibid., 196, 197.

90 Ibid., 249, 251.

91 Ibid., 281, 282.

92 Ibid., 289, 290.

93 Arnheim, *Visual Thinking*, 145, 148.

94 Kohler, *Gestalt Psychology*, 269, 272.

95 Goldstein, *Cognitive Psychology*, 288.

96 Ibid., 288–90.

97 Wilson, *Biophilia*, 77.

98 Alexander, *Process of Creating Life*, 472.

7. The Universal Quality of Fractal Expression

1 Rudolf Arnheim, *Visual Thinking* (Berkeley: University of California Press, 2004), 156.

2 David Seamon and Arthur Zajonc, eds., *Goethe's Way of Science* (Albany: State University of New York Press, 1998), 41.

3 Ibid., 292.

4 Rudolf Steiner, *Nature's Open Secret* (Washington, D.C.: Steiner Books, 2000), 67.

5 Arnheim, *Visual Thinking*, 270.

6 Ibid., 162.

7 Christopher Alexander, *The Nature of Order: The Process of Creating Life* (Berkeley, CA: Center for Environmental Studies, 2003), 456, 457.

8 Alexander, *The Nature of Order: The Phenomenon of Life* (Berkeley, CA: Center for Environmental Studies, 2001), 427, 428.

9 David Seamon and Arthur Zajonc, eds., *Goethe's Way of Science* (Albany: State University of New York Press, 1998), 115.

10 Steiner, *Nature's Open Secret*, 16, 17.

11 Seamon and Zajonic, *Goethe's Way of Science*, 62.

12 Caroline Van Eck, "Goethe and Alberti: Organic Unity in Nature and Architecture," *The Structurist* 35/36 (1995): 22.

13 Steiner, *Nature's Open Secret*, 17.

14 Ibid., 266.

15 Seamon and Zajonic, *Goethe's Way of Science*, 62.

16 Arnheim, *Visual Thinking*, 236.

17 Steiner, *Nature's Open Secret*, 67.

18 Ibid., 122.

19 Stephen Wolfram, *A New Kind of Science* (Champaign, IL: Wolfram Media, 2002), 4, 5.

20 Ibid., 298.

21 Ibid., 386–91.

22 Ibid., 718, 719.

23 Ibid., 697.

24 Arnheim, *Visual Thinking*, 169, 170.

25 Ibid., 170.

26 Ibid., 174.

27 Ibid., 193.

28 Nathan Cabot Hale, *Abstraction in Art and Nature* (New York: Dover, 1993), 26, 31, 32, 105, 163.

29 Paul Zygas and Linda Nelson Johnson, *The Phoenix Papers*, vol. 2, *The Natural Pattern of Structure* (Tempe: Arizona State University Press, 1995), 17, 104.

30 Steiner, *Nature's Open Secret*, 190–96.

31 Ibid., 188.

32 Ibid., 198.

33 Ibid., 156, 180.

34 Seamon and Zajonic, *Goethe's Way of Science*, 267, 268.

35 Steiner, *Nature's Open Secret*, 51.

36 Ibid., 54, 55.

37 Ibid., 258.

38 Ibid., 15.

39 Ibid., 14.

40 Ibid., 13.

41 Hale, *Abstraction in Art and Nature*, 15.

42 Malcolm Budd, *An Aesthetic Appreciation of Nature* (New York: Oxford University Press, 2002), 33, 34, 112.

43 Arnheim, *Visual Thinking*, 168.

44 Hale, *Abstraction in Art and Nature*, 14.

45 Arnheim, *Visual Thinking*.

46 Ibid., 192.

47 Ibid., 172, 173.

48 Ibid., 308.

49 Dick Oliver, *Fractal Vision* (Boston: Sams, 1992), 212.

50 Seamon and Zajonic, *Goethe's Way of Science*, 283.

51 Ibid., 281.

52 Ibid., 281–86.

53 Arnheim, *Visual Thinking*, 68.

54 Ibid., 108, 109.

55 Ibid., 182.

56 Ibid., 129.

57 Ibid., 227.

58 Ibid., 161.

59 Christopher Alexander, *Notes on the Synthesis of Form* (Cambridge, MA: Harvard University Press, 1964), 8.

60 Arnheim, *Visual Thinking*, 185, 186.

61 Seamon and Zajonic, *Goethe's Way of Science*, 40, 41.

62 Steiner, *Nature's Open Secret*, 127.

63 Ibid., 222.

64 Arnheim, *Visual Thinking*, 297.

65 Robert Williams, *The Geometrical Foundation of Natural Structures* (New York: Dover, 1972), 20.

66 Arnheim, *Visual Thinking*, 161.

67 Steiner, *Nature's Open Secret*, 62, 68.

68 Ibid., 180, 181.

69 Ibid., 50.

70 Seamon and Zajonic, *Goethe's Way of Science*, 185, 186.

71 Steiner, *Nature's Open Secret*, 185, 186.

72 Arnheim, *Visual Thinking*, 108.

73 Ibid., 137.

74 Ibid., 188.

75 Ibid., 161.

76 Ibid., 23.

77 Ibid., 41.

78 Ibid.

79 Wolfgang Kohler, *Gestalt Psychology* (New York: Liveright, 1992), 256, 257.

80 Werner Biaser, *Nature in Building: Rudolf Steiner in Dornach* (New York: Birkhauser, 2002), 9.

81 Kohler, *Gestalt Psychology*, 198, 199.

82 Eli Bornstein, "Notes on the Mechanical and Organic in Art and Nature," *The Structurist* 35/36 (1995): 46.

83 Arnheim, *Visual Thinking*, 128.

84 Ibid., 208.

85 Ibid., 216.

86 Ibid., 136, 137.

87 Ibid., 137.

88 Ibid., 150, 151.

89 Ibid., 138, 139.

90 Paolo M. Portoghesi, *Nature and Architecture* (Milan, Italy: Skira, 2000), 286.

91 Arnheim, *Visual Thinking*, 108.

92 Ibid., 148.

93 Rudolf Arnheim, *The Dynamics of Visual Form* (Berkeley: University of California Press, 1977), 45, 69.

94 Arnheim, *Visual Thinking*, 276.

95 Alexander, *Notes on the Synthesis of Form*, 85–92.

96 Arnheim, *Visual Thinking*.

97 Richard Weston, *Modernism* (London: Phaidon Press, 1996), 65.

98 Harry Holtzman and Martin James, eds., *The New Art—The New Life: The Collective Writings of Piet Mondrian* (Cambridge, MA: Da Capo Press, 1993), 82.

8. The Abstract Trajectory to the Fractal Modernist Form

1 Richard Weston, *Modernism* (London: Phaidon Press, 1996), 26.

2 Ibid., 41.

3 Ibid., 42, 43.

4 Ibid., 35–38.

5 Ibid., 43–44.

6 Ibid., 65–70.

7 Ibid., 81–88.

8 Ibid., 145.

9 Carsten-Peter Warneke, *De Stijl* (Cologne, Germany: Benedikt Taschen, 1994), 16.

10 Weston, *Modernism*, 92–94.

11 Warneke, *De Stijl*, 90.

12 Weston, *Modernism*, 97.

13 Warneke, *De Stijl*, 134–35.

14 D. Brett King and Michael Wertheimer, *Max Wertheimer and Gestalt Theory* (Edison, NJ: Transaction, 2007), 157–59.

15 Ibid., 370.

16 Ibid., 157–59.

17 Weston, *Modernism*, 169.

18 Ibid., 190.

19 Ibid., 9.

20 Philip Steadman, *The Evolution of Designs: Biological Analogy in Architecture and the Applied Arts* (New York: Routledge, Taylor and Francis, 2008), 9.

21 Ibid., 11, 13.

22 Le Corbusier, *Towards a New Architecture* (New York: Dover, 1986), 31.

23 Ibid., 73

24 Ibid., 73.

25 Ibid., 31.

26 Rudolf Arnheim, *The Dynamics of Architectural Form* (Berkeley: University of California Press, 1977), 134.

27 Caroline Van Eck, "Goethe and Alberti: Organic Unity in Nature and Architecture," *The Structurist* 35/36 (1995): 26.

28 Weston, *Modernism*, 168.

29 Peter Carter, *Mies van der Rohe at Work* (London: Phaidon Press, 1974), 61.

30 Paul Goldberger, *The Skyscraper* (New York: Alfred A. Knopf, 1981), 107.

31 Carl Bovill, *Fractal Geometry in Architecture and Design* (Basel, Switzerland: Birkhauser, 1996), 119–44.

32 Rudolf Arnheim, *Visual Thinking* (Berkeley: University of California Press, 1969), 161.

33 Ibid., 174, 175.

34 Christopher Alexander, *Notes on the Synthesis of Form* (Cambridge, MA: Harvard University Press, 1964), 8.

35 Arnheim, *Visual Thinking*, 227.

9. Nature's Generative Character

1 "Alan Mathison Turing," http://www.thocp.net/biographies/turing_alan.html.

2 "The Alan Turing Internet Scrapbook," http://www.turing.org.uk/turing/scrapbook/ machine.html.

3 http://www.archilab.org/public/2000/catalog/skavya/xkavyaen.htm.

4 "Gottfried Wilhelm Leibniz (1646–1716)," http://www.friesian.com/leibniz.htm.

5 Stephen Wolfram, *A New Kind of Science* (Champaign, IL: Wolfram Media, 2002), 2, 3.

6 Ibid., 298.

7 Ibid., 716.

8 Ibid., 5.

9 Ibid., 772.

10 Ibid.

11 Ibid., 400–9.

12 Ibid., 413–17.

13 Ibid., 425.

14 Ibid., 28.

15 Ibid., 108.

16 Ibid., 110.

17 "Zuse's Thesis: The Universe Is a Computer," http://www.idsia.ch/~juergen/digitalphysics.html.

18 Wolfram, *A New Kind of Science*, 465.

19 Ibid., 471.

20 Ibid., 516–18.

21 Ibid., 397, 398.

22 "A New Kind of Science," http://serendip.brynmawr.edu/exchange/node/1977.

23 "The Altenberg 16: An Exposé of the Evolution Industry," *Scoop*, http://www.scoop.co.nz/stories/HL0806/S00237.htm.

24 Wolfram, *A New Kind of Science*, 16.

25 Chris Lucas, "Self-Organization FAQ," http://psoup.math.wisc.edu/archive/sosfaq.html.

26 Wolfram, *A New Kind of Science*, 210.

27 Alberto Estevez, *Genetic Architectures* (Santa Fe, NM: Lumen Books, 2003), 53.

28 Lucas, "Self-Organization FAQ."

29 "About Emergent," http://www.emergentarchitecture.com/about.php?id=1.

30 Peter A. Corning, "The Re-emergence of 'Emergence': A Venerable Concept in Search of a Theory," http://www.complexsystems.org/publications/pdf/emergence3.pdf.

31 "About Emergent."

32 Christopher Alexander, *The Nature of Order: The Process of Creating Life* (Berkeley, CA: Center of Environmental Structure, 2003), 312.

33 Michael Hansmeyer, "Algorithms in Architecture," http://mh.portfolio.com/Algorithms_Architecture/pls.html.

34 Martin Hemberg and Una-May O'Reilly, "Integrating Generative Growth and Evolutionary Computation for Form Exploration," http://people.csail.mit.edu/unamay/publications-dir/gpem_hemberg.pdf.

35 "What Is Xfrog?," http://www.xfrogdownloads.com/greenwebNew/products/xfrog.htm.

36 Stephen Todd and William Latham, *Evolutionary Art and Computers* (Maryland Heights, MO: Academic Press, 1992), 4.

37 Ibid., 63, 64.

38 Ibid., 216.

39 Hemberg and O'Reilly, "Integrating Generative Growth."

40 John Frazer, "Digital Code Scripts for Generative and Evolutionary Design: De Identitate," http://generativedesign.com/asialink/de6.htm.

41 Ibid.

42 Ibid.

43 Ibid.

44 William Mitchell, *The Logic of Architecture* (Cambridge, MA: MIT Press, 1990), ix, x.

45 Ibid., 23.

46 Robert Williams, *The Geometrical Foundation of Natural Structure* (New York: Dover, 1972), 15–18.

47 Michael Barnsley, *Fractals Everywhere* (Boston: Academic Press, 1988), xx.

48 Heinz-Otto Peitgen, Hartmut Jurgens, and Dietmar Saupe, *Fractals for the Classroom* (New York: Springer, 1991), viii.

49 Ibid., 255, 256.

50 Frazer, "Digital Code Scripts."

51 Melanie Mitchell, *An Introduction to Genetic Algorithms* (Cambridge, MA: MIT Press, 1998), 5, 6.

52 Todd and Latham, *Evolutionary Art and Computers*, 64.

53 Mitchell, *An Introduction to Genetic Algorithms*, 10, 11.

54 Ibid., 27.

55 Dick Oliver, *Fractal Vision* (Boston: Sams, 1992), 87–96.

56 Todd and Latham, *Evolutionary Art and Computers*, 98.

11. The Fractal Confluence of Science and Art

1 Leonard Shlain, *Art and Physics: Parallel Visions in Space, Time and Light* (New York: William Morrow, 1993), 431.

2 Ibid., 35, 36.

3 Ibid., 16.

4 Patricia Railing, "The Machine Is No More Than a Brush: Morphology of Art and the Machine in Russian Avant-Garde Theory and Practice," *The Structurist* 35/36 (1995): 55.

5 Richard Weston, *Modernism* (London: Phaidon Press, 1996), 65.

6 Shalain, *Art and Physics,* 158.

7 Ibid., 189, 191.

8 Nathan Cabot Hale, *Abstraction in Art and Nature* (New York: Dover, 1993), 217.

9 Shalain, *Art and Physics,* 43,44.

10 Joshua Taylor, *Futurism* (Garden City, NY: Doubleday, 1961), 11.

11 Umberto Boccioni, "Plastic Dynamism," http://www.391.org/manifestod/umbertoboccioni_plasticdynmism.htm.

12 Taylor, *Futurism,* 15.

13 Rudolf Arnheim, *Visual Thinking* (Berkeley: University of California Press, 1969), 182.

14 http://www.391.org/manifestos/19131215umbertoboccioni_plasticdynamism.htm

15 Taylor, *Futurism,* 13.

16 "Architecture and Society: A Study of Architecture and Society from Ancient Greece to the Present," University of Arizona School of Architecture, http://cala.arizona.edu/courses/arc103/trad103/tutorials/architecture_history/problem_sets/20th_century/deconstruction/01t.html.

17 Kostas Terzidis, *Algorithmic Architecture* (New York: Architectural Press, 2006), 120.

18 Weston, *Modernism,* 61.

19 David Seamon and Arthur Zajonc, eds., *Goethe's Way of Science* (Albany: State University of New York Press, 1998), 99, 106.

20 Railing, "The Machine Is No More Than a Brush," 50.

21 Charles Jencks, *The Architecture of the Jumping Universe* (London: Academy, 1997), 55.

22 Steven Harrod Buhner, *The Secret Teaching of Plants* (Rochester, VT: Bear, 2004), 260.

23 Railing, "The Machine Is No More Than a Brush," 50.

24 Mitchell Whitelaw, "The Abstract Organism: Towards a Prehistory for A-life Art," http://creative.canberra.edu.au/mitchell/papers/abstractorganism.pdf.

25 Charles Harrison and Paul Wood, eds., *Art in Theory, 1900–1990: An Anthology of Changing Ideas* (Hoboken, NJ: Wiley Blackwell, 1998), 166, 176.

26 Railing, "The Machine Is No More Than a Brush," 52.

27 Ibid., 49.

28 Manuel Corrada, "Mechanical and Organic Form in the Theory and Art of El Lissitzky," *The Structurist* 35/36 (1995): 60, 61.

29 John Milner, *Kazimir Malevich and the Art of Geometry* (New Haven, CT: Yale University Press, 1996), 192–94.

30 Tony Robbin, *Fourfield: Computers, Art and the 4th Dimension* (New York: Bulfinch Press, 1992), 27.

31 Ibid., 28–31.

12. The Spectrum of Architecture's Relationship to Nature

1 Frank Lloyd Wright, *An Autobiography: Frank Lloyd Wright* (Pittsburgh, PA: Horizon Press, 1943), 27.

2 Ibid., 36.

3 Ibid., 45.

4 Ibid., 27.

5 Ibid., 594.

6 Ibid., 145.

7 Ibid., 205.

8 Ibid., 126.

9 Peter Blake, *The Master Builders* (New York: W. W. Norton, 1975), 305.

10 Anthony Alofsin, *Frank Lloyd Wright: The Lost Years, 1910–1922* (Chicago: University of Chicago Press, 1994), 263.

11 Blake, *Master Builders*, 296.

12 Alofsin, *The Lost Years*, 263.

13 Wright, *An Autobiography*, 357.

14 Frank Lloyd Wright, *An Organic Architecture: The Architecture of Democracy* (Cambridge, MA: MIT Press, 1939).

15 Wright, *An Autobiography*, 365.

16 Ibid., 372.

17 Ibid., 293.

18 Wright, *An Organic Architecture*, 2.

19 Frank Lloyd Wright, *The Japanese Print* (Pittsburgh, PA: Horizon Press, 1967), 18.

20 Wright, *An Autobiography*, 217.

21 Wright, *Japanese Print*, 16; Wright, *An Autobiography*, 219–24.

22 Alofsin, *The Lost Years*, 90.

23 Ibid., 108.

24 Ibid., 109–19.

25 Ibid., 4, 5.

26 Ibid., 270.

27 Ibid., 264, 270, 274.

28 Wright, *An Autobiography*, 170, 171.

29 Ibid., 363.

30 Ibid., 172.

31 Ibid., 372, 373.

32 Ibid., 361.

33 Ibid., 367.

34 Ibid., 358, 368.

35 Ibid., 239, 282.

36 *Frank Lloyd Wright at Hull House: On "The Art and Craft of the Machine"* (Chicago: Hull House Museum).

37 Ibid.

38 Wright, *An Autobiography*, 60.

39 Ibid., 72, 251–54.

40 Ibid., 181.

41 Paul Zygas and Linda Nelson Johnson, *Frank Lloyd Wright: The Phoenix Papers*, vol. 2, *The Natural Pattern of Structure* (Tempe: Arizona State University Press, 1995), 42.

42 Wright, *Japanese Print*, 16, 17.

43 Wright, *An Autobiography*, 205.

44 Ibid., 204.

45 Wright, *Japanese Print*, 19, 21, 81.

46 Wright, *An Autobiography*, 168.

47 Ibid., 108, 181.

48 Ibid., 368.

49 Donald Hoffman, *Frank Lloyd Wright's Fallingwater* (Mineola, NY: Dover, 1978), 85.

50 Alofsin, *The Lost Years*, 127.

51 Ibid., 120.

52 Wright, *Japanese Print*, 16.

53 Alofsin, *The Lost Years*, 121, 122.

54 Ibid., 11, 12.

55 Blake, *Master Builders*, 357.

56 Wright, *Japanese Print*, 15, 16.

57 Wright, *An Organic Architecture*, 2, 3, 8.

58 Wright, *An Autobiography*, 163.

59 Patrick Meehan, ed., *Truth against the World: Frank Lloyd Wright* (New York: John Wiley, 1987).

60 Wright, *An Autobiography*, 576.

61 Wright, *Japanese Print*, 19.

62 Ibid., 28.

63 Wright, *An Autobiography*, 163.

64 Ibid., 111.

65 Ibid., 333.

66 Ibid., 279.

67 Blake, *Master Builders*.

68 Wright, *Japanese Print*, 66.

69 Wright, *An Autobiography*.

70 Alofsin, *The Lost Years*, 90.

71 Wright, *Japanese Print*, 14.

72 Ibid., 29.

73 William Curtis, *Le Corbusier Ideas and Forms* (London: Phaidon Press, 1986), 16.

74 Blake, *Master Builders*.

75 Curtis, *Le Corbusier Ideas and Forms*, 18.

76 Le Corbusier, *Modulor 2* (New York: Birkhauser, 1958), 296.
77 Curtis, *Le Corbusier Ideas and Forms*, 227.
78 Ibid., 19.
79 Ibid., 21.
80 Ibid., 18, 19.
81 Ibid., 21.
82 Jacque Guiton, *The Ideas of Le Corbusier on Architecture and Urban Planning* (New York: George Braziller, 1981), 113, 114.
83 Ibid., 71.
84 Curtis, *Le Corbusier Ideas and Forms*, 13.
85 Ibid., 23.
86 Ibid., 30, 33.
87 Blake, *Master Builders*, 14, 15.
88 Curtis, *Le Corbusier Ideas and Forms*, 33, 34.
89 Ibid., 48.
90 Ibid., 51.
91 Ibid., 43.
92 Le Corbusier, *Towards a New Architecture* (New York: Dover, 1986), 73.
93 Le Corbusier, *Modulor 2*, 19.
94 Curtis, *Le Corbusier Ideas and Forms*, 33.
95 Ibid., 53.
96 Blake, *Master Builders*, 17.
97 Le Corbusier, *Towards a New Architecture*, 102.
98 Guiton, *Ideas of Le Corbusier*, 114.
99 Le Corbusier, *Modulor 2*, 17.
100 Le Corbusier, *Modulor* (New York: Birkhauser, 1958), 71.
101 Ibid., 156, 207.
102 Curtis, *Le Corbusier Ideas and Forms*, 164.
103 Le Corbusier, *Modulor*, 30, 37.
104 Le Corbusier, *Towards a New Architecture*, 218.
105 Curtis, *Le Corbusier Ideas and Forms*, 53.
106 Le Corbusier, *Towards a New Architecture*, 31.
107 Le Corbusier, *Modulor*, 55.
108 Ibid., 18, 19.
109 Ibid., 72.
110 Ibid., 78.
111 Le Corbusier, *Modulor 2*, 93.
112 Curtis, *Le Corbusier Ideas and Forms*, 28.
113 Le Corbusier, *Modulor 2*, 148, 149.
114 Le Corbusier, *Modulor*, 224, 225.
115 Le Corbusier, *Towards a New Architecture*.
116 Guiton, *Ideas of Le Corbusier*, 83; Le Corbusier, *Modulor 2*, 148.
117 Guiton, *Ideas of Le Corbusier*, 86.
118 Le Corbusier, *Modulor*, 32.
119 Guiton, *Ideas of Le Corbusier*, 61.
120 Wright, *An Autobiography*, 575.
121 Le Corbusier, *Modulor 2*, 25.
122 Ibid., 79, 80.
123 Wright, *An Autobiography*, 363.
124 Ibid., 339.
125 Wright, *An Organic Architecture*, 9.
126 Ibid., 39.

Selected Bibliography

Alexander, Christopher. *The Nature of Order: Phenomenon of Life*. Berkeley, CA: Center for Environmental Studies, 2001.

———. *The Nature of Order: The Process of Creating Life*. Berkeley, CA: Center for Environmental Structure, 2003.

———. *Notes on the Synthesis of Form*. Cambridge, MA: Harvard University Press, 1964.

Alofsin, Anthony. *Frank Lloyd Wright: The Lost Years, 1910–1922*. Chicago: University of Chicago Press, 1994.

Arnheim, Rudolf. *The Dynamics of Architectural Form*. Berkeley: University of California Press, 1984.

———. *The Dynamics of Architectural Form*. Berkeley: University of California Press, 1977.

———. *Visual Thinking*. Berkeley: University of California Press, 2004.

Barnsley, Michael. *Fractals Everywhere*. Boston: Academic Press, 1988.

Bayer, Patricia. *Art Deco Architecture*. New York: Harry N. Abrams, 1992.

Biaser, Werner. *Nature in Building: Rudolf Steiner in Dornach*. New York: Birkhauser, 2002.

Blake, Peter. *The Master Builders*. New York: W. W. Norton, 1975.

Bornstein, Eli. "Notes on the Mechanical and Organic in Art and Nature." *The Structurist* 35/36, (1995): 20–26, 44–63.

Bovill, Carl. *Fractal Geometry in Architecture and Design*. Basel, Switzerland: Birkhauser, 1996.

Budd, Malcolm. *An Aesthetic Appreciation of Nature*. New York: Oxford University Press, 2002.

Buhner, Steven Harrod. *The Secret Teachings of Plants*. Rochester, VT: Bear, 2004.

Carter, Peter. *Mies van der Rohe at Work*. London: Phaidon Press, 1974.

Clayton, Susan, and Susan Opotow, eds. *Identity and the Natural Environment: The Psychological Significance of Nature*. Cambridge, MA: MIT Press, 2003.

Corrada, Manuel. "Mechanical and Organic Form in the Theory and Art of El Lissitzky." *The Structurist* 35/36 (1995): 57–63

Curtis, William. *Le Corbusier Ideas and Forms*. London: Phaidon Press, 1986.

Estevez, Alberto. *Genetic Architectures*. Santa Fe, NM: Lumen Books, 2003.

Goldberger, Paul. *The Skyscraper*. New York: Alfred A. Knopf, 1981.

Grabow, Stephen. "Organic and Mechanical Form Principals." *The Structurist* No. 35/36. (1995): 4–12

Guiton, Jacque. *The Ideas of LeCorbusier on Architecture and Urban Planning*. New York: George Braziller, 1981.

Hale, Nathan Cabot. *Abstraction in Art and Nature*. New York: Dover, 1993.

Harrison, Charles, and Paul Wood, eds., *Art in Theory 1900–1990: An Anthology of Changing Ideas*. Hoboken, NJ: Wiley Blackwell, 1998.

Hoffman, Donald. *Frank Lloyd Wright's Fallingwater*. Mineola, NY: Dover, 1978.

Holtzman, Harry, and Martin James, eds., *The New Art—The New Life: The Collective Writings of Piet Mondrian*. Cambridge, MA: Da Capo Press, 1993.

Jenks, Charles. *The Architecture of the Jumping Universe*. London: Academy, 1997.

Kellert, Stephen. *Building for Life*. Washington, D.C.: Island Press, 2005.

Kellert, Stephen, and Edward Wilson. *The Biophilia Hypothesis*. Washington, D.C.: Island Press, 1995.

King, D. Brett, and Michael Wertheimer. *Max Wertheimer and Gestalt Theory*. Edison, NJ: Transaction, 2007.

Kohler, Wolfgang. *Gestalt Psychology*. New York: Liveright, 1992.

Laseau, Paul, and James Tice. *Frank Lloyd Wright: Between Principle and Form*. New York: Van Nostrand Reinhold, 1992.

Le Corbusier. *Modulor*. New York: Birkhauser, 1958.

———. *Modulor 2*. New York: Birkhauser, 1958.

———. *Towards a New Architecture*. New York: Dover, 1986.

Mandelbrot, Benoit. *The Fractal Geometry of Nature*. New York: W. H. Freeman, 1983.

Meehan, Patrick, ed. *Truth against the World: Frank Lloyd Wright*. New York: John Wiley, 1987.

Milner, John. *Kazimir Malevich and the Art of Geometry*. New Haven, CT: Yale University Press, 1996.

Mitchell, Melanie. *An Introduction to Genetic Algorithms*. Cambridge, MA: MIT Press, 1998.

Mitchell, William. *The Logic of Architecture*. Cambridge, MA: MIT Press, 1990.

Oliver, Dick. *Fractal Vision*. Boston: Sams, 1992.

Pearce, David. *New Organic Architecture (The Breaking Wave)*. Berkeley, CA: University of California Press, 2001.

Peitgen, Heinz-Otto, Hartmut Jurgens, and Dietmar Saupe, *Fractals for the Classroom*. New York: Springer, 1991.

Peterson, Ivan. *The Mathematical Tourist*. New York: W. H. Freeman, 1998.

Portoghese, Paolo M. *Nature and Architecture*. Milan, Italy: Skira, 2000.

Railing, Patricia. "The Machine Is No More Than a Brush: Morphology of Art and the Machine in Russian Avant-Garde Theory and Practice." *The Structurist* 35/36(1995): 49–56.

Robbin, Tony. *Fourfield: Computers, Art and the 4th Dimension*. New York: Bulfinch Press, 1992.

Seamon, David, and Arthur Zajonc, eds. *Goethe's Way of Science*. Albany: State University of New York Press, 1998.

Shalain, Leonard. *Art and Physics: Parallel Visions in Space, Time and Light*. New York: William Morrow, 1993.

Steiner, Rudolf. *Architecture*. Vancouver, BC: Sophia Brooks, 2004.

———. *Architecture as a Synthesis of the Arts*. London: Steiner Books, 1999.

———. *Nature's Open Secret*. Washington, D.C.: Steiner Books, 2000.

Thompson, D'Arcy. *On Growth and Form*. New York: Cambridge University Press, 1961.

Todd, Stephen, and William Latham. *Evolutionary Art and Computers*. Maryland Heights, MO: Academic Press, 1992.

Van Eck, Caroline. "Goethe and Alberti: Organic Unity in Nature and Architecture." *The Structurist* 35/36 (1995): 20–26.

Warneke, Carsten-Peter. *De Stijl*. Cologne, Germany: Benedikt Taschen, 1994.

Weston, Richard. *Modernism*. London: Phaidon Press, 1996.

Williams, Robert. *The Geometrical Foundation of Natural Structure*. New York: Dover, 1972.

Wilson, Edward. *Biophilia*. Cambridge, MA: Harvard University Press, 1986.

Wolfram, Stephen. *A New Kind of Science*. Champaign, IL: Wolfram Media, 2002.

Wright, Frank Lloyd. *An Autobiography: Frank Lloyd Wright*. Pittsburgh, PA: Horizon Press, 1943.

———. *An Organic Architecture: The Architecture of Democracy*. Cambridge, MA: MIT Press, 1939.

———. *The Japanese Print*. Pittsburgh, PA: Horizon Press, 1967.

Zygas, Paul, and Linda Nelson Johnson. *The Phoenix Papers*, vol. 2, *The Natural Pattern of Structure*. Tempe: Arizona State University Press, 1995.

Index

The letter *f* following a page number refers to a figure.